'At last, a text on criminal law written in appropriate language, but also with enough detail, to engage students of criminology and related courses. The book is clearly structured with question breaks and regular recaps that will clearly enhance student understanding'.

– **Dr Ian Marsh**, Liverpool Hope University

Criminal Law for Criminologists

Criminal Law for Criminologists uses theoretical and practical research to bridge the gap between 'the law in the books' (criminal law doctrine) and 'the law in action' (criminal justice process). It introduces the key policies and principles that drive criminal law in England and then explains the law itself in terms of relevant statute and case law. Starting with an outline of the basic principles and theories of criminal law and criminal justice, the author goes on to discuss:

- Criminal law and criminal justice in a historical perspective,
- General principles of criminal law, including actus reus and mens rea,
- Specific types of criminal offence, including property, homicide, sexual, public order, and drug offences,
- An overview of defences to crime,
- An appendix outlining essential legal skills.

In examining the links between the worlds of criminal law and criminal justice, *Criminal Law for Criminologists* brings a fresh perspective to this field of research. Written in a clear and direct style, this book will be essential reading for students of criminology, criminal justice, law, cultural studies, social theory, and those interested in gaining an introduction to criminal law.

Noel Cross is Programme Leader in Criminal Justice in the School of Justice Studies at Liverpool John Moores University. He became a programme leader in 2011. He has worked at Liverpool John Moores University since 2002. He holds a BA in Jurisprudence from the University of Oxford, an MA in Applied Criminal Justice and Criminology from the University of Swansea, and a PhD in Applied Social Studies from the University of Swansea. Aside from criminal law, his research interests include youth justice, zemiology, and the links between crime and power.

Criminal Law for Criminologists

Principles and Theory in
Criminal Justice

Noel Cross

Routledge
Taylor & Francis Group

LONDON AND NEW YORK

First published 2020
by Routledge
2 Park Square, Milton Park, Abingdon, Oxon OX14 4RN

and by Routledge
52 Vanderbilt Avenue, New York, NY 10017

Routledge is an imprint of the Taylor & Francis Group, an informa business

© 2020 Noel Cross

British Library Cataloguing-in-Publication Data
A catalogue record for this book is available from the British Library

Library of Congress Cataloging-in-Publication Data
Names: Cross, Noel, author.
Title: Criminal law for criminologists : principles and theory in
    criminal justice / Noel Cross.
Description: Abingdon, Oxon ; New York, NY : Routledge, 2020. |
    Includes bibliographical references and index. |
Identifiers: LCCN 2019056077 | ISBN 9781138606906 (hardback) |
    ISBN 9781138606913 (paperback) | ISBN 9780429467431
    (ebook)
Subjects: LCSH: Criminal law—England. | Criminologists—
    England—Handbooks, manuals, etc.
Classification: LCC KD7869.6 .C76 2020 | DDC 345.42—dc23
LC record available at https://lccn.loc.gov/2019056077

ISBN: 978-1-138-60690-6 (hbk)
ISBN: 978-1-138-60691-3 (pbk)
ISBN: 978-0-429-46743-1 (ebk)

Typeset in Garamond
by Apex CoVantage, LLC

Printed and bound by CPI Group (UK) Ltd, Croydon, CR0 4YY

Contents

Illustrations

Figure

Tables

Acknowledgements

When it comes to writing books, no criminologist is an island, and this book is no exception. I would like to thank my family for providing support and encouragement when I most needed it. Dr Karen Corteen and Dr Rachael Steele from the Criminal Justice team at Liverpool John Moores University took time out to read and comment on the book, and this gave me the belief to keep going, when I had very little left of my own. I also want to thank all of the students, past and present, on my Criminal Law and Criminal Justice module on the BA Criminal Justice and LLB Law and Criminal Justice programmes for giving me the opportunity and inspiration to teach a subject about which I am passionate. Finally, yet importantly, I want to thank all of the editorial team at Routledge for the opportunity to write this book and for their help on the journey towards completing it.

Cases

A (Conjoined Twins), Re [2001] 3 All ER 1
Abdul-Hussain [1999] Crim LR 570
Abdullahi [2007] 1 WLR 225
Adams v Camfoni [1929] 1 KB 95
Adebolajo [2014] EWCA Crim 2779
Adomako [1995] 1 AC 171
Airedale NHS Trust v Bland [1993] AC 789
Aitken [1992] 4 All ER 541
Albert v Lavin [1982] AC 546
Ali [1995] Crim LR 303
Ali [2008] EWCA Crim 716
Allen [1988] Crim LR 698
Alphacell v Woodward [1972] AC 824
Ambler [1979] RTR 217
Anderson and Morris [1966] 2 QB 110
Anderton v Ryan [1985] AC 560
Arobieke [1988] Crim LR 314
Asif [2008] EWCA Crim 3348
Asmelash [2013] EWCA Crim 157
Assange v Swedish Prosecution Authority [2011] EWHC 2849 (Admin)
Attorney-General v Able [1984] QB 795
Attorney-General for Northern Ireland v Gallagher [1963] AC 349
Attorney-General's Reference (No.1 of 1974) (1974) 59 Cr App Rep 203
Attorney-General's Reference (No.1 of 1975) [1975] QB 773
Attorney-General's References (Nos. 1 & 2 of 1979) [1980] QB 180
Attorney-General's Reference (No.4 of 1980) [1981] 1 WLR 705
Attorney-General's Reference (No.6 of 1980) [1981] QB 715
Attorney-General's Reference (No. 2 of 1983) [1984] QB 456
Attorney-General's Reference (No.1 of 1992) [1993] 1 WLR 274
Attorney-General's Reference (No.3 of 1992) [1994] 1 WLR 409
Attorney-General's Reference (No. 3 of 1994) [1997] 3 WLR 421
Attorney-General's Reference (No.3 of 1998) [2000] QB 401

Attorney-General's Reference (No.2 of 1999) [2000] QB 796
Austin (FC) and another v Metropolitan Police Commissioner [2009] UKHL 5
B [2013] EWCA Crim 3
B v DPP [2000] 2 AC 428
B, R v DPP [2007] EWHC 739 (Admin)
B & S v Leathley [1979] Crim LR 314
Bailey [1983] 2 All ER 503
Bainbridge [1960] 1 QB 129
Ball [1989] Crim LR 730
Barnes [2005] 1 WLR 910
Batt [1994] Crim LR 592
Becerra and Cooper (1976) 62 Cr App Rep 212
Belfon [1976] 3 All ER 46
Bell [1984] 3 All ER 842
Bennett [1995] Crim LR 877
Bezzina; Codling; Elvin [1994] 3 All ER 964
Bird [1985] 1 WLR 816
Birmingham [2002] EWCA Crim 2608
Blackman [2017] EWCA Crim 190
Blackshaw [2011] EWCA Crim 2312
Blake [1997] 1 All ER 963
Blaue [1975] 3 All ER 446
Blayney v Knight [1975] Crim LR 237
Bloxham [1983] AC 109
BM [2018] EWCA Crim 560
Bogacki [1973] QB 832
Bollom [2004] 2 Cr App Rep 6
Bourne (1952) 36 Cr App Rep 125
Bow (1976) 64 Cr App Rep 54
Bowen [1996] 4 All ER 837
Bowsher [1973] RTR 202
Boyea [1992] Crim LR 574
Brady [2007] Crim LR 564
Bratty v Attorney-General for Northern Ireland [1963] AC 386
Bree [2007] 2 All ER 676
Brennan [2014] EWCA Crim 2387
Brook [1993] Crim LR 455
Brooker v DPP [2005] EWHC 1132
Brown [1985] Crim LR 212
Brown [1994] 1 AC 212
Bryce [2004] 2 Cr App Rep 35
Bryson [1985] Crim LR 699
Bunch [2013] EWCA Crim 2498
Burgess [1991] 2 QB 92

Statutes

Accessories and Abettors Act 1861
Aggravated Vehicle-Taking Act 1992
Animal Welfare Act 2006
Antisocial Behaviour Act 2003
Antisocial Behaviour, Crime and Policing Act 2014
Anti-Terrorism, Crime and Security Act 2001
Children and Young Persons Act 1933
Computer Misuse Act 1990
Coroners and Justice Act 2009
Corporate Manslaughter and Corporate Homicide Act 2007
Coroners and Justice Act 2009
Counter-Terrorism Act 2008
Counter-Terrorism and Security Act 2015
Crime and Courts Act 2013
Crime and Disorder Act 1998
Crime (Sentences) Act 1997
Criminal Attempts Act 1981
Criminal Damage Act 1971
Criminal Justice Act 1967
Criminal Justice Act 1988
Criminal Justice Act 1991
Criminal Justice Act 2003
Criminal Justice and Court Services Act 2000
Criminal Justice and Courts Act 2015
Criminal Justice and Immigration Act 2008
Criminal Justice and Police Act 2001
Criminal Justice and Public Order Act 1994
Criminal Law Act 1967
Criminal Law Act 1977
Customs and Excise Management Act 1979
Domestic Violence, Crime and Victims Act 2004
Drugs Act 2005

Chapter 1

Introduction

Chapter overview

Introduction: what is the point of studying criminal law if you are a
    criminology or criminal justice student?
Approaching criminal law in principle and practice
Approaching criminal justice in principle and practice
Conclusion: a road map for the rest of the book
Further reading

Chapter aims

After reading Chapter 1, you should be able to understand:

- The basic principles of criminal law
- The basic principles of criminal justice
- The key theories which try to explain what criminal law does
- The key theories which try to explain what criminal justice does

Introduction: what is the point of studying criminal law if you are a criminology or criminal justice student?

This book focuses on English criminal law and its relationships to the study
areas of criminology and criminal justice. The book explains how criminal
law defines crime and also how these definitions compare to developments in
criminological theory, and how those involved in criminal justice use criminal
law in practice as they respond to crime. Throughout the book, where the text

talks about a defendant or victim in a particular criminal law case, the words 'defendant' and 'victim' will be abbreviated to 'D' and 'V', respectively. When referencing criminal law cases where one party to the case is the Crown, the text simply gives the other party name – so, for example, instead of writing *R v Woollin* [1999] AC 82, the text will just say *Woollin*, and so will the bibliography.

Criminal law defines certain kinds of behaviour as being unlawful and therefore provides a framework and a rulebook for criminal justice agencies who respond to crime in a range of different ways. However, do criminal justice organisations stick to the rules set out by criminal law? How do they respond to the social problem of crime – by using criminal law itself, or by using other values and ideas? The book aims to bridge the gap between criminal law and criminal justice to provide a better understanding of both subject areas while using both theoretical and practical knowledge as a way of bridging that gap.

Some writers (e.g. Hillyard and Tombs 2004; Pemberton 2007) have argued that criminal law is not useful to criminology and criminal justice because it wrongly focuses on individual responsibility and so overlooks social harms committed by states and organisations which are just as socially damaging as individual wrongdoing. In contrast, this book will argue that criminal law and criminal justice need each other to survive and therefore should be studied side by side (Zedner 2011). The gap between them has traditionally been wide in terms of writers on each side overlooking knowledge and ideas produced by the other side (Nelken 1987; Lacey 2007). However, without criminal law, criminal justice's main purpose – enforcement of criminal law – would disappear. In addition, without criminal justice to enforce it, criminal law would lose much of its power to shape and maintain order in society. It is also true that each side has lessons that it could learn from the other. For example, criminology and criminal justice can give criminal law a better understanding of how to work towards a fairer society; and the criminal law can focus criminal justice and criminology's attention on which kinds of behaviour society should and should not regard as crimes (Zedner 2011).

The next section of this chapter introduces basic principles relating to criminal law in England in terms of what criminal law is and what makes it distinctive as a social phenomenon.

Approaching criminal law in principle and practice

Defining criminal law

Farmer (2008) argues that there are two main approaches to defining criminal law. The first approach is that criminal law is made up of behaviours which can be seen as moral wrongs against the community (e.g. Duff 2007), or behaviours for which it is the community's job to punish and which deserve the powerful response of a criminal conviction (Lamond 2007). The first problem with this view is that 21st-century criminal law extends beyond behaviours which the public agree should be considered crimes (like murder and rape) to include behaviours which are less obviously morally wrong, such as using a mobile phone while driving. The second problem with this view is that it assumes a strong consensus in society about what is and is not morally wrong – a consensus that is not present in modern societies like England today (Wilson 2012). This does not mean that criminal law never reflects public morality – only that we cannot fully explain modern criminal law using moral beliefs (cf. Devlin 1965).

The harm principle is an alternative approach to the idea of criminal law reflecting community values. The harm principle argues that criminal law does, and should, target behaviour that causes physical harm, psychological harm, or serious offence to another person (Feinberg 1984). As with the morality approach to law, one problem with the harm principle is that it cannot explain everything that criminal law currently defines as a crime. The harm principle seemingly cannot explain what Ashworth (2008) calls the preventive function of criminal law – the law's labelling certain kinds of behaviour as carrying a risk of social harm or danger and therefore deserving of public condemnation and punishment. Nor can the harm principle explain the increasing number of regulatory offences within criminal law. One example is entering into an arrangement with someone you have reasonable cause to believe is under age 16, where the arrangement gives that person the chance of winning an animal as a prize (Animal Welfare Act 2006, s.11(3)). This does not mean that we should assume that criminal law never regulates behaviour that is objectively harmful (Hall and Winlow 2015: 89). However, criminal law's scope is so wide that it is now difficult to see which types of behaviour are most harmful to society simply by looking at criminal law. A final problem with the harm principle is that it is vague and does not give any guidance about how to weigh the seriousness of different kinds of harm, how to judge them, or how to balance them (Harcourt 1999: 193). Some critical criminologists, for example Pemberton (2015), take a very different view of harm as a trigger for social response, but their ideas about harm do not come from the law itself. Instead, Pemberton and others take a wider approach to defining social harm based on harmful events that prevent humans from flourishing and which are the product of human action or inaction (Yar 2012: 63). These harms can be damaging to physical or mental health, damaging to a person's autonomy, or relational (i.e. about social exclusion or discrimination), but are preventable through political and economic decisions about social conditions and are often the direct result of capitalist political economies (Pemberton 2015: 9–10). On this view, harm goes far beyond what criminal law would define as harmful, to include issues such as poverty, racism, and social exclusion (ibid.).

The second definition of substantive criminal law, drawing on the work of Williams (1955), is that it is simply the part of the law that deals with behaviour defined as criminal, and results in punishment by the State when a person is found guilty of breaking the law. In other words, criminal law is different from other kinds of law (like civil law, which deals with other forms of behaviour that result in some form of compensation after a finding of guilt) because it uses a different procedure to respond to people who break it. Criminal law accepts that it is fragmented and diverse in nature. However, it uses the criminal justice process to impose consistency and objectivity on itself and to present an image of itself to society as being consistent and objective (Farmer 1996). This hides the reality that criminal law is not as objective or standardised as it presents itself to be (Norrie 2014). In fact, criminal law has a range of functions. Some of these functions are instrumental, such as the idea of the rule of law discussed next; some are ideological, such as the prioritising of the interests of the powerful in society over those of the powerless (Lacey 1993). The following chapters of this book identify these functions, as criminal law and criminal justice are analysed as part of the same social process of criminalisation (Lacey and Zedner 2017), or regulating bad or risky behaviours.

The standard and burden of criminal proof

An example of the distinctive nature of criminal law procedure lies in the standard of proof needed to find guilt in each case. Criminal law establishes guilt by evidence of guilt beyond reasonable doubt. The civil law establishes guilt by evidence of guilt on the balance of probabilities, which requires a lower standard of proof and therefore less evidence indicating guilt than proof beyond reasonable doubt. Linked to this is the idea of the burden of proof being on the prosecution in criminal law (*Woolmington v DPP* [1935] AC 462). This means that D is innocent until the police and prosecutors have enough evidence to prove beyond reasonable doubt in court that D is guilty of all the different elements of the criminal charge(s) brought against them. Traditionally, this means that they will have to prove the guilty conduct (actus reus) specified by the definition of the offence and also the guilty state of mind (mens rea) which is specified. The principle is the foundation of the adversarial system of criminal justice that exists in England, where the prosecution and defence compete against each other to persuade the courts that their evidence is more convincing than the other side's.

Criminal law and punishment

Criminal law is distinctive from other types of law not simply because it imposes punishment on those who break it. This also happens in other types of law, as well as elsewhere in life, such as when a referee sends a player off the field in a football match for breaking the rules of the game. What makes criminal law distinctive is that it also 'labels' people as being criminal, communicating the message to them that they have broken the moral rules of the community through the process of conviction (Duff 2001, 2007). The intention of criminal law is therefore to create stigma through conviction and punishment for prohibited behaviours (Ashworth 2000).

Criminal law and the rule of law

The principle of the rule of law is also fundamental to understanding English criminal law and criminal justice. Under the rule of law, no one can be punished unless they have breached the law as it is clearly and currently defined and they have been warned that the conduct they have been accused of is criminal (*Rimmington* [2006] 1 AC 459). The breach must also be proved in a court of law. Finally, everyone (including those who make the law) is subject to the rule of law, unless the law itself gives special status to an individual or group (Simester et al. 2016: Chapter 2).

Sources of criminal law

Criminal law in England comes from three main sources. The first is common law. This is law that judges make and develop when they decide cases, in line with the rules on precedent. Precedent means that a particular court has to follow an earlier court's decision based on the same law and the same facts as the case it is currently deciding and made at a higher court level or (usually) at the same level as itself. However, a court does not have to follow decisions made at lower levels. The diagram that follows shows the structure of the appeal process in England and how precedent works:

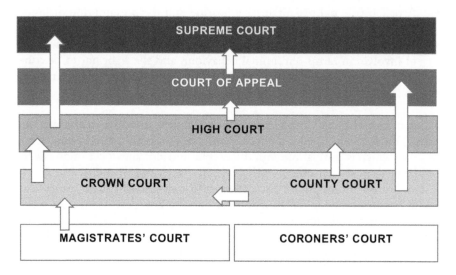

Figure 1.1 The English court appeal system

The second source of criminal law is statute law. This is law that Parliament creates and implements in the form of Acts of Parliament, or statutes. Statute law can decriminalise old offences, create new offences, re-define or change criminal offences that already exist, or bring together old pieces of legislation on the same topic. All new criminal offences must now be created by statute law, not by the courts through the common law (*Jones and Milling* [2007] 1 AC 136), although courts used to be able to use common law to create offences, and some offences (such as murder) are still defined by common law today. However, even where a statute defines a criminal offence, courts will often decide the details of that offence through their own case-by-case decisions, especially where there is some confusion over what a statute means in practice.

The third source of law is law that develops from the obligation of substantive criminal law to comply with European human rights law as contained in the European Convention on Human Rights ('ECHR' hereafter). Since Parliament passed the Human Rights Act 1998, individuals have the right to complain to courts in England when they feel that substantive criminal law has breached their human rights. The occurrence of miscarriages of justice, for example, where a person is convicted and punished for a criminal offence which they did not commit, involves serious breaches of human rights and has been seen as being a normal and routine feature of criminal justice today (Naughton 2007: 4). Because of the Human Rights Act, courts must interpret statute law in a way that is compatible with human rights legislation (s.3). Key ECHR provisions that are relevant to criminal law include:

- Article 2 (the right to life);
- Article 6 (the right to a fair legal hearing and the presumption of innocence for defendants); and
- Article 7 (the right to know exactly what the offence someone is accused of involves in terms of criminal behaviour, and the right not to be convicted under law which was not in effect when the act being punished was done).

S.6 of the Human Rights Act requires public authorities, including the police, the Crown Prosecution Service and the courts (discussed next) to act in a way which is compatible with the ECHR and also allows common law to be changed in line with the ECHR (*H* [2002] 1 Cr App Rep 59).

The Brexit referendum of 2016 resulted in a majority of participants voting in favour of the United Kingdom leaving the European Union. As such, there is considerable uncertainty over whether the ECHR will continue to influence English criminal law, and over how (if at all) the ECHR will influence that criminal law. It is important to remember, though, that the ECHR is part of a different legal system, managed by the Council of Europe, to the European Union.

Substantive criminal law, in all its forms, develops through the decisions of individuals and organisations. Therefore, what counts as 'crime' can and does change over time. For example, the Coalition Government created an estimated 1760 new criminal offences in England, Wales, and Scotland in 2010–11 alone (Chalmers and Leverick 2013: 550). This apparent expansion in criminal law's reach has led some writers to argue that criminal law criminalises too much (e.g. Husak 2008).

On the other hand, there are types of behaviour which used to be crimes but which no longer are. Examples include the Sexual Offences Act 1967, which partially decriminalised homosexual behaviour between adult men and a wide range of historical offences, such as eavesdropping, scolding, and wearing felt hats, all of which were crimes during the late 16th century (Sharpe 2014: 73–4). From these examples, it is clear that crime itself is a social construct (Reiner 2007: 25–6). No behaviour is criminal until an individual or group of people decides to make it criminal (Christie 2004). As a result, the boundaries of criminal behaviour have changed constantly over time, in line with changes in public opinion, political parties' views, and social and economic conditions (Lacey 1995; Duff et al. 2010). Sometimes these changes occur in a principled and rational way, but, more often, such changes have caused confusion and inconsistency in criminal law (Sanders et al. 2010: 8), and most key writers agree that criminal law has more than one function (e.g. Fletcher 1978; Ashworth 2008). The book will focus on criminal law's historical development in various places throughout this book, particularly in Chapter 2.

Study exercise 1.1

Using Internet resources and statute books, find three examples of offences that have been decriminalised and three examples of offences that have been created in England since 1997. Why do you think each of these offences was criminalised or decriminalised? Do you agree with the decision to criminalise or decriminalise each one?

Theories of criminal law

Clarkson (2005: 254–67) summarises the key theoretical approaches to the purposes of criminal law, as follows:

- The 'law and economics' approach, which states that criminal law is there to deter 'economically inefficient' acts which do not help the economy (e.g. stealing a car rather than buying one), and to regulate such behaviour, given that individual offenders choose to commit a crime of their own free will.

- The 'enforcement of morality' approach, which states that criminal law is and should be there to criminalise behaviour which is against the common moral values of society (see Devlin 1965; cf. Hart 1963).
- The 'paternalistic' approach, which states that criminal law is there and should be there to prevent behaviour which causes harm either to offenders themselves or to others.
- The 'liberal' approach, which states that criminal law is there and should be there only to prevent harm or serious offence caused by offenders to others (see Feinberg 1984; Feinberg 1985).
- The 'radical' approach, which states that criminal law is there to protect the interests of the powerful in society and to hide social conflict by confusing society about its true purpose (e.g. Kelman 1981).
- The 'risk management' approach, which states that criminal law is there to manage the risk to the public created by dangerous situations or behaviour (Feeley and Simon 1994).

As Clarkson (ibid.) goes on to explain, these principles offer reasons for allowing different kinds of behaviour to be criminalised which compete with each other. As a result, a criminologist analysing criminal law must consider the possibility that more than one theoretical approach is capable of explaining criminal law.

Study exercise 1.2

Using Internet resources, research the case of Stephen Gough, the so-called 'Naked Rambler', and the legal and criminal justice response to his behaviour. Do you think that Stephen Gough should be guilty of a crime? If so, on what grounds would you criminalise him? How (if at all) should he be punished?

The next section of the chapter provides a guide to the theory and practice of criminal justice.

Approaching criminal justice in principle and practice

Defining criminal justice

Davies (2015: 11) states that 'the content of criminal law provides the starting point of the criminal justice system by defining behaviour that is to be regulated through the use of criminal law'. However, this statement by itself does not reflect the complex reality of criminal justice, as Davies goes on to argue, for two main reasons.

Firstly, just as criminal law itself is built and developed socially and politically, often in a more disjointed way than it first appears, so the criminal justice process of enforcing the law is not carried out equally for all crimes and all criminal offences. The historical development of criminal justice and its institutions will be discussed at various points throughout the book, and especially as the focus of Chapter 2, as a way of showing its development alongside socio-economic and political conditions. Critical criminologists have argued that some types of criminal behaviour are more likely to be investigated and prosecuted than others and that this prioritising reflects the interests of powerful people in society, rather than the level of harm caused to society (e.g. Tombs and Whyte 2015). Secondly, although criminal justice is sometimes referred to as a 'system', some have questioned whether it is organised and unified enough to be called a 'system' at all (e.g. Pullinger 1985).

Who plays a part in criminal justice practice?

Criminal justice is made up of a variety of agencies and organisations, each with their own responsibilities, values, goals, and areas of decision-making authority (Lacey 1994: 4). As Newburn (2017: 579–82) shows, all of the following agencies have a role to play in the process of criminal justice:

- The police, who have the power to stop, search, arrest, interrogate, and charge suspects.
- The Crown Prosecution Service, whose role it is to decide whether there is sufficient evidence and public interest to prosecute a suspect, and, if there is enough evidence, to prosecute the case in court.
- Agencies who deal with those whom the courts have sentenced. These include:
  - Youth Offending Teams (who work with offenders aged between 10 and 17);
  - The National Probation Service (who will supervise all offenders in the community from 2021 onwards, with private sector companies providing some rehabilitation services, following the reversal of the partial privatisation of probation services (through Community Rehabilitation Companies) in 2014 (Grierson 2019);
  - HM Prison Service, which aims to rehabilitate people who are sentenced to prison as well as containing them securely and safely (Wahidin 2013: 190).
- The magistrates' courts, who hear and sentence all summary offences, as well as some triable 'either way' offences. Triable either way offences can

be dealt with at either the magistrates' or Crown courts, in terms of trials, sentencing, or both. Lay magistrates, drawn from the community, who sit in panels of two or three and are advised on law by a court legal adviser, hear most cases in the magistrates' courts. In 2018, there were just over 16,000 lay magistrates hearing cases, compared with only 310 district judges and deputy district judges, professional judges who hear cases alone (Courts and Tribunals Judiciary 2018). Lay magistrates are representative of the general population in terms of ethnic minority and gender proportions (Courts and Tribunals Judiciary 2014) but are more likely to be from a middle- or upper-social-class background than a lower-class background (Morgan and Russell 2000). In total, magistrates' courts handled 93.4% of all court trials in the year to September 2016 (Ministry of Justice 2017);

- The Crown Courts, who hear and sentence all indictable-only offences (which can only be dealt with at Crown Courts), as well as some triable either way offences. In the Crown Court, a judge decides on the law, and a jury of 12 people decide on the facts of the case, (i.e. whether someone is guilty or not guilty). Judges in the Crown Court make decisions on which evidence will be admissible in court; oversee the examination and cross-examination of evidence in court; advise the jury on the law which applies in a case; and sum up the cases for juries at the end of the trial (Otton 2002). Crown Court judges are not representative of the wider population in terms of race or gender (Courts and Tribunals Judiciary 2014) or in terms of social class (Darbyshire 2007);
- The Criminal Cases Review Commission, an organisation which investigates possible miscarriages of justice in terms of people being wrongfully convicted and/or sentenced;
- Community Safety Partnerships, multi-agency partnerships (involving representation from the police, local authorities, and probation, among others) which monitor local crime problems and develop local-level strategies for reducing crime;
- The Criminal Injuries Compensation Authority, which pays compensation to victims of violent crime; and
- The Parole Board, which makes decisions about whether prisoners should be released from custody or returned to custody following earlier release.

Even this is not a complete list of those involved in criminal justice. There are also a range of public sector and voluntary sector agencies which assist the victims of crime during their case's progression through the process (Cook and Davies 2017: 400–1; Shapland 2018). Defence solicitors and barristers represent defendants in courts and present arguments in favour of the defendant being found not guilty of the charges brought against them. The government has a great deal of influence over criminal justice policy, which in turn influences criminal justice practice day-to-day in various ways (Hamerton and Hobbs 2014). The government controls policy directly, through government departments which are responsible for different parts of criminal justice (like the Ministry of Justice and the Home Office), and also indirectly, through organisations which are linked to government (such as the National Youth Justice Board, which oversees youth justice policy in England). The media play a key part, not only in reporting on and shaping people's perceptions of criminal justice but also in influencing the operation of criminal justice itself (Marsh and Melville 2014).

The public also play a vital role in criminal justice at every stage of the process. Firstly, they play a key role in reporting crime to the police. Members of the public can, since the Police Reform Act 2002, become community support officers, and in doing so use many of the powers that can normally be used only by full-time police officers (Jones et al. 2017). They can also be Special Constables, who help the full-time police in their day-to-day work. The majority of magistrates sitting in the magistrates' court are lay magistrates – members of the public who, after receiving training, hear and sentence court cases (Campbell et al. 2019). Crown Court juries are made up of 12 members of the public. The public play a range of important roles in working with those convicted in court. For example, the public can act as mentors, helping young people and volunteers by monitoring the behaviour of young people who have been sentenced in court, as prison visitors in the adult criminal justice process, or as part of voluntary sector organisations which can now assume a range of responsibilities for community-based supervision of offenders. The public can also be victims of, or witnesses to, crime – reporting crime to police, giving evidence in court, and taking part in restorative justice, which often aims to bring offenders and victims together either as part of the offender's punishment after they have been convicted by the courts, or as an alternative to court punishment (Johnstone 2011: ch.5).

Study exercise 1.3

Draw a flowchart illustrating the different stages of the criminal justice process, including the individuals and agencies who you think have a say at each stage.

Theories of criminal justice

King (1981: 12–31) outlines the key theoretical approaches to the purposes of criminal justice and the typical features which these theories would produce in practice if they were applied:

- The 'due process' model, shown by equality between the defence and the prosecution in the process, rules protecting the defendant against error or abuse of power, and the presumption of the defendants' innocence until they are proven guilty.

- The 'crime control' model, shown by disregard of legal controls, implicit presumption of guilt, support for the police, and a high conviction rate (Packer 1968).
- The 'medical' model, shown by individualised responses to crime (so that each offender receives an intervention package tailored to meet their needs and circumstances), treatment of the social causes behind offending rather than punishment of the offence, and discretion and expertise of decision-makers (Garland 1985).
- The 'bureaucratic' model, shown by the promotion of speed and efficiency, the minimisation of conflict between people working in criminal justice and of money spent on the process, and the importance of and acceptance of records (Bottoms and McClean 1976).
- The 'status passage' model, shown by the public shaming of the defendant, court values which reflect (or claim to reflect) community values, and criminal justice agents' control over the process.
- The 'power' model, shown by the reinforcement of class values through criminal justice, the deliberate alienation and suppression of the defendant, the presence of paradoxes and contradictions between the rhetoric and the performance of criminal justice, and the ignorance of social harm caused by inequality in society (e.g. Sim et al. 1987).

In addition to these six models, Davies (2015: 27–32) adds a further two:

- The 'just deserts' model, shown by offenders being punished according to the blameworthiness and harmfulness of their actions, the recognition of offenders' basic human rights, the need for establishment of the offender's blameworthiness before punishment, and the recognition of the right of society to punish those who have offended. The concept of proportionality, where the sentence given balances the perceived seriousness of the offence, relates closely to this model (von Hirsch 1976, 1993).
- The 'risk management' model, shown by the monitoring and control of offenders based on the risk they pose to society and their previous offending history, the use of surveillance and supervision to reduce crime and change offending behaviour, and the use of longer sentences for offenders who are seen as being particularly dangerous (e.g. Garland 2001).

Roach (1999) adds two further interconnected models:

- The 'punitive victims' rights' model, which claims to prioritise the rights of victims by punishing offenders on the basis of upholding victims' rights and responding to the risks of victimisation.

- The 'non-punitive victims' rights' model, which uses non-punitive measures such as restorative justice to give victims control over their crime (Christie 1977), and to bring victims and offenders together to resolve conflict (Braithwaite 1989).

Two final 'hybrid' models have also been put forward:

- The 'social ordering' model, which sees criminal justice as a related but not entirely co-ordinated set of practices geared to the construction and maintenance of social order. Viewed this way, criminal justice has both instrumental features (real-life practices) and also symbolic features (its effects on people's attitudes and emotions). The decisions of individuals and the social context in which those decisions are made are important in terms of understanding it, and its power lies not only in what criminal justice agents and agencies can do but also in the beliefs and values which influence how they do it (Lacey 1994: 28–34).
- The 'radical pluralist' model, which argues that criminal justice has a range of values and that the State has a disproportionate influence on the operation and development of both, but that the State does not always manage to enforce its own values and interests through criminal justice policy and practice (Cavadino et al. 2013).

Conclusions: a roadmap for the rest of the book

Drawing on the work of Clarkson (2005), Johnstone and Ward (2010), and Hopkins Burke (2012) we can summarise some key theoretical approaches to understanding criminal law, criminology and criminal justice, in terms of what they do and should do, which will form a framework for analysing criminal law and criminal justice in the rest of the book. Later chapters will use these models in analysing general principles of criminal law and criminal justice (Chapters 3–4 and 10) and analysing specific criminal offences and the response to them (Chapters 5–9). These models are as follows:

- The 'liberal' approach, which supports the limitation of criminal law on the prevention of harm caused by offenders to others. It supports the punishment of offenders in a limited and proportionate way on the basis that people make the choice to commit crime (e.g. Feinberg 1984; von Hirsch 1993) or have breached the moral rules of the community (e.g. Devlin 1965; cf. Hart 1963).
- The 'deterministic' approach, which states that offenders are not fully responsible for their crime for social, biological, or psychological reasons

and so should have their punishment limited or replaced by treatment (e.g. Slobogin 2005).

• The 'radical' approach, which states that criminal law and criminal justice are there to protect the interests of the powerful in society and to hide social conflict (Box 1983). It focuses on social and economic inequality as a key influence on criminal behaviour at all levels of society (Reiner 2007), sees criminal law and criminal justice as fundamentally unequal and flawed due to divisions in society (Norrie 2014), and advocates greater punishment for the crimes of the powerful (Tombs and Whyte 2015).

• The 'restorative' approach, which states that criminal law and criminal justice exclude victims from the process of conflict resolution (Christie 1977) when they should in fact be working towards bringing offenders and victims together to resolve conflict in non-punitive settings (Braithwaite 1989).

• The 'risk management' approach, which states that criminal law is there to manage the risk to the public created by dangerous situations or behaviour (Feeley and Simon 1994; Garland 2001) and to hold criminally responsible those who present a risk to society, by assessing their character (Lacey 2016). The approach leads to greater use of administrative, regulatory, and contractual responses to control behaviour, outside the formal criminal law itself (Ashworth and Zedner 2010). Other results include a criminal justice drive towards efficiency in terms of time and money, as well as greater surveillance and social control, through criminal punishment (Cohen 1985) and preventive measures like CCTV over those seen as being particularly risky in society.

• The 'radical hybrid realist' model, drawing on the work of Hopkins Burke (2012). This model argues that power is contested at different levels of society but recognises that although the powerful have disproportionate influence over the development of criminal law and criminal justice, those at lower levels of society also have influence over its development, and, at times, the interests of the powerful and less powerful are shared. The model recognises the role played by social conditions in explaining crime and justifying punishment while also recognising that individuals have some choice over their criminal behaviour. This model shares some of the concerns and values of all five models defined earlier, without seeing any one of them as explaining everything about criminal law and criminal justice, or seeing any of them as providing a complete blueprint for reform of either.

We can represent the theoretical viewpoints within criminal law and criminal justice that the chapter has discussed on a roadmap, which is shown in Table 1.1.

Table 1.1 The theoretical roadmap for this book

Subject area and subject theory	Roadmap theory
Criminal law – law and economics	Liberal
Criminal law – liberal	
Criminal justice – due process	
Criminal justice – just deserts	
Criminal justice – status passage	
Criminal justice – punitive victims' rights	
Criminal law – paternalistic	Deterministic
Criminal justice – medical	
Criminal law – radical	Radical
Criminal justice – power	
Criminal justice – non-punitive victims' rights	Restorative
Criminal law – risk management	Risk management
Criminal law – enforcement of morals	
Criminal justice – crime control	
Criminal justice – bureaucratic	
Criminal justice – risk management	
Criminal justice – social ordering model	Radical hybrid realist
Criminal justice – radical pluralism	

Key points

- Criminal law in England covers a wide range of criminal behaviour and is a social construct in that it can and does change in nature according to time and place
- Criminal law is based around the idea that individuals are responsible for their criminal actions and that everyone is equal in the eyes of the law
- A wide range of individuals and agencies have a say in how English criminal justice operates
- There are a wide range of theories trying to explain what criminal law and criminal justice do and should do
- It is possible to identify a range of theoretical models which could be used to bring explanations of criminal law and criminal justice together

Further reading

Davies, M. (2015), *Davies, Croall and Tyrer's Criminal Justice* (5th ed.): chs.1 and 2. Harlow: Pearson.

Horder, J. (2016), *Ashworth's Principles of Criminal Law* (8th ed.): ch.1. Oxford: OUP.

Lacey, N., and Zedner, L. (2017), 'Criminalization: Historical, Legal, and Criminological Perspectives', in Liebling, A., Maruna, S., and McAra, L. (eds.), *The Oxford Handbook of Criminology* (6th ed.). Oxford: OUP.

Padfield, N., and Bild, J. (2016), *Text and Materials on the Criminal Justice Process* (5th ed.): ch.1. Abingdon: Routledge.

Wells, C., and Quick, O. (2010), *Lacey, Wells and Quick's Reconstructing Criminal Law* (4th ed.): ch.1. Cambridge: CUP.

References

Ashworth, A. (2000), 'Is the Criminal Law a Lost Cause?' *Law Quarterly Review*, **116**(2): 225–56.

Ashworth, A. (2008), 'Conceptions of Overcriminalization', *Ohio State Journal of Criminal Law*, **5**: 407–25.

Ashworth, A., and Zedner, L. (2010), 'Preventive Orders: A Problem of Under-Criminalization?' in Duff, R.A., Farmer, L., Marshall, S.E., Renzo, M., and Tadros, V. (eds.), *The Boundaries of the Criminal Law*. Oxford: OUP.

Bottoms, A.E., and McClean, J.D. (1976), *Defendants in the Criminal Process*. London: Routledge.

Box, S. (1983), *Power, Crime and Mystification*. London: Tavistock.

Braithwaite, J. (1989), *Crime, Shame and Reintegration*. Cambridge: CUP.

Campbell, L., Ashworth, A., and Redmayne, M. (2019), *The Criminal Process* (5th ed.). Oxford: OUP.

Cavadino, M., Dignan, J., and Mair, G. (2013), *The Penal System: An Introduction* (5th ed.). London: Sage.

Chalmers, J., and Leverick, F. (2013), 'Tracking the Creation of Criminal Offences', *Criminal Law Review*: 543–60.

Christie, N. (1977), 'Conflicts as Property', *British Journal of Criminology*, **17**(1): 1–19.

Christie, N. (2004), *A Suitable Amount of Crime*. London: Routledge.

Clarkson, C.M.V. (2005), *Understanding Criminal Law* (4th ed.). London: Sweet and Maxwell.

Cohen, S. (1985), *Visions of Social Control*. Cambridge: Polity Press.

Cook, I.R., and Davies, P. (2017), 'Supporting Victims and Witnesses', in Harding, J., Davies, P., and Mair, G. (eds.), *An Introduction to Criminal Justice*. London: Sage.

Courts and Tribunals Judiciary (2014), *Judicial Diversity Statistics 2014*. Available online at: www.judiciary.gov.uk/publications/judicial-diversity-statistics-2014/. Accessed 24 May 2018.

Courts and Tribunals Judiciary (2018), *Magistrates' Courts*. Available online at: www.judiciary.gov.uk/you-and-the-judiciary/going-to-court/magistrates-court/. Accessed 24 May 2018.

Darbyshire, P. (2007), 'Where Do English and Welsh Judges Come From?' *Cambridge Law Journal*, **66**(2): 365–88.

Davies, M. (2015), *Davies, Croall and Tyrer's Criminal Justice* (5th ed.). Harlow: Pearson.

Devlin, P. (1965), *The Enforcement of Morals*. Oxford: OUP.

Duff, R.A. (2001), *Punishment, Communication and Community*. Oxford: OUP.

Duff, R.A. (2007), *Answering for Crime: Responsibility and Liability in the Criminal Law*. Oxford: Hart.

Duff, R.A., Farmer, L., Marshall, S.E., Renzo, M., and Tadros, V. (2010), 'Introduction: The Boundaries of the Criminal Law', in Duff, R.A., Farmer, L., Marshall, S.E., Renzo, M., and Tadros, V. (eds.), *The Boundaries of the Criminal Law*. Oxford: OUP.

Farmer, L. (1996), 'The Obsession with Definition: The Nature of Crime and Critical Legal Theory', *Social and Legal Studies*, **5**(1): 57–73.

Farmer, L. (2008), 'Definitions of Crime', in Cane, P., and Conaghan, J. (eds.), *The New Oxford Companion to Law*. Oxford: OUP.

Feeley, M.M., and Simon, J. (1994), 'Actuarial Justice: The Emerging New Criminal Law', in Nelken, D. (ed.), *The Futures of Criminology*. London: Sage.

Feinberg, J. (1984), *The Moral Limits of the Criminal Law, Volume 1: Harm to Others*. New York: OUP.

Feinberg, J. (1985), *The Moral Limits of the Criminal Law, Volume 2: Offence to Others*. New York: OUP.

Fletcher, G.F. (1978), *Rethinking Criminal Law*. Boston: Little, Brown and Co.

Garland, D. (1985), *Punishment and Welfare*. Aldershot: Gower.

Garland, D. (2001), *The Culture of Control: Crime and Social Order in Contemporary Society*. Oxford: OUP.

Grierson, J. (2019), 'Probation Will Be Renationalised After Disastrous Grayling Reforms', *The Guardian*, 26 May. Available online at: www.theguardian.com/society/2019/may/16/part-privatisation-probation-sevices-to-be-reversed-offender-management-nationalised-chris-grayling. Accessed 11 June 2019.

Hall, S., and Winlow, S. (2015), *Revitalizing Criminological Theory: Towards a New Ultra-Realism*. Abingdon: Routledge.

Hamerton, C., and Hobbs, S. (2014), *The Making of Criminal Justice Policy*. Abingdon: Routledge.

Harcourt, B. (1999), 'The Collapse of the Harm Principle', *Journal of Criminal Law and Criminology*, **90**(1): 109–94.

Hart, H.L.A. (1963), *Law, Liberty and Morality*. Oxford: OUP.

Hillyard, P., and Tombs, S. (2004), 'Beyond Criminology?' in Hillyard, P., Pantazis, C., Tombs, S., and Gordon, D. (eds.), *Beyond Criminology: Taking Harm Seriously*. London: Pluto Press.

Hopkins Burke, R. (2012), *Criminal Justice Theory: An Introduction*. Abingdon: Routledge.

Horder, J. (2016), *Ashworth's Principles of Criminal Law* (8th ed.). Oxford: OUP.

Husak, D. (2008), *Overcriminalization: The Limits of the Criminal Law*. Oxford: OUP.

Johnstone, G. (2011), *Restorative Justice: Ideas, Values, Debates* (2nd ed.). Abingdon: Routledge.

Johnstone, G., and Ward, T. (2010), *Law and Crime*. London: Sage.

Jones, T., Newburn, T., and Reiner, R. (2017), 'Policing and the Police', in Liebling, A., Maruna, S., and McAra, L. (eds.), *The Oxford Handbook of Criminology* (6th ed.). Oxford: OUP.

Kelman, M. (1981), 'Interpretive Construction in the Substantive Criminal Law', *Stanford Law Review*, **33**(4): 591–673.

King, M. (1981), *The Framework of Criminal Justice*. London: Croom Helm.

Lacey, N. (1993), 'A Clear Concept of Intention: Elusive or Illusory?' *Modern Law Review*, **56**(5): 621–42.

Lacey, N. (1994), 'Introduction: Making Sense of Criminal Justice', in Lacey, N. (ed.), *Criminal Justice: A Reader*. Oxford: OUP.

Lacey, N. (1995), 'Contingency and Criminalisation', in Loveland, I. (ed.), *Frontiers of Criminality*. London: Sweet and Maxwell.

Lacey, N. (2007), 'Character, Capacity, Outcome: Toward a Framework for Assessing the Shifting Pattern of Criminal Responsibility in Modern English Law', in Dubber, M., and Farmer, L. (eds.), *Modern Histories of Crime and Punishment*. Stanford, CA: SUP.

Lacey, N. (2016), *In Search of Criminal Responsibility: Ideas, Interests and Institutions*. Oxford: OUP.

Lacey, N., and Zedner, L. (2017), 'Criminalization: Historical, Legal, and Criminological Perspectives', in Liebling, A., Maruna, S., and McAra, L. (eds.), *The Oxford Handbook of Criminology* (6th ed.). Oxford: OUP.

Lamond, G. (2007), 'What Is a Crime?' *Oxford Journal of Legal Studies*, **27**(4): 609–32.

Marsh, I., and Melville, G. (2014), *Crime, Justice and the Media* (2nd ed.). Abingdon: Routledge.

Ministry of Justice (2017), *Criminal Justice System Statistics Quarterly: September 2016* (overview table 3.1). Available online at: www.gov.uk/government/uploads/system/uploads/attachment_data/file/591932/oveview-tables-september-2016.xlsx. Accessed 24 May 2018.

Morgan, R., and Russell, N. (2000), *The Judiciary in the Magistrates' Courts*. Home Office/LCD Occasional Paper No.66. London: Home Office/Lord Chancellor's Department.

Naughton, M. (2007), *Rethinking Miscarriages of Justice: Beyond the Tip of the Iceberg*. Basingstoke: Palgrave Macmillan.

Nelken, D. (1987), 'Criminal Law and Criminal Justice: Some Notes on Their Irrelation', in Dennis, I.H. (ed.), *Criminal Law and Justice*. London: Sweet and Maxwell.

Newburn, T. (2017), *Criminology* (3rd ed.). Abingdon: Routledge.

Norrie, A. (2014), *Crime, Reason and History* (3rd ed.). Cambridge: CUP.

Otton, P. (2002), 'The Role of the Judge in Criminal Cases', in McConville, M., and Wilson, G. (eds.), *The Handbook of the Criminal Justice Process*. Oxford: OUP.

Packer, H.L. (1968), *The Limits of the Criminal Sanction*. Stanford, CA: SUP.

Padfield, N., and Bild, J. (2016), *Text and Materials on the Criminal Justice Process* (5th ed.): ch.1. Abingdon: Routledge.

Pemberton, S. (2007), 'Social Harm Future(s): Exploring the Potential of the Social Harm Approach', *Crime, Law and Social Change*, **48**(1): 27–41.

Pemberton, S. (2015), *Harmful Societies: Understanding Social Harm*. Bristol: Policy Press.

Pullinger, H. (1985), 'The Criminal Justice System Viewed as a System', in Moxon, D. (ed.), *Managing Criminal Justice*. London: Home Office.

Reiner, R. (2007), *Law and Order: An Honest Citizen's Guide to Crime and Control*. Cambridge: Polity Press.

Roach, K. (1999), 'Four Models of the Criminal Process', *Journal of Criminal Law and Criminology*, **89**(2): 671–716.

Sanders, A., Young, R., and Burton, M. (2010), *Criminal Justice* (4th ed.). Oxford: OUP.

Shapland, J. (2018), 'Interventions and Services for Victims of Crime', in Walklate, S. (ed.), *Handbook of Victims and Victimology* (2nd ed.). Abingdon: Routledge.

Sharpe, J.A. (2014), *Crime in Early Modern England, 1550–1750* (revised 2nd ed.). Harlow: Pearson.

Sim, J., Scraton, P., and Gordon, P. (1987), 'Introduction: Crime, the State and Critical Analysis', in Scraton, P. (ed.), *Law, Order and the Authoritarian State*. Milton Keynes: Open University Press.

Simester, A.P., Spencer, J.R., Stark, F., Sullivan, G.R., and Virgo, G.J. (2016), *Simester and Sullivan's Criminal Law: Theory and Doctrine* (6th ed.). Oxford: Hart.

Slobogin, C. (2005), 'The Civilization of Criminal Law', *Vanderbilt Law Review*, **58**(1): 121–67.

Tombs, S., and Whyte, D. (2015), *The Corporate Criminal: Why Corporations Must Be Abolished*. Abingdon: Routledge.

von Hirsch, A. (1976), *Doing Justice: The Choice of Punishments*. New York: Hill and Wang.

von Hirsch, A. (1993), *Censure and Sanctions*. Oxford: OUP.

Wahidin, A. (2013), 'The Prison Enterprise', in Hucklesby, A., and Wahidin, A. (eds.), *Criminal Justice* (2nd ed.). Oxford: OUP.

Wells, C., and Quick, O. (2010), *Lacey, Wells and Quick's Reconstructing Criminal Law* (4th ed.). Cambridge: CUP.

Williams, G. (1955), 'The Definition of Crime', *Current Legal Problems*, **8**: 107–30.

Wilson, W. (2012), 'Participating in Crime: Some Thoughts on the Retribution/Prevention Dichotomy in Preparation for Crime, and How to Deal with It', in Reed, A., and Bohlander, M. (eds.), *Participation in Crime: Domestic and Comparative Perspectives*. Abingdon: Routledge.

Yar, M. (2012), 'Critical Criminology, Critical Theory, and Social Harm', in Hall, S., and Winlow, S. (eds.), *New Directions in Criminological Theory*. Abingdon: Routledge.

Zedner, L. (2011), 'Putting Crime Back on the Criminological Agenda', in Bosworth, M., and Hoyle, C. (eds.), *What Is Criminology?* Oxford: OUP.

Chapter 2

Perspectives on the history of criminal law and criminal justice

Chapter overview

Introduction
Perspectives on the history of criminal law in England
Perspectives on the history of criminal justice in England
Conclusions: linking discussion to the roadmap theories
Further reading

Chapter aims

After reading Chapter 2, you should be able to understand:

- The advantages of using historical sources as a source of knowledge about the theory and practice of criminal law and justice
- The limitations of using historical sources as a source of knowledge about the theory and practice of criminal law and justice
- Key perspectives on the historical development of criminal law
- Key perspectives on the historical development of criminal justice

Introduction

This chapter will introduce you to different ways of thinking about the historical development of criminal law and justice in England. There are a range of benefits connected with using a historical perspective to understanding criminal law and justice. Firstly, using historical knowledge and ideas helps us to see how criminal law and justice are social institutions whose scope and values link closely with political, social, and economic trends in wider society.

Secondly, using historical sources shows us that the issues and problems relating to crime now, and society's fear of crime, occurred in the past as well (e.g. Pearson 1983). Thirdly, using history in this way also reminds us that, since criminal law and justice systems changed radically at different points in the past, our current responses to crime in the form of criminal law and criminal justice may not be the only ones which are appropriate and effective (Sharpe 2001: 146). For all of these reasons, studying criminal law and criminal justice from a historical perspective can give us a better understanding of how they work today.

However, there are important limitations to remember when looking at historical sources of information on criminal law and justice. There are significant gaps in terms of missing historical information. Manuel Eisner (2017: 567–8), in his study of long-term trends in homicide in England since 1200, shows that homicide is the type of crime which was most likely to be recorded in judicial statistics. Information on other types of crime is more limited, and even homicide statistics are not fully reliable because of limitations in law enforcement and the underrepresentation of some social groups in homicide statistics (ibid.). Secondly, as Chapter 1 argued, what counts as 'crime' can and has regularly changed over time. There were significant overlaps between concepts of crime and sin in 18th-century England, with church courts prosecuting offences against social order and influencing how secular courts responded to harmful behaviour (Sharpe 2001: 112). There were also sharp differences between what the State thought of as 'crime' and what local communities thought of as 'crime'. The transformation of various forms of previously legal customary behaviour into crimes punishable by death through the 'Bloody Code' of the 18th and early 19th centuries (Hay 1975) is a key example of differing viewpoints on the definition of crime at different levels of society in England. As a result, the reliability of criminal statistics from the past is always limited in terms of giving a full and complete picture of crime, just as today's crime statistics are. Finally, it is important to remember that records of prosecutions and convictions in court almost certainly do not give us an accurate measure of how much crime there was in society at a particular time (Sharpe 2014; Godfrey et al. 2008: 48). There was a 'dark figure' of unrecorded crime in the past, just as there is today (see Chapter 3 for more discussion of this issue in relation to actus reus).

The remaining sections of this chapter, while taking the limitations of historical crime data into account, look at knowledge and perspectives on criminal law and justice as they operated in the past in England.

Perspectives on the history of criminal law in England

Johnstone and Ward (2010) argue that before the emergence of a centrally organised system of criminal law, village-style communities regulated what we would now see as being criminal behaviour on a local basis, and the response taken depended on whether the crime took place between community members or between strangers. Local communities dealt with crime in a wide variety of ways, ranging from verbal warnings to exclusion from the community and death (ibid: 31). Violent acts of vengeance were more common as a response to crimes committed by strangers, as a means of maintaining honour and meeting social obligations between lords and their followers (Berman 1983). However, a system of compensation for crime gradually displaced the usage of vengeance with a detailed system of different financial penalties due for different types of physical injury, for example (Miller 2006).

Following the Norman Conquest, the State made increasing efforts to increase its power and intervene in disputes between individuals, firstly by taking a percentage of the compensation owed as payment for settling disputes between individuals, and then by demanding full payment of compensation to itself, thereby making financial gains as well as increasing its power over society (McAuley and McCutcheon 2000). Norman kings struggled to impose law and order on English society, but from the early 14th century onwards, an increasingly formalised and extensive system of criminal law and justice emerged, with the aims of encouraging individual participation in a wealth-generating, competitive market economy and controlling lower-class threats to State power (Hall 2012: 20–4). Hall (ibid.) also uses the impact of the emerging capitalist economy on individuals to explain the long-term decline in homicide rates since the 14th century, and to explain the long-term increase in property-based crime over the same period. In Hall's view, violence needed to decrease to allow a competitive capitalist economy to develop, but this capitalist economy also promoted individual selfishness and financial competitiveness in a way that encouraged financially orientated crimes such as fraud and theft.

Johnstone and Ward (2010: 36–9) discuss the move towards modern criminal law and justice by pointing towards the key influence of the Church's view of crime as specifically sinful behaviour which needed to be punished, and towards the secular criminal courts presenting themselves as objective and above society, in the same way as the Church did. Importantly, they do not only rely on the development of capitalism and its impact on society as an explanation for how English criminal law developed. Johnstone and Ward (ibid: 39–42) go on to point to the development of mens rea, or the mental element necessary to prove liability for some types of crime (see Chapter 4 for more details) as a practical response to a number of issues. Firstly, introducing mens rea limited Church immunity from criminal prosecution. Secondly, mens rea acted as a way of distinguishing felonies (often capital offences) from less serious misdemeanours. Thirdly, mens rea was also a way of ensuring that those who lacked capacity for crime (such as young children) did not receive punishment.

It is important to note, however, that before the 19th century, mens rea was concerned with the objective idea of judging a person's malice or bad character rather than what was going on in a person's head at the time they committed a crime, in psychological terms (Horder 1997; Lacey 2007). It is also important to note that criminal law had already prioritised the control of the lower levels of society by the 1500s. These attempts at social control intensified at times of demographic pressure (such as increases in the birth rate) and religious and social unrest, as public fear of crime increased (Sharpe 2014: 250–4). For example, sumptuary laws, which regulated which colours and types of clothing lower- and middle-class people could wear, emerged as early as the 1300s and were well established by the 1500s (Hall 2012: 22).

By the 1600s, criminal law developed and controlled by the Crown was expanding to include offences against religion and morality, which Church courts had previously regulated. By this time, criminal law was divided into three categories – treason, felonies, and misdemeanours. Treasonous offences, comprising offences against the monarch and the Church, were the most serious crimes and were punishable by death. As well as crimes involving homicide, treason included a wide range of offences which would not be seen as being criminal today, such as sodomy and witchcraft (Horder 2016: 24–5). The felony category was similarly wide, including well-known crimes such as murder, but also less serious offences such as causing a nuisance on a highway or bridge (ibid.). The concept of felony considerably expanded through the criminalisation of previously legal and customary behaviour relating to property ownership as capital offences during the 18th century (Radzinowicz 1948; Thompson 1975).

Norrie (2014: ch.2) traces the development of criminal law in the first half of the 19th century to a set of rules responding to socially harmful behaviour on the basis that offenders had freedom of choice over whether or not to commit crime and so deserved punishment on the basis of having made the choice to commit crime. It is at this point that we see criminal law developing the idea of mens rea as a way of determining criminal responsibility. It replaced an assessment of a person's character based on local knowledge that was capable of disproving evidence of guilt (Lacey 2001, 2007). Criminal law reformers such as Jeremy Bentham attempted to limit the scope of criminal law to make it more humane, to remove the influence of religious beliefs over it, and to make it more logical and easier to understand. These attempts culminated in the partial codification of the English criminal law in a series of statutes from 1861 (Horder 2016: 32–4), although this did not reduce the scope or the punitivism of criminal law.

Indeed, the increased development of another criminal law function, namely, regulating socially risky forms of behaviour (Wiener 1990; Farmer 1997), changed the shape of criminal law. One important way in which criminal law started to control risk was by introducing statutory strict liability offences which did not require proof of subjective fault from the mid-19th century onwards and which are still central to criminal law today (Horder 2014; Norrie 2014: ch.5). The criminalisation of attempted crime for the first time during the 19th century was another way in which criminal law moved towards regulating risk (Fletcher 1978). Other forms of behaviour seen as offensive to Victorian ideas about respectability, such as prostitution, became crimes during the early 19th century. Older offences such as breach of the peace were prosecuted more often than before (Johnstone and Ward 2010: 57–8), and new offences criminalising mere 'suspicious behaviour' became part of criminal law from 1824 onwards (Crowther 2007: 34). Such developments were linked closely with the increasing tendency in English society to blame lower-class people for criminal activity, at first simply on the grounds of their class, and later on a mixture of biological and physical factors beyond an individual person's control and urban environmental conditions (Emsley 2013: chs. 3–5). This resulted in greater surveillance of lower-class behaviour, both on the streets and in the workplace (Godfrey et al. 2008: ch.7), but far less criminal law attention focussed on white-collar crimes committed by the middle and upper classes, despite the evidence that this kind of crime (especially fraud) was widespread in England in the 19th century (Emsley 2013: 6–9).

Definitions of mens rea did not change throughout the rest of the 19th century (Smith 1998), and it was not until the mid-20th century that criminal law decisively shifted towards punishing people on the basis of subjective, individual psychological fault. This shift links closely to the introduction of universal voting rights and the resulting portrayal of all members of society as being equal citizens in political discourse (Ramsay 2006).

Since the Second World War, successive governments have introduced a wide range of new offences to criminal law. For example, 786 new criminal offences became part of English law in 1951–52, and another 634 in 2010–11 (Chalmers et al. 2015). This trend has led some writers to question whether all of these behaviours needed to be criminalised (Ashworth and Zedner 2008; Husak 2008), as well as to criticise the fact that many new criminal offences are not scrutinised in detail by Parliament before becoming part of criminal law and are badly defined (Chalmers and Leverick 2013). This more recent history of English criminal law, from the end of the Second World War onwards, will be a key theme in later chapters, as the book discusses principles and rules in different areas of criminal law in more detail. For now, though, the rest of this chapter considers different perspectives and knowledge on the historical development of criminal justice in England.

Study exercise 2.1

During the 19th century, criminal law tried to distance itself from issues of religion and morality. Do you think it is ever possible to keep morality out of criminal law?

Perspectives on the history of criminal justice in England

Just as State control over criminal law itself began to increase from the early 14th century onwards, so did its control over the enforcement of criminal law through criminal justice. Over time, the State took the process of justice away from victims (Christie 1977), so the Crown could keep compensation money for itself in the form of fines and therefore increase power financially as well as in terms of social authority (McAuley and McCutcheon 2000). The establishment of magistrates (justices of the peace) in the Justices of the Peace Act 1361, in a role that involved the administration of justice (Logan 2017a), displayed the delegation of power to hear criminal trials from central royal authority to the local, community level. From then on, the State gradually delivered an increasingly centralised and efficient criminal justice framework. However, the State did not have dominance over the response to crime until a much later point in history. The development and usage of duelling as a middle- and upper-class method of resolving conflicts between the 1600s and early 1800s is evidence of continuing access to justice outside the formal criminal court process (Banks 2017), as is the usage of violent community punishments, or 'rough music', for wrongdoers as late as the 18th century in England (Thompson 1991).

Looking first at the historical development of policing in England, it is true that the first professional police force was not established until 1829, in London; before this policing was the responsibility of local parish constables (Johnstone and Ward 2010: 52) who were mostly unpaid volunteers, sometimes supported by paid watchmen (Godfrey et al. 2008: ch.4). Rawlings (1999: 32) points to the role played by John and Henry Fielding in campaigning for an organised criminal justice (more specifically, policing) response to crime of the kind that individuals and communities could not provide in the aftermath of the crime panic of 1748. The transition to professional policing was a gradual process, lasting from the late 18th century to 1856, when a professional police force became mandatory for each local authority area (Emsley 2013: 227). Even then, police duties included more than just responding to crime. Police also engaged in general social regulation, inspecting lodging houses and surveying roads, for example (Johnston 1992: 5).

Traditional police historians such as Critchley (1967) explained the transition to professional policing as a natural progression in efficiency and as a response to parish constables' failure to cope with increased crime rates driven by industrialisation. These writers pointed to the tradition of community policing in the professional area and the reliance on policing by consent rather than by force, in support of their reform-supporting view. However, revisionist historians like Storch (1976) argued that the professional police were more concerned with socially controlling the poor in society and with disciplining behaviour that was traditionally seen as a legal custom (such as gambling and drinking) than with improving conditions in society. Gatrell (1980: 250) takes a different view, arguing that although most viewed the police with great suspicion by in the 1830s, by the mid-19th century people at all levels of society accepted the access to justice given to them by police presence (see also Emsley 2013: 253). The police also assumed the role of prosecuting crime, which was previously the role of the victim – a role that gave them considerable power to define the limits of criminality (Tennant 2017).

Turning to knowledge about criminal courts in England, in the medieval era, while what we would recognise as court processes did operate, they did so alongside other, more physical ways of proving guilt. These were trials of ordeal, involving trial by fire, water, or hot iron, and although such processes were easy to manipulate, and often showed bias against women, they were still in use in England as late as the 17th century (Cole and Osidipe 2017: 265–6). Sharpe (2014) points to striking similarities in felony prosecution patterns between the 14th and 18th centuries. Most prosecutions were for low-level property offences, and murder was the only other regularly prosecuted felony. Prosecutions for arson, rape, and other felonies were very rare, although Sharpe also points out that prosecutions for regulatory offences were regular, and increased at times of social unrest and increases in numbers of poor people in England from the 14th century onwards (ibid.). Sharpe also points to the decline in prosecutions for serious violence between the 13th and 20th centuries but also shows a similar decline in prosecutions for property offences from the early 17th century through to the mid-19th century. Building on Sharpe's arguments, Emsley (2013: 29) suggests that prosecutions increased in times of political and social unrest (such as the Napoleonic Wars with France) because victims were more fearful and because offenders took advantage of the increased opportunities to commit different kinds of crime.

Gatrell (1980) also demonstrates the decline in recorded theft and violence in England between the 1830s and 1910s and claims that the introduction of a professionalised police force and a more centralised judicial system had an influence on this apparent drop in crime. Gatrell's argument here is that the poor in society did not benefit from economic growth and could not resist the controls placed upon them by police, court, and welfare policies. Gatrell combines this explanation with the argument that in the second half of the 19th century, the poor in English society did not experience long-term unemployment and rising food prices at the same time. Considering these societal changes together, it is not surprising that recorded crime rates declined. For Hall (2012: ch.2), rates of violence and homicide decreased from the 14th century onwards. Hall argues that this occurred not so much because of the kind of civilising and moralising processes identified by Eisner (2017) but rather because the values of capitalism encouraged people to favour property crime over violent crime and also because the punishments for property crime were more lenient than for violent offences. Hall, using a psychodynamic approach, highlights the 'special liberty' and psychological selfishness encouraged by capitalism in support of this view.

Another interesting issue is the decline in the number of prosecutions of women for serious offences after the mid-18th century. Feeley and Little (1991) argued that while women made up 40–45% of felony defendants at the Old Bailey courts for most of the 18th century, by 1900 they comprised only around 15%. Feeley and Little argue that these figures represent an actual decline in female offending, brought on by changing social conditions and greater informal social control affecting women's lives from the early 19th century onwards. However, it is always difficult to tell whether historical crime statistics are a result of changing public attitudes to crime, variations in reporting practices, or genuine changes in patterns of offending (Godfrey and Lawrence 2014).

Marxist accounts point to the increasing use of criminal justice by the social elite as a tool for protecting their own interests and as a tool for denying social equality to the lower classes, arguing against the earlier work of Radzinowicz, which focussed mainly on the continual process of positive reform within English criminal justice (Smith 2007). Logan (2017a) points out that magistrates traditionally came from upper- and middle-class backgrounds – it was not until 1906 when the abolition of the property qualification took place, allowing working-class people to become magistrates, and a similar property qualification limited those eligible for jury service until as late as 1974 (Logan 2017b). Thompson (1975) and Hay (1975) argued that the increase in the use of pardons and mercy to offset the increase in capital offences in criminal law in the 18th and early 19th centuries was another means of extending the elite classes' social control over others in society. Hay (ibid.) also points to the sharp increase in capital offences in criminal law in the 18th century, many of which focussed on the protection of ruling-class property by criminalising behaviour previously seen as customary by the poor in society.

Langbein (1983) strongly criticised Hay's work. Looking at data from London courts in the 1750s, Langbein argues that there is no evidence of regular prosecutions for new criminal offences designed to increase the power of the social elite, as Hay claims. Instead, the prosecutions in Langbein's data mostly related to offences that had been felonies since medieval times (see also Innes and Styles (1986)). Langbein also argues against Hay's claim that only the social elite had the power to prosecute others. Langbein shows that victims of the offences in his sample (who had to prosecute their own offences privately in court at that time) were mostly not from the ruling classes. Langbein (1983) and Beattie (1986) also show that juries often tried to limit the scope of criminal law in a principled and rational way, with increasing levels of guidance from judges as the 19th century went on (Logan 2017b), and did not automatically act in line with ruling-class interests. Langbein's later work (2003) argues that due process safeguards like defence lawyers and the exclusion of hearsay evidence emerged during the 18th century as a way of correcting mistakes and inconsistencies occurring at the pre-trial stage. However, felony defendants could not have legal representation until 1836 (Griffiths 2017), and courts heard 20 to 30 cases per day on average in the late 18th century (Lacey 2008: 13), so there was little sense of court defendants being innocent until proven guilty at this point.

The work of King (2000) and that of Brewer and Styles (1980) support the view that people from a wide range of social backgrounds could use criminal justice as a means of responding to harm against them. Innes and Styles (1986) also point out how difficult it sometimes was for the ruling classes to bring new criminal offences into the law through Parliamentary legislation. Finally, Beattie (1986) shows how much discretion magistrates and juries had not only in deciding on guilt but also at the pre-trial stage in terms of investigating, and even dismissing, cases before court. The widespread use of mercy in criminal justice, in the form of pardons (with or without conditions) to mitigate sentencing (Strange 2017) is further evidence of how much discretion existed.

Overall, it is clear that the State and the ruling classes had increasing levels of influence over the criminal court process from the 14th century onwards. However, it is also clear that criminal justice could be, and was, used by every level of society as a tool in the response to criminal harm and was more the result of class conflict and the usage of individual discretion (King 2000) than a weapon for social control by the elite (Smith 2007: 607). One example of how the State attempted to impose its own view of how criminal justice should work, but was forced to back down in the face of contrasting attitudes elsewhere in society, is the case of *Dudley and Stephens* (1884) 14 QBD 273, in which two sailors were on trial for the murder of one of their crewmates. Dudley, Stephens, and two others were adrift in a small boat in the South Atlantic for 19 days with very little food. They selected the weakest crewmember, killed him, ate his body and drank his blood (Emsley 2013: 5). Dudley and Stephens's actions sound horrific, but so-called 'survival cannibalism' was a long-standing custom among sailors (Simpson 1984). The judges reflected ruling-class sensibilities by refusing to allow a defence of necessity to Dudley and Stephens (Norrie 2014) but then reduced the mandatory death sentence to six months' imprisonment, indirectly recognising the lower-class custom in punishment without fully acknowledging it as part of the law.

Study exercise 2.2

Read the competing accounts of 18th-century criminal law and criminal justice in England by Hay (1975) and Langbein (1983). Which account do you find more convincing, and why?

Turning finally to the usage of criminal punishment in England through history, the traditional Whig view is that there was a gradual move from various forms of corporal punishment working together with wide usage of capital punishment, to a more humane and rational approach based around prison and other ways of limiting personal freedom. The gradual decline in the use of benefit of clergy as a way for literate adult males to avoid the death sentence for felonies, and its final abolition in 1823 (Turner 2017a), might support this view of steady progress towards consistency and fairness in criminal punishment.

Foucault (1977), on the other hand, in a more Marxist-influenced account, examines the changes in punishment techniques during the 18th and 19th centuries, arguing that there was a shift from often-brutal forms of corporal and capital punishment towards greater use of the prison. Foucault argues that this change occurred because using punishment (both in prison and wider society) to psychologically discipline individuals' behaviour was a more effective way of controlling lower-class people and exploiting their ability to work in a way which profited the elite in society. Garland (1985) points to the increasing focus on rehabilitation of offenders through expert decision-making, inside and outside prison, from the mid- to late-19th century onwards – although non-rehabilitative sentences, such as fines and corporal punishment, were still evident even in this welfare-driven policy era.

Sharpe (2014) points to a decline in the usage of corporal punishment intended to shame the offender publicly, such as whipping or the stocks, between 1550 and 1750. Sharpe argues that houses of correction were used to discipline the behaviour of petty offenders in England through hard labour from the mid-16th century onwards (ibid.), a fact which contradicts Foucault's claim that a change in criminal justice terms towards discipline and social control did not occur until the 18th century. Hall (2012: 27) also argues that changes in punishment had been gradually occurring over a longer period than Foucault had claimed.

Writers have also debated whether the transition to transportation and prison, and away from public and violent forms of punishment like public hanging, was driven by a desire to make criminal punishment more humane. Seal (2017) points to evidence of execution becoming less and less of a public spectacle during the 19th century, as prisoners no longer had a procession to their execution and no longer gave a speech to spectators before their hanging took place. Beattie (1986) argues that the idea of increasing humanity in punishment is at least partially true. Gatrell (1994), in a more critical approach, looks at the attitudes towards public hanging from a variety of different social viewpoints before concluding that the State ended executions in public to avoid the criticisms of justice from the crowds who attending public hangings and because of their own indifference towards the circumstances of offenders who were hanged. As a result, Gatrell doubts whether changes in punishment occurred for humanitarian reasons. Even Rawlings (1999: 65), who acknowledges the importance of reformers like John Howard in improving prison conditions and encouraging less frequent use of the death penalty, argues that without an increasingly strong and centralised criminal justice process, these reformers would have found it much harder to get their voices heard. There was a move to regard the appropriate aim of punishment, inside and outside prison, as being rehabilitation, because crime was the result of biological and social factors beyond the individual offender's control (Garland 1985). This trend emerged in the late 19th century and continued to be important until the mid-20th century.

Rawlings (1999) and Emsley (2011) continue the story of English criminal justice's development through the 20th century. Later chapters will say more about the modern era of criminal justice, but here the discussion can identify some key trends. Firstly, there were the increasing attempts at State centralisation and control over criminal justice policy and practice (Garland 1985), to the point where efficiency became a measure of success in itself and not simply a way of achieving other criminal justice aims. However, this trend did not and could not remove the discretion which criminal justice agencies and individuals had, and still have, over how criminal justice is carried out (see, for example, Godfrey et al. (2008: ch.4) for the significant discretion involved in police work, past and present). Nonetheless, the State changed the face of criminal punishment throughout the 20th century by introducing a series of non-custodial penalties to complement imprisonment and the fines. After a steady increase in the number of non-custodial penalties available from the 1940s onwards, there has more recently been a streamlining of sentencing options, so that since 2005, they comprise absolute discharges, conditional discharges, compensation orders, fines, community orders, and suspended sentence orders (Mair 2017: 285). Nevertheless, without the individual decision-making of thousands of criminal justice practitioners, especially probation workers, such punishments could not be enforced in practice.

Secondly, from the 1950s onwards, and in the context of a rise in recorded crime which began at that time and continued at an increasing rate into the mid-1990s (Reiner 2007: 64–6), there was a decline in criminal justice policy-makers' belief that offenders could be successfully rehabilitated and that crime could be removed from society (Garland 2001). Thirdly, in a return to historical views from the early 19th century, there was an increasing political tendency from the 1970s to treat individuals as being fully responsible for their offending behaviour. Such a tendency focuses on the individual motive and opportunity which partially explains crime, but ignores the effects of social and economic factors, such as changes in technology, and more broadly the impact of a neoliberal, consumerist, free-market economy on social exclusion and individual attitudes towards offending (Young 1999; Reiner 2007: 80–90; Hall 2012).

Finally, and in close connection with the third trend, some writers have detected increasing levels of public fear of crime in the face of increasing policy focus on security and reducing risk (Reiner 2007: 114–6) and an increasingly tough approach to punishing crime, pointing to rising prison usage and punishment intended to shame offenders as evidence (Garland 2001; Pratt 2002). Matthews (2005) provides an important critique of this alleged increase in punitivism. He shows that punishment is more diverse and less excessive in nature than Garland and Pratt have claimed, and points to evidence suggesting that public opinions on criminal justice are not as punitive as they appear to be. Matthews' work (see also Zedner 2002) is an important reminder that trends in criminal justice policy are often nothing new historically speaking, often overstated in their influence, and often overly pessimistic in denying that a different, and better, criminal justice (and wider social order) is possible (Young 1992; Malloch and Munro 2013).

Study exercise 2.3

Find information on the usage of different types of criminal justice punishment in England in 1998, 2008, and 2018. Do the trends in punishment usage over the past 20 years reflect Garland's argument that criminal punishment is becoming increasingly harsh?

Conclusions: linking discussion to the roadmap theories

What can different perspectives on the historical development of English criminal law and criminal justice tell us about how these institutions developed? The first point is to reiterate the points made in this chapter's introduction about the limitations of historical evidence on criminal law and criminal justice. It is clear that statistics on prosecution, conviction, and punishment cannot explain everything about criminal law and criminal justice in England, simply because, in the past as now, some crime – maybe most crime – was neither recorded nor punished. However, studying the history of criminal law and criminal justice in this way can help to explain how these institutions look now. Just as importantly, historical study can generate ideas about how they can work in a fairer and more effective way in the future. The argument here is therefore that the advantages of studying historical data about criminal law and criminal justice outweigh the disadvantages.

The chapter's overview of criminal law and criminal justice in England through history clearly shows that the liberal group of roadmap theories has been very influential in the development of both. The chapter has also shown how closely the development of both criminal law and criminal justice link to changing social, political, religious, and economic conditions over time. Criminal law has always centred on individual responsibility for criminal behaviour in terms of controlling crime and deterring people from committing it. Through judging people based on their character and the shift towards criminal liability for serious offences based on psychological mens rea, as well as the enforcement of public morals, criminal law has always expressed its own values and functions in this liberalist way. Criminal justice has taken a very similar path through history. Punishment, like criminal law, focussed on deterrence and physical punishments in medieval and early modern times, and usage of the death penalty persisted well into the 20th century. Even the more recent shift to the risk management model in punishment detected by writers like Feeley and Simon (1992) and Garland (2001) connects to the liberal approach. Such a preventive approach may focus on trying to control the behaviour of whole groups of people, but it still relies on trying to change the offending perspectives of individuals, and views individuals as free to make decisions and responsible for their criminal actions. As such, it links closely with the traditional liberal approach (Carvalho 2017) – a theme which later chapters in the book will discuss in more depth.

However, the story of criminal law and criminal justice in England through history is not only one of liberal and risk management values. Work from writers such as Hay (1975) pointed to the influence of ruling-class interests over criminal law and criminal justice, with the aim of extending the power of the elite and repressing other social groups. The approach of Hay clearly fits in with the radical group of theories on the roadmap and supports the argument of Norrie (2014) and others that criminal law and criminal justice's liberal appearance hides their bias in favour of the ruling class in society. However, other historical work shows that there have always been limits to the ruling class influence over criminal law and justice, important though that influence is. The evidence of Beattie (1986) and King (2000), among others, demonstrates that discretion over the direction of criminal law and justice, at a variety of different societal levels, is a feature throughout their history in England. At different points, that discretion was used in a way which reflected deterministic theories, with the aim of rehabilitating offenders rather than simply punishing them (Garland 1985), as well as in a way which focussed on punishment and deterrence.

It is therefore clear that the history of both criminal law and criminal justice is one where radical, social power-based values competed with liberal ideas about responsibility for crime, as well as a variety of other theoretical concerns. As a result, the radical hybrid realist theories, which see criminal law and justice as having a series of values and as being the result of conflict between the powerful State and other groups at different levels of society, offer the most realistic explanation of their historical development. Later chapters will discuss whether the same theoretical approach applies to the current landscape of criminal law and criminal justice, starting with an analysis of actus reus in Chapter 3.

Key points

- The development of both criminal law and criminal justice in England is closely linked with changing social, political, religious, and economic conditions
- Criminal law in England became increasingly organised and increasingly under State control from the 13th century onwards
- Criminal law in England gradually became more focussed on disciplining the behaviour of the poor in society, and this trend became increasingly important from the mid-19th century onwards
- The extent of ruling-class influence over the different stages of criminal justice in England has been the subject of extensive academic debate since the 1970s
- Criminal justice underwent a change from physical, deterrent forms of punishment to more humane, but also more psychological, disciplinary forms of punishment from the 16th century onwards – but the process of change was gradual and inconsistent
- While liberal and power-based interpretations of criminal justice history play a prominent role, the radical hybrid realist roadmap theories introduced in Chapter 1 offer the most complete and realistic account of criminal law and justice's historical development

Further reading

Emsley, C. (2013), *Crime and Society in England, 1750–1900* (4th ed.). Abingdon: Routledge.

Garland, D. (1985), *Punishment and Welfare*. Aldershot: Gower.

Hay, D., Linebaugh, P., Rule, J.G., Thompson, E.P., and Winslow, C. (eds.) (1975), *Albion's Fatal Tree: Crime and Society in Eighteenth-Century England*. London: Allen Lane.

Langbein, J.H. (1983), 'Albion's Fatal Flaws', *Past and Present*, **98**(1): 96–120.

Sharpe, J.A. (2014), *Crime in Early Modern England, 1550–1750* (revised 2nd ed.). Harlow: Pearson.

References

Ashworth, A., and Zedner, L. (2008), 'Defending Criminal Law: Reflections on the Changing Character of Crime, Procedure and Sanctions', *Criminal Law and Philosophy*, **2**(1): 21–51.

Banks, S. (2017), 'Duelling', in Turner, J., Taylor, P., Morley, S., and Corteen, K. (eds.), *A Companion to the History of Crime and Criminal Justice*. Bristol: Policy Press.

Beattie, J.M. (1986), *Crime and the Courts in England, 1660–1800*. Oxford: OUP.

Berman, H.J. (1983), *Law and Revolution: The Formation of the Western Legal Tradition*. Cambridge, MA: HUP.

Brewer, J., and Styles, J. (1980), 'Introduction', in Brewer, J., and Styles, J. (eds.), *An Ungovernable People: The English and Their Law in the Seventeenth and Eighteenth Centuries*. London: Hutchinson.

Carvalho, H. (2017), *The Preventive Turn in Criminal Law*. Oxford: OUP.

Chalmers, J., and Leverick, F. (2013), 'Tracking the Creation of Criminal Offences', *Criminal Law Review*: 543–60.

Chalmers, J., Leverick, F., and Shaw, A. (2015), 'Is Formal Criminalisation Really on the Rise? Evidence from the 1950s', *Criminal Law Review*: 177–91.

Christie, N. (1977), 'Conflicts as Property', *British Journal of Criminology*, 17(1): 1–19.

Cole, B., and Osidipe, T. (2017), 'Criminal Courts', in Harding, J., Davies, P., and Mair, G. (eds.), *An Introduction to Criminal Justice*. London: Sage.

Critchley, T.A. (1967), *A History of Police in England and Wales, 900–1966*. London: Constable.

Crowther, C. (2007), *An Introduction to Criminology and Criminal Justice*. Basingstoke: Palgrave Macmillan.

Eisner, M. (2017), 'Interpersonal Violence on the British Isles, 1200–2016', in Liebling, A., Maruna, S., and McAra, L. (eds.), *The Oxford Handbook of Criminology* (6th ed.). Oxford: OUP.

Emsley, C. (2011), *Crime and Society in Twentieth-Century England*. Harlow: Pearson.

Emsley, C. (2013), *Crime and Society in England, 1750–1900* (5th ed.). Abingdon: Routledge.

Farmer, L. (1997), *Criminal Law, Tradition and Legal Order: The Genius of Scots Law, 1747 to the Present*. Cambridge: CUP.

Feeley, M.M., and Little, D.L. (1991), 'The Vanishing Female: The Decline of Women in the Criminal Process, 1687–1912', *Law and Society Review*, 25(4): 719–57.

Feeley, M.M., and Simon, J. (1992), 'The New Penology: Notes on the Emerging Strategy of Corrections and Its Implications', *Criminology*, 30(4): 449–74.

Fletcher, G.F. (1978), *Rethinking Criminal Law*. Boston: Little, Brown and Co.

Foucault, M. (1977), *Discipline and Punish: The Birth of the Prison*. Harmondsworth: Penguin.

Garland, D. (1985), *Punishment and Welfare*. Aldershot: Gower.

Garland, D. (2001), *The Culture of Control: Crime and Social Order in Contemporary Society*. Oxford: OUP.

Gatrell, V.A.C. (1980), 'The Decline of Theft and Violence in Victorian and Edwardian England', in Gatrell, V.A.C., Lenman, B., and Parker, G. (eds.), *Crime and the Law: The Social History of Crime in Western Europe Since 1500*. London: Europa.

Gatrell, V.A.C. (1994), *The Hanging Tree*. Oxford: OUP.

Godfrey, B.S., and Lawrence, P. (2014), *Crime and Justice Since 1750*. Abingdon: Routledge.

Godfrey, B.S., Lawrence, P., and Williams, C.A. (2008), *History and Crime*. London: Sage.

Griffiths, C.C. (2017), 'Advocacy in Criminal Trials', in Turner, J., Taylor, P., Morley, S., and Corteen, K. (eds.), *A Companion to the History of Crime and Criminal Justice*. Bristol: Policy Press.

Hall, S. (2012), *Theorizing Crime and Deviance*. London: Sage.

Hay, D. (1975), 'Property, Authority and Criminal Law', in Hay, D., Linebaugh, P., Rule, J.G., Thompson, E.P., and Winslow, C. (eds.), *Albion's Fatal Tree: Crime and Society in Eighteenth-Century England*. London: Allen Lane.

Hay, D., Linebaugh, P., Rule, J.G., Thompson, E.P., and Winslow, C. (eds.) (1975), *Albion's Fatal Tree: Crime and Society in Eighteenth-Century England*. London: Allen Lane.

Horder, J. (1997), 'Two Histories and Four Hidden Principles of Mens Rea', *Law Quarterly Review*, 113(1): 95–119.

Horder, J. (2014), 'Bureaucratic Criminal Law: Too Much of a Good Thing?' in Duff, R.A., Farmer, L., Marshall, S.E., Renzo, M., and Tadros, V. (eds.), *Criminalization: The Political Morality of Criminal Law*. Oxford: OUP.

Horder, J. (2016), *Ashworth's Principles of Criminal Law* (8th ed.). Oxford: OUP.

Husak, D. (2008), *Overcriminalization: The Limits of Criminal Law*. Oxford: OUP.

Innes, J., and Styles, J. (1986), 'The Crime Wave: Recent Writing on Crime and Criminal Justice', *Journal of British Studies*, **25**(4): 380–435.

Johnston, L. (1992), *The Rebirth of Private Policing*. London: Routledge.

Johnstone, G., and Ward, T. (2010), *Law and Crime*. London: Sage.

King, P. (2000), *Crime, Justice and Discretion in England, 1740–1820*. Oxford: OUP.

Lacey, N. (2001), 'In Search of the Responsible Subject: History, Philosophy and Social Sciences in Criminal Law Theory', *Modern Law Review*, **64**(3): 350–71.

Lacey, N. (2007), 'Character, Capacity, Outcome: Toward a Framework for Assessing the Shifting Pattern of Criminal Responsibility in Modern English Law', in Dubber, M., and Farmer, L. (eds.), *Modern Histories of Crime and Punishment*. Stanford, CA: SUP.

Lacey, N. (2008), *The Prisoner's Dilemma: Political Economy and Punishment in Contemporary Democracies*. Cambridge: CUP.

Langbein, J.H. (1983), 'Albion's Fatal Flaws', *Past and Present*, **98**(1): 96–120.

Langbein, J.H. (2003), *The Origins of Adversary Criminal Trial*. Oxford: OUP.

Logan, A. (2017a), 'Magistrates', in Turner, J., Taylor, P., Morley, S., and Corteen, K. (eds.), *A Companion to the History of Crime and Criminal Justice*. Bristol: Policy Press.

Logan, A. (2017b), 'Juries', in Turner, J., Taylor, P., Morley, S., and Corteen, K. (eds.), *A Companion to the History of Crime and Criminal Justice*. Bristol: Policy Press.

Mair, G. (2017), 'Community Sentences', in Harding, J., Davies, P., and Mair, G. (eds.), *An Introduction to Criminal Justice*. London: Sage.

Malloch, M., and Munro, W. (eds.) (2013), *Crime, Critique and Utopia*. London: Palgrave Macmillan.

Matthews, R. (2005), 'The Myth of Punitiveness', *Theoretical Criminology*, **9**(2): 175–201.

McAuley, F., and McCutcheon, J. (2000), *Criminal Liability*. Dublin: Round Hall Sweet and Maxwell.

Miller, W.I. (2006), *Eye for an Eye*. Cambridge: CUP.

Norrie, A. (2014), *Crime, Reason and History* (3rd ed.). Cambridge: CUP.

Pearson, G. (1983), *Hooligan: A History of Respectable Fears*. Basingstoke: Palgrave Macmillan.

Pratt, J. (2002), *Punishment and Civilisation*. London: Sage.

Radzinowicz, L. (1948), *A History of English Criminal Law, Volume I*. London: Stevens.

Ramsay, P. (2006), 'The Responsible Subject as Citizen: Criminal Law, Democracy and the Welfare State', *Modern Law Review*, **69**(1): 29–58.

Rawlings, P. (1999), *Crime and Power: A History of Criminal Justice 1688–1998*. Harlow: Longman.

Reiner, R. (2007), *Law and Order: An Honest Citizen's Guide to Crime and Control*. Cambridge: Polity Press.

Seal, L. (2017), 'Capital Punishment (England and Wales)', in Turner, J., Taylor, P., Morley, S., and Corteen, K. (eds.), *A Companion to the History of Crime and Criminal Justice*. Bristol: Policy Press.

Sharpe, J.A. (2001), 'Crime, Order and Historical Change', in Muncie, J., and McLaughlin, E. (eds.), *The Problem of Crime* (2nd ed.). London: Sage/Open University Press.

Sharpe, J.A. (2014), *Crime in Early Modern England, 1550–1750* (revised 2nd ed.). Harlow: Pearson.

Simpson, A.W.B. (1984), *Cannibalism and the Common Law*. Chicago: UCP.

Smith, B.P. (2007), 'English Criminal Justice Administration, 1650–1850: A Historiographical Essay', *Law and History Review*, **25**(3): 593–634.

Smith, K.J.M. (1998), *Lawyers, Legislators and Theorists: Developments in English Criminal Jurisprudence, 1800–1957*. Oxford: OUP.

Storch, R.D. (1976), 'The Policeman as Domestic Missionary: Urban Discipline and Popular Culture in Northern England, 1850–1880', *Journal of Social History*, **9**(4): 481–502.

Strange, C. (2017), 'Mercy', in Turner, J., Taylor, P., Morley, S., and Corteen, K. (eds.), *A Companion to the History of Crime and Criminal Justice*. Bristol: Policy Press.

Tennant, M. (2017), 'The "New" Police', in Turner, J., Taylor, P., Morley, S., and Corteen, K. (eds.), *A Companion to the History of Crime and Criminal Justice*. Bristol: Policy Press.

Thompson, E.P. (1975), *Whigs and Hunters: The Origin of the Black Act*. London: Allen Lane.

Thompson, E.P. (1991), *Customs in Common: Studies in Traditional Popular Culture*. London: Merlin Press.

Turner, J. (2017a), 'Benefit of Clergy', in Turner, J., Taylor, P., Morley, S., and Corteen, K. (eds.), *A Companion to the History of Crime and Criminal Justice*. Bristol: Policy Press.

Wiener, M. (1990), *Reconstructing the Criminal: Culture, Law and Policy in England, 1830–1914*. Cambridge: CUP.

Young, J. (1999), *The Exclusive Society*. London: Sage.

Young, P. (1992), 'On the Importance of Utopias in Criminological Thinking', *British Journal of Criminology*, **32**(4): 423–37.

Zedner, L. (2002), 'Dangers of Dystopias in Penal Theory', *Oxford Journal of Legal Studies*, **22**(2): 341–66.

Chapter 3

Actus reus and mens rea I

General principles

Chapter aims

After reading Chapter 3, you should be able to understand:

- The basic meanings of actus reus and mens rea
- The key criminal law principles which are included within the concepts of actus reus and mens rea
- How actus reus and mens rea are constructed and represented in crime statistics

- How the police, CPS, and courts use actus reus and mens rea in criminal justice practice
- How victims of crime who report actus reus and mens rea are treated by the criminal justice process
- How the evidence on actus reus and mens rea in criminal law and criminal justice fits in with the theoretical models introduced in Chapter 1

Introduction

This chapter will begin the explanation and analysis of the concepts of actus reus, or 'guilty act', and mens rea, or 'guilty mind', by looking at how these concepts relate to individual liability for a completed crime. Chapter 4 will then look at how actus reus and mens rea work in relation to crimes which are not complete, or which have been committed by more than one person.

The term 'actus reus' literally means 'guilty act', constituting 'the package of behaviour which forms the substance of a criminal prohibition' (Wilson 2017: 69). The term 'mens rea' literally means 'guilty mind', and refers to a blameworthy state of mind on the part of the defendant (Herring 2019: 65) – in other words, what the defendant is thinking or planning at the time when they are committing the offence. However, neither actus reus or mens rea is as straightforward as these definitions imply.

Actus reus means more than just 'guilty acts'. It also includes a range of other behaviour requirements, defined in each criminal offence. For example, the actus reus of theft is taking someone else's property, and the actus reus of murder is unlawfully killing another person. But, as these two examples show, the types of illegal behaviour vary greatly between different types of offence. Herring (2016: 71) distinguishes between four different actus reus requirements – the 'four Cs':

- Conduct. Here, the actus reus involves illegal behaviour – (e.g. perjury) a crime which involves lying when giving evidence in court.
- Circumstances. Here, the actus reus involves behaviour performed in a particular scenario which makes it illegal. For example, the crime of criminal damage involves damaging or destroying property 'belonging to someone else', so the key circumstance here is that the property does not belong to the perpetrator.
- Context. Here, it is an internal or 'state of mind' element which makes the behaviour a criminal offence. For example, the crime of rape involves sexual intercourse – but done without the victim's consent, which makes it illegal. Here, the lack of consent is not something that can be 'seen'. The victim's state of mind is what counts.

- Consequences. Here, the actus reus involves producing an illegal result through behaviour – (e.g. murder) where the conduct causes the unlawful death of someone else. If the consequence was not caused by the defendant's behaviour, the offence is not proved (e.g. *White* [1910] 2 KB 124).

Since the term 'actus reus' covers so many different types of criminal behaviour in criminal law, most criminal offences will only have some of the 'four Cs', not all of them. For example, context is not relevant to the crime of murder – D would still be guilty of murder even if V asked, or even begged, D to kill them, as long as all of the actus reus and mens rea requirements were present.

Literally, 'mens rea' means 'guilty mind'. It refers to the internal thoughts which, when combined with actus reus, make up the definition of the most serious crimes – in other words, what the defendant is thinking or planning at the time when they are committing the offence. Not all crimes require mens rea, though. Strict liability offences only require actus reus, but not mens rea, for at least one element of the offence. These will be discussed later in this chapter.

The first part of this chapter explains the rules of actus reus and mens rea in more detail. The second part of the chapter discusses the ways in which criminal justice uses the concepts of actus reus and mens rea – using the police, the Crown Prosecution Service (CPS), and the criminal court process as examples, as well as considering crime victims' relationship with these agencies. Normally, criminal law sees actus reus and mens rea as separate and separable concepts (Duff 1990). However, the argument here is that criminal justice does not react to criminal behaviour by separating actions and mental responsibility in this way. Instead, it makes a judgment about a person's criminal blameworthiness which brings together mental state and behaviour (Wells and Quick 2010: 119).

Actus reus: the law

Key actus reus principles

No mens rea without actus reus

Often, in criminal law, crime is committed when there is a combination of actus reus and mens rea (see later in this chapter for a discussion of mens rea). The actus reus for each crime must be established. It is not enough that the mens rea for the crime was present if the actus reus was not committed as well (*Deller* (1952) 36 Cr App Rep 184). Criminal law in England and Wales, as Baker (2015: 250–1) explains, insists on some expression of someone's criminal thoughts through their actions before it will intervene to punish them.

Voluntary acts

Not all illegal acts count as actus reus. Acts must be voluntary before they can be considered as criminal behaviour. If the defendant has no control over their physical actions for some reason, and commits a crime while 'out of control' in this way, then there is no actus reus. In *Hill v Baxter* [1958] 1 QB 277, the Court of Appeal stated that if a swarm of killer bees attacked the defendant while driving, and the bees caused the defendant to lose control of the car and hit a pedestrian crossing the road, the defendant would not commit any actus reus because their actions were not voluntary.

In a situation like this, the defendant is conscious but has lost control over their physical actions. In other cases, though, the defendant might be unconscious. For example, they may be sleepwalking or suffering from various medical or psychological conditions, such as hypoglycaemia (Simester et al. 2016). The 'voluntary act' principle can apply in these circumstances to remove the actus reus, just as it can where D is fully conscious.

Actus reus and 'status offences'

Actus reus does not have to be about doing something. It can also be about status – being something or somewhere that is prohibited by criminal law, or possessing something that is prohibited. Examples include possession of a prohibited drug (Misuse of Drugs Act 1971 s.5(1) – see also Chapter 9 for further discussion of drugs-related criminal offences). Occasionally, the lack of the requirement of voluntary action can lead to what seem to be very unfair convictions under status offences, where the defendant appeared to have no control over where they were. Two good examples of this are *Larsonneur* (1933) 24 Cr App Rep 74 and *Winzar v Chief Constable of Kent* (1983), *The Times*, 28th March.

Actus reus and omissions

In a few situations, someone can be convicted and punished for *not* doing something – for an omission rather than an act. The courts have made people liable for omissions where the omission has caused a crime in the following situations:

- Where the defendant has voluntarily agreed to take care of the victim but has failed to take reasonable steps to do so (e.g. *Stone and Dobinson* [1977] QB 354).
- Where a parent has failed to look after their child to a reasonable standard (e.g. *Downes* (1875) 13 Cox CC 111).
- Where it is the defendant's duty to do something as part of their job contract, but the defendant does not do it and criminal harm results (e.g. *Pittwood* (1902) 19 TLR 37).

- Where the defendant has duties as part of their public office (e.g. as a police officer) but does not carry them out and criminal harm results (e.g. *Dytham* [1979] QB 722).
- Where the defendant has created a dangerous situation accidentally or unknowingly but then realises that it is dangerous and does not take steps to remove the danger and criminal harm results (e.g. *Fagan v MPC* [1969] 1 QB 438; *Miller* [1983] 2 AC 161; *Santana-Bermudez* [2004] Crim LR 471). This principle now extends to situations where the defendant should have known that they had created a dangerous situation in *Evans* [2009] EWCA Crim 650.
- Where statute law has created an offence that includes omission liability. There are no general rules that decide whether omissions liability is part of a statutory offence, but there is a trend towards accepting omissions liability for an ever-greater range of offences (Child and Ormerod 2017: 50). Offences of failing to wear a seatbelt and failing to stop after a vehicle accident, under the Road Traffic Act 1988, are just two examples of statutory omissions liability.

In some cases there seems to be very little difference between an act and an omission. For example, in *Speck* [1977] 2 All ER 859, D was guilty of gross indecency with a child because his failure to stop her from doing what she did was seen by the court as an 'invitation to continue' the gross indecency. On the other hand, in *Airedale NHS Trust v Bland* [1993] AC 789, the House of Lords decided that a victim of the Hillsborough disaster who had been in a coma for three years and who had no chance of recovery should be allowed to die by doctors ceasing to feed and medicate him through tubes. The court stated that this would be an omission (which would not lead to criminal liability for murder) rather than a deliberate act of killing by the doctors at the hospital (which would lead to liability).

Study exercise 3.1

Compare and contrast the arguments of Ashworth (1989) and Williams (1991) on how far liability for omissions should go in criminal law. Which argument do you think is better and why?

Actus reus and causation

Result crimes require the defendant to cause a prohibited consequence. There has to be a 'chain of causation' between what the defendant did and the illegal result. For example, for murder and manslaughter, the prohibited result is the unlawful death of another person. There are two types of causation in criminal law. These are factual causation and legal causation. Both factual and legal causation need to be proved before causation can be established.

Factual causation is sometimes known as 'but for' causation, because proving it involves asking whether the prohibited result would have occurred if the defendant's act had not happened. For example, in *White*, despite the defendant's attempt to kill the victim, the victim would have died regardless of the defendant's act, so the factual chain of causation was not there. *Dalloway* (1847) 2 Cox CC 273 shows that where the defendant could not have done anything to prevent the victim's death, they are not guilty, even where, as in this case, the defendant's conduct was blameworthy in itself. The Supreme Court in *Hughes* [2013] 1 WLR 2461, overruling *Williams* [2011] 1 WLR 588, decided that even where a defendant did not have driving insurance and/or a driving licence, they could not be convicted of causing death while driving under these circumstances unless their driving had been at fault in some way.

For factual causation, the defendant's act does not have to be the only cause of the prohibited result, or even the main cause. It only has to be an 'operating and substantial' cause of the result. In *Pagett* (1983) 76 Cr App Rep 279, the main cause of the victim's death was the police firing bullets at her, but the defendant was still guilty of manslaughter because he had been using the victim as a human shield while firing at the police. In *Environment Agency v Empress Car Co (Abertillery) Ltd* [1999] 2 AC 22, the defendant company was convicted of polluting a river, even though a third party had maliciously and deliberately opened the tap on the company's tank of diesel, causing the diesel to leak into the river. The House of Lords said that as the vandalism was foreseeable by a reasonable person, the defendant company had still caused the prohibited outcome, despite the voluntary damage caused by the third party here.

Proving legal causation involves asking the question: if factual causation is present, are there any other legal principles which will break the chain of causation and remove liability for the prohibited outcome? Firstly, was there an independent and voluntary act by a third party which broke the chain of causation? In *Pagett* (see earlier discussion), the Court of Appeal decided that the police's act of firing at the victim was only a 'reflex', not a voluntary independent act. As a result, the police did not break the chain of causation, and the defendant was still guilty of manslaughter. In some situations, an independent third party act is capable of breaking the chain of causation, as in *Rafferty* [2007] EWCA Crim 1846, where the later drowning of V by D's accomplices broke the chain linking the defendant's earlier robbery and assault of the victim and the victim's death.

A second category of 'third party intervention' involves the victim dying after receiving poor medical treatment for injuries originally caused by the defendant. *Smith* [1959] 2 QB 35 stated that if what D did is still a 'substantial and operative cause' of V's death, even poor medical treatment will not break the chain (see also *Cheshire* [1991] 3 All ER 670 and *Malcherek* [1981] 2 All ER 422). On the other hand, doctors' treatment of the victim in *Jordan* (1956) 40 Cr App Rep 152 did break the causation chain because the treatment had been 'palpably bad'. The defendant was therefore not guilty of causing the victim's death – but *Jordan* was an exceptional case in terms of how bad the doctors' treatment of the victim was.

The third category of 'third party intervention' cases involves situations where the defendant has assisted the victim to take drugs in some way, the victim has voluntarily taken the drugs, and the victim has died because of taking them. There was some uncertainty in the law during the 1990s and early 2000s about whether or the defendant was responsible for causing unlawful death in this situation. The House of Lords resolved the confusion in *Kennedy (No.2)* [2007] 3 WLR 612. This case decided that where D prepares drugs and gives them to V to take, and V dies as a result of taking the drugs, D is not guilty of manslaughter as long as V made a 'voluntary and informed' decision to take the drugs.

A fourth category involves V, previously injured by D, contributing to his or her own death by some kind of neglect or intervention. The basic rule here is that D has to 'take the victim as they find them'. Any physical or psychological characteristics that might make V more vulnerable to harm are irrelevant, as long as what D did is still a 'substantial and operative cause' of V's death. This principle is illustrated by *Holland* (1841) 2 Mood & R 351, *Blaue* [1975] 3 All ER 446, and *Dear* [1996] Crim LR 595. The courts have rejected attempts to construct causation between D and V where the harm causing V's death was the combined acts of the defendant and others (*Carey* [2006] EWCA Crim 17). The courts have also broken the causation chain where D's harm was seen only as part of the background to the independent act causing V's death (*Dhaliwal* [2006] 2 Cr App Rep 348).

Where V is injured, or killed, trying to escape from D, the escape will only break the chain of causation if it was not 'reasonably foreseeable'. Therefore, if an ordinary person who was present at the scene would not have expected the victim to try to escape, then the chain of causation will be broken (*Pitts* (1842) Car & M 284 and *Roberts* (1971) 56 Cr App Rep 95). D must have actually committed a *crime* that caused V to try to escape, however (*Arobieke* [1988] Crim LR 314). Causation is also possible where D frightens V to death. D can be liable for murder or manslaughter in such a case, depending on their mens rea (*Towers* (1874) 12 Cox CC 530 and *Hayward* (1908) 21 Cox CC 692).

> **Study exercise 3.2**
>
> Read a media account of the events surrounding the fire at the Grenfell
> Tower block in West London on 14th June 2017, in which 72 people
> died. Using factual and legal causation principles, should any individual
> or group be held criminally responsible for the deaths of the victims?
> Does the causation law go far enough in blaming the people who you
> believe should be held legally responsible for the victims' deaths at
> Grenfell?

Mens rea: the law

Key mens rea principles

Direct and oblique intent

The phrase 'mens rea' refers to the state of mind of D while they are committing a criminal offence. Some offences can only be committed with intent
as mens rea (murder or theft, for example). There are two types of intent
in criminal law. The first is *direct intent*. This occurs where someone aims,
desires, or makes the decision to bring about a particular consequence that is
prohibited (*Mohan* [1976] QB 1). Where there is evidence beyond reasonable
doubt that D wanted to commit a particular crime, or tried or made an effort
to make the crime happen, they have direct intent.

However, intent also has another meaning in criminal law in England and
Wales. This is either *indirect intent* or *oblique intent*. This occurs where there
is evidence beyond reasonable doubt that D did not have direct intent but did
foresee a chance that the crime might happen because of what they did. The
question is how much of a chance of the crime happening D has to foresee
before criminal law decides that there is intention. This is a vitally important
question where an offence requires intent as mens rea, such as murder.

The House of Lords has struggled to define the boundary between indirect
intent and recklessness in the murder cases of *Moloney* [1985] 1 AC 905, *Hancock and Shankland* [1986] 1 AC 455, and then *Nedrick* [1986] 1 WLR 1025,
which tried to consolidate the guidelines set out in the two previous cases. It
said that juries were only entitled to find indirect intent where D foresaw the
prohibited outcome as a 'virtually certain' consequence of their actions. This
test takes into account the 'naturalness' of the prohibited outcome as a result
of D's actions (from the *Moloney* test) and the level of probability of the prohibited outcome as a result of D's actions (from the *Hancock* test). If someone
realised the outcome was 'almost inevitable', that would be strong evidence
that indirect intent was there. However, foresight of death or grievous bodily

harm was still only 'evidence'. It was still up to the jury to decide whether it actually amounted to intent in each case, based on the evidence presented to them during the trial. This last point was confirmed in *Woollin* [1999] AC 82, as it was interpreted in *Matthews and Alleyne* [2003] 2 Cr App Rep 30 – so that foresight of virtual certainty is only evidence from which juries can infer intent, but do not have to. As the law currently stands, therefore:

• The lower limit of indirect intent is foresight by D of the prohibited outcome as a virtually certain result of their actions;
• If D does not have this level of foresight, there cannot be any intent;
• But even where foresight of a virtual certainty is proved, the jury does not have to convict;
• Finally, if a jury finds that D has foreseen the prohibited outcome as a 'morally certain' outcome of their actions (meaning that the level of foresight is higher than a virtual certainty), then under *Moloney* they have to convict.

Study exercise 3.3

How easy does the law's current definition of intent make it for juries to understand what intent means legally?

Intent and motive

Criminal law has stated that D's good motive is irrelevant as long as they have the intent required – so that they would still be guilty if they intentionally committed a crime for a good reason. In *Yip Chiu-Cheung v R* [1995] 1 AC 111, the court stated that an undercover police officer, if he had been prosecuted, would have been guilty of conspiracy because he had planned to smuggle drugs with D. This was the case even though the police officer only did this in an attempt to trap and arrest D in the act of smuggling the drugs (see also *Sood* [1998] EWCA Crim 254).

There are some cases where criminal law has allowed good motive as a defence against criminal intent, however. In *Steane* [1947] KB 997, the Court of Appeal decided that D was not guilty of assisting the enemy during wartime even though he intentionally made radio broadcasts for the Nazis during the Second World War, because the court judged his intention to be saving his family from a concentration camp rather than assisting the enemy. And in *Re A (Conjoined Twins)* [2001] 2 WLR 480, doctors were given permission to operate to separate conjoined twins, in the knowledge that not separating the twins would almost certainly result in both twins dying, where they foresaw the death of the weaker twin as being a virtually certain consequence of the operation.

> **Study exercise 3.4**
>
> Should the law ever allow good motive to be used as a defence? If so, in what circumstances?

Transfer of malice

Where D has the right actus reus and mens rea for a particular criminal offence, but the offence has a different 'target' (either a person or property) from the one which D intended to hit, then D is still guilty of the offence (*Saunders and Archer* (1573) 2 Plowd 473; *Latimer* (1886) 17 QBD 359). This is the transfer of malice principle. However, the principle does not work where D has the actus reus of one crime, but the mens rea of another (*Pembliton* (1874) LR 2 CCR 119).

Contemporaneity

Generally, the actus reus and the mens rea of an offence must happen at the same time in order for someone to be guilty of that offence, even if they only coincide for a very short time (e.g. *Styles* [2015] EWCA Crim 619). However, if the actus reus is a continuing act, and D has the right mens rea during that continuing act, then they can still be guilty. In *Thabo-Meli* [1954] 1 WLR 228, D was guilty of murder where he attacked V with a wooden club and then threw the victim over a cliff, thinking V was already dead. In fact V died later from exposure at the bottom of the cliff. D's actus reus was held to be continuing from when he first attacked V until after he had thrown V over the cliff, and as he had the right mens rea (intent to do grievous bodily harm or kill) during this continuing act, he was guilty of murder. This principle has also been applied to unlawful act manslaughter in *Church* [1966] 1 QB 59 and *Le Brun* [1991] 4 All ER 673, and to non-fatal assaults in *Fagan v MPC* [1969] 1 QB 439 and *Santana-Bermudez* [2004] Crim LR 471. In *Attorney-General's Reference (No.4 of 1980)* [1981] 1 WLR 705, one of several acts committed by D caused V's death, but it could not be confirmed which one actually had. The court said that this did not matter as long as each act was enough to establish a conviction for manslaughter, which was true in this case.

Recklessness

Recklessness is not about aiming or meaning to commit a crime, as intention is, but instead only requires taking a risk that the crime will be committed because of the defendant's actions. Criminal law will not punish every risk of a crime being committed, though. The risk needed for criminal liability must be unjustifiable – whether a risk is justifiable or not is decided based upon how socially beneficial taking that risk is (Child and Ormerod 2017: 109).

The law on criminal recklessness is there to punish people who take unnecessary risks which end up causing damage or harm. There are two specific types of criminal recklessness. The first type of recklessness is 'subjective recklessness'. Subjective recklessness is proved where a defendant foresaw a risk of the actus reus of the crime occurring (damage, injury, and so on) but took that risk anyway, resulting in the causing of the actus reus. As long as D foresees some risk, it does not matter how large a risk D foresees (*Brady* [2007] Crim LR 564). This type of recklessness was used in the case of *Cunningham* [1957] 2 QB 396. The second type of recklessness is 'objective recklessness'. Objective recklessness is proved where a reasonable person in D's position would have foreseen an 'obvious and serious' risk of the actus reus occurring as a result of the risk that D took. It also includes subjective recklessness as described earlier. This type of recklessness first appeared in the cases of *Caldwell* [1982] AC 341 and *Lawrence* [1982] AC 510. The objective type of recklessness labels a wider range of behaviour as being criminally blameworthy than the subjective type. This is true because there is no need for D to have actually foreseen the risk of causing the actus reus under the objective test, as long as a reasonable person in D's position would have seen an obvious and serious risk of the crime occurring. Under the subjective test, if D did not foresee a risk of the actus reus being caused, there can be no recklessness.

Before *Caldwell*, the courts applied the subjective recklessness test to cases of assault (*Cunningham* itself) and criminal damage (*Stephenson* [1979] 1 QB 695; cf. *Parker* [1976] 63 Cr App Rep 211), as well as to other crimes that could be committed recklessly. After *Caldwell*, the courts began to apply the wider objective recklessness test instead of the subjective recklessness test for offences such as criminal damage. However, *G and R* [2003] 3 WLR 1060 overruled *Caldwell* for cases of criminal damage. In *G and R*, the House of Lords gave a range of reasons for preferring the subjective recklessness test to the objective recklessness test. These included:

• Subjective recklessness focuses on what Ds were actually thinking about at the time of the offence, or their 'blameworthy' thoughts. This makes punishing people for crimes based on their recklessness fairer, especially for serious crimes. This is so because they have seen the risk of what could happen because of their behaviour but continued with that behaviour regardless.

• Subjective recklessness avoids discrimination against those who cannot see the risks they create, for reasons that are not their fault – such as children and the mentally ill. Both of these groups were convicted and punished under objective recklessness (e.g. *Elliott v C* [1983] 1 WLR 939, *Bell* [1984] 3 All ER 842) because, although they could not understand the 'obvious and serious' risks which they were taking, a reasonable person in their position would have seen those risks. As a result, bringing back the subjective recklessness test would be fairer to vulnerable people in society in terms of not punishing them for taking risks that they did not realise they were taking.

- Subjective recklessness also avoids the confusion of a necessary feature of objective recklessness – the so-called 'lacuna'. This is another way of saying that there is a 'loophole' in the law allowing some defendants to escape liability. Here, what the lacuna means is that where D sees the risk but thinks they have eliminated it completely (but in fact have not done so), then they cannot be objectively reckless, because they have foreseen the risk, but cannot be subjectively reckless either because they have not 'gone ahead' with the risk. The loophole was never successfully used to avoid liability in a case – but in cases like *Chief Constable of Avon and Somerset v Shimmen* (1986) 84 Cr App Rep 7, its applicability was considered.
- Finally, juries (and presumably magistrates too) can be trusted to tell whether a defendant is telling the truth or not if they claim not to have seen the risk, based on the evidence of the defendant's actions.

However, objective recklessness has not disappeared completely. If someone is voluntarily intoxicated because they have taken alcohol or other drugs of their own free will, and committed a crime whilst intoxicated, then they are treated in law as having foreseen the risk and gone ahead anyway, even if their intoxication meant that they did not actually see the risk themselves (*Heard* [2007] EWCA Crim 125). Therefore, in these situations, objective recklessness still plays a part in criminal law.

Study exercise 3.5

Make a list of the advantages of subjective and objective recklessness. Which do you think should be used by criminal law and why? Should the law use them both together, and, if so, which should the law use in which circumstances?

Negligence

Negligence is about an objective standard of behaviour, which the defendant falls below and is liable for a criminal offence as a result. In recent times, negligence has been used as the mens rea for an increasingly wide range of crimes, especially offences that have become statutory, like rape under the Sexual Offences Act 2003, and new statutory offences, such as harassment under the

Protection from Harassment Act 1997. Negligence also plays a role in criminal law in relation to strict liability offences, which this chapter discusses next. Many statutory strict liability offences provide a defence where the defendant has exercised 'due diligence'. In other words, if someone can prove that they were not negligent, they will be acquitted.

Study exercise 3.6

Using an Internet statute database, find five other offences that require negligence as mens rea. Do you agree that all of the offences should have this type of mens rea?

Strict liability

Strict liability offences only require actus reus to be proved to secure a conviction, not mens rea. Strict liability is used for statutory offences (i.e. offences that have been created by Parliament under statute law). Where the mens rea requirements for these offences are not clear in the original statute, the courts have had to decide whether the offence is completely strict liability, partly strict liability, or not strict liability at all, based on the words of the statute. The aim of this section is to explain how the courts make this decision, by examining the series of guidelines that they use.

It is important to remember three preliminary points about strict liability. Firstly, some offences can be strict liability for one or more parts of the actus reus but require mens rea for other parts of it. A good example of how this works is the comparison of the cases of *Hibbert* (1869) LR 1 CCR 184 and *Prince* (1875) LR 2 CCR 154. Secondly, other parts of the actus reus still have to be proved even if no mens rea is needed, including causation. The courts have taken a wide view of what counts as causation for strict liability offences (*Environment Agency v Empress Car Co*). Thirdly, sometimes Parliament will intervene with new legislation to make an offence strict liability even though the courts have said that it requires mens rea, as it did with a range of sexual offences in the Sexual Offences Act 2003.

Considering these points, the chapter will now discuss principles that help the courts to decide when to use strict liability. Firstly, in criminal law there is a presumption that an offence will require mens rea (*Sweet v Parsley* [1970] AC 132). Under *B v DPP* [2000] 2 AC 428, there needs to be a 'compellingly clear' or 'necessary' implication that the statute is strict liability – (i.e. that strict liability was clearly what Parliament had in mind when it created the legislation). If the statute states that mens rea is required, then there is no possibility that the offence can be strict liability. However, if there is no indication on this issue in the statute either way, this does not rule out the use of strict liability for that offence. If some parts of an offence require mens rea and other parts do not, that is good evidence that the parts which do not require mens rea are strict liability (*K* [2002] 1 AC 462). Courts need to look at the overall scheme and aims of a statute and consider that when making a decision on strict liability (*G* [2009] 1 AC 92).

However, the courts still have discretion to decide one way or the other where the legislation is not completely clear on whether an offence is strict liability or not. There are some statutory words which, when used in legislation, point towards mens rea being needed (like 'knowingly') or towards strict liability (like 'sell'). Offences involving possessing something, such as controlled drugs, are normally partially strict. Once the prosecution has proved that a defendant knows about possessing a particular item, such as a box or container, in criminal law's eyes the defendant possesses whatever is contained inside that item, such as drugs, even if they do not know about what is inside (*Warner v MPC* [1969] 2 AC 256).

If the offence is 'truly criminal', and serious enough to involve a 'breach of morality', it is more likely to need mens rea than if it is just a regulatory offence designed to improve societal behaviour (*Gammon Ltd v A-G for Hong Kong* [1985] AC 1). The more serious the offence is, the more serious the punishment for it will be, and the more likely it is that mens rea will be needed (*B v DPP*). However, in *Howells* [1977] QB 614, the offence was possession of a firearm that carried a maximum punishment of five years' imprisonment – but the offence was strict liability. Even if an offence can result in a prison sentence, it does not necessarily mean that such an offence will require mens rea. In *Blake* [1997] 1 All ER 963, the offence was 'truly criminal' because it carried a two-year maximum prison sentence, but in *Harrow LBC v Shah* [1999] 3 All ER 302, the same maximum sentence did not make the offence 'truly criminal'. These two cases show how different strict liability guidelines can conflict and take priority over one another in different case scenarios.

If the offence aims to guard against serious social harm in some way, it is more likely to receive the label of strict liability (*Gammon*). For example, *Blake* was a strict liability case because the public could be jeopardised by the emergency services not receiving 999 calls because of pirate radio stations blocking their radio transmissions. Similarly, *Smedleys v Breed* [1974] AC 839 and *Hobbs v Winchester Corp* [1910] 2 KB 471 were both cases which involved food contamination, and both were classed as strict liability. *Bezzina; Codling; Elvin* [1994] 3 All ER 964 were cases involving the offence of failing to control dangerous dogs – again this was a strict liability offence due to the public safety issue. However, *Robinson-Pierre* [2013] EWCA Crim 2396 emphasised that even in strict liability offences there has to be proof of an act or omission from the defendant that caused the prohibited state of affairs to happen. In *G* [2009], the offence involved child sexual abuse and was strict liability as a result. In *Jackson* [2006] EWCA Crim 2380, the court saw the offence of flying an aircraft at too low a level as involving a risk to public safety and therefore strict liability. Finally, *Alphacell v Woodward* [1972] AC 824 and *Southern Water Authority v Pegrum* [1989] Crim LR 442 both involved water pollution, and in both cases, the offences were strict.

The easier it is for someone to comply with the requirements of the statutory offence, the more likely it is that the offence will be labelled as strict liability. *Lim Chin Aik v R* [1963] AC 160, *Bowsher* [1973] RTR 202, and *Matudi v R* [2003] EWCA Crim 697 are examples of this principle. Similarly, if the offence aims at regulating people who are in a particular business or profession, rather than at regulating the behaviour of the public, then it is more likely to be strict liability. In *Sweet v Parsley* the offence was aimed at the public, and this was one reason why the offence required mens rea; but in *Pharmaceutical Society of Great Britain v Storkwain* [1986] 1 WLR 903, the offence was aimed at a particular industry and was strict.

The more vulnerable the likely victims of the offence are, the more likely the offence is to be strict liability. The contaminated food and pollution cases (discussed earlier) are good examples of this because everyone needs food to eat and air to breathe but has very little protection against people and organisations who harm them through damaging these 'essentials'. Another example is *Harrow LBC v Shah*, where the court classified the offence of selling lottery tickets to those under age 16 as strict to protect children from the dangers of gambling.

However, vulnerability of victims is not conclusive in terms of whether an offence is strict liability. In *Sheppard* [1981] AC 394, the House of Lords decided that an offence of wilful neglect of a child required mens rea. In *B v DPP* the offence of inciting a child under the age of 14 to commit gross indecency was held to require mens rea, so that the defendant would not be guilty if he made an honest mistake about the girl's age. In *B*, the House of Lords pointed out that although the statute was partly aimed at protecting vulnerable children from paedophiles, the offence could also involve children of similar ages sexually experimenting with one another consensually (as in fact it did in this particular case). *K*, which also involved a sexual offence (indecent assault) and a mistake as to age, followed the decision in *B*. Parliament later made these offences ones of strict liability by statute in the Sexual Offences Act 2003. However, the points made in *B* and *K* about the effect of vulnerable victims and the balancing of different strict liability principles in the same case are still important.

Study exercise 3.7

Simester (2005) argues that it is fair to impose strict liability for offences where no social stigma is attached to the criminal offence, but that it is not fair to impose it where stigma does exist. Do you think the current law on strict liability fits in with Simester's argument?

Actus reus and mens rea in criminal justice practice

Actus reus, mens rea, and the construction of crime

As shown in Chapter 1, there is no behaviour which is automatically criminal. Behaviour must be criminalised in either common law or statute law, and a range of individuals, social groups, and factors play a part in deciding which behaviour will be outlawed by criminal law, and how criminal law will define actus reus and mens rea in relation to particular criminal behaviours.

The key players in this process are summarised by Wells and Quick (2010: ch.2). Firstly, the public and their opinions play a part in a variety of ways. The public vote for politicians and governments which introduce new laws, and politicians attach great importance to appealing to public opinion on acceptable and unacceptable behaviour (Bottoms 1995). The public also report some crimes more than others, perceive some kinds of behaviour as being more dangerous than others (Lacey 1995), and fear certain types of criminal behaviour more than others (Farrall et al. 2009). The media also plays a crucial part in both shaping public opinion on crime and reporting it (Marsh and Melville 2014). Secondly, Parliament, judges, magistrates, and their clerks all create and interpret the meaning of actus reus and mens rea in practice. Thirdly, the Home Office and the Ministry of Justice introduce and develop new criminal laws and policies.

Fourthly, the power of the Attorney General and the Director for Public Prosecutions to allow particular types of prosecution to be brought gives them the power to determine what is and is not actus reus and mens rea. Next, the Lord Chief Justice, the senior criminal judge in England and Wales, plays a key role in developing sentencing policy through issuing guidelines on how particular offences should be sentenced (working alongside other members of the Sentencing Council), as well as hearing criminal appeal cases. Both of these roles help to determine the shape of actus reus and mens rea. Finally, pressure groups such as Liberty, the pro-human rights organisation, the Law Commission, and the Association of Chief Police Officers (ACPO) all put forward their own views on how criminal law should look, and sometimes these views become part of criminal law. All of these different individuals and agencies play a key part in the development of actus reus and mens rea, as well as how they are applied in criminal justice practice.

How accurately do the crime statistics that are available from the government (and other sources) reflect the number of 'actus reuses' and 'mens reas' which are committed in England and Wales? The Office of National Statistics publishes crime statistics annually. Crime statistics are taken from the Crime Survey for England and Wales (referred to hereafter as 'CSEW') – the results of a survey asking a selected group of children and adults in England and Wales about their recent experiences of being victims of crime (Maguire and

McVie 2017). In 2014, the government decided that police crime statistics were no longer reliable enough to be part of annual crime statistics, due to changes in police recording practices over time. Crime Survey for England and Wales data for the year ending in December 2017 showed an estimated 10.6 million crimes had been committed in England and Wales in the previous year. In addition, there was an estimated 660,000 offences against children aged between 10 and 15 (ONS 2019a).

These crime statistics are often portrayed as being an accurate representation of all the crime that exists in England and Wales at any given time – for example, by the tabloid press – but the reality is very different. While the CSEW does pick up some of the 'dark figure' of crime which is not reported to the police, there are several other categories of crime which it does not cover – for example, 'victimless' crimes such as drug-dealing, and crimes against businesses (Maguire and McVie 2017). There are also some other types of offences which the CSEW cannot cover because of the way in which it operates. The most obvious example is homicide, where the victims of the crime are dead and so impossible to interview. Only police records can give information about homicides. The CSEW also limits the number of incidents recorded per victim to five (Maguire and McVie 2017: 174), which may seriously underestimate the experiences of some victims for whom victimisation is a constant experience (Genn 1988).

As a result, crime statistics cannot measure the full extent of actus reus and mens rea being committed. They simply give a partial picture of it. Crime statistics, like criminal laws, are social constructions. What is included or excluded from them changes over time. Both criminal law and crime statistics do not only reflect changes in society's views on what should and should not be criminalised, and liberal views on the maximisation of individual people's freedom to live their lives as they wish. They also reflect the interests of the powerful and their attempts to hold onto their position of power in society (Lacey and Zedner 2017).

Study exercise 3.8

Read an account of how the Crime Survey for England and Wales works on the Office for National Statistics website. Could the survey's methodology improve to make it more accurate in capturing as many actus reuses as possible? If so, how?

The next section of the chapter considers the relationship between actus reus, mens rea, and policing.

Actus reus, mens rea, and the police

The power of the police to intervene in people's lives to enforce criminal law, in terms of powers to stop, search, arrest, detain, and interrogate those it suspects of committing an actus reus and mens rea, is largely governed by the Police and Criminal Evidence Act 1984 (hereafter 'PACE'). PACE set out the police's powers in legislation and has widened many of them (Campbell et al. 2019) but has also introduced formal 'rights' for defendants for the first time, attempting to reach a balance between crime control and due process.

S.1 of PACE allows police officers to stop and search persons and vehicles if they have a reasonable suspicion that they will find stolen or prohibited articles, illegal drugs, or a weapon. PACE Code of Practice A gives protection against its abuse by police. For example, stops and searches must be based on objective evidence and cannot be carried out merely as a result of prejudice on age, gender, race, or other grounds (Home Office 2015: para. 2.2). However, section 60 of the Criminal Justice and Public Order Act 1994 allows the police to stop and search without reasonable grounds for suspicion over a 24-hour period where there is 'general anticipation of violence' (Wells and Quick 2010: 43). In addition, the police can authorise stopping and searching vehicles and people without reasonable suspicion in a specified area or place in connection with the prevention of terrorism (section 47A of the Terrorism Act 2000 as amended by the Terrorism Act 2000 (Remedial) Order 2011). Under sections 1–11 of the Criminal Justice and Police Act 2001, the police can also give a penalty notice for disorder, of either £60 or £90, for a range of minor offences, such as being drunk in a public place, threatening behaviour, or theft to the value of £100 or less.

Under section 110 of the Serious Organised Crime and Police Act 2005, which replaces section 24 of PACE, a police officer can arrest someone without a warrant for any offence which that person is committing, or about to commit, or for any offence which the officer reasonably suspects that person is committing or about to commit. These powers can normally only be used where a police officer has reasonable grounds for believing that one of a list of reasons applies, including preventing the suspect from causing injury or damage. PACE Code of Practice G emphasises that the use of the power of arrest must be necessary and that officers must consider whether less intrusive ways of achieving their objectives can be used instead (Home Office 2012: para. 1.3).

Police also have the basic right to detain suspects (PACE s.41ff) and question them (s.66) – but, again, PACE limits these powers in various ways. The police must take a suspect to a police station as soon as possible after arrest. Once they are at the station, they should be brought to a custody officer as soon as is practicable, and the police can only detain a suspect for a maximum of 36 hours before either charging or releasing them (Criminal Justice Act 2003 s.7, amending PACE ss.41–42). If they consider it necessary, the police can apply to a magistrates' court to detain the suspect for further 'blocks' of 36 hours, up to a maximum of 96 hours (PACE s.43–44). Throughout the custody period, a custody officer should review the suspect's detention, after six hours initially, and then every nine hours after that. Section 34 of the Criminal Justice and Public Order Act 1994 states that if a person relies on a fact or defence in their trial that they could reasonably have been expected to mention during a police interview, then the court can draw 'adverse inferences' from this. Extended pre-charge detention is also available in cases involving terrorist offences, under the Terrorism Act 2000 as amended, and the maximum time allowed to detain a suspect before charge is 14 days (Protection of Freedoms Act 2012).

There has been a great deal of debate among criminologists about how well PACE works in terms of balancing crime control and due process. One body of critical research has argued that PACE has done very little to close the gap between criminal law and criminal justice in terms of the response to actus reuses and mens reas of which the police are aware. McConville et al. (1991) argued that PACE had very little impact on the police's behaviour in terms of stretching the concept of criminal behaviour in the form of actus reus and mens rea. Instead, police 'working rules', or patterns of using informal discretion, were what mattered in terms of how criminal law was used. These working rules were based around the 'crime control' approach to criminal justice, whereby obtaining as many convictions as possible was prioritised, even if this meant some innocent people being convicted along the way. They pointed out that the police were a prosecution agency, and aimed to construct a case for the prosecution focusing on evidence that pointed to guilt rather than presenting all available evidence (including evidence that suggested innocence).

McConville et al. (1991) argued, as a result, that detention of suspects was automatically authorised, as custody officers tended not to question what other officers claimed, and that suspects were either informed of their rights at the police station in a way that they did not understand or were not informed of their rights at all (ibid.). They also highlighted the key role of confession evidence in the process of crime control, since this removes or greatly reduces the need for supporting evidence indicating guilt (Sanders et al. 2010), as well removing the need for the case to go to trial at court (which in turn saves time and money). Jackson (2008), in a similar vein, argues that PACE meant a more open and transparent process of detention at the police station but that PACE also allowed more people to be detained in custody and questioned there, turning the PACE process from one of investigation to one of testing and examining accusations against defendants. Jackson (ibid.) is also critical of the low standard of legal advice available to defendants in the police station, arguing that this further prioritises crime control values over due process values.

Not all academic writers agree with McConville et al.'s views about how the police use their powers in practice. Dixon (1999) argues that due process-based law such as PACE can have, and has had, an impact on police practice, by structuring that practice according to a set of rules and reducing the misuse of power. Maguire (2002), meanwhile, while acknowledging the difficulties PACE has had in changing usage of police discretion in practice – for example, in terms of implementing independent checks on police activity while detaining and questioning suspects – points out that PACE has been valuable in introducing a clear legal structure for police activities which was lacking before its implementation. Morgan (1995) also criticises the arguments of McConville et al. in particular, claiming that their study deliberately highlights evidence which shows the police (and PACE's influence) in a negative light and plays down evidence which suggests that PACE had made a difference to police behaviour in their study (see also Smith 1997, 1998).

The evidence of police usage of their powers clearly shows that they are not necessarily effective tools for detecting actus reus and mens rea. In the year to March 2017, the police carried out 303,845 stops and searches in England and Wales, a fall of 21% compared with the previous year – but only 17% of stops and searches led to an arrest (Home Office 2017a: 17). Over the same time, 48% of investigations which the police recorded were closed without a suspect being identified, and only 11% of cases resulted in someone being charged (Home Office 2017b: 16). Ashworth and Zedner (2008) estimated that at least half of the people who receive penalty notices for disorder would not have received a caution or prosecution otherwise, and Young (2008) points to a net-widening process caused by the introduction of penalty notices.

The statistical evidence on apparent racial bias in police usage of stop, search, and arrest powers also supports McConville et al.'s view that police practice distorts the response to actus reus and mens rea. Phillips and Bowling show that while those from black and ethnic minority backgrounds are less likely to be stopped and searched than they were in the first decade of the 21st century, they were still four times as likely to be stopped and searched as white people in 2015 (2017: 199). Black British people were eight times as likely to be stopped and searched as white people in 2016–17 (Home Office 2017a: 7). Bowling and Phillips (2002) argue that this imbalance is due to a mixture of direct and indirect police discrimination. Reiner's (2010) view is that police work can never be politically neutral because criminal law and criminal justice reinforce social divisions and because the police's role is to support State power.

A final point about the nature of police work relates to the increasing level of private sector involvement in policing work. While privatised policing is nothing new, and was common throughout the 18th century in England (Johnston 1992), it has played an increasingly important role in taking over functions of public policing in the past two decades. Jones et al. (2017: 784–6) identify a number of reasons for this development. These include economic cutbacks to public expenditures on policing, the growing privatisation of urban space, the direct privatisation of police functions such as managing custody suites, and the increasing prevalence of cybercrime in society.

Study exercise 3.9

List and explain three changes which you would make in order to reform police powers in PACE. What principles would you use to explain these changes?

Actus reus, mens rea, and the Crown Prosecution Service

The Crown Prosecution Service (hereafter 'CPS') decides whether or not a case should proceed to the court stage after the police have charged a suspect, and selects appropriate charges in cases which it does take to court. The police consult their local CPS branch before deciding whether to charge a suspect, and pass on details of the case to the CPS. The local Principal Crown Prosecutor then allocates the case to a member of their team, and only the Principal Crown Prosecutor has the power to decide whether to continue with the case. Next, the CPS must provide a constant review of the progress made with each case in terms of the quantity and quality of evidence obtained. Finally, the CPS makes the decision whether or not to prosecute, using the Code for Crown Prosecutors (Crown Prosecution Service 2013) as a guide, using two key tests: whether or not there is sufficient evidence to provide a realistic prospect of conviction if the case reaches court, and whether or not prosecution is in the public interest. The CPS's task in principle is to 'close the gap' between actus reus and mens rea in the law and in criminal justice in two ways. The first way is by ensuring that there is enough evidence to prove that the right person is matched up with an actus reus and mens rea. The second way is by ensuring that an appropriate offence charge is found to match the criminal behaviour committed.

HM Crown Prosecution Service Inspectorate (2015) found that in 2014, 91.5% of prosecuted cases in England and Wales met the two key tests. However, other evidence suggests that the CPS faces operational and institutional problems which limit its effectiveness in bringing actus reus, mens rea and criminal justice closer together. One problem is the Code for Crown Prosecutors itself. In theory, it is supposed to provide all of the guidance that CPS workers need to make the decision on whether or not to prosecute. Yet Hoyano et al. (1997) found that the language used in the Code became more simplified each time that a new version of the Code was published. Rogers (2006) was also critical of the Code for not making it clear that prosecutors should have a reason for wanting an accused person's punishment.

The tests used to decide whether to prosecute have also been criticised as unhelpful. The Code (Crown Prosecution Service 2013) defines the 'realistic prospect of conviction' test as being an objective test: is a court more likely than not to convict based on the evidence available, and on the admissibility and reliability of that evidence? Yet this test over-simplifies the wide discretion that courts have to decide on admissibility of evidence, and to decide the facts of the case in different ways. Sanders (2016: 87) argues that many cases charged under the 'realistic prospect' test do not receive the full CPS review that the Code for Crown Prosecutors requires. Sanders also points to the lack of CPS investigatory powers, which limit its ability to challenge incorrect police decisions about actus reus and mens rea (ibid: 89). Economic factors also affect the CPS's ability to label people with the right actus reus and mens rea accurately. Between 2013 and 2018, the CPS lost 1000 staff and lost £86m from its annual budget (Dearden 2018a). The CPS's 'public interest' test also hides the reality of the presumption in favour of prosecution unless there are factors present that are against prosecution, and the CPS reliance on (sometimes very limited) police information on whether prosecution would be in the public interest or not (Sanders 2016).

Other research indicates that the CPS takes cases that are evidentially weak to court more often than the evidence from the HM Crown Prosecution Inspectorate cited earlier suggests. In Baldwin's (1997) study, early warning signs about prosecutions ending in acquittal in court were noticed by the CPS in 87.3% of the judge-ordered acquittals (where the judge orders a jury to acquit a defendant during the course of a trial), and in 73.1% of the judge-directed acquittals (where a judge orders a defendant's acquittal before the jury has been sworn in at the start of a trial). Problems have also arisen regarding the accountability of the CPS for its decisions. Campbell et al. (2019) show that weaknesses have been found in terms of recording CPS decisions and in terms of communication of vital information from person to person within the CPS.

Study exercise 3.10

Research the CPS decision to drop historical sexual offence charges against the former Labour MP Lord Janner in 2015. Do the facts of this case support Sanders' (2016) views of CPS practice?

The CPS is not the only criminal justice agency that prosecutes for criminal offences. Some agencies are responsible for investigating and prosecuting certain types of criminal offences. The Health and Safety Executive, whose role it is to regulate standards of safety in the workplace, is one example of such an agency. Others include the Serious Fraud Office, which, as its name suggests, responds to serious cases of fraud, and the Environment Agency, which responds to crimes of environmental damage. Many of the offences that these agencies deal with are ones of strict liability. Making an offence strict liability makes it easier to prosecute, but investigatory agencies have very limited financial and staff resources compared with the CPS (Tombs and Whyte 2007: 123). This may explain why these agencies have a very different attitude towards prosecution compared to the police and CPS. As Hawkins (2002) points out, they use prosecution as a last resort and tend to use it only where the organisation has broken the law repeatedly or was clearly at fault for their offences. The agencies therefore use a strategy of encouraging companies to self-regulate and comply with the law (Hawkins 1984). Often these agencies respond to crimes committed by companies and organisations (see Chapter 4). From the point of prosecution more generally, though, it is interesting to note how few cases result in prosecution by these agencies. For example, the Health and Safety Executive prosecuted only 554 cases in 2016–17 (Health and Safety Executive 2018: 11).

Actus reus, mens rea, and the courts

The following sections consider how actus reus and mens rea are used in criminal justice practice by considering the key stages and agencies in the pre-sentence criminal process, starting with court plea decisions.

Court trials and pleas

Sanders et al. (2010: Chapter 8) show that over 90% of cases in the magistrates' court end up with the defendant either pleading guilty or being found guilty in their absence, and that only around 25% of cases in the Crown Court actually reach the jury trial stage. One reason for the low rate of trials in both courts is the problem of so-called 'cracked trials', when the defendant changes their plea to guilty on the day when the trial is due to start, or when the prosecution offers no evidence at this point. Another reason is 'ineffective trials', when a trial does not go ahead as planned due to delays caused by the prosecution, the defence, or the court, and a new hearing has to be scheduled. Between October and December 2017, 15% of trials in the Crown Court were ineffective and 35% were cracked (Ministry of Justice 2018a), while in the magistrates' court, 15% of trials were ineffective and 38% were cracked (ibid). A key factor in the number of cracked trials is the number of last-minute guilty pleas by defendants, as Sanders et al. (2010: ch.8) point out.

In order to explain the high rate of guilty pleas, some criminologists have argued that in the magistrates' court, the emphasis is on processing cases as quickly as possible, and maintaining social power over the 'criminal classes' rather than making sure that defendants' guilt is proved beyond reasonable doubt (e.g. Carlen 1976; McBarnet 1981). Parker et al. (1989) pointed to the emphasis on local 'court culture' (i.e. the patterns of decision-making which particular individuals or groups of magistrates rely on when considering guilt in cases) in magistrates' decision-making rather than on application of the formal rules. They argued that the magistrates in their study tended to be heavily in favour of the prosecution's case and conviction. Brown (1991) argued that in deciding on defendants' innocence or guilt in cases, magistrates often stereotyped and depersonalised the facts of each individual offence and offender to speed up the process of justice.

Sanders et al. (2010) argue that the main reason for the high number of guilty pleas is the amount of pressure which is put on defendants to plead guilty – not only by the prosecution but also by the defence solicitor or barrister. This pressure can come in the form of plea-bargaining (where a defendant is offered a less serious sentence in exchange for pleading guilty) or charge-bargaining (where the defendant is offered a less serious charge in exchange for pleading guilty). Pressure can be put on defendants by both prosecution and defence lawyers, to choose a magistrates', rather than a Crown Court's, trial on the grounds of more lenient sentences, fewer delays, and fewer cost penalties, and to plead guilty even where there are doubts about their legal guilt (Bottoms and McClean 1976; Baldwin and McConville 1977). In some court cases, the defendants will be factually guilty of the offence with which they have been charged and will plead guilty to reflect their responsibility through actus reus and mens rea so as to take advantage of the sentencing discount that an early guilty plea offers them. But research evidence suggests that the court process overall offers the scope for an individual to be put under pressure to plead guilty to an offence for which they did not have the required actus reus and mens rea, through the process of plea-bargaining (McConville 2002).

Study exercise 3.11

Spend a morning or afternoon observing cases in a magistrates' court near you. Do you agree with McBarnet (1981) that magistrates are more concerned about resolving cases quickly than about proving defendants' guilt beyond reasonable doubt? What factor(s) influenced your answer?

Legal representation in court

Both prosecution and defence lawyers have considerable influence over the course of the court process, not just through their use of plea-bargaining and charge bargaining (discussed earlier) but also in other ways. These include their knowledge of criminal law itself and the reactions of particular judges or juries, their questioning of witnesses during examination of their own witnesses and cross-examination of the other side's witnesses, and the quality of their preparation for a case. For the purposes of this discussion, the role played by the defence lawyer is particularly important because it is the defence solicitor or barrister who has the responsibility of ensuring that the prosecution proves that the defendant has the required actus reus and mens rea for an offence beyond reasonable doubt.

In terms of preparation for cases, the evidence on its quality is mixed. In Zander and Henderson's (1993) study of the Crown Court, 44% of defence barristers said their brief had previously been returned by someone else, and 25% of defence barristers in contested cases had received the brief later than 4pm on the day before the trial was due to start. McConville et al. (1994), meanwhile, found evidence that some defence practices in their study encouraged or created guilty pleas against their client's wishes, or used language in court which made it clear to magistrates that their client was not telling the truth. They found that the solicitors who took this approach did so because they believed certain clients or social groups were guilty, or because they did not want to upset the police or the courts with which they worked. Therefore, there was no point in defending their clients fully.

McConville et al. mentioned the fact that solicitors were not using legal aid, the financial support available to defendants to help them secure legal representation in court, effectively enough. This issue has become more important as the government's legal aid budget was cut by £450m per year through the Legal Aid, Sentencing and Punishment of Offenders Act 2012 (Joyce 2017: 255), reducing the number of solicitors who offer legal aid services to defendants and increasing the number of unrepresented defendants in the courts. While the evidence discussed earlier does not suggest that all defence solicitors ignore due process in their work, it does point to the fact that in practice, this aspect of court justice has the potential to move away from a pure consideration of a defendant's responsibility for crime through actus reus and mens rea, in favour of saving time and money.

Evidence

Evidence plays a crucial role in understanding the links between actus reus and mens rea in criminal law and how it is used in criminal justice practice. This is true especially because mens rea involves what is going on in a defendant's head at the time of the offence, and the easiest way to prove this is through evidence of their external behaviour at that time. Both the prosecution and the defence can call and examine witnesses on their side, as well as cross-examine witnesses on the other side, to help them disprove the other side's version of events. Newburn (2017: 695) identifies a number of different types of evidence which can be given in court:

- Oral testimony on the witness stand, which is traditionally seen as being the best and most reliable form of evidence in an adversarial system.

- Documentary evidence, such as witness statements.
- Exhibits, such as weapons and clothing.
- Audio and photographic materials, such as CCTV footage.
- Eyewitness testimony from an observer of the facts.
- A defendant's confession made earlier in the criminal process.
- Expert testimony by psychiatrists or doctors on specialist matters.

Evidence clearly plays a vital role in proving a person's criminal liability in terms of mens rea (and actus reus) beyond reasonable doubt. Sanders (1987) argued that the move towards subjective mens rea, which has increased since the time he was writing in the form of the abolition of *Caldwell* recklessness, may encourage the police and courts to place too much emphasis on confession evidence which may have been obtained illegally at the police station, despite PACE regulations outlawing this practice. The relaxation of the restrictions on hearsay evidence in the Criminal Justice Act 2003 can be seen as a move towards allowing a greater range of evidence to be used by the CPS, and increasing the risk that innocent people will be wrongly convicted on the basis of unreliable or fabricated evidence. Similarly, allowing the prosecution to make adverse inferences about the defence's case in court where the defence has not complied with the disclosure rules set out in the 2003 Act arguably gives the prosecution an unfair advantage in court, given the advantages of State resources in the criminal process over limited defence time and legal aid funding (Leng 2002). However, Redmayne (2004) found widespread non-compliance with the disclosure rules by defence lawyers.

Another important issue in how the court process uses evidence to link a defendant to actus reus and mens rea is the role played by expert and scientific evidence. Roberts (2013) points out that while evidence from these sources has undoubtedly benefited criminal justice by securing rightful convictions in many cases, juries and magistrates wrongly see such evidence as being conclusive simply because it has come from experts or scientists. This can lead to miscarriages of justice, and so evidence interpretation by the court process is vital. Roberts also shows that scientific evidence can have a number of limitations, particularly from the point of view of proving mens rea, since even apparently clear evidence such as fingerprints or DNA does not tell the court anything about the mens rea involved in the crime – for example, whether it was committed intentionally, recklessly, negligently, or accidentally.

Study exercise 3.12

Read an account of the internal CPS review of June 2018 into disclosure of evidence to the defence and its impact on ineffective trials (e.g. Davies and Dodd 2018). Why do you think these disclosure failings occurred?

Miscarriages of justice and appeals

Newburn (2017: 697) discusses the series of high-profile miscarriages of justice, where the criminal process convicted people of crimes that those people did not commit, since the Second World War in England. These cases included the 'Guildford Four', the 'Birmingham Six' (all wrongly convicted of terrorist offences), and, after PACE was implemented, the 'Cardiff Three'. Newburn (ibid: 698) also shows how the government established the Criminal Cases Review Commission (CCRC) in 1997 to investigate miscarriages of justice in terms of new evidence casting doubt on a criminal conviction. Nobles and Schiff (2000) show that the law and the media have different ideas about miscarriages of justice, with the law's understanding of the extent and nature of miscarriages confined to the legal process itself. Naughton (2007: 42) adds the number of appeals at Crown Court from decisions in the magistrates' court (which he calls 'mundane' miscarriages) and the number of appeals at the Court of Appeal from decisions in the Crown Court (which he calls 'routine' miscarriages) to the small number of cases sent back to the Court of Appeal by the CCRC. Naughton concludes, based on this analysis, that there are 18 known miscarriages of justice occurring every day in English courts, and so miscarriages are a normal rather than an exceptional feature of criminal justice.

Appeals can be made against conviction on three different grounds: an error in how the judge or clerk applied the law, an error of fact such as a conviction on unsafe evidence, and an error in the trial process, such as a biased summing up to the jury by the judge. Figure 1.1 in Chapter 1 shows which court(s) hear appeals at which stages in the criminal process. In 2017, the Crown Court allowed only 43% of appeals against verdict in the magistrates' court and only 48% of appeals against sentence (Ministry of Justice 2018). In 2015–16, the Court of Criminal Appeal allowed only 36% of appeals against conviction but allowed 71% of appeals against sentence (Courts and Tribunals Judiciary 2017).

Sanders et al. (2010: ch.10) point to the inconsistency of the appeals process, as well as its failure to uncover enough miscarriages of justice due to criminal justice agencies' breaking of the rules. The appeals process is a double-edged sword in terms of how actus reus and mens rea is proved. On the one hand, it provides a potential way of restoring someone's legal innocence if their mens rea has been mistakenly 'proved' in their original court case. On the other hand, it could also mean that people who really did have actus reus and mens rea could be wrongly set free due to a mistake in the court process.

Study exercise 3.13

Using Internet sources, find out about the role played by expert evidence in the miscarriage of justice shown in the Sally Clark murder case. How do you think this miscarriage of justice happened? Do you think that anything could have been done to prevent the miscarriage from occurring in the first place?

Actus reus, mens rea, and victims

The reporting of crime to criminal justice agencies by victims is vital in 'closing the gap' between the occurrence of actus reus and mens rea and the prosecution, conviction, and punishment of people for breaking the law. Most crimes come to the police's attention via the public, and victims of crime play a vital role in giving evidence in court which forms the basis of successful prosecution. The Crime Survey for England and Wales (CSEW) estimates that only 40% of crime that it records is also reported to the police. Clarkson et al. (1994) identified key reasons for victims not reporting crimes to the police as including the victim's perception that their crime is not detectable, the victim's reluctance to have their own conduct scrutinised, and fear of reprisals. The CSEW has its own limitations in terms of which actus reuses and mens reas it records (discussed earlier in this chapter). It is clear, then, that there is a considerable difference in number between the actus reuses and mens reas experienced by victims and those identified and responded to in the criminal justice process.

Some criminologists (e.g. Spalek 2017) argue that the police have traditionally been slow to recognise the needs of victims who report their crimes, especially victims who are vulnerable on the grounds of their age, gender, ethnicity, or class. The Victims' Code of Practice, launched in 2004 and most recently revised in 2015 (Ministry of Justice 2015), makes it clear that police should keep victims updated with information on progress being made with their case and carry out a needs assessment for further help and support where appropriate. However, the Code does not offer any enforceable rights for victims (Cook and Davies 2017: 396–8), and the Witness Charter, which provides standards of care that witnesses can expect from criminal justice agencies, similarly lacks enforceable rights (Joyce 2017: 500).

As well as having rights to information about their case from the CPS under the Code, victims also now have the right to review a CPS decision not to charge, following the case of *Killick* [2011] EWCA Crim 1608, and the procedure for seeking a review is part of the Victims' Code (Howey 2017: 249). The victim's interest must be balanced against the CPS's main two tests for deciding whether to prosecute a case – (i.e. the public interest in prosecution and the prospect of a realistic conviction). These tests will take priority over the interests of the victim, and, if there were a conflict between the two, would be decisive in reaching a decision on prosecution.

The Youth Justice and Criminal Evidence Act 1999 introduced a range of measures designed to help vulnerable victims and witnesses before and during the court process. These measures included screening witnesses from the accused, giving evidence by live video link, the removal of barristers' and judges' wigs and gowns, video-recorded evidence, and giving evidence through an intermediary (Hall 2013: 212). Adler (2013: 305), having reviewed the evidence on the effectiveness of these measures, concludes that they have made a positive difference to victims' and witnesses' experiences, but also argues that there are limits to how effective the measures are. Burton et al. (2006), meanwhile, found that the measures for vulnerable witnesses were not available nationwide and that the police and the CPS had great difficulty in identifying who was and was not 'vulnerable' and eligible for the special measures under the 1999 Act, excluding many victims who really were vulnerable in the process.

This is perhaps inevitable in an adversarial criminal justice process such as the one used in England (Ellison 2001), where recent legislation takes the view that conditions can only improve for victims by making them worse for defendants (Jackson 2003). Past research showed that vulnerable victims, such as victims of sexual offences, children, and the mentally disordered felt 're-victimised' and traumatised by the giving of evidence under cross-examination, due to the hostile adversarial attitudes of solicitors and barristers (Chambers and Millar 1987; Morgan and Zedner 1992; Temkin 2002). There is also evidence that the traditionally hostile and unfair treatment given to the victims of sexual violence, for example, has continued after the 1999 Act (Kelly et al. 2005).

The government also introduced Victim Personal Statements (VPS) nationally in 2001 as a way of allowing victims to explain how crimes have affected them physically, emotionally, psychologically, and financially – but VPS is only considered by a court following a defendant's conviction (Joyce 2017: 501). Community Impact Statements (CIS), introduced in 2009, allow witnesses to express their feelings about a crime in a similar way. Sanders et al. (2001) were heavily critical of the pilot VPS, pointing out that the police and courts ignored most statements and that the statements had little or no impact on sentencing – meaning that most victims who engaged with VPS felt disappointed after doing so.

Overall, the measures designed to make things easier for victims giving evidence may damage due process for defendants by excluding some evidence that they could otherwise have used to disprove the charges against them, while not making giving evidence in court easier for victims (Ellison 2001).

Study exercise 3.14

Read the articles by Sanders et al. (2001) and Chalmers et al. (2007). Which article do you think gives the most accurate account of the effectiveness of VPS?

Conclusions: linking discussion to the roadmap theories

The emphasis on acts being voluntary and requiring mens rea to go with them points to criminal law view of actus reus as being a liberal one. On this liberal roadmap view, individuals are to remain free from any social or political interference as long as they do not break the law (Norrie 1996, 2014), and criminal law only punishes where there is individual responsibility through having the right mens rea that is provable (Hart 1968). However, criminal law's usage of actus reus and mens rea is not as liberal as it appears to be. Actus reus can involve being somewhere or possessing something that criminal law will not allow. Similarly, criminal law also punishes people for omissions, in certain limited circumstances. These are social uses of actus reus, hidden by the general 'voluntary act' principles commonly associated with actus reus (Norrie 2014). Similarly, in causation, the liberal roadmap view involves holding a defendant responsible for what happens to the victim as a result of their actions, unless a third person's voluntary act intervenes to break the chain (Hart and Honoré 1985). However, the law has also made moral judgments about people's behaviour in terms of causation by blaming them for not calling for help after a family member's drug overdose, in terms of causing that other person's death (*Evans*). This shows that actus reus is about something more than protecting the vulnerable in society. It is also about regulating the social order, in line with the radical roadmap theory, and making moral judgments about the behaviour of certain types of 'undesirable' people, regardless of their liability under liberal principles (Norrie 1991, 2014).

Turning to mens rea, in terms of intent, as Lacey (1993) has pointed out, intent in criminal law is currently defined widely. Intent includes not just cases where people have aimed or planned to do what they did, but also cases where people did not aim or plan the offence, instead foreseeing the prohibited outcome as a moral or virtually certain outcome of their actions. Norrie (2014) argues that the law has included foresight within the definition of intent, while leaving magistrates and juries to decide whether it applies case-by-case, to cover up the difficult social and moral decisions that have to be made on whether someone deserves to be held criminally responsible for the consequences of their actions. On this view, intent in criminal law is not just about liberal principles of individual responsibility that deserve to be punished. It is also about having the discretion to make moral judgments about individuals' responsibility in a way that reflects radical, power-based roadmap ideas about society and reinforces social inequality. In *G and R*, the House of Lords supported a subjective view of recklessness which again made criminal law look liberal, by only blaming people for their recklessness where they saw the risk themselves and went on to take that risk anyway. However, as Duff (1990) has argued, sometimes it is right to blame people who did not think about the risks they were taking. The objective recklessness test set up in *Caldwell* allowed the law to do this but meant that people who were not capable of appreciating the risks that they were taking (e.g. *Elliott v C, Bell*) still received criminal punishment for their actions. This was one of the key reasons why *G and R* overruled *Caldwell* – punishing defendants like this made the law look less liberal. However, it is arguable that criminal law on recklessness is still trying to make moral, risk-based judgments about the behaviour of particular defendants by mixing subjective and objective recklessness. This is visible in *G and R* itself, where the stated exception to the subjective recklessness test is where a defendant cannot see the risk of their actions because they are voluntarily intoxicated.

The liberal view of criminal law and criminal justice presents strict and corporate liability as being an exception to the rules of mens rea and individual responsibility where the activity of individuals or groups presents a real danger to public safety or vulnerable victims. However, the reality of how strict liability is used in practice shows that it is far from being exceptional in criminal law. Ashworth and Blake's (1996) research showed that 40% of offences triable in the Crown Court were strict liability – and the majority of these offences carried maximum prison sentences of more than six months. The use of strict liability in this way raises questions about whether criminal law and criminal justice uses it fairly (Duff 2005; Horder 2016). More recently, strict liability has moved beyond its roots as a response to corporate offending (Norrie 2014: ch.5) to cover a wide range of offences, from gun ownership to sexual assault. Norrie argues that these decisions represent an attempt to inject the morality and interests of the powerful in society into the law in a range of different situations.

Turning now to criminal justice, the liberal view of crime statistics as being an accurate picture of crime hides a range of social issues which decide which actus reuses will be included in criminal statistics and which will not. In terms of how the police and the CPS use the rules on actus reus set out in the liberally centred criminal law, McConville et al. (1991) argued that the legal rules (such as PACE), which claim to provide a balance between two sides of the liberal roadmap in the shape of crime control and due process, have very little impact in practice. Others such as Choongh (1997) and Hillyard and Gordon (1999) argue that the police use their power to extend social control and social exclusion as far as possible, bringing together the risk management and power roadmap theories.

However, the argument here is that police and CPS work, like criminal law, have a conflicting set of aims in terms of how it uses actus reus and mens rea. Sometimes due process wins, but at other times criminal justice practice is characterised by the radical or risk management models. A similar picture emerges in pre-sentence court processes, where the traditional due process features of that process (defendants' rights to bail, to choose mode of trial and not to be convicted on the basis of hearsay evidence, for example) have been eroded by government legislation and policy that prioritise risk management roadmap-based efficiency in terms of saving time and money in dealing with court cases, not just as a way of achieving justice and due process but as a goal in its own right. This has led to a large number of defendants volunteering to give up their right to have their criminal responsibility tested in a court, after being offered a range of incentives and coercive tactics to plead guilty, such as lesser charges and sentencing discounts. All of these are factors could explain the apparent regularity of miscarriages of justice, not all of which are put right through the criminal appeals process.

This conflict and confusion in police, CPS, and court work is particularly significant for victims. Victims of crime have a set of needs of their own when they inform criminal justice of an actus reus and mens rea which has affected their lives, but those needs can be very different from victims' needs. The conflict that results can lead to victims' expectations being frustrated in their dealings with criminal justice agencies, while also reducing due process for defendants in some cases.

When considering criminal law and criminal justice's perspectives on actus reus and mens rea, a range of roadmap models are relevant, but the radical hybrid realist model comes closest to capturing how pre-sentence criminal justice works. The radical hybrid realist model recognises that the powerful in society have significant (but not conclusive) influence over criminal law and criminal justice, and its recognition of a range of competing and conflicting sets of values influencing the operation of both.

Key points

- Actus reus is a concept used in criminal law to decide which types of behaviour should be labelled as criminal – but it is not only concerned with positive actions
- Mens rea is a concept used in criminal law to decide how responsibility should be allocated for crimes and takes a variety of different forms in different criminal offences – sometimes it is not required at all, in strict liability offences
- Police powers such as arrest are regulated by the Police and Criminal Evidence Act, but there is an ongoing academic debate about how much of an influence law has on police work and about how fairly the police use their powers
- Criminal prosecution work is mostly handled by the Crown Prosecution Service, although other agencies prosecute particular offences as well – both types of agency have been criticised by academics for limitations in fairness and effectiveness

- Pre-sentence court processes are characterised by due process values in principle, but these values have been eroded by recent risk-based policies such as limited acceptance of hearsay evidence
- Criminal justice acknowledges victims of crime by the introduction of measures such as victim personal statements – but academicians have raised doubts about how much these measures have succeeded in meeting victims' needs
- There is evidence of liberal, deterministic, power-based, and risk-based roadmap models playing a role in criminal law and justice, but the radical hybrid realist roadmap theory offers the most complete and realistic account of how criminal law and justice use actus reus and mens rea to respond to harmful behaviour

Further reading

Campbell, L., Ashworth, A., and Redmayne, M. (2019), *The Criminal Process* (5th ed.). Oxford: OUP.

Norrie, A. (2014), *Crime, Reason and History* (3rd ed.): chs.3–7. Cambridge: CUP.

Sanders, A., Young, R., and Burton, M. (2010), *Criminal Justice* (4th ed.). Oxford: OUP.

Wells, C., and Quick, O. (2010), *Lacey, Wells and Quick's Reconstructing Criminal Law: Text and Materials* (4th ed.): ch.2. Cambridge: CUP.

Wilson, W. (2017), *Criminal Law* (6th ed.): chs.4–8. Harlow: Pearson.

References

Adler, J. (2013), 'Psychology and Criminal Justice', in Hucklesby, A., and Wahidin, A. (eds.), *Criminal Justice* (2nd ed.). Oxford: OUP.

Ashworth, A. (1989), 'The Scope of Criminal Liability for Omissions', *Law Quarterly Review*, **105**(3): 424–59.

Ashworth, A., and Blake, M. (1996), 'The Presumption of Innocence in English Criminal Law', *Criminal Law Review*: 306–17.

Ashworth, A., and Zedner, L. (2008), 'Defending the Criminal Law: Reflections on the Changing Character of Crime, Procedure and Sanctions', *Criminal Law and Philosophy*, **2**(1): 21–51.

Baker, D.J. (2015), *Glanville Williams' Textbook on Criminal Law* (4th ed.). London: Sweet and Maxwell.

Baldwin, J., and McConville, M. (1977), *Negotiated Justice*. London: Martin Robertson.

Bottoms, A.E. (1995), 'The Philosophy and Politics of Punishment and Sentencing', in Clarkson, C.M.V., and Morgan, R. (eds.), *The Politics of Sentencing Reform*. Oxford: Clarendon Press.

Bottoms, A.E., and McClean, J.D. (1976), *Defendants in the Criminal Process*. London: Routledge.

Bowling, B., and Phillips, C. (2002), *Racism, Crime and Justice*. Harlow: Longman.

Brown, S. (1991), *Magistrates at Work*. Buckingham: Open University Press.

Burton, M., Evans, R., and Sanders, A. (2006), 'Implementing Special Measures for Vulnerable and Intimidated Witnesses: The Problem of Identification', *Criminal Law Review:* 229–40.

Campbell, L., Ashworth, A., and Redmayne, M. (2019), *The Criminal Process* (5th ed.). Oxford: OUP.

Carlen, P. (1976), *Magistrates' Justice*. London: Martin Robertson.

Chalmers, J., Duff, P., and Leverick, F. (2007), 'Victim Statements: Can Work, Do Work (For Those Who Bother to Make Them)', *Criminal Law Review:* 360–79.

Chambers, G., and Millar, A. (1987), 'Proving Sexual Assault: Prosecuting the Offender or Persecuting the Victim?' in Carlen, P., and Worrall, A. (eds.), *Gender, Crime and Justice*. Milton Keynes: Open University Press.

Child, J.J., and Ormerod, D. (2017), *Smith, Hogan and Ormerod's Essentials of Criminal Law* (2nd ed.). Oxford: OUP.

Choongh, S. (1997), *Policing as Social Discipline*. Oxford: Clarendon.

Clarkson, C.M.V., Cretney, A., Davis, G., and Shepherd, J.P. (1994), 'Assault: The Relationship Between Seriousness, Criminalisation and Punishment', *Criminal Law Review:* 4–20.

Cook, I.R., and Davies, P. (2017), 'Supporting Victims and Witnesses', in Harding, J., Davies, P., and Mair, G. (eds.), *An Introduction to Criminal Justice*. London: Sage.

Courts and Tribunals Judiciary (2017), *Court of Appeal (Criminal Division) Annual Report 2015–16*. Available online at: www.judiciary.gov.uk/publications/court-of-appeal-criminal-division-annual-report-2015-16/. Accessed 30 May 2018.

Crown Prosecution Service (2013), *The Code for Crown Prosecutors* (7th ed.). London: Crown Prosecution Service.

Davies, C., and Dodd, V. (2018), 'CPS Chief Apologises Over Disclosure Failings in Rape Cases', *The Guardian*, 5 June. Available online at: www.theguardian.com/law/2018/jun/05/scores-of-uk-sexual-offence-cases-stopped-over-evidence-failings. Accessed 18 July 2019.

Dearden, L. (2018a), 'UK's "Creaking" Criminal Justice System Needs Urgent Funding Increase, Outgoing CPS Head Alison Saunders Says', *The Independent*, 28 October. Available online at: www.independent.co.uk/news/uk/crime/crime-prosecutions-uk-police-cps-budget-cuts-criminal-justice-system-alison-saunders-a8605276.html. Accessed 18 July 2019.

Dixon, D. (1999), 'Police Investigative Procedures: Changing Legal and Political Contexts of Policing Practices', in Walker, C., and Starmer, K. (eds.), *Miscarriages of Justice: A Review of Justice in Error*. London: Blackstone Press.

Duff, R.A. (1990), *Intention, Agency and Criminal Liability*. Oxford: Blackwell.

Duff, R.A. (2005), 'Strict Liability, Legal Presumptions and the Presumption of Innocence', in Simester, A. (ed.), *Appraising Strict Liability*. Oxford: OUP.

Ellison, L. (2001), *The Adversarial Process and the Vulnerable Witness*. Oxford: OUP.

Farrall, S., Jackson, J., and Gray, E. (2009), *Social Order and the Fear of Crime in Contemporary Times*. Oxford: OUP.

Genn, H. (1988), 'Multiple Victimisation', in Maguire, M., and Pointing, J. (eds.), *Victims of Crime: A New Deal?* Milton Keynes: Open University Press.

Hall, M. (2013), 'Victims in the Criminal Justice Process', in Hucklesby, A., and Wahidin, A. (eds.), *Criminal Justice* (2nd ed.). Oxford: OUP.

Hart, H.L.A. (1968), *Punishment and Responsibility*. Oxford: OUP.

Hart, H.L.A., and Honoré, T. (1985), *Causation in the Law* (2nd ed.). Oxford: OUP.

Hawkins, K. (1984), *Environment and Enforcement: Regulation and the Social Definition of Pollution*. Oxford: Clarendon.

Hawkins, K. (2002), *Law as Last Resort: Prosecution Decision-Making in a Regulatory Agency*. Oxford: OUP.

Health and Safety Executive (2018), *Health and Safety at Work: Summary Statistics for Great Britain, 2018*. Available online at: www.hse.gov.uk/statistics/overall/hssh1718.pdf. Accessed 21 May 2019.

HM Crown Prosecution Service Inspectorate (2015), *Five Year Review and Annual Report 2014–15*. London: HM Crown Prosecution Service Inspectorate.

Herring, J. (2016), *Criminal Law: Text, Cases and Materials* (7th ed.). Oxford: OUP.

Herring, J. (2019), *Criminal Law* (11th ed.). London: Palgrave Macmillan.

Hillyard, P., and Gordon, D. (1999), 'Arresting Statistics: The Drift to Informal Justice in England and Wales', *Journal of Law and Society*, **26**(4): 502–22.

Home Office (2012), *PACE Code of Practice G – Revised Edition*. Norwich: The Stationery Office.

Home Office (2015), *PACE Code of Practice A – Revised Edition*. Norwich: The Stationery Office.

Home Office (2017a), *Police Powers and Procedures, England and Wales, Year Ending 31st March 2017* (2nd ed.). Statistical Bulletin 20/17. London: Home Office.

Home Office (2017b), *Crime Outcomes in England and Wales, Year Ending 31st March 2017* (2nd ed.). Statistical Bulletin 09/17. London: Home Office.

Horder, J. (2016), *Ashworth's Principles of Criminal Law* (8th ed.). Oxford: OUP.

Howey, A. (2017), 'Prosecution and the Alternatives', in Harding, J., Davies, P., and Mair, G. (eds.), *An Introduction to Criminal Justice*. London: Sage.

Hoyano, A., Hoyano, L.C.H., Davis, G., and Goldie, S. (1997), 'A Study of the Impact of the Revised Code for Crown Prosecutors', *Criminal Law Review*: 556–64.

Jackson, J. (2003), 'Justice for All – Putting Victims at the Core?' *Journal of Law and Society*, **30**(2): 309–26.

Jackson, J. (2008), 'Police and Prosecutors After PACE: The Road from Case Construction to Case Disposal', in Cape, E., and Young, R. (eds.), *Regulating Policing*. Oxford: Hart.

Johnston, L. (1992), *The Rebirth of Private Policing*. London: Routledge.

Jones, T., Newburn, T., and Reiner, R. (2017), 'Policing and the Police', in Liebling, A., Maruna, S., and McAra, L. (eds.), *The Oxford Handbook of Criminology* (6th ed.). Oxford: OUP.

Joyce, P. (2017), *Criminal Justice* (3rd ed.). Abingdon: Routledge.

Kelly, L., Lovett, J., and Regan, L. (2005), *A Gap or Chasm?* Home Office Research Study 293. London: Home Office.

Lacey, N. (1993), 'A Clear Concept of Intention: Elusive or Illusory?' *Modern Law Review*, **56**(5): 621–42.

Lacey, N. (1995), 'Contingency and Criminalisation', in Loveland, I. (ed.), *Frontiers of Criminality*. London: Sweet and Maxwell.

Lacey, N., and Zedner, L. (2017), 'Criminalization: Historical, Legal, and Criminological Perspectives', in Liebling, A., Maruna, S., and McAra, L. (eds.), *The Oxford Handbook of Criminology* (6th ed.). Oxford: OUP.

Leng, R. (2002), 'The Exchange of Information and Criminal Disclosure', in McConville, M., and Wilson, G. (eds.), *The Handbook of the Criminal Justice Process*. Oxford: OUP.

Maguire, M. (2002), 'Regulating the Police Station: The Case of the Police and Criminal Evidence Act 1984', in McConville, M., and Wilson, G. (eds.), *The Handbook of the Criminal Justice Process*. Oxford: OUP.

Maguire, M., and McVie, S. (2017), 'Crime Data and Criminal Statistics: A Critical Reflection', in Liebling, A., Maruna, S., and McAra, L. (eds.), *The Oxford Handbook of Criminology* (6th ed.). Oxford: OUP.

Marsh, I., and Melville, G. (2014), *Crime, Justice and the Media* (2nd ed.). Abingdon: Routledge.

McBarnet, D. (1981), *Conviction: Law, the State and the Construction of Justice*. Basingstoke: Macmillan.

McConville, M. (2002), 'Plea Bargaining', in McConville, M., and Wilson, G. (eds.), *The Handbook of the Criminal Justice Process*. Oxford: OUP.

McConville, M., Hodgson, J., Bridges, L., and Pavlovic, A. (1994), *Standing Accused*. Oxford: OUP.

McConville, M., Sanders, A., and Leng, R. (1991), *The Case for the Prosecution: Police Suspects and the Construction of Criminality*. London: Routledge.

Ministry of Justice (2015), *Code of Practice for Victims of Crime*. London: Ministry of Justice.

Ministry of Justice (2018), *Criminal Court Statistics Quarterly: September to December 2017*. Available online at: https://assets.publishing.service.gov.uk/government/uploads/system/uploads/attachment_data/file/695408/ccsq-bulletin-oct-dec-2017.pdf. Accessed 25 May 2018.

Morgan, J., and Zedner, L. (1992), *Child Victims: Crime, Impact and Criminal Justice*. Oxford: Clarendon.

Morgan, R. (1995), 'Damned If They Do, Damned If They Don't: *The Case for the Prosecution*', in Noaks, L., Levi, M., and Maguire, M. (eds.), *Contemporary Issues in Criminology*. Cardiff: University of Wales Press.

Naughton, M. (2007), *Rethinking Miscarriages of Justice: Beyond the Tip of the Iceberg*. Basingstoke: Palgrave Macmillan.

Newburn, T. (2017), *Criminology* (3rd ed.). Abingdon: Routledge.

Nobles, R., and Schiff, D. (2000), *Understanding Miscarriages of Justice*. Oxford: OUP.

Norrie, A. (1991), 'A Critique of Legal Causation', *Modern Law Review*, **54**(5): 685–701.

Norrie, A. (1996), 'The Limits of Justice: Finding Fault in the Criminal Law', *Modern Law Review*, **59**(4): 540–56.

Norrie, A. (2014), *Crime, Reason and History* (3rd ed.). Cambridge: CUP.

ONS (2019a), *Crime in England and Wales, Year Ending March 2019*. Available online at: www.ons.gov.uk/peoplepopulationandcommunity/crimeandjustice/bulletins/crimeinenglandandwales/yearendingmarch2019#. Accessed 18 July 2019.

Parker, H., Sumner, M., and Jarvis, G. (1989), *Unmasking the Magistrates*. Milton Keynes: Open University Press.

Phillips, C., and Bowling, B. (2017), 'Ethnicities, Racism, Crime and Criminal Justice', in Liebling, A., Maruna, S., and McAra, L. (eds.), *The Oxford Handbook of Criminology* (6th ed.). Oxford: OUP.

Redmayne, M. (2004), 'Disclosure and Its Discontents', *Criminal Law Review*: 441–62.

Reiner, R. (2010), *The Politics of the Police* (4th ed.). Oxford: OUP.

Roberts, P. (2013), 'Forensic Science and Criminal Justice', in Hucklesby, A., and Wahidin, A. (eds.), *Criminal Justice* (2nd ed.). Oxford: OUP.

Rogers, J. (2006), 'Restructuring the Exercise of Prosecutorial Discretion in England', *Oxford Journal of Legal Studies*, **26**(4): 775–803.

Sanders, A. (1987), 'Some Dangers of Policy-Oriented Research: The Case of Prosecutions', in Dennis, I.H. (ed.), *Criminal Law and Justice*. London: Sweet and Maxwell.

Sanders, A. (2016), 'The CPS: 30 Years On', *Criminal Law Review*: 82–98.

Sanders, A., Hoyle, C., Morgan, R., and Cape, E. (2001), 'Victim Impact Statements: Can't Work, Won't Work', *Criminal Law Review*: 447–58.

Sanders, A., Young, R., and Burton, M. (2010), *Criminal Justice* (4th ed.). Oxford: OUP.

Simester, A.P., Spencer, J.R., Stark, F., Sullivan, G.R., and Virgo, G.J. (2016), *Simester and Sullivan's Criminal Law: Theory and Doctrine* (6th ed.). Oxford: Hart.

Smith, D.J. (1997), 'Case Construction and the Goals of the Criminal Process', *British Journal of Criminology*, **37**(3): 319–46.

Smith, D.J. (1998), 'Reform or Moral Outrage: The Choice Is Yours', *British Journal of Criminology*, **38**(4): 616–22.

Spalek, B. (2017), *Crime Victims: Theory, Policy and Practice* (2nd ed.). London: Palgrave Macmillan.

Temkin, J. (2002), *Rape and the Legal Process* (2nd ed.). Oxford: OUP.

Tombs, S., and Whyte, D. (2007), *Safety Crimes*. Cullompton: Willan.

Wells, C., and Quick, O. (2010), *Lacey, Wells and Quick's Reconstructing Criminal Law: Text and Materials* (4th ed.). Cambridge: CUP.

Williams, G. (1991), 'Criminal Omissions: The Conventional View', *Law Quarterly Review*, **107**(1): 86–98.

Wilson, W. (2017), *Criminal Law* (6th ed.). Harlow: Pearson.

Young, R. (2008), 'Street Policing After PACE: The Drift to Summary Justice', in Cape, E., and Young, R. (eds.), *Regulating Policing: The Police and Criminal Evidence Act 1984 – Past, Present and Future*. Oxford: Hart.

Zander, M., and Henderson, P. (1993), *The Crown Court Study*. Royal Commission on Criminal Justice Study No.19. London: HMSO.

Chapter 4

Actus reus and mens rea II
Alternative forms of criminal
responsibility

Chapter overview

Introduction
Alternative forms of criminal responsibility: the law
    Corporate liability
    Vicarious liability
    Complicity
    Inchoate offences
    Terrorism and organised crime offences
    State crimes
Alternative forms of criminal responsibility and criminal justice
    Corporate liability and criminal justice
    Complicity, inchoate offences, and criminal justice
    Terrorist offences, organised crime offences, and criminal justice
    State crimes and criminal justice
Conclusions: linking discussion to the roadmap theories
Further reading

Chapter aims

After reading Chapter 4, you should be able to understand:

- The principles governing corporate and vicarious liability in criminal law
- Which forms of complicity liability exist in criminal law, and what the actus reus and mens rea requirements are for each form
- Which forms of inchoate liability exist in criminal law, and what the actus reus and mens rea requirements are for each form
- How the law defines terrorist offences, organised crime offences, and state crimes

- How criminal justice enforces the different types of criminal liability
- How the evidence on the forms of liability in criminal law, which are discussed in this chapter, and the criminal justice response to these forms of liability, fits in with the roadmap theories introduced in Chapter 1

Introduction

Chapter 4 continues the discussion of actus reus and mens rea principles but from a different angle than in Chapter 3. In the first part of this chapter, the focus will be on how criminal law responds to crimes where the situation does not involve one individual person committing one or more full criminal offences. This can occur either where more than one person can be held criminally responsible for an offence (corporate liability, complicity, and the inchoate offences of assisting crime and conspiracy) or where someone has failed to complete the commission of an offence (the inchoate offence of attempt). It can also occur in the context of terrorism and state crime, types of criminality that are regulated by international law as well as domestic law. The criminal justice section of the chapter then considers criminal justice responses to these types of offending.

Alternative forms of criminal liability: the law

Corporate liability

Corporate liability involves the conviction and punishment of whole companies or organisations for particular offences, rather than just individuals. However, corporate liability can be proved only in limited and specific circumstances. The basic rule for establishing corporate liability is the 'identification principle', established in *Tesco v Nattrass* [1972] AC 153. To establish corporate liability, the prosecution must prove that there was a 'directing or controlling mind' which had the right actus reus and mens rea. In other words, there must be one person in charge of the organisation who has both the actus reus and mens rea required for the offence before the whole company can be convicted. If no one involved with the company has the right actus reus and mens rea, then the company cannot be held liable for the offence. The mens rea of more than one person cannot be put together to create the mens rea which is needed for a corporate offence (*Attorney-General's Reference (No.2 of 1999)* [2000] QB 796).

Two other approaches to corporate liability in criminal law do not rely on the identification principle. These are offences that specifically target corporations, and offences that criminalise a failure to prevent harmful behaviour from occurring (Child and Ormerod 2017: 30). An example of legislation imposing specific corporate liability for a particular offence, and which also uses 'failure to prevent' offences, is the Corporate Manslaughter and Corporate Homicide Act 2007, which deals with the offence of corporate manslaughter (see Chapter 7 for more details).

Study exercise 4.1

Do you agree with the identification principle as the basis for deciding on corporate liability? If not, what principle(s) would you use instead?

Vicarious liability: the law

Vicarious liability is based around someone's responsibility for an offence because of another person's actus reus and mens rea, not D's own. Often vicarious liability is imposed for strict liability offences (see Chapter 3), so these areas of the law are also linked. As with strict liability, it is often statutes that the courts have to interpret to decide whether vicarious liability applies, based on the words used in that statute.

The courts take certain words used in statutes to indicate that vicarious liability should apply. For example, statutes prohibiting the 'selling' of certain goods in certain situations are often held to include vicarious liability, as in *Tesco v Brent LBC* [1993] 2 All ER 718. However, vicarious liability only applies where an employee is acting within the scope of their authority as part of the job (*Adams v Camfoni* [1929] 1 KB 95).

The offences to which vicarious liability can attach are not always strict liability, though. Where the offence does require mens rea, the employer must have the right mens rea, as well as the employee, to be vicariously liable. The exception to this is where the employer has fully delegated their responsibilities to the employee in the law's eyes, so that the employee has completely taken the place of the employer at the time of the offence (*Vane v Yiannopoullos* [1965] AC 486). In such a case, the employer is still vicariously liable.

Study exercise 4.2

Is it ever fair to impose vicarious liability on employers for offences that they themselves have not committed? If so, under what circumstances should vicarious liability apply?

Complicity: the law

The law on complicity is complex. Complicity liability deals with who is criminally responsible (and for what they are criminally responsible) when more than one person is involved in the same crime. The law is made more confusing because there are complicity offences based on the law in section 8 of the Accessories and Abettors Act 1861, and offences based on the law in the Serious Crime Act 2007, running alongside each other.

There are three basic points to note about complicity. Firstly, the law differentiates between main, or principal, offenders and secondary offenders. The main offender is the person who directly commits the crime (i.e. the one who causes it). The secondary offender is the person who helps or encourages the main offender to commit the crime. Secondly, under the 1861 legislation, if the actus reus of the main offence is not committed, then the secondary offender cannot be guilty. This is because secondary liability relies on derivative liability (*Thornton v Mitchell* [1940] 1 All ER 339). There is detailed discussion of the inchoate offences in the 2007 Serious Crime Act relating to assisting or encouraging crime in the inchoate offences section of this chapter. However, be aware at this point that these inchoate offences can act as an alternative to the 1861 legislation offences relating to complicity. For the purposes of prosecution, the 2007 legislation has one key advantage over the 1861 legislation. This is that under the 2007 legislation, there is no need to wait until the main offence has occurred before prosecuting someone for assisting or encouraging the crime. Finally, the legislation that defines secondary offender liability under s.8 of the Accessories and Abettors Act 1861 (and s.44 of the Magistrates' Courts Act 1980 if the offence is in the magistrates' court) states that secondary offenders can receive the same sentence, up to and including the maximum sentence allowed for each offence, as the main offenders can. Section 58 of the Serious Crime Act 2007 states the same principle for the 2007 offences of assisting or encouraging crime.

Secondary liability: actus reus

The basic actus reus required for secondary liability is an act (or omission) which assists or encourages the main crime. There are four types of secondary liability listed in the Accessories and Abettors Act 1861 – aiding, abetting, counselling, and procuring. D only has to commit one of the four types of actus reus to be guilty (*Ferguson v Weaving* [1951] 1 KB 814).

Aiding means that a secondary offender has given some kind of help or support to the main offender (e.g. *Bainbridge* [1960] 1 QB 129). Aiding can happen either before or during the commission of the main offence (*Coney* (1882) LR 8 QBD 534). For aiding, there is no need for D's actions to be the 'but for' cause of the main offence. However, there does have to be some kind of 'causal link' between D helping and the main offender committing the offence (*Bryce* [2004] 2 Cr App Rep 35). This is a question for the jury or magistrates to decide on the facts. However, the secondary offender's act must actually help the main offender to commit the offence (*Attorney-General v Able* [1984] QB 795). The secondary offender is still guilty even if the main offender does not know about, or does not want, the help that the secondary offender has given.

Coney shows that the secondary offender's presence at the scene of the crime without doing or saying anything can only be evidence suggesting that the actus reus for aiding has been committed, but not conclusive proof. More recent cases such as *Robinson v R* [2011] EWCA Crim 916 and *L v CPS* [2013] EWHC 4127 (Admin) have required a positive act of assistance from the secondary offender, rather than just presence at the scene of the crime, to prove the actus reus of aiding. 'Positive assistance' in this context occurs where the main offender is encouraged by the secondary offender's presence and the secondary offender realises that this is the case. Aiding can also occur by omission. *Tuck v Robson* [1970] 1 WLR 741 shows that if D has a legal duty to stop someone from doing something illegal and does not fulfil that duty, then that defendant is liable as a secondary offender.

In terms of actus reus, abetting and counselling both involve some kind of help or encouragement being given to the main offender by D, either by words, actions, or omissions occurring before or during the main offence. There is no need for 'but for' causation (*Attorney-General v Able*), but there must be a causal link between the actions of D and the actions of the main offender (*Bryce*). Unlike aiding, for D to be guilty of abetting or counselling, the main offender must know that they are acting within the scope of D's encouragement or approval (*Calhaem* [1985] QB 808). In *Luffman* [2008] EWCA Crim 1379, for example, D had provided the main offender with a gun and bullets for use in killing the victim. The law on whether D can abet or counsel simply by being present at the scene of the crime is similar to that for aiding (discussed earlier). *Clarkson* [1971] 1 WLR 1402 stated that there has to be 'encouragement in fact'. However, not much 'encouragement' is required in order for a secondary offender to be liable on the facts of this case. Simply clapping or cheering would be enough.

Procuring means 'to produce by endeavour' (*Attorney-General's Reference (No.1 of 1975)* [1975] QB 773). To procure a main offence, D must cause it in some way. A causal link between D's actions and the main offender's crime is therefore needed for the actus reus. No consensus between the defendant and the main offender is necessary for procuring, and there is no need for D to be encouraging or assisting the main offender's crime.

Secondary liability: mens rea

There are four mens rea requirements for secondary liability. Firstly, D has to intend to encourage or assist the main offence (*National Coal Board v Gamble*

[1959] 1 QB 11). The motive for helping is not relevant. As long as D intends to help the main offender and knows the essential facts of the main offence (see next), they will be guilty. Secondly, D has to realise that their acts are capable of assisting or encouraging the main offender *(Bryce)*.

Thirdly, D must have knowledge of the key elements of the main crime – in other words, they must also have mens rea regarding the consequences of the help that they are giving. This means that the court must look at the main offender's mens rea in cases of this kind, as well as the secondary offender's. *Jogee* [2016] UKSC 8 decided that D, as a secondary offender, must 'intend' that the main offender will commit the crime with the right mens rea. *Jogee* overruled a series of earlier cases, including *Chan Wing-Siu* [1985] 1 AC 168 and *Powell; English* [1999] 1 AC 1, all of which stated that D only had to foresee a real (substantial) risk (i.e. be subjectively reckless) that the main offender would commit the crime, and would have the right mens rea while committing it. Foresight of the main offender committing the crime is now only evidence that a jury could use to find an intention to assist or encourage.

Study exercise 4.3

Do you think the change to the rules on the mens rea needed for secondary offenders in *Jogee* has made the law a) fairer on defendants, b) easier to understand for juries, and c) more effective in regulating the social harm caused by gang criminality?

Finally, D must know the essential facts of the offence which the main offender commits *(Ferguson v Weaving)*. In terms of how much D has to know about the circumstances of the main offence, *DPP for Northern Ireland v Maxwell* [1978] 1 WLR 1350 says that D is only liable if the main crime committed is on a 'shopping list' of crimes which D foresaw might be committed. Therefore, if D knows one or more of a range of offences will take place but is unsure exactly which offence will occur, they would still be guilty if one or more of these offences occur, and if D knows the general class of the main offence, but not the specific one, they would again be guilty.

Where the assisting or encouragement of crime occurs by omission, D's mens rea must include the following characteristics:

- Knowledge that the main offender was committing the crime;
- Deliberately 'turning a blind eye' to the crime; and
- Knowledge that by doing so D was encouraging the main offender to commit the crime *(JF Alford Transport Ltd* [1997] 2 Cr App 326).

Study exercise 4.4

Read the case of *Gnango* [2011] UKSC 59. Do you think Gnango should have been convicted of assisting or encouraging murder based on the facts of the case? Do you think that he would still be guilty after the *Jogee* decision?

Before the decision in *Jogee*, the law also recognised another category of complicity liability known as 'joint enterprise' or 'joint unlawful enterprise'. A joint unlawful enterprise meant that there is an express or implied agreement to commit crime together between two or more people (*Anderson and Morris* [1966] 2 QB 110). *Powell; English* decided that where there is a joint unlawful enterprise, everyone involved in it is liable for the crimes that result from the plan. *Jogee* made it clear that joint unlawful enterprises were an example of secondary liability for assisting or encouraging crime, not a separate form of criminal liability. However, the court in *Jogee* did state that if one person in the enterprise acts outside the plan in a way that the secondary offender could not have contemplated, the secondary offender is not liable for the crime that person commits – but in a case of murder, they could still be guilty of the lesser offence of manslaughter.

Defences to secondary liability

In some situations, it is possible for someone to withdraw from being a secondary offender and avoid liability for the crimes that take place partly because of earlier assistance or encouragement. To withdraw successfully from secondary liability, D has to give a clear warning of withdrawal to the others involved in the crime that will take place (*Becerra and Cooper* (1976) 62 Cr App Rep 212), or has to do something to try to stop the others from carrying out their plan, like calling the police (*Grundy* [1977] Crim LR 543). As *Rook* [1993] 2 All ER 955 shows, the withdrawal from the enterprise must be clear and unambiguous. It is not enough, for example, for D not to turn up at the arranged day, time, and place of the planned crime without clearly explaining to the others involved that they do not want to be involved in the crime anymore.

The law on withdrawal is slightly different where the crime that D is assisting or encouraging is unplanned and spontaneous – a group of people suddenly and violently attacking an individual, for example. *O'Flaherty* [2004] Crim LR 751 states that in a situation like this D does not need to say clearly to the others that they are withdrawing from the crime. All D needs to do is to leave the scene of the crime. It is a question of fact for the jury or magistrates to decide in cases like this whether D has done enough to withdraw from the crime based on all the available evidence. *Rafferty* [2007] EWCA Crim 1846 is a good example of a case where the court decided that D had done enough to withdraw. *Jogee* fully supported this principle.

The second defence to secondary liability is the so-called 'victim principle', which states that victims cannot be guilty of assisting or encouraging crimes against themselves. The principle was used in *Tyrrell* [1894] 1 QB 710. However, the victim principle only applies to offences that aim to protect a particular type of victim. It does not apply generally in criminal law on complicity (*Gnango*).

Study exercise 4.5

Why do you think the law sometimes lets people withdraw from complicity liability?

The next section of this chapter moves on to look at the law on inchoate offences.

Inchoate offences: the law

Making sense of inchoate offences

Inchoate offences are a specific group of types of liability, covering situations where D has not completed the full actus reus and mens rea for a particular offence but has taken some steps towards completing the actus reus and mens rea required. The key question in this context is how far criminal law allows people to go towards committing the full offence before it criminalises their behaviour. To answer this question, the actus reus and mens rea requirements for different types of inchoate liability will now be explained. At the outset, it is important to note that there are three different types of inchoate offences – attempt, conspiracy, and incitement. Attempt and conspiracy 'attach' to individual offences, so that D has to be charged with, for example, attempted burglary rather than simply attempted crime generally. However, incitement is an offence on its own as 'encouraging or assisting crime' under the Serious Crime Act 2007. Statute law now covers most of the principles defining all three types of inchoate offences. The discussion of the law will begin by taking a closer look at criminal attempts, followed by conspiracy and incitement.

Attempt: actus reus

An attempt means that D has tried to complete the actus reus and mens rea for a particular offence but has not fully succeeded. The question is how far

D has to go towards completing the actus reus of the offence before their conduct counts as a criminal attempt. Following various attempts by the common law to set guidelines on when an attempt had been committed (e.g. *Robinson* [1915] 2 KB 342 and *DPP v Stonehouse* [1978] AC 55), the actus reus of attempt is now defined by the Criminal Attempts Act 1981. S.1(1) of the Act states that the actus reus of attempt is any act which is 'more than merely preparatory to the commission of the offence', so that D has 'embarked upon the crime proper' (*Gullefer* [1990] 1 WLR 1063). This issue, as the Act states, is a question of fact, which means that juries and magistrates have to decide on a case-by-case basis whether D has gone beyond what is 'merely preparatory' in committing an offence, taking the offence and the circumstances of the case into account. The discretion given to courts in deciding what is and is not an attempt has led to contrasting decisions since the Criminal Attempts Act became law. Therefore, for example, Ds were guilty of attempts in *Jones* [1990] 1 WLR 1057, *Attorney-General's Reference (No.1 of 1992)* [1993] 1 WLR 274, and *Tosti* [1997] Crim LR 746. On the other hand, Ds were not guilty in *Campbell* (1991) 93 Cr App Rep 350 and *Geddes* [1996] Crim LR 894.

Attempt: mens rea

The Criminal Attempts Act 1981 s.1(1) states that intention to commit the full offence is the mens rea required for attempts. This includes both direct and oblique forms of intent (see discussion in Chapter 3). The situation is more complex where there is more than one element to the actus reus of the offence which needs mens rea, and there has been disagreement over mens rea requirements for offences like these. *Khan* [1990] 1 WLR 813 stated that there must be intent to commit the 'core act' in the actus reus, and that the same mens rea is needed for the full offence for the other parts of actus reus. *Attorney-General's Reference (No.3 of 1992)* [1994] 1 WLR 409 claimed to follow the decision in *Khan* but took a different approach to defining mens rea for attempt than the one in *Khan* by stating that D must 'intend to supply whatever is missing from the completion of the offence'. However, *Pace* [2014] EWCA Crim 186 stated that D needed to have intention to commit all of the elements of the offence that they are attempting to commit. *Pace* is a narrower definition of the mens rea for attempt than the one in *Khan*, but it did not overrule either of the two earlier cases, meaning that there are now three competing definitions of the mens rea for attempt in criminal law.

Attempt and impossibility

Can someone be legally guilty of attempting to commit an offence that is impossible to commit in reality? Ss. 1(2) and 1(3) of the Criminal Attempts Act 1981 show that even if an offence is factually impossible, D who fulfils the actus reus and mens rea criteria is still guilty of attempt. There has been confusion in the law over whether D is guilty where they do something thinking that it is an offence but where facts that they do not know about mean that committing the intended crime is impossible in the circumstances. In *Shivpuri* [1987] AC 1 the House of Lords decided that impossible attempts like this are still attempts in criminal law, overruling the earlier House of Lords case of *Anderton v Ryan* [1985] AC 560, which took the opposite view only a year earlier.

Study exercise 4.6

Should the law convict people of attempting impossible crimes, or is this just prosecuting 'thought crime'?

Conspiracy: actus reus

The actus reus for most conspiracies is defined by Criminal Law Act 1977. The only common law conspiracies still present in the law relate to conspiracy to defraud (see *Scott v Metropolitan Police Commissioner* [1975] AC 819) and conspiracy to corrupt public morals (see *Shaw v DPP* [1962] AC 220). S.1(1) states that the actus reus for a statutory conspiracy is 'an agreement by two or more people' to follow 'a course of conduct *necessarily* amounting to the commission of an offence by one or more of them'. The offence is complete once the agreement has formed. There has to be proof of a definite agreement, however. Proof of ongoing discussions working towards an agreement to commit the full offence is not enough (*Walker* [1962] Crim LR 458). There is no conspiracy where the only parties to the agreement are husband and wife; where the only other party to the agreement is under the age of 10, the minimum age of criminal responsibility in England and Wales; or where the only other party to the agreement is the intended victim of the planned offence (s.2(2)).

Conspiracy: mens rea

There are three elements in the mens rea for statutory conspiracy, according to *Saik* [2006] 2 WLR 993. Firstly, there must be an intention to make the agreement. Secondly, under s.1(1) of Criminal Law Act 1977, there has to be an intention to do the act which is prohibited by the full offence. Thirdly, under s.1(2), there has to be intention or knowledge that a fact or circumstance which is necessary for the commission of the substantive offence will exist when the agreement is carried out.

Each person involved in the conspiracy must have intention that the full offence will occur (*Yip Chiu-Cheung v R* [1995] 1 AC 111). The parties to the conspiracy are only liable for the intended consequences of their planned course of conduct (*Siracusa* (1990) 90 Cr App Rep 340). D does not have to intend to play an active role in the planned course of conduct in order to be guilty of conspiracy. As long as the intention that the full offence will occur is present, and D intends to go along with the other parties' activity in pursuing the course of conduct without doing anything to prevent them from following it, then D is guilty of conspiracy (*Siracusa; Yip*). *Clark* [2012] EWCA Crim 1220 shows that D does not have to know all of the details of the criminal conspiracy in which they were involved as long as they shared a common criminal purpose with their co-conspirators.

If there is a conditional agreement to carry out an offence if something else happens, then the parties still have the mens rea for conspiracy as long as the offence is the aim of the agreement, and the offence would necessarily be committed if the conspiracy was carried out (*Jackson* [1985] Crim LR 442). However, if the aim of the agreement is something else other than the offence, and something that does not necessarily involve the commission of an offence, then the parties do not have the mens rea for conspiracy, even if they foresee the offence as a possible way of bringing about the agreement (*Reed* [1982] Crim LR 819).

Conspiracy and impossibility

S.1(1)(b) of Criminal Law Act 1977, which was inserted by s.5 of the Criminal Attempts Act 1981, states that impossibility is no defence to a statutory conspiracy. In this way, the law on impossibility in relation to statutory conspiracy is the same as it is in relation to attempt.

Study exercise 4.7

Do you think the current conspiracy laws give a reasonable prospect of convicting the leaders of terrorist organisations such as ISIL?

Incitement: actus reus

The Serious Crime Act 2007 introduced new offences of 'encouraging or assisting crime', which replaced the previous common law on incitement. Bear in mind that under s.49(1) of the Act, the actus reus for these offences is proved as soon as the encouragement or assistance has taken place with the right mens rea (see next). It does not matter whether or not the full offence is actually committed later. This shows the difference between the new offences and complicity liability (discussed earlier in this chapter), under which the full offence must be carried out before D can be liable. However, there is the potential for overlap between these provisions and the law on complicity, which could cause confusion in criminal law and criminal justice in the future.

The basis of the actus reus under the new legislation is doing an act (or an omission under s.47(8)) that is factually capable of assisting or encouraging a criminal offence (ss.44–45), or that is factually capable of assisting or encouraging more than one criminal offence (s.46). D has a defence if they can prove that they had knowledge of the circumstances and that their actions were reasonable in the light of these circumstances. They also have a defence if they can prove that they had a reasonable belief in the existence of certain circumstances and that their actions were reasonable in the light of the circumstances as D believed them to be (s.50). Therefore, in this case, the normal burden of proof switches from the prosecution to the defence.

Incitement: mens rea

Again the Serious Crime Act 2007 governs this issue. The offence under s.44 (discussed earlier) requires mens rea of intention to assist or encourage the commission of the full offence. The offence under s.45 (which has the same actus reus as the one under s.44) requires the lesser mens rea of belief that the full offence will be committed and belief that the act will assist or encourage the commission of the full offence. Similarly, the offence under s.46 (assisting or encouraging more than one offence) requires mens rea of D's belief that one or more offences will be committed and D's belief that the act will assist or encourage the commission of one or more of the offences. The case of S [2011] EWCA Crim 2872 emphasised that prosecutors should only use the s.46 offence when D's act is capable of assisting or encouraging more than one offence. S also made it clear that D only needs a belief that one of the offences will (not just might) be committed, and does not have to know that the act that D encourages is an offence, or who is going to commit the offence, or whom the victim will be.

Incitement and impossibility

Under s.49(1) of the Serious Crime Act 2007, D is still guilty of incitement even if the offence is factually impossible to commit in the circumstances, as long as D believes that the full offence will be committed and believes that what they are doing will encourage or assist that offence.

Study exercise 4.8

Make a list of three differences, in terms of actus reus, mens rea, and impossibility, between the old law and the new law under the Serious Crime Act 2007.

Terrorism and organised crime offences: the law

As Joyce (2017: 582) points out, the very concept of terrorism is difficult to define precisely. It is also true that those who commit terrorist acts include individuals acting spontaneously, as well as groups and networks of varying organisation and size (Innes and Levi 2017: 455). Even so, terrorist offences are included here because of their links to group activity, as well as because of their distinctive focus on terrorism as communicative violence designed to intimidate those beyond immediate victims (ibid: 457). McLaughlin (2001: 293–4) shows how States transformed the concept of violence aimed at bringing political change into the concept of terrorism during the 20th century, because the term 'terrorism' makes it easier to impose moral and ideological censure on certain types of behaviour. The legislative response to terrorism toughened up in line with successive events perceived as being terrorism in England itself, such as the IRA bombing campaigns of the 1970s, 1980s, and 1990s, and the terrorist attacks in London on 7th July 2005. Despite the contested nature of terrorism, English criminal law does provide a definition of it, as well as a range of specific terrorist offences, many of them inchoate. Only specific terrorist and organised crime offences within English criminal law are considered here, but bear in mind that there are also an extensive range of powers aimed at seizing the assets of those accused of terrorism, in the Terrorism Act 2000 and in later legislation.

S.1 of the Terrorism Act 2000 defines terrorism as serious violence, serious property damage, endangerment to another's life, creation of serious risk to the health and safety of the public or to a section of the public, or serious interference with or disruption to an electronic system. The use or threat of one or more of these actions must be designed to influence the government, or to intimidate the public or a section of the public (unless firearms or explosives are involved, in which case there is no need to prove this criterion). The use or threat must be made for advancing a political, religious, racial, or ideological cause.

In the years since 2000, various specific anti-terrorist offences have been introduced, many of them inchoate (see Lowe 2018: chs.2 and 3 for more details). S.1 of the Terrorism Act 2006 criminalises the encouragement of others (intentionally or recklessly) to commit, prepare, or instigate terrorist acts. S.5 of the Terrorism Act 2006 makes it an offence for someone to engage in preparation for acts of terrorism or to assist others in preparation for acts of terrorism. The mens rea for this offence is an intention to commit one or more acts of terrorism, and the maximum sentence for this offence is life imprisonment. Section 58 of the Terrorism Act 2000 criminalises collecting, or making a record of, information likely to be useful to a person committing or preparing an act of terrorism, or to possess a document or record containing information of that kind. The maximum sentence for this offence is 10 years' imprisonment. Section 2 of the Terrorism Act 2006 makes it an offence to distribute a terrorist publication (i.e. one which is likely to be useful to a person committing or preparing an act of terrorism) with the intention of encouraging terrorist acts. The maximum sentence for this offence is seven years' imprisonment. There are also various other offences aimed at criminalising the support of terrorist activity. In the Terrorism Act 2000, these include being a member of a proscribed terrorist organisation (s.11), wearing a uniform connected with such an organisation (s.13), or supporting one by organising or addressing meetings (s.12), by giving and receiving financial support, or by laundering the financial proceeds of terrorism (ss.15–18).

Other offences in the 2000 and 2006 Acts criminalise various levels of actual involvement in terrorist activity. These include:

- Giving or receiving training in weapon usage, either generally (s.54 of the 2000 Act) or specifically for the purposes of terrorism (s.6 of the 2006 Act);
- Directing the activities of a terrorist organisation (s.56 of the 2000 Act);
- Possessing an article for terrorist purposes (s.57 of the 2000 Act); or
- Attendance at a place where training for the purposes of terrorism is being provided, knowing or believing that this is the purpose of the training (s.8 of the 2006 Act).

Finally, it is also important to note that even if someone is charged with an offence that is not specifically anti-terrorist, they could still be convicted of an offence with 'terrorist connections'. This could occur if their offence appears on the list of offences in Schedule 2 of the Counter-Terrorism Act 2008 (murder for example), and the trial judge decides that the offence should be labelled in this way. If the judge does decide to impose the 'terrorist connections' label, this can be treated as an aggravating factor when sentencing, and can also lead to removal of the normal rule of parole at the halfway point of a prison sentence.

Turning to organised crime, it is defined by the National Crime Agency (the organisation responsible for responding to it) as serious crime planned, coordinated, and conducted by people working together often (but not necessarily) for financial gain; most of the activities considered by UK policymakers to be associated with organised crime are regulated by existing types of criminal law offence. These include drugs offences, firearms offences, child exploitation and abuse, cybercrime, and slavery and human trafficking (now regulated in England and Wales by the Modern Slavery Act 2015). However, Section 45 of the Serious Crime Act 2015 introduces a specific new offence of participating in the activities of an organised crime group. If a person takes part in activities that they know or reasonably suspect are criminal activities of an organised crime group, or will help an organised crime group to carry on its activities, they are guilty of this offence. 'Criminal activities' are defined as offences which constitute an offence punishable with seven years' imprisonment or more in England and Wales, but can be committed in other countries, too, as long as they would equate to an offence of this kind if they had been committed in England and Wales. The criminal activities must be carried out in order to obtain any gain or benefit. An organised crime group is defined as a group which carries on criminal activities as its purpose, or one of its purposes, and has at least three members (although D does not have to know any of the group's members). This offence has a maximum sentence of five years' imprisonment.

Study exercise 4.9

Draw a flowchart showing the development of anti-terrorist legislation in English criminal law since 2000. Then, using Internet research, find out what anti-terrorist criminal law is like in a country outside England. What similarities and differences can you see between the legislative frameworks in England and your other chosen country?

State crimes: the law

The State, defined as the centralised governmental organisation that has control over the legitimate use of force (such as criminal punishment) within a defined geographical area, can also be responsible for crime as an organisation. An obvious barrier to the response to state crime is that states are responsible for defining criminal law in their area of governance, so they can (in theory) redefine that law, or the response to it, to make their criminal acts legal. As a result, international law, such as international treaties, defines crimes that states, and individuals who are part of states, can commit. Such law therefore covers the behaviour of the English state and those who represent it.

State crime is a relatively new branch of criminal law, with most offences only created after the Second World War (Cassese et al. 2013: 3–4). State crime can include the misdeeds of government institutions and agencies, powerful individuals acting in the name of the state, and those acting criminally as enabled by the state powers vested in them (Ross 2017). As Green and Ward (2004) show, state crime now covers the following key types of criminal behaviour:

- War crimes, in terms of breaches of rules on when a state can declare war, as well as breaches of rules on conduct during a war (see Pena-Neira and Quiroga 2017);
- Crimes against humanity, meaning a serious, large-scale and organised attack on the dignity of a civilian population in war or peacetime, which can include behaviours such as murder, rape as a weapon of war (Aginam 2017), torture, or persecution (Cassese et al. 2013: 90–2);
- Torture (see Tembo 2017a);
- Genocide (see Turner 2017b);
- State-sponsored terrorist activity (see Tembo 2017b); and
- Various forms of financial crime, such as State-sponsored theft and fraud through corruption.

Study exercise 4.10

Draft a piece of legislation covering the regulation of state crime. What offences would you include? What punishments would you use for your offences and why?

Alternative forms of criminal liability and criminal justice

Corporate liability and criminal justice

Norrie (2014: ch.5) traces the development of corporate and vicarious liability (a development that has a close connection to the emergence of strict liability at the same time) in criminal law from the shift in the law's focus to regulating working-class offending in the 19th century. Norrie argues that those who shaped criminal law, focusing on individual mental blameworthiness for crime, did not think that criminal law would also need to regulate criminal behaviour by those from a middle- and upper-class social background, through the activities of businesses. A related problem was the general reluctance of magistrates and juries to convict others who tended to be from their own social class. Once it became clear that businesses could cause as much (if not more) social harm as individual criminals from a lower-class background, two different strategies developed to deal with corporate crime.

The first strategy identified by Norrie is differentiation – marking out corporate crime as 'different' from 'real crime' by making them strict liability and removing mens rea requirements. This approach is visible in the offences contained in the Health and Safety at Work Act 1974, such as an employer's failure to ensure the health, safety, and wellbeing of their employees at work, as well as in a long line of historical strict liability offences from the second half of the 19th century which were aimed at corporations (Johnstone and Ward 2010: 114). The second strategy is assimilation – treating corporate crime as 'real crime' by requiring mens rea as part of corporate offences. This approach is visible in the 'controlling mind' identification principle (discussed earlier).

Norrie argues that both strategies are problematic in terms of conveying the social harm caused by corporate crime. The use of differentiation and strict liability allows companies to deny that their crime is a serious or 'real' crime. This is a fundamentally misleading image when, as Tombs (2017) points out, corporate crime can and does include such severe instances of social harm as:

- Environmental pollution of water and air;
- Financial crimes like tax evasion;
- Crimes against the consumer such as illegal marketing;
- Crimes against employees such as violation of wage laws; and
- Crimes against the public such as the sinking of the P&O *Herald of Free Enterprise* ferry at Zeebrugge in 1987, killing 193 people, which was caused by the P&O company's failure to provide a safe operating system and a coherent approach to health and safety (Wells 2001: 48–51).

It is unsurprising, given its scope, that corporate crime has a significant psychological and financial impact on society, as well as causes physical harm (Tombs 2017).

The differentiation strategy's effectiveness is further undermined by the seemingly lenient approach to regulating corporate crime by those agencies that are responsible for responding to it, such as the Health and Safety Executive (HSE), which is responsible for investigating and prosecuting breaches of health and safety legislation in the workplace and therefore do the work normally done by both the police and the Crown Prosecution Service in the criminal justice process. There is evidence that the HSE and other regulatory agencies do take corporate mens rea into account by only prosecuting companies that repeatedly and deliberately break the law (e.g. Richardson 1987). However, the fact that these agencies tend to prosecute corporate law-breaking only as a last resort after warnings and inspections have failed to change behaviour (Hawkins 2002) portrays the response to corporate crime as being weak. It is also true that the HSE's resourcing by the government was reduced by 40% between 2011–12 and 2014–15, with the number of HSE inspections declining by 69% and the number of HSE convictions declining by 60% over the same period (Tombs 2017: 139–40). Even fining companies severely for corporate wrongdoing is problematic because companies can change their corporate identity and can pass the costs of fines onto the public by making employees redundant or transferring their business activities to another jurisdiction (Fisse and Braithwaite 1993).

The assimilation strategy also has encountered serious difficulties in practice. All but the smallest corporations will have responsibility for the running of the business spread among a variety of management staff, so that there will be no 'controlling mind' to which to attribute mens rea (Clarkson 1996). As a result, many prosecutions for high-profile cases of corporate killing failed in the 1980s and 1990s (Almond 2007: 287–8). The Corporate Manslaughter and Corporate Homicide Act 2007 tried to combine the differentiation and assimilation approaches, as discussed in Chapter 8, but has been criticised for its limited scope, widespread exemptions from liability, and over-reliance on individual liability rather than corporate liability (Gobert 2008). These problems illustrate the challenges that corporate liability present to traditional views of criminal law and criminal justice as treating all crimes and offenders equally. Writers such as Norrie (2014) are pessimistic about the ability of even radical reforms like enforced company nationalisation (Box 1983) and probation through court-appointed monitors of corporate activity (Fisse and Braithwaite 1993) to respond to corporate criminality meaningfully, given current socio-economic and political conditions.

Study exercise 4.11

What sort of system of punishment do you think would be most effective in reducing the social harm caused by corporate offending?

Complicity, inchoate offences, and criminal justice

Neither complicity nor inchoate offences have always been part of criminal law. They became part of criminal law through the decision of judges within the criminal justice process, rather than through Parliament-generated statute law. Taking the English law on attempt for example, there was no general rule that attempting a crime was a crime in itself until Lord Mansfield created the rule in the case of *Schofield* (1784) Cald 397, and later cases followed that decision until the doctrine established itself firmly by the mid-19th century (Sayre 1928: 834–6).

In a similar vein, Sayre (1922) also shows how the offence of conspiracy started off as a statutory administrative offence intended to deter people from making false accusations in court. However, a line of court decisions starting with the *Poulterer's Case* (1611) 9 Coke 55b decided that agreements to commit crimes were crimes in themselves, even if the actual crime did not take place – and by the 18th century, agreements to commit immoral acts, and not just crimes, were also criminal conspiracies (Jarvis and Bisgrove 2014: 262).

Spicer (1981) points to the criminal justice tendency to make conspiracies easier to prove by relaxing the evidential requirements, and to use conspiracy charges after the full offence has been committed to make conviction easier, rather than using them to try to prevent future crime from occurring. Jarvis and Bisgrove (2014) also point to the modern-day tendency of prosecution agencies to try to cut corners when charging cases, by assuming that there was only one conspiracy when in fact there was more than one, and assuming a common criminal purpose between all of those accused, when in fact there was no such common purpose. In this way, criminal justice enforcement practice in the area of inchoate offences shapes the meaning of criminal law itself (Wells and Quick 2010: 305).

Crewe et al. (2015) clearly illustrate the damaging impact of complicity law on the lives of those convicted of this type of offence. Crewe et al. found that of the prisoners sentenced to life imprisonment for murder that they surveyed at HMP Whitemoor, 51% had been convicted under complicity law and 33% did not know whether they had been convicted under complicity law or not. Crewe et al. also found that three times as many BME prisoners had been convicted of murder under complicity laws as in the general population and that those convicted of murder through complicity received longer minimum sentence tariffs than others. Almost three-quarters of surveyed prisoners did not believe themselves to be morally guilty of murder. Almost half were in the process of appealing either their conviction, their sentence, or both. Crewe et al.'s argument is therefore that the law on complicity acts as an ethnic and social 'vacuum cleaner', sweeping the economically and socially disadvantaged into prison without a fair and consistent process of justice.

Study exercise 4.12

Draw up a list of arguments for and against the idea that the decision in *Jogee* will improve the social discrimination found in the criminal justice enforcement of complicity law by Crewe et al. in their study.

Terrorist offences, organised crime offences, and criminal justice

The usage of a robust criminal justice response to terrorist activity is not a recent development in England. The Troubles in Northern Ireland were the trigger for a series of special criminal justice measures, such as the extension of police stop and search powers, detention without trial, and telephone taps (Newburn 2017: 970). Critical criminologists such as Hillyard (1993) have seen these powers as excessive and at times brutal abuses of due process, with no conclusive proof of increased effectiveness compared with normal criminal justice processes.

The pattern of departing from normal criminal justice processes in favour of a more punitive and risk-based approach in response to high-profile incidents of terrorism became increasingly regular following 9/11. Innes and Levi (2017: 464) track the constant development of new anti-terrorist legislation since 2001, including:

- The Anti-Terrorism, Crime and Security Act 2001, which introduced detention without trial, later overturned by court decisions;
- The Prevention of Terrorism Act 2005, which introduced control orders that had the power to restrict suspects' movement and communication with others severely. Control orders were overturned by the High Court on human rights grounds in 2006 and have since been replaced by Terrorism Prevention and Investigation Measures (TPIMs), which perform most of the same control functions;
- The Terrorism Act 2006, which extended the duration of allowable detention of suspects without charge from 14 to 28 days;
- The Counter-Terrorism Act 2008, which allowed police to continue questioning of suspects after charging them;
- The Terrorist Asset-Freezing Act 2010; and
- The Counter-Terrorism and Security Act 2015.

Clear patterns are visible in this legislation in terms of an increase in police powers, but also in terms of an increasing focus on the seizure of financial assets as a way of disrupting terrorist activities in England and elsewhere. Innes and Levi (2017: 468–70) question the effectiveness of these policies. They cite the very low numbers of terrorist finance prosecutions since 2001 and the small-scale and local nature of recent terrorist attacks such as the Manchester Arena bombing of 22nd May 2017 and the London Bridge attack of 3rd June 2017, neither of which needed significant financial resources or international finance transfer to be carried out.

Such limitations point to the need to work with communities on a more local level to divert vulnerable groups away from terrorist activity. However, the governments Prevent strategy, which aims to reduce terrorism in this way, has been controversial. Millings' (2013) research found that young Asian men saw Prevent as being exclusionary and polarising, wrongly labelling whole communities as being part of the problem of terrorism. Millings pointed to the crucial role played by the police in denying social belonging and acceptance to young Asian men in relation to police implementation of the Prevent strategy on a local level.

The criminal justice response to organised crime has largely mirrored its response to terrorism. This is in part due to the belief of policy-makers that both forms of crime are increasingly multi-national in nature, that both forms of crime require extensive financial support to operate, and that both forms of crime are increasing in frequency and severity. In the organised crime context, such beliefs have led to specialist law enforcement agencies such as the National Crime Agency, which was set up in 2013 as an organisation whose role is to tackle the types of serious and organised crime mentioned earlier in this chapter, on a national and international level. The National Crime Agency reported that there were 4,629 mapped organised crime groups operating in the UK at the end of 2017 (National Crime Agency 2018: 8), a reduction of over 20% in number compared with 2017.

The same report acknowledges the limitations of this statistic as a measure of how much organised and serious crime exists in the UK, however. The NCA believes that modern slavery, human trafficking, child sexual abuse, firearms offences, and drugs offences (which are facilitated through 'county lines' and the exploitation of children to supply drugs across different areas of the country – see Coomber and Moyle 2018), all of which are commonly linked to organised crime, are increasing gradually and consistently in occurrence. These data support the view of Hobbs (1995, 2013), who argues that socioeconomic processes like globalisation and neoliberalism have made organised crime normal and increasingly flexible in society, where it was previously restricted to professional criminals. On this view, it is virtually impossible for even specialist organised crime agencies such as the NCA to have a meaningful impact on the incidence of this socially harmful group of offences.

Study exercise 4.13

How, if at all, do you think Brexit will affect the ability of criminal justice to respond effectively to terrorism and organised crime in England?

State crimes and criminal justice

Green and Ward (2017: 441) argue that the scale of state crime is staggering when we consider even rough estimates of civilians killed by their own governments. Rummel calculated that governments murdered 262 million people during the 20th century (ibid), and more recently, the Syrian Human Rights network estimates that between 2011 and 2018, the various factions in the Syrian Civil War have killed 222,114 civilians (Syrian Network for Human Rights Network 2019).

Crimes on this scale point to the need for an international response in which countries such as England must play a meaningful part. Johnstone and Ward (2010: 171) identify three types of international response to state crime:

*   International criminal law and its associated tribunals, such as the International Criminal Court (ICC) (see Close 2017);

- Universal jurisdiction, where states try to punish state crimes committed outside their own country; and
- Transitional justice, where state crimes that were committed under a previous regime are tried and punished in the same country.

Johnstone and Ward (ibid.) note the difficulties in finding meaningful punishment to fit the enormous scale of state crime. Punishing individuals for state crime, as the ICC has tried to do, downplays the organisational dynamics behind state crime. This approach also assumes that the decision-making behind state crime is rational, and risks trivialising state crime conflicts by punishing one individual for hundreds or thousands of deaths. On the other hand, punishing groups under joint enterprise law makes it more difficult to work out exactly how blameworthy individuals really are.

Another problem facing the regulation of state crime through criminal justice is the fact that international criminal courts take conflicts away from victims and communities by trying cases in another country. Doing this 'steals' victims' conflicts away from them and makes it harder for victims' voices to be heard (Christie 1977). Roche (2005) has argued that the kinds of local level, informal truth commissions seen in Northern Ireland and South Africa make it easier to listen to victims and condemn offenders effectively. Using processes that are more informal might also reduce the ability of the public to deny that the horrors of state crime exist worldwide, and force the public to acknowledge the widespread civic level of compliance and passive acceptance of state crime (Cohen 2001). Such an approach might also avoid the political issues often faced by international criminal courts in terms of the pressure on them to comply with the interests of powerful countries such as the USA, whose government policies have consistently favoured war and invasion over the use of formal and informal justice as a response to state crime. The Iraq war of 2003 is representative of the approach of American policy and is itself an example of the range of social harm done by state crime (Walklate 2017).

Overall, it seems that local level, restorative responses to state crime are the most effective way of responding to it, offering a range of approaches under the banner of reconciliation (White 2017). However, giving victims a voice and raising public awareness to avoid widespread denial in this way is not a sufficient response by itself. To address the immense social harm caused by state crime meaningfully, it is also necessary to bring about the wider political, social, and economic change that removes the exclusion and division on a local, national, and international level, which so often acts as the trigger for the worst excesses of state crime, both violent and financial. Such exclusion allows the victims of state crime to be labelled as 'other' and makes it easier for state crime to be justified by those who commit it. Such 'othering' is visible in a range of state crime examples provided by Green and Ward (2017: 445–7) such as the genocides in Rwanda and Myanmar, the endemic corruption in Papua New Guinea, and even the floods caused by Hurricane Katrina in the USA in 2005 – an apparently 'natural disaster' actually caused by State corruption. We also need to consider the efficiency and high levels of organisation present in state crimes such as genocide and the close links with the structures of the modern state itself (Turner 2017b) when thinking about the most effective responses to state crime.

Study exercise 4.14

How would you use the media to increase public awareness of the nature and extent of state crime around the world?

Conclusions: linking discussion to the roadmap theories

Alternative forms of criminal liability represent a departure from the liberal roadmap idea of an individual being responsible for completed crime. The development of collective responsibility for crime (complicity, conspiracy, incitement) was not the inevitable result of a purely liberal approach to defining criminal law. Rather, these forms of criminal liability emerged because of historical decision-making by powerful social groups to regulate the morally risky and dangerous behaviour of the relatively powerless in society and thereby to secure their own social, economic, and political interests. As such, we can see how the liberal model's focus on individual responsibility links together with the risk management model to explain the general trend of expanding criminal law's scope in the creation of a range of new terrorist and organised crime offences, for example.

A closer look at these areas of criminal law shows how the law enhances its liberal appearance while simultaneously reserving its power to morally condemn those it sees as being worthy of blame. Therefore, in the law of complicity, *Jogee* focussed on the need for a secondary offender to intend that a crime is committed, while *Gnango* saw D convicted on a moral rather than a logically and coherently legal basis, generating considerable academic debate about whether the case had reached the right outcome (Virgo 2012; Mirfield 2013). In the law of attempt, magistrates and juries receive the freedom to make a moral judgment about whether or not D has gone beyond merely preparing to commit the actus reus of a crime and so has begun to attempt it. However, they are constrained by the need for intention to commit all elements of the crime as the mens rea for attempts following *Pace*, which represents another link back to the liberal roadmap model of insisting on clear individual responsibility for crime.

In areas where criminal behaviour reinforces and advances the interests of powerful groups in society, the response of criminal law has been hesitant.

Legislation defining corporate offending is confused and lacking in overall purpose. It struggles to choose between an approach of strict liability differentiation, which plays down the seriousness of corporate offending, and an approach of assimilation that struggles to balance individual and collective responsibility for offending behaviour within organisations (Norrie 2014) and therefore shows the limits of the liberal roadmap model in explaining the aims of criminal law. Despite the invisibility of much corporate crime to criminal law and justice, campaigns from the families of its victims have helped to change public attitudes to this type of crime, showing that a power-based response is not inevitable (Tombs 2017).

Statutory legislation regulating group behaviour that is international in scope and threatens whole sections of society, such as financial organised crime, terrorism, and human trafficking, is a key and regular feature of modern criminal law. This shows a continued commitment from criminal law to using the risk management roadmap model to regulate risky and harmful behaviour, ideally before such behaviour actually takes place. An interesting contrast lies in the lack of domestic legislation designed to regulate state crime, which is committed in the interests of the powerful in society. English criminal law engages with the response to state crime in a passive way by promising commitment to upholding international criminal law on the domestic level, rather than actively tackling these crimes itself.

Switching the focus to criminal justice, the struggle of criminal justice agencies to enforce criminal law's regulation of these alternative types of criminal liability is clear. Taking corporate crime first, radical criminologists like Steve Tombs have pointed to the delegation of responsibility for investigation and prosecution of corporate offences away from the police and onto separate agencies such as the Health and Safety Executive. These agencies never had the extent of financial and staff resources that the police and the Crown Prosecution Service can call upon, and have suffered the same kind of budget cutbacks as the mainstream criminal justice agencies in the past decade. It is therefore hardly surprising that so few cases of corporate offending reach court, and even fewer result in punishment. A small number of prosecutions have led to success in securing criminal justice in a few cases involving corporate killing – although question marks remain over whether justice is served by the imposition of financial penalties in response to such severe harm.

The story of the criminal justice response to organised crime is one of bureaucratic consolidation of power over enforcement in the hands of the National Crime Agency, focusing on liberal and risk management ideas but overlooking the localised and flexible nature of much organised crime and its roots in wider social and economic processes like globalisation and neoliberalism (Hobbs 2013). Meanwhile, the general failure by English criminal justice to respond to state crime (committed in England or elsewhere) reinforces the radical, power-based roadmap model of criminal law and criminal justice, and it is interesting that the most effective responses to state crime around the world have been community-focussed and based around the ideas found in the restorative roadmap model. Finally, as Crewe et al. (2015) show, in sentencing terms, criminal justice takes a risk management approach to those convicted under complicity law, with social injustice the clear result.

Overall, then, we can see from this chapter that there is far more to criminal law and criminal justice's response to alternative forms of criminal liability than the liberal roadmap model, despite initial appearances. Both criminal law and criminal justice use a variety of roadmap models in their responses, as different groups in society compete to promote their interests. It is perhaps the radical hybrid realist model that comes closest to capturing the range of values that drive criminal law and justice, while still acknowledging the truths that there are significant limits to what either institution can do to address the social harm caused by crime without wider social and political change, and that the most powerful in society do not always succeed in promoting their interests through criminal law and justice.

Key points

- There are various forms of criminal liability which do not rely on individual responsibility for a completed criminal offence
- These forms cover individual responsibility within the context of group offending (complicity, state crime, terrorism, organised crime, and corporate liability) and individual responsibility for an incomplete offence (inchoate offences)
- Legislative decision-making has expanded the scope of criminal law in the areas of terrorism and organised crime, while judicial decision-making has tended to emphasise individual responsibility within group offending
- Criminal justice has tended to use risk management to respond to offending in these areas, often resulting in harsh punitivism in cases of complicity
- Both criminal law and criminal justice have struggled to accept and reflect the social, economic, and political contexts which lie behind these types of crime
- There is evidence of liberal, radical, and risk management-based roadmap models playing a role in these areas of criminal law and justice, but the radical hybrid realist roadmap theory introduced in Chapter 1 offers the most complete and realistic account of how criminal law and justice use alternative forms of criminal liability to respond to harmful behaviour

Further reading

Crewe, B., Liebling, A., Padfield, N., and Virgo, G. (2015), 'Joint Enterprise: The Implications of an Unfair and Unclear Law', *Criminal Law Review*: 252–69.

Green, P., and Ward, T. (2017), 'Understanding State Crime', in Liebling, A., Maruna, S., and McAra, L. (eds.), *The Oxford Handbook of Criminology* (6th ed.). Oxford: OUP.

Hobbs, D. (2013), *Lush Life: Constructing Organised Crime in the UK*. Oxford: Clarendon.

Innes, M., and Levi, M. (2017), 'Making and Managing Terrorism and Counter-Terrorism: The View from Criminology', in Liebling, A., Maruna, S., and McAra, L. (eds.), *The Oxford Handbook of Criminology* (6th ed.). Oxford: OUP.

Tombs, S. (2017), *Social Protection After the Crisis: Regulation Without Enforcement*. Bristol: Policy Press.

References

Aginam, O. (2017), 'Rape as a Weapon of War', in Morley, S., Turner, J., Corteen, K., and Taylor, P. (eds.), *A Companion to State Power, Liberties and Human Rights*. Bristol: Policy Press.

Almond, P. (2007), 'Regulation Crisis: Evaluating the Potential Legitimizing Effects of "Corporate Manslaughter" Cases', *Law and Policy*, **29**(3): 285–310.

Box, S. (1983), *Power, Crime and Mystification*. London: Tavistock.

Cassese, A., Baig, L., Fan, M., Gaeta, P., Gosnell, C., and Whiting, A. (2013), *Cassese's International Criminal Law* (3rd ed.). Oxford: OUP.

Child, J.J., and Ormerod, D. (2017), *Smith, Hogan and Ormerod's Essentials of Criminal Law* (2nd ed.). Oxford: OUP.

Christie, N. (1977), 'Conflicts as Property', *British Journal of Criminology*, **17**(1): 1–19.

Clarkson, C.M.V. (1996), 'Kicking Corporate Bodies and Damning Their Souls', *Modern Law Review*, **59**(4): 557–72.

Close, J. (2017), 'International Criminal Courts', in Morley, S., Turner, J., Corteen, K., and Taylor, P. (eds.), *A Companion to State Power, Liberties and Human Rights*. Bristol: Policy Press.

Cohen, S. (2001), *States of Denial: Knowing About Atrocities and Suffering*. Cambridge: Blackwell.

Coomber, R., and Moyle, L. (2018), 'The Changing Shape of Street Level Heroin and Crack Supply in England: Commuting, Holidaying and Cuckooing Drug Dealers Across "County Lines"', *British Journal of Criminology*, **58**(6): 1323–42.

Crewe, B., Liebling, A., Padfield, N., and Virgo, G. (2015), 'Joint Enterprise: The Implications of an Unfair and Unclear Law', *Criminal Law Review*: 252–269.

Fisse, B., and Braithwaite, J. (1993), *Corporations, Crime and Accountability*. Cambridge: CUP.

Gobert, J. (2008), 'The Corporate Manslaughter and Corporate Homicide Act 2007 – Thirteen Years in the Making, But Was It Worth the Wait?' *Modern Law Review*, **71**(3): 413–33.

Green, P., and Ward, T. (2004), *State Crime: Governments, Violence and Corruption*. London: Pluto Press.

Green, P., and Ward, T. (2017), 'Understanding State Crime', in Liebling, A., Maruna, S., and McAra, L. (eds.), *The Oxford Handbook of Criminology* (6th ed.). Oxford: OUP.

Hawkins, K. (2002), *Law as Last Resort: Prosecution Decision-Making in a Regulatory Agency*. Oxford: OUP.

Hillyard, P. (1993), *Suspect Community*. London: Pluto Press.

Hobbs, D. (1995), *Bad Business: Professional Criminals in Modern Britain*. Oxford: OUP.

Hobbs, D. (2013), *Lush Life: Constructing Organised Crime in the UK*. Oxford: Clarendon.

Innes, M., and Levi, M. (2017), 'Making and Managing Terrorism and Counter-Terrorism: The View from Criminology', in Liebling, A., Maruna, S., and McAra, L. (eds.), *The Oxford Handbook of Criminology* (6th ed.). Oxford: OUP.

Jarvis, P., and Bisgrove, M. (2014), 'The Use and Abuse of Conspiracy', *Criminal Law Review*: 261–77.

Johnstone, G., and Ward, T. (2010), *Law and Crime*. London: Sage.

Joyce, P. (2017), *Criminal Justice* (3rd ed.). Abingdon: Routledge.

Lowe, D. (2018), *Terrorism: Law and Policy*. Abingdon: Routledge.

McLaughlin, E. (2001), 'Political Violence, Terrorism and States of Fear', in Muncie, J., and McLaughlin, E. (eds.), *The Problem of Crime* (2nd ed.). London: Sage/Open University Press.

Millings, M. (2013), 'Policing British Asian Identities: The Enduring Role of the Police in Young British Asian Men's Situated Negotiation of Identity and Belonging', *British Journal of Criminology*, **53**(6): 1075–92.

Mirfield, P. (2013), 'Guilt by Association: A Reply to Professor Virgo', *Criminal Law Review*: 577–83.

National Crime Agency (2018), *National Strategic Assessment of Serious and Organised Crime 2018*. London: National Crime Agency.

Newburn, T. (2017), *Criminology* (3rd ed.). Abingdon: Routledge.

Norrie, A. (2014), *Crime, Reason and History* (3rd ed.). Cambridge: CUP.

Pena-Neira, S., and Quiroga, T. (2017), 'War Crimes', in Morley, S., Turner, J., Corteen, K., and Taylor, P. (eds.), *A Companion to State Power, Liberties and Human Rights*. Bristol: Policy Press.

Richardson, G. (1987), 'Strict Liability for Regulatory Crime: The Empirical Evidence', *Criminal Law Review*: 295–306.

Roche, D. (2005), 'Truth Commission Amnesties and the International Criminal Court', *British Journal of Criminology*, **45**(4): 565–81.

Ross, J.I. (2017), 'State Crime', in Morley, S., Turner, J., Corteen, K., and Taylor, P. (eds.), *A Companion to State Power, Liberties and Human Rights*. Bristol: Policy Press.

Sayre, F.B. (1922), 'Criminal Conspiracy', *Harvard Law Review*, **35**(4): 393–427.

Sayre, F.B. (1928), 'Criminal Attempts', *Harvard Law Review*, **41**(7): 821–59.

Spicer, R. (1981), *Conspiracy: Law, Class and Society*. London: Lawrence and Wishart.

Syrian Network for Human Rights (2019), *Casualties*. Available online at: http://sn4hr.org/. Accessed 31 January 2019.

Tembo, E.B. (2017a), 'Torture', in Morley, S., Turner, J., Corteen, K., and Taylor, P. (eds.), *A Companion to State Power, Liberties and Human Rights*. Bristol: Policy Press.

Tembo, E.B. (2017b), 'State Terrorism', in Morley, S., Turner, J., Corteen, K., and Taylor, P. (eds.), *A Companion to State Power, Liberties and Human Rights*. Bristol: Policy Press.

Tombs, S. (2017), *Social Protection After the Crisis: Regulation Without Enforcement*. Bristol: Policy Press.

Turner, J. (2017b), 'Genocide', in Morley, S., Turner, J., Corteen, K., and Taylor, P. (eds.), *A Companion to State Power, Liberties and Human Rights*. Bristol: Policy Press.

Virgo, G. (2012), 'Joint Enterprise Liability Is Dead: Long Live Accessorial Liability', *Criminal Law Review*: 850–70.

Walklate, S. (2017), 'State Harm', in Morley, S., Turner, J., Corteen, K., and Taylor, P. (eds.), *A Companion to State Power, Liberties and Human Rights*. Bristol: Policy Press.

Wells, C. (2001), *Corporations and Criminal Responsibility* (2nd ed.). Oxford: OUP.

Wells, C., and Quick, O. (2010), *Lacey, Wells and Quick's Reconstructing Criminal Law: Text and Materials* (4th ed.). Cambridge: CUP.

White, L. (2017), 'Post-Conflict Reconciliation', in Morley, S., Turner, J., Corteen, K., and Taylor, P. (eds.), *A Companion to State Power, Liberties and Human Rights*. Bristol: Policy Press.

Chapter 5

Property offences

Chapter aims

After reading Chapter 5, you should be able to understand:

- The actus reus requirements, mens rea requirements, and available defences for the offences of theft, vehicle theft, fraud, burglary, criminal damage, and robbery in criminal law
- How criminal justice responds to these types of property offences
- How the evidence on these property offences in criminal law and criminal justice fits in with the roadmap theories introduced in Chapter 1

Introduction

Chapter 5 discusses the main types of criminal offences against property. This chapter explains the property offences of theft, vehicle theft, fraud, burglary, criminal damage, and robbery in terms of their legal definitions, before placing them in their criminal justice contexts.

Property offences: the law

Theft

Statutory definition

Theft is defined by the Theft Act 1968 s.1(1) as the dishonest appropriation of property belonging to another person, with the intention to permanently deprive that other person of it.

Actus reus

The actus reus of theft has three elements. The first is an 'appropriation'. 'Appropriation' is defined by s.3(1) of the Theft Act as an assumption of the rights of the owner of the property. *DPP v Gomez* [1993] AC 442 decided that there can be an appropriation even where V consents to D taking their property, following *Lawrence* [1972] AC 626.

Gomez also decided that an assumption of any (not all) of the property owner's rights was enough to count as an appropriation. So what the law says is an appropriation is more than just taking someone's property without their consent. *Hinks* [2001] 2 AC 241 extends the meaning of appropriation further by stating that it can occur even where the victim has made a valid gift of the property to D, as long as D has the right mens rea for theft. This means that even though the civil law would not see D's conduct as illegal, criminal law could still convict D of theft.

The second element of the actus reus is property, so the question here is what the law counts as being property for the purposes of theft. S.4(1) of the 1968 Theft Act includes money, all personal property, all real property, and all things in action. The courts have also decided that confidential information, such as the questions on a future exam paper, is not property (*Oxford v Moss* (1978) 68 Cr App Rep 183) and that corpses are not property unless they have been treated or prepared, for example for medical teaching (*Kelly* [1998] 3 All ER 741).

The third element of the actus reus of theft is that the property 'belongs to another'. Under s.5(1) of the 1968 Act, this does not only include the property's owner but also whoever is in possession of it at the time of the theft, whoever is in control of it at the time of the theft, a trustee of the property, or anyone with a 'proprietary interest' in the property. The phrase 'belonging to another' is therefore widely defined by criminal law and can cover property which is owned by the thief and property which its owner did not know about. This is shown by *Turner (No. 2)* (1971) 55 Cr App Rep 336 and *Woodman* [1974] QB 354, respectively. In *Goodwin* [1996] Crim LR 262, D did not 'own' money which he had dishonestly won from a slot machine using foreign coins. The money still belonged to the owner of the machine. *Smith* [2011] 1 Cr App Rep 30 shows that property still belongs to someone even if it is illegal to possess that property – for example, as here, where the property is prohibited drugs.

Study exercise 5.1

Should it be theft to touch a tin of beans in a supermarket without taking them off the shelf, as long as you have the right mens rea?

Mens rea

There are two elements to the mens rea of theft. Firstly, under s.1 of the Theft Act 1968, D must commit the actus reus dishonestly. S.2 of the Act gives three scenarios where conduct is not dishonest, but it does not define dishonesty. *Ghosh* [1982] QB 1053 used a mixed subjective/objective test for dishonesty. Under *Ghosh*, D must be dishonest according to standards of reasonable honest people (the objective part), and D must realise that what they did was dishonest according to those standards (the subjective part). However, in *Ivey v Genting Casinos (UK) Ltd* [2017] UKSC 67, the Supreme Court stated that the subjective part of the *Ghosh* test was no longer good law. The test for dishonesty in theft is now an objective one. This objective test cannot be altered to take into account the standards of the market or business in which D works (*Hayes* [2015] EWCA Crim 1944), so D cannot claim that their actions were honest according to the standards of their profession if a reasonable, honest member of the public would see their actions as dishonest.

The second element of the mens rea for theft is that D must have 'an intention to permanently deprive' V (the person to whom the property belongs) of that property. 'Intention' here means the same as it normally does in criminal law. Only intention to deprive *permanently* is normally enough mens rea, however. If D intends to return the property, even after having it for a long time, there cannot be an intention to permanently deprive.

Even if this is the case, D can still be guilty of theft under s.6 of the Theft Act 1968. S.6 states that where D intends to treat the property as their own regardless of the property owner's rights, or where they borrow or lend the property but the borrowing or lending is for a period and in circumstances making it equivalent to an outright taking or disposal, they still have the intention to permanently deprive which is needed. *Lloyd* [1985] QB 829 states that borrowing property can only count as an intention to permanently deprive under s.6 where D only returns the property after all the 'goodness and virtue' has been taken out of it. S.6 can also apply where D treats the property as their own to dispose of – as happened in *Velumyl* [1989] Crim LR 299, *DPP v Lavender* [1994] Crim LR 297, and most recently *Raphael* [2008] EWCA Crim 1014. 'Conditional intent' can also be enough to be intention to permanently deprive – so that if D opens a door or bag, and the jury or magistrates believe that D was about to steal whatever was inside if they thought it was valuable, D would still be guilty of attempted theft (*Attorney-General's References (Nos. 1 & 2 of 1979)* [1980] QB 180).

Study exercise 5.2

Make a list of types of behaviour you would consider dishonest. Then ask someone else to make a list of dishonest behaviour. Are the two lists the same or different? What implications do you think this has for juries and magistrates who have to decide whether behaviour is dishonest in practice?

Vehicle theft

Although in some cases it is clear that D intended to permanently deprive V of their vehicle, it can be difficult to prove that D had this intention, which means that the mens rea of theft would not be proved. As a result, s.12 of the Theft Act 1968 creates a separate offence. The offence is committed where D takes a vehicle, or 'conveyance', without having the consent of the owner or any other lawful authority, for D's own or another's use, or, knowing that any conveyance has been taken without such authority, drives it or allows themselves to be carried in or on it. Therefore, s.12 creates two offences – one of taking, and another of driving or allowing oneself to be carried in or on a vehicle that has been taken. D has a defence where they believe that they have lawful authority to take the vehicle, or that they would have the owner's consent if the owner knew about the taking and the surrounding circumstances.

In addition, s.12A of the Act, inserted by the Aggravated Vehicle-Taking Act 1992, creates an offence of aggravated vehicle-taking. This offence occurs where D commits the basic taking without consent offence in relation to a 'mechanically propelled' vehicle. It also needs to be proved that, at any time after the vehicle is unlawfully taken (either by D or someone else) and before it was recovered, the vehicle was driven, or injury or damage was caused, in one or more of a list of given circumstances. These circumstances are defined in s.12(A)(2) as:

- Dangerous driving of the vehicle on a road or other public place;
- An accident causing injury or death to someone which was caused by the driving of the vehicle; an accident causing damage to any property other than the vehicle which was caused by the driving of the vehicle;
- Or damage to the vehicle itself.

D has a defence where they can prove that the driving, accident, or damage occurred before they committed the basic offence; or that they were neither in, on, nor in the immediate vicinity of the vehicle when the driving, accident, or damage occurred.

Study exercise 5.3

'The actus reus and mens rea requirements of the aggravated vehicle-taking offence are a fair response to people who go out joyriding in stolen cars'. Discuss this statement.

Fraud

Statutory definition

The offence of fraud is now defined by s.1 of the Fraud Act 2006. Under s.1, the general offence of fraud can be committed in one of three ways. These are: dishonestly making a false representation (under s.2 of the 2006 Act); dishonestly failing to disclose information which D has a legal duty to disclose (s.3); and dishonestly abusing a position of trust (s.4). The 2006 Act also introduces a new general offence of obtaining services by deception in s.11, again to replace the previous range of specific offences covering this type of behaviour, where D persuades V through fraud to do something for them without paying for it.

Fraud by making a false representation – actus reus and mens rea

The actus reus of this offence is making any representation as to fact or law, or anyone's state of mind, which is untrue or misleading. The representation can be expressly made in terms of what D says or does. But it can also be implied from what D says or does, as shown in the pre-Fraud Act cases of *DPP v Ray* [1974] AC 370 and *Lambie* [1982] AC 449, which show that a false representation can be made where D uses a credit card to buy goods in a shop, knowing that their card account is overdrawn. The representation can be made to a computer or any other machine, as well as to a person. The mens rea is that D must dishonestly make the false representation, and must also intend to make a gain through the representation, to cause a loss to V, or to expose V to the risk of loss. 'Dishonesty' and 'intention' mean the same here as they do for the offence of theft. The gain and loss apply only to money or other property, either real or personal. An example of s.2 in action is *Asif* [2008] EWCA Crim 3348, where D was convicted because he had lied about having a clean driving licence, which he needed in order to get a particular job.

Fraud by failing to disclose information – actus reus and mens rea

The actus reus of this type of fraud is failure to disclose information to V which D has a legal duty to disclose, for example, because of a contractual obligation, a fiduciary relationship, or their status as V's employer. The mens rea for the offence is that D must fail to disclose the information dishonestly, and must also intend to make a gain at V's expense, cause loss to V, or expose V to the risk of loss as a result of failing to disclose the information. The mens rea is therefore the same as for the s.2 offence discussed earlier. An example of s.3 in action is *Daley* [2010] EWCA Crim 2193, where D was convicted because he failed to disclose previous criminal convictions on a job application, as he was legally required to do.

Fraud by abuse of a position of trust – actus reus and mens rea

For this offence, the actus reus is an abuse by D, either by act or by omission, of a position where they are expected to protect someone else's (V's) financial interests, or are expected not to act against them. The mens rea for the offence is that D must dishonestly abuse their position of trust and must also intend to make a gain at V's expense, cause a loss to V, or expose V to a risk of loss by doing so. An example of s.4 in action is *Marshall* [2009] EWCA Crim 2076, where D, a care home worker, was convicted of fraud because he misused some of the care home residents' bank accounts for personal financial gain. In *Valujevs* [2015] 3 WLR 109, the Court of Appeal emphasised that s.4 applies only where D has assumed control and responsibility over another person's finances and abuses that control. It does not apply to business relationships generally.

Obtaining services by deception – actus reus and mens rea

For this offence, the services can be obtained by D either for themselves or for someone else. There are four elements to the actus reus. Firstly, D has to obtain services by an act. Secondly, D's act must cause the services to be provided. Thirdly, the services must be made available on the basis that they have been paid for, are being paid for, or will be paid for. Fourthly, D must obtain the services without any payment having been made, or without paying for them in full.

There are two elements to the offence's mens rea. Firstly, when D obtains the services, they must know that the services are being made available on the basis that they have to be paid for, or might have to be paid for. Secondly, D must have the intention not to pay for the services, or not to pay for them in full.

Study exercise 5.4

'The Fraud Act 2006 effectively criminalises lying because it does not require loss to the victim, and as such is too wide in terms of criminalisation'. Discuss this statement.

Burglary

Statutory definition

The Theft Act 1968 defines several types of burglary. Under s.9(1)(a), D is guilty of burglary if they enter a building or part of building as a trespasser and with intent to commit theft, grievous bodily harm (GBH), or criminal damage. Under s.9(1)(b), D is guilty of burglary if, after entering a building or a part of a building as a trespasser, they commit theft, attempted theft, GBH, or attempted GBH while inside. S.26 of the Criminal Justice Act 1991 amended s.9 to distinguish between domestic burglary, committed in buildings where people live, and non-domestic burglary. It is a question of fact in courts as to whether property that has been burgled is domestic or not (*Flack* [2013] EWCA Crim 115). S.10 of the Theft Act 1968 defines a more serious form of burglary, aggravated burglary, as a burglary committed while D has a firearm, imitation firearm, any offensive weapon, or any explosive with him at the time. Both the s.9(1)(a) and the s.9(1)(b) forms of burglary can be committed in this aggravated form.

Actus reus – entry

In both forms of burglary, the prosecution has to prove that D entered the building as a trespasser. The question here is how far D has to go before they have committed an 'entry' into the building. *Collins* [1973] QB 100 stated that D had to have made an 'effective and substantial entry' into the building as a trespasser, and that this was a question for magistrates or juries to decide on the facts of each case. However, *Brown* [1985] Crim LR 212 decided that entry only had to be effective, and not substantial, without actually overruling *Collins*. *Ryan* [1996] Crim LR 320 again stated that D's entry only has to be effective, and could be effective even if not all of D's body had actually entered the building.

Actus reus – trespass

Trespassing, in civil law terms, means being on someone else's property or land without their permission. Questions about the actus reus of trespass in burglary cases have centred around what happens when D has some level of permission to be in a particular building but then goes further in trespassing terms than they are allowed to. *Jones and Smith* [1976] 3 All ER 54 shows that where D enters a building where they have general permission to be, but enters knowing that they are going further than they are allowed to go in the building, or entered being subjectively reckless about whether they were doing this, then D is trespassing. *Walkington* [1979] 2 All ER 716 states that it is possible to trespass in a *part* of a building, which does not have to be a separate room from the part of the building where D has permission to be.

Actus reus – building or part of a building

What D enters as a trespasser must be a building or part of a building. In most cases it is obvious that a structure counts as a building. However, the issue is not always clear. S.9(4) of the 1968 Act states that inhabited vehicles or vessels can count as buildings for the purposes of burglary, but in other cases, the courts have decided whether or not a structure counts as a building on a case-by-case basis, taking into account, for example, how permanent a structure is. This can mean differing outcomes on similar sets of facts, as *B & S v Leathley* [1979] Crim LR 314 and *Seekings and Gould* [1986] Crim LR 167 show. In *Coleman* [2013] EWCA Crim 544, the court decided that inhabited boats and caravans counted as buildings.

Mens rea – entry, trespass, and other requirements

Collins sets out the mens rea requirements for both types of burglary. Under s.9(1)(a), the prosecution must prove that at the time of D's entry into the building, they knew that they had entered as a trespasser, or were subjectively reckless about whether they had entered as a trespasser or not, and also that they had an intention to commit theft, GBH, or criminal damage while inside. Under s.9(1)(b), the prosecution must prove that at the time when D committed the offence of theft, attempted theft, GBH, or attempted GBH, they knew that they had entered as a trespasser, or were subjectively reckless about whether they had entered as a trespasser or not. The right actus reus and mens rea requirements for the offence which they committed are also necessary. As with theft, a conditional intent is enough mens rea for burglary, under *Walkington* and *Attorney-General's References (Nos. 1 & 2 of 1979)*.

Aggravated burglary – actus reus and mens rea

Aggravated burglary has to be either the s.9(1)(a) or s.9(1)(b) type, with the actus reus and mens rea requirements that each type has. In addition, D must have a firearm or imitation firearm, offensive weapon, or explosive with them. For the s.9(1)(a) type of burglary, D has to have had the aggravating item with them at the time when they entered the property as a trespasser (*Francis* [1982] Crim LR 363). For the s.9(1)(b) type of burglary, D has to have had the aggravating item with them at the time when they committed the offence of theft, attempted theft, GBH, or attempted GBH inside the property (*O'Leary* (1986) 82 Cr App Rep 341).

Study exercise 5.5

Should any entry into another person's property with the right mens rea count as burglary, even if someone only puts his or her arm inside the property and causes little or no damage to the property in doing so?

Criminal damage

Statutory definition

Criminal damage is defined by s.1(1) of the Criminal Damage Act 1971 as where D, without lawful excuse, destroys or damages any property belonging to another and does so either intending to destroy or damage any such property, or being reckless as to destroying or damaging it. S.1(3) creates a separate offence where D without lawful excuse, destroys or damages any property belonging to another by fire and does so either intending to destroy or damage any such property, or being reckless as to destroying or damaging it (commonly known as arson). Either of these offences can also be committed in aggravated form under s.1(2), where D commits criminal damage either intentionally or recklessly, endangering life. In addition, under s.2, D commits an offence if they make threats to destroy or damage property with a known likelihood of endangering life by doing so, and under s.3, D commits an offence if they have an article intending without lawful excuse to use it to destroy or damage property belonging to another.

Under s.5(2) of the Act, two categories of behaviour which provide a 'lawful excuse', and so act as defences to a criminal damage charge, are given. Firstly, D has a defence where they believe that the owner of the property would consent to its damage or destruction. Secondly, D has a defence where they take reasonable action because they believe that there is an immediate need to protect either their own or someone else's property. Under s.5(3), D's belief must be subjective and honest in both cases.

Finally, s.10 of the 1971 Act defines what counts as 'property belonging to another' for the purposes of criminal damage. The definition of property is similar to the one in the definition of theft, except that it includes land where the theft definition of property does not. However, it does not include intangible property or things in action. 'Belonging to another' includes anyone who has custody or control of the property, who has a proprietary right or interest in it, who has a charge on it, or who has the right to enforce a trust to which the property is subject.

Actus reus

As the definition discussed earlier shows, the 1971 Act defines s.1(1) criminal damage's actus reus as being the destruction or damage of property, and the Act also defines what 'property' means and what 'belonging to another' means. But it does not define 'damage'. *Hardman v CC of Avon and Somerset* [1986] Crim LR 330 shows that temporary damage to property can still count as damage, especially if the damage costs money to repair. *Morphitis v Salmon* [1990] Crim LR 48 also shows that either permanent or temporary physical damage can count, as can either permanent or temporary damage to the usefulness or value of the property (*Fiak* [2005] EWCA Crim 2381). Whether damage has occurred is a question of fact for the magistrates or jury and partially depends on the nature of the property which has been damaged. What counts as damage is an objective test – as long as D intends to act, it is irrelevant that D does not realise that what they have done amounts to illegal damage (*Seray-Wurie v DPP* [2012] EWHC 208 (Admin)).

For the offence of aggravated criminal damage under s.1(2), the property does not have to belong to someone else (*Merrick* [1995] Crim LR 802). For the offence of threatening to destroy or damage property under s.2, the test is whether a reasonable person would regard D's words or actions as a threat to damage property (*Cakmak* [2002] Crim LR 581).

Mens rea

S.1(1) states that for the basic form of criminal damage under ss.1(1) and 1(3), D must have intended or been reckless as to the destruction or damage of property and must also have knowledge or belief that the property belongs to another. Mens rea for both of these issues must be proved (*Smith* [1974] 1 All ER 632). For aggravated criminal damage under s.1(2), as well as the mens rea requirements for the basic criminal damage offence, the prosecution also needs to prove that D intended or was reckless as to the endangerment of someone's life as a result of the criminal damage. *G* [2003] decided that for criminal damage offences, subjective recklessness was needed. *Steer* [1988] AC 111 shows that the endangerment to life must be proved to have resulted from the criminal damage itself, not from D's actions which caused the criminal damage. According to *Dudley* [1989] Crim LR 57, the prosecution does not have to prove that anyone's life actually was endangered by D's criminal damage, as long as D had the right mens rea for the offence. The property that endangers V's life does not have to be the same property which D damages (*Attorney-General's Reference (No.3 of 1992)* [1994] 1 WLR 409). *Wenton* [2010] EWCA Crim 2361 shows that the endangerment of life must be caused by the act of damage and must not arise from a separate act.

Defences

S.5 of the 1971 Criminal Damage Act (discussed earlier) defines the defences to the basic form of criminal damage. *Hunt* (1978) 66 Cr App Rep 105 and *Hill and Hall* (1989) 89 Cr App Rep 74 state that whether D did the damage 'in order to protect property' is an objective test. The test is whether D's actions could reasonably be said to protect the property, although it is also based on D's subjective belief in the reasonableness of their actions. *DPP v Blake* [1993] Crim LR 586 states that D's actions must not be too remote from the property to be reasonably capable of protecting it. This case also shows that D must honestly and subjectively believe that a living person had consented or would consent to the damage to the property in order to use the defence under s.5(2)(a) of the 1971 Act. The honest and subjective belief is the most important factor in this defence, and it does not matter if that honest belief occurred while intoxicated (*Jaggard v Dickinson* [1981] 1 QB 527), or combined with a dishonest and criminal purpose (*Denton* [1981] 1 WLR 1446).

In *Jones and Milling* [2007] 1 AC 136, the defendants criminally damaged an RAF base as a protest against the Second Iraq War, and as an attempt to prevent the aircraft at the base from taking part in the war. They claimed the general defence of prevention of crime, because they argued that the war was illegal under the international law crime of aggression. The House of Lords decided that even if the war was illegal in this way, a crime against international law was not a crime that could act as a defence to a charge of criminal damage in English law.

Study exercise 5.6

Which defences to criminal damage should the law allow, if any? Give reasons for your answer.

Robbery

Statutory definition

Under s.8(1) of the Theft Act 1968, robbery is defined as theft where D, immediately before or at the time of the theft, uses force on V or seeks to put V in fear of being subjected to unlawful force then and there, in order to steal.

Actus reus and mens rea

Robinson [1977] Crim LR 173 shows that all of the actus reus and mens rea requirements of theft have to be proved before robbery itself can be proved, because robbery requires an offence of theft to be taking place. In addition, D needs to use unlawful force, or put V in fear of immediate unlawful force, immediately before or at the time of the theft. This means that the actus reus and mens rea of an offence against the person – common assault or any more serious violent offence – also need to be proved in terms of occurring immediately before or at the time of the theft.

Dawson [1976] Crim LR 692 shows that whether or not force occurred immediately before or during the theft is a question of fact for the jury to decide. Robbery is complete at the time of appropriation (*Corcoran v Anderton* (1980) 71 Cr App Rep 104). Any use of force, including express and implied threats of force, is enough to prove robbery in principle, even if the victim is not put in fear (*B, R v DPP* [2007] EWHC 739 (Admin)). As such, even very slight force could be enough for the actus reus, although some levels of force will be so slight that they are not enough to prove robbery, as *P v DPP* [2012] EWHC 1657 (Admin), where D snatched a cigarette from V's hand without touching V, shows. The force or threat of force must have occurred in order to steal. *Hale* (1979) 68 Cr App Rep 415 and *Lockley* [1995] 2 Cr App Rep 554 explain that whether or not the theft has been committed is also a question of fact for the jury to decide. If the force or threat occurs after the theft has been committed, then robbery has not been committed. However, as *Hale* and *Lockley* show, the law will extend the time of the theft to prove robbery for as long as the theft is continuing 'in practical terms'. Finally, where D has a right to claim the property that they take by force, no robbery occurs, even though D realises that they have no right to use force in order to reclaim the property that is theirs (*Robinson*).

Study exercise 5.7

Should robbery be limited to cases where D uses violence of actual bodily harm (ABH) or worse?

Property offences and criminal justice

Theft and criminal justice

In the year to March 2019, the Crime Survey for England and Wales recorded no change in the levels of theft in England and Wales, after a long period of decreasing rates since 1995 (ONS 2019a: 49). Theft remains a volume crime, however, as 43.7% of all offences recorded by the CSEW in 2017–18 were theft-related (ONS 2019a: 24). Although the CSEW does not cover theft from businesses, the British Retail Consortium estimated that in 2017, the direct cost of retail crime was £700m in 2017, with customer theft increasing by 15% compared with the previous year, and now amounting to over £0.5bn (British Retail Consortium 2018).

However, the conviction rate for theft offences was 87.8% in 2018, a higher conviction rate than for any other offence group apart from drugs offences and public order offences; and the custody rate for theft in 2018 was 30.1% (Ministry of Justice 2019: table Q1.3). Research has suggested that the average value of stolen goods is £88, and that the average theft is unplanned (Speed and Burrows 2006). If this is an accurate picture of the typical thief, then on average, according to current Sentencing Council sentencing guidelines (Sentencing Council 2015), sentences for theft should normally range between a discharge and a fine. This suggests that the current custody rate for theft offences is excessively punitive. Only around 1.6% of CSEW-recorded theft offences result in court proceedings, and 75% of theft cases recorded by police were closed without any suspect being identified in the year to March 2018 (Home Office 2018a: 8), pointing to the limited ability of criminal justice to regulate theft in practice.

Study exercise 5.8

In what circumstances (if any) do you think that shoplifters should be jailed?

Vehicle theft and criminal justice

Police-recorded vehicle offences showed an increase of 3% (457,433 offences) in the year to March 2019, largely due to a 10% increase in recorded theft of a vehicle. CSEW-recorded vehicle-related theft showed no statistically significant change over this period (ONS 2019a: 19–20), although longer-term trends show that vehicle-related theft recorded by the CSEW (and the British Crime Survey before it) decreased by 79% between 1995 and 2017 (ONS 2019a: 24). These statistics need to be analysed carefully, however.

Aside from the general differences between police and CSEW statistics in terms of how they are collected, both sets of data include thefts *from* vehicles (which, legally, are ordinary theft under s.1 of the Theft Act 1968), as well as theft *of* vehicles under either s.1 or s.12 and s.12A of the 1968 Act. Theft of a car carries a high economic cost – £10,290 on average in 2015–16, when the costs of crime prevention, replacing loss, and criminal justice intervention are included (Heeks et al. 2018: 6).

Light et al.'s (1993) study on car thieves showed that boredom, peer pressure, and thrill-seeking were key reasons why offenders became involved in car theft. The study also found that vehicle security features (or the lack of them) played a part in deciding which cars to steal. However, the study also highlighted that the offenders generally came from a background characterised by unemployment, social deprivation, and limited social and economic opportunities (ibid: 21). Desistance from offending was far more due to becoming older and more emotionally mature than to the deterrent effect of being caught by the police, going to court, and possibly going to prison, which was low even for offenders who had actually been to prison (ibid: 69). Therefore, while recent Home Office research points to the effectiveness of situational crime prevention measures like steering locks and vehicle immobilisers in reducing theft of and from vehicles (Morgan et al. 2016), it also shows that such measures have made crime less likely but have not made criminal justice detection more likely. In addition, CSEW data show that people living in rented accommodations and living in urban areas are more likely to be the victims of vehicle-related theft than other social groups (ONS 2017). It therefore seems likely that social and economic factors affect both the likelihood of committing vehicle-related theft and the likelihood of being victimised by it.

Study exercise 5.9

List three reasons why you think police-recorded vehicle theft has increased recently. Explain your answers.

Fraud and criminal justice

The CSEW recorded no significant change in the amount of fraud in England and Wales in 2017–18 (ONS 2019a: ch.10). Such figures may not indicate an increase in the social harm caused by fraud, but they do not tell the whole story. There are significant problems in measuring the extent of fraud due to differences in how data is collected by different agencies, reluctance of victims to report their offence, and a lack of awareness that fraud has occurred. What we do know is that the range of types of fraud is extensive, ranging from benefit fraud, through consumer fraud, to tax and insider dealing frauds

(Newburn 2017: 405–6). The CSEW also reported substantial increases in consumer fraud (34% rise) and 'other fraud' (109% rise), as well as a 13% increase in reported remote-purchase plastic card fraud (ONS 2019a: ch.10). The 2017 Annual Fraud Indicator estimated that fraud cost the UK at least £190bn in 2017, including fraud against the public sector, private sector, charities, and individuals – more than the current government spends on health and defence combined (Experian 2017: 3). Of course, this is only a measure of the financial crime that fraud, online and offline, causes. Victims of fraud may also experience psychological harm caused by the stress of losing money and the embarrassment of being defrauded (Tcherni et al. 2016: 907). It therefore seems that the costs of fraud to its victims and the public generally, particularly through forms of online fraud such as identity theft and phishing, are huge, and seemingly outweigh the costs of shoplifting, the most common form of recorded theft (discussed earlier).

Given the extensive social harm caused by fraud, a criminal justice response to it might be expected to treat offenders harshly. However, the reality of the response to fraud is more complex. Levi (2002) notes that the police, who investigate most frauds, often have difficulties in gathering the documentary evidence needed to investigate fraud thoroughly. He also notes that even though there is a specialist investigation and prosecution agency which deals with large-scale fraud, the Serious Fraud Office (SFO), which has the power to require information from suspects and others and compel them to answer its questions, the SFO has very limited staff and financial resources compared with the losses it is investigating and the funds available to some of the corporations and individuals it is investigating (ibid: 430).

Other criminologists have pointed to the higher cautioning rate for corporate fraud offences compared with more 'traditional' forms of crime such as theft, and lighter sentences for corporate offenders who commit fraud than others (Croall 2001). Finally, Cook (1989) has pointed out that although benefit fraud costs the UK far less than tax fraud in economic terms, it is punished more harshly by criminal justice. For example, Cook found that many of those convicted of benefit fraud in her study had to pay a fine as well as pay back the stolen money. By contrast, those accused of tax fraud were often not prosecuted by the Inland Revenue in exchange for paying back the money they owed.

Study exercise 5.10

Find one media report of benefit fraud and another media report of income tax fraud. Based on what you have read, do you think that there is class-based bias in criminal justice's response to different types of fraud? Give reasons for your answer.

Burglary and criminal justice

In 2017–18, the number of burglaries recorded by police in England and Wales decreased by 1% compared with the previous year (ONS 2019a: 7), and the number of domestic burglaries recorded by the CSEW decreased by 3% in 2017–18 compared with 2016–17, also showing a decrease of 72% since 1995 (ibid: 24). Given these apparently significant decreases in the number of burglaries, it is easy to overlook the often-extensive harm suffered by the victims of this offence. The pioneering study by Maguire and Bennett (1982) highlighted the psychological effects of domestic burglary on its victims. Maguire and Bennett found that the emotional impact on victims of domestic burglary was often severe and was perceived as being worse than the financial loss they suffered. Over 25% of victims in the study said that they had suffered serious or quite serious shock, and two-thirds had their lives affected for some weeks after the offence, despite very little evidence of violence. Donaldson (2003), in his study on the elderly victims of burglary, found that those who had been burgled were two and a half times more likely to die or have to move to a nursing home within two years than those of a similar age who had not been burgled. Kearon and Leach (2000) have argued that the impact of burglary on its victims is so great because burglary involves an invasion of the home and the possessions and objects that people have in their homes. When someone's personal space and possessions are invaded in this way, they feel as if they have been the victim of violence against their own bodies. This may explain the feelings of victims reported by the studies discussed earlier.

Government survey research into the causes of domestic burglary has tended to focus on individual characteristics and behaviour which is perceived to increase the risk of being victimised, and situational crime prevention. For example, the 2018 CSEW claimed that 63% of domestic burglary victims in England and Wales in the previous year had no or less-than-basic home security. This compared with 37% who had at least basic security measures (ONS 2019b: Table 14).

However, research from burglars themselves draws attention to the roots of burglary in issues relating to social harm. Hearnden and Magill (2004) found that the need to get money to buy drugs was the main reason given by convicted burglars for their most recent burglary, while Bennett and Wright (1984) highlighted the complex relationship between individual choice to commit burglary and wider social factors. In their study, alcohol and drug use sometimes provided encouragement to commit 'spur of the moment' burglaries, but, on other occasions, addiction to alcohol or drugs provided the main motivation to offend in order to obtain more money to feed these addictions. Mawby (2001: ch.7) points out that successful burglary reduction programmes such as the Kirkholt Project and the Burglary Reduction Initiative in Plymouth combined situational target-hardening measures with targeting of resources on the social problems which were identified as being key causes of burglary locally, particularly drug abuse and debt.

> ### Study exercise 5.11
>
> Read Hearnden and Magill's (2004) research findings. Do you think, after reading them, that situational factors (e.g. strong locks on doors and windows) or social factors (e.g. drug abuse and unemployment) are more important in trying to reduce the amount of burglaries that occur?

Criminal damage and criminal justice

Criminal damage, like theft, is a volume crime. The CSEW estimated 1,097,000 incidences of criminal damage in England and Wales in 2017–18, with no significant changes from the previous year, while the police recorded a 1% decrease in offences over the same period (ONS 2019a: 6). The CSEW also showed a 68% reduction in offences since 1995 (ibid: 24), with a 44% reduction in offences recorded by police over the same period (ibid: 32), a similar reduction in other property offences that we have discussed earlier in this chapter.

Studying conviction and sentencing trends for criminal damage reveals interesting trends. The conviction rate was 70.2% in 2018, a decrease of 2.9% compared with 2017 (Ministry of Justice 2019: table Q1.3), and while the numbers sentenced at all courts have decreased by 82% in the 10 years following 2008, the average custodial sentence length has doubled over the same period (ibid: table Q5.3). These data suggest a more punitive criminal justice approach at the sentencing stage, although it is important to remember that the offence category of criminal damage covers a wide range of behaviour, from minor vehicle damage to arson, intentionally endangering life.

In fact, criminal justice has struggled to provide a consistent approach to the wide range of social behaviour covered by the category of criminal damage. At the most serious end of the harm scale, there is the social damage caused by arson. The Arson Prevention Forum (2017) calculated that 47 deaths had resulted from deliberate fires in England in the previous year, as well as around 1000 injuries, and estimated the economic cost of arson to be around £1.45bn. Faced with this level of harm, it is difficult to argue against a criminal justice approach based on punishment. But criminal damage also includes a range of other types of behaviour whose criminality and social harmfulness is less obvious. Graffiti is clearly regarded as criminal damage by criminal law and justice. Yet the art created by artists such as Banksy, which often consists of stencils spray-painted onto (other people's) walls, regularly sells for thousands of pounds at auction and arguably adds value to the property to which it is added (Edwards 2009). Other types of criminal damage are viewed as being outside the scope of the offence as it is defined under the Criminal Damage Act 1971, because the property is intangible or because it does not clearly belong to another, yet can still cause extensive damage in reality. Examples would include cybercrime in the form of computer misuse causing damage to intangible property (such as hacking and the use of viruses, which is now criminalised under the Computer Misuse Act 1990 as amended – see Herring 2019: 259–63) and the intentional or reckless degradation of the earth's resources through pollution or habitat destruction on which green criminology focuses (Potter 2017). These types of damage are often linked to corporate activity, affecting the lives of the least powerful most noticeably, and yet are responded to leniently by criminal justice agencies (Brisman and South 2017).

Study exercise 5.12

Should the law and criminal justice classify some graffiti as art and therefore not punish it as criminal damage? If so, where would you draw the line between damage and art? Would you prosecute Banksy, for example?

Robbery and criminal justice

Robbery is an example of an offence which is low volume and more accurately captured by police data than by the CSEW as a result. In 2017–18, police-recorded robbery offences rose by 17% compared with the previous year, continuing a medium-term upward trend and mirroring a non-significant 29% CSEW increase (ONS 2019a: 2) but was still 5% lower than in 2007–8 (ibid: 32).

Robbery, as it is legally defined, is a combination of a property offence (theft) and any violent offence, and so it covers a very wide range of behaviour, from professionally organised armed robberies involving kidnap or serious injury through to children demanding small amounts of money from one another on school playgrounds. There is also a great deal of overlap between minor robbery and theft from the person (Ashworth 2002), even though robbery is an offence which can only be dealt with at the Crown Court and carries a maximum sentence of life imprisonment. This overlap is especially important because most robberies are so-called 'muggings' involving personal possessions being snatched from a victim without much force being used. Although robberies involving the use of knives have increased recently, it is still true that almost 80% of robberies recorded by police in 2017–18 did not involve knives (ONS 2019a: 46) and only 2% of personal robberies in

2015–16 involved the use of a firearm (ONS 2016: 14). As Matthews (2002) explains, improvements in crime prevention measures from businesses that were traditionally targets of robbery (e.g. banks, building societies, and post offices), such as intruder alarms, CCTV, and tighter security for the transport of money to and from business premises, meant that there were fewer professional armed robbers at the start of the 21st century than ever before.

Robbery offending and victimisation are both unusually clustered in terms of where offenders and victims live and who they are. Recorded robbery is typically concentrated in urban areas, especially London, where 41% of recorded robberies occurred in 2017–18, but only 16% of recorded crime overall occurred (ONS 2019a: 20). The robbery 'hot spots' are in areas more likely to be socio-economically deprived. Harrington and Mayhew (2001) found that nearly half of all victims in their study were under 18 and that 77% of incidents were male-on-male.

These data – when combined with the high custody rate for robberies in court, standing at 68.9%, higher than for any other offence group (Ministry of Justice 2019: table Q1.3) – indicate a risk-based criminal justice approach assuming a rational choice to offend. However, Matthews (2002: 37) found that a significant number of the armed commercial robbers in his study were either drunk or on drugs at the time of their robbery, and in a large percentage of cases the robbers were desperate for money, either to clear debts or to fund a drug habit. This meant that many of the robbers in Matthews' study only had a vague idea of how much money was available from their victims and an even vaguer idea of what security measures were there to prevent them from committing robbery. Wright et al.'s (2006) study into street robbers again rejects the rational choice approach to explaining why robbery is committed. Instead, the research found that the robbers interviewed were heavily involved in 'street culture', which often meant that they felt desperate and had an immediate need for cash, to which robbery offered a solution. Crucially, though, most of the robbers did not think about the consequences of their actions as individualist crime prevention supporters would predict. Instead, robbery had a range of cultural causes for the study's participants, from maintaining personal reputation, through obtaining money for alcohol or drugs, to seeking informal justice for earlier harm suffered.

Study exercise 5.13

Presdee (2005) argues that robbery is best understood as an expression of young people's need for excitement in their lives, as a form of rebellion against social control, and as a response to the increasingly consumerist society in which we live. If Presdee is right, what implications would this have for the way in which criminal justice should respond to robbery?

Conclusions: linking discussion to the roadmap theories

The development of theft and fraud, in terms of their definition in criminal law since the Theft Act 1968 was introduced, points to a stretching of the scope of criminal law, based on individual responsibility and risk assessment, which fits with the risk management roadmap model. In the context of theft, *Gomez* and *Hinks* extended the concept of appropriation, as far as situations where the victim legally transfers property to the defendant under civil law. Bogg and Stanton-Ife (2003) interpreted *Hinks* as a decision that, in line with the liberal roadmap theory, enforced the rights of vulnerable victims not to suffer financial exploitation. Concern with protecting the vulnerable in society is a valuable goal for criminal law. This argument is harder to sustain, however, when we consider the fact that around 98% of all theft offences do not reach court and so cannot be regulated by this legal decision. Another problem is the confusing overlap between theft and fraud that decisions like *Gomez* created (Shute and Horder 1993).

The new fraud offences created by the Fraud Act 2006 could be said to have the same tendency of widening the scope of criminal law based on risk management models. As Ormerod (2007) points out, the new offences do not need proof of any causal link between deception and obtaining property, or of the effects of the false representation on the victim. The inclusion of exposing V to the risk of a loss means that reckless fraud is criminalised, a feature which again extends the scope of criminal law.

The widening of the scope of the actus reus in both theft and fraud has meant more of an emphasis on the mens rea requirement of dishonesty. The law has allowed the magistrates or jury to decide whether D's behaviour was dishonest in each case, and by defining dishonesty (under the *Ghosh* test as interpreted by *Ivey*) as anything that the community would think was dishonest. In this way, the law claims to reflect moral views on what is and is not dishonesty which everyone in the community shares. However, as Norrie (2014: 51–3) shows, there is no agreement in society about what counts as dishonesty. To give one example, downloading music via the Internet without paying for it is seen as theft by criminal justice, yet a report published in 2013 estimated that at least a third of people in the UK consumed at least one item of online content illegally over the previous three months (Ofcom/Kantar Media 2013: 3). Similarly, the data on theft and fraud discussed earlier show that they are widespread in society. Yet the law chooses to cover up the social conflict on this issue by claiming that the community always agrees on what dishonesty is.

Elsewhere in property offences law, the first trend has been one of widening the scope of criminal behaviour, focusing on risk management, in terms of both actus reus and mens rea requirements. In burglary, for example, the actus reus requirements of trespass and entry have been steadily reduced in terms of actual criminal behaviour in cases such as *Jones and Smith* and *Ryan*, leading to an increasing emphasis on mens rea. In robbery, an offence which carries a maximum sentence of life imprisonment, the scope of the offence's actus reus means everything from snatching and then dropping a bag from someone's arm to a well-organised, professional armed raid causing economic and physical harm.

In criminal damage, criminal law has also moved towards risk-based criminality by allowing people to be convicted, and potentially punished severely, for damaging property with the owner's permission, even if the risk is created for a short period and is eliminated immediately, as happened in *Merrick* [1995] Crim LR 802 (Wells and Quick 2010: 414). As Wells and Quick (ibid) also point out, the image created by the legal definition of criminal damage is one of the destruction of tangible goods – the smashed bus shelter or the indelible inner-city graffiti, for example. However, it does not label the damage caused by the pollution of air and water, offences which are far more likely to be committed by middle- and upper-class offenders, as being 'criminal' in the same way. Criminal law has also interpreted the defences to criminal damage in a way that suggests the influence of the radical roadmap model. On one hand, in *Jaggard v Dickinson* [1981] QB 527, the defence of 'lawful excuse' was allowed for a drunken belief in the owner's consent to damage. On the other hand, the Ds in *Hill* and *Jones and Milling* were not allowed to use the defence of prevention of crime where they committed criminal damage in an attempt to prevent politically and legally questionable activity such as the invasion of Iraq in 2003. Criminal damage law therefore takes a risk management approach to responding to damage committed by individuals which threaten the social order, while effectively ignoring arguably more harmful conduct by those who are not seen as being socially dangerous. In this way, the radical and risk management models mesh together when explaining the current state of the law.

In terms of criminal justice's enforcement of these offences, a major problem for the risk management approach of criminal law (as shown with other offences in previous chapters) has been the low number of cases which are reported, recorded, cleared up, and punished. Crime and conviction statistics also do not reveal the social context of attitudes towards theft generally, and shoplifting in particular. Some writers have argued that there is a contradiction between the society in which we live, which is increasingly materialistic and organised by the need to buy and consume more and more personal possessions, and the moral disapproval of shoplifting shown by criminal law and criminal justice (Presdee 2005; Hall 2012). Overall, the response to shoplifting by criminal justice is more characterised by liberal, individualistic ideas of crime control and power-driven responses to the harm caused to the powerful in society than by due process and the reflection of the social harm and inequality that drives the commission of shoplifting, such as unemployment and drug abuse (Cook 2006).

The response to fraud seems to be quite different, however. Critical crimi-nologists have used the low rate of serious fraud prosecutions and convictions to argue that the criminal justice response to fraud is characterised by the rad-ical roadmap theory, so that, for example, the SFO's 'soft' response is aimed at protecting and maintaining the power and wealth of those who commit serious fraud (e.g. Tombs 2017). This is a convincing argument, and there is some clear evidence of differences in criminal justice's response based on the social class of the fraudster (Cook 1989). However, it overlooks the fact that fraud is not in the interests of capitalism and making more profit generally, something that can benefit many groups in society, not just the powerful (Levi 1987; Nelken 2012: 637–8). Nor does the approach reflect the fact that many fraud victims' first priority will be to recover the money they have lost rather than to see their offender being punished harshly (Levi and Pithouse 1992). Also, businesses rely on having a good reputation which is damaged just by the process of publicly appearing in court (Fisse and Braithwaite 1985). These factors may explain why sentencing patterns differ for higher-class fraudsters.

These data indicate that there is not one roadmap model that is in control in this area of criminal law and criminal justice. Instead, there seems to be a complex mixture of liberal and risk-management responses attempting to respond to the social harm caused by these crimes. It also seems that the radical model can also play a part in the criminal justice response to these property offences, alongside the liberal and risk management models. This is suggested, for example, by the apparent reluctance of criminal justice to pros-ecute corporations that commit tax evasion offences. Therefore, the radical hybrid realist model is the best explanatory roadmap for a system of regulat-ing property offences which is influenced by power-based issues, but also by other theoretical ideas.

Key points

- Despite recent reform in the law on fraud, there remains significant overlap in the behaviour criminalised by theft and fraud offences
- Criminal damage definitions have needed to be updated by further legislation to respond to cybercrime and environmental crime
- The scope of burglary and robbery in terms of how they are defined by criminal law has generally increased in the past 50 years
- Rates of property offending have remained stable in England and Wales recently, after a long period of decline

- Most property offences are not responded to by criminal justice, and there is some evidence of class bias in the criminal justice regulation of different types of fraud
- The traditionally liberal approach to regulating property crime in criminal law and justice has been displaced to some extent by risk management and radical influences, and the current picture is one of a range of theoretical influences, best explained by the radical hybrid realist roadmap model

Further reading

Levi, M. (2017), 'The Criminal Pursuit of Serious White-Collar Crimes', in Carlen, P., and Ayres Franca, L. (eds.), *Alternative Criminologies*. Abingdon: Routledge.

Loveless, J., Allen, M., and Derry, C. (2018), *Complete Criminal Law* (6th ed.): chs.12–14. Oxford: OUP.

Mawby, R.I. (2001), *Burglary*. Cullompton: Willan.

Presdee, M. (2005), 'Volume Crime and Everyday Life', in Hale, C., Hayward, K., Wahidin, A., and Wincup, E. (eds.), *Criminology*. Oxford: OUP.

Wells, C., and Quick, O. (2010), *Lacey, Wells and Quick's Reconstructing Criminal Law* (4th ed.): section IV. Cambridge: CUP.

References

Arson Prevention Forum (2017), *State of the Nation Report 2017*. Available online at: http://stoparsonuk.org/arson/documents/Arson-Prevention-Forum-Booklet.pdf. Accessed 14 June 2019.

Ashworth, A. (2002), 'Robbery Re-Assessed', *Criminal Law Review*: 851–72.

Bennett, T., and Wright, R. (1984), *Burglars on Burglary: Prevention and the Offender*. Aldershot: Gower.

Bogg, A.L., and Stanton-Ife, J. (2003), 'Protecting the Vulnerable: Legality, Harm and Theft', *Legal Studies*, **23**(3): 402–22.

Brisman, A., and South, N. (2017), 'Green Criminology', in Liebling, A., Maruna, S., and McAra, L. (eds.), *The Oxford Handbook of Criminology* (6th ed.). Oxford: OUP.

British Retail Consortium (2018), *2017 Retail Crime Survey: Summary*. Available online at: https://brc.org.uk/media/249703/2017-crime-survey-short-story_fa_63_v11.pdf. Accessed 17 July 2019.

Cook, D. (1989), *Rich Law, Poor Law: Different Responses to Tax and Supplementary Benefit Fraud*. Milton Keynes: Open University Press.

Cook, D. (2006), *Criminal and Social Justice*. London: Sage.

Croall, H. (2001), *Understanding White Collar Crime*. Buckingham: Open University Press.

Donaldson, R. (2003), *Experiences of Older Burglary Victims*. Home Office Research Findings No. 198. London: Home Office.

Edwards, I. (2009), 'Banksy's Graffiti: A Not So Simple Case', *Journal of Criminal Law*, **73**(4): 345–61.

Experian (2017), *Annual Fraud Indicator 2017*. Nottingham: Experian.

Fisse, B., and Braithwaite, J. (1985), *The Impact of Publicity on Corporate Offenders*. Albany, NY: SUNY Press.

Hall, S. (2012), *Theorizing Crime and Deviance*. London: Sage.

Harrington, V., and Mayhew, P. (2001), *Mobile Phone Theft*. Home Office Research Study No.235. London: Home Office.

Hearnden, I., and Magill, C. (2004), *Decision-Making by Burglars: Offenders' Perspectives*. Home Office Research Findings No.249. London: Home Office.

Heeks, M., Reed, S., Tafsiri, M., and Prince, S. (2018), *The Economic and Social Costs of Crime* (2nd ed.). Home Office Research Report No.99. London: Home Office.

Herring, J. (2019), *Criminal Law* (11th ed.). London: Palgrave Macmillan.

Home Office (2018a), *Crime Outcomes in England and Wales, Year Ending March 2018*. Statistical Bulletin HOSB No.10/18. London: Home Office.

Kearon, A., and Leach, R. (2000), 'Invasion of the "Body Snatchers": Burglary Reconsidered', *Theoretical Criminology*, **4**(4): 451–72.

Levi, M. (1987), *Regulating Fraud: White-Collar Crime and the Criminal Process*. London: Tavistock.

Levi, M. (2002), 'Economic Crime', in McConville, M., and Wilson, G. (eds.), *The Handbook of the Criminal Justice Process*. Oxford: OUP.

Levi, M. (2017), 'The Criminal Pursuit of Serious White-Collar Crimes', in Carlen, P., and Ayres Franca, L. (eds.), *Alternative Criminologies*. Abingdon: Routledge.

Levi, M., and Pithouse, A. (1992), 'The Victims of Fraud', in Downes, D. (ed.), *Unravelling Criminal Justice*. Basingstoke: Palgrave Macmillan.

Light, R., Nee, C., and Ingham, H. (1993), *Car Theft: The Offender's Perspective*. Home Office Research Study No.130. London: Home Office.

Loveless, J., Allen, M., and Derry, C. (2018), *Complete Criminal Law* (6th ed.). Oxford: OUP.

Maguire, M., and Bennett, T. (1982), *Burglary in a Dwelling*. London: Heinemann.

Matthews, R. (2002), *Armed Robbery*. Cullompton: Willan.

Mawby, R.I. (2001), *Burglary*. Cullompton: Willan.

Ministry of Justice (2019), *Criminal Justice System Statistics Quarterly, September 2018 – Overview Tables*. Available online at: https://assets.publishing.service.gov.uk/government/ uploads/system/uploads/attachment_data/file/780613/overview-tables-sept-2018.ods. Accessed 21 March 2019.

Morgan, N., Shaw, O., Feist, A., and Byron, C. (2016), *Reducing Criminal Opportunity: Vehicle Security and Vehicle Crime*. Home Office Research Report No.87. London: Home Office.

Nelken, D. (2012), 'Corporate and White-Collar Crime', in Maguire, M., Morgan, R., and Reiner, R. (eds.), *The Oxford Handbook of Criminology* (5th ed.). Oxford: OUP.

Newburn, T. (2017), *Criminology* (3rd ed.). Abingdon: Routledge.

Norrie, A. (2014), *Crime, Reason and History* (3rd ed.). Cambridge: CUP.

Ofcom/Kantar Media (2013), *Online Copyright Infringement Tracker Wave 4 (Covering Period March 2013 to May 2013): Overview and Key Findings*. Available online at: www.ofcom. org.uk/_data/assets/pdf_file/0034/78919/oci_main_report_w4_final.pdf. Accessed 28 March 2019.

ONS (2016), *Offences Involving Weapons*. Available online at: www.ons.gov.uk/ peoplepopulationandcommunity/crimeandjustice/compendium/focusonviolentcrimeands exualoffences/yearendingmarch2015/chapter3offencesinvolvingtheuseofweapons. Accessed 27 March 2019.

ONS (2017), *Overview of Vehicle-Related Theft: England and Wales*. Available online at: www.ons.gov.uk/peoplepopulationandcommunity/crimeandjustice/articles/overviewofvehiclerelatedtheft/2017-07-20. Accessed 21 March 2019.

ONS (2019a), *Crime in England and Wales, Year Ending March 2019*. Available online at: www.ons.gov.uk/peoplepopulationandcommunity/crimeandjustice/bulletins/crimeinenglandandwales/yearendingmarch2019. Accessed 21 March 2019.

ONS (2019b), *Nature of Crime: Burglary*. Available online at: www.ons.gov.uk/peoplepopulationandcommunity/crimeandjustice/datasets/natureofcrimeburglary. Accessed 27 March 2019.

Ormerod, D. (2007), 'The Fraud Act 2006 – Criminalising Lying', *Criminal Law Review*: 193–219.

Potter, G.R. (2017), 'Green Criminology', in Morley, S., Turner, J., Corteen, K., and Taylor, P. (eds.), *A Companion to State Power, Liberties and Human Rights*. Bristol: Policy Press.

Presdee, M. (2005), 'Volume Crime and Everyday Life', in Hale, C., Hayward, K., Wahidin, A., and Wincup, E. (eds.), *Criminology*. Oxford: OUP.

Sentencing Council (2015), *Theft Offences: Definitive Guideline*. London: Sentencing Council.

Shute, S., and Horder, J. (1993), 'Thieving and Deceiving: What Is The Difference?' *Modern Law Review*, **56**(4): 548–54.

Speed, M., and Burrows, J. (2006), *Sentencing in Cases of Theft from Shops (Sentencing Advisory Panel Research Report no.3)*. London: Sentencing Advisory Panel/Morgan Harris Burrows.

Tcherni, M., Davies, A., Lopes, G., and Lizotte, A. (2016), 'The Dark Figure of Online Property Crime: Is Cyberspace Hiding a Crime Wave?' *Justice Quarterly*, **33**(5): 890–911.

Tombs, S. (2017), *Social Protection After the Crisis: Regulation Without Enforcement*. Bristol: Policy Press.

Wells, C., and Quick, O. (2010), *Lacey, Wells and Quick's Reconstructing Criminal Law: Text and Materials* (4th ed.). Cambridge: CUP.

Wright, R., Brookman, F., and Bennett, T. (2006), 'The Foreground Dynamics of Street Robbery in Britain', *British Journal of Criminology*, **46**(1): 1–15.

Non-fatal assaults

Chapter aims

After reading Chapter 6, you should be able to understand:

- Which non-fatal, non-sexual assault offences are in criminal law
- What the actus reus and mens rea requirements are for each offence
- How the criminal offences designed to deal with harassment and stalking work

- What the consent defence is in the context of assault, and how it works
- How criminal justice, in terms of the police, CPS, courts, and punishment agencies respond to non-fatal assaults
- How the evidence on non-fatal assaults in criminal law and criminal justice fits in with the theoretical models introduced in Chapter 1

Introduction

This chapter discusses non-fatal, non-sexual offences against the person – offences of assault, which do not result in death. The first part of this chapter explains the law on non-fatal assaults in detail, examining its basis in the Offences against the Person Act 1861 (referred to as 'OAPA' hereafter in this chapter). The second part of the chapter then contextualises the law by examining how it is used in criminal justice practice, and how the roadmap models in Chapter 1 explain criminal law and criminal justice responses to these types of violence.

Non-fatal assaults: the law

Common assault

Actus reus

Common assault is now defined as a criminal offence in s.39 of the Criminal Justice Act 1988, although the common law offence is still in operation (*DPP v Taylor; Little* [1992] 1 All ER 299), and the actus reus is the same for both the statutory and the common law offences. The actus reus of assault is that D must cause V to 'apprehend immediate application of unlawful violence to the body', according to *Venna* [1976] QB 421. V must fear that they will suffer unlawful violence in the immediate future, rather than later (*Tuberville v Savage* (1669) 1 Mod Rep 3). *Logdon v DPP* [1976] Crim LR 121 emphasises that as long as V is in fear, it does not matter if the violence is not actually possible in the reality of the circumstances. This also means that if V does not fear unlawful violence, then the actus reus of assault has not been committed, even if V actually does suffer unlawful violence which has been caused by D (*Lamb* [1967] 2 QB 981). *Fagan v MPC* [1969] 1 QB 438 shows that assault can be committed by omissions as well as acts. The important case of *Ireland; Burstow* [1998] AC 147 made it clear that assault can be committed by words alone.

The threat of violence does not have to be capable of being carried out immediately, in the sense of the next few seconds. In *Smith v Chief Superintendent of Woking Police Station* (1983) 76 Cr App Rep 234, V saw D through a closed and locked window. D was guilty of assault even though it would have taken him some time to get through the window and cause unlawful violence to V. *Ireland; Burstow* extends this principle further. Here, V, fearing the 'possibility' of immediate violence was enough to meet the actus reus requirements for assault. This could occur where, for example, D makes threatening phone calls to V, and V does not know exactly where D is but fears that D might be close enough to carry out the threat of unlawful violence immediately.

Mens rea

Venna [1976] emphasised that common assault can be committed either intentionally or recklessly. *Savage; Parmenter* [1991] 1 AC 699 states that subjective recklessness is required, so that D must see the risk of V apprehending immediate unlawful violence, and continue with their actions anyway.

Study exercise 6.1

Do we still need the offence of common assault in criminal law now that we have offences of harassment and stalking?

Battery

Actus reus

The actus reus of battery is causing application of unlawful force to V's body *(DPP v Taylor; Little)*. As with common assault, the actus reus of battery is defined in s.39 of the Criminal Justice Act 1988 but is also a common law offence. Any force applied to someone else's body can be enough for the actus reus of battery – at least in theory. The actus reus of battery is normally direct application of force *(Fagan v MPC)*. A few cases extend this principle to situations where D has not directly applied force to V's body but has still 'caused' unlawful force to be applied. Examples include *Martin* (1881) 8 QBD 54, *DPP v K* [1990] 1 WLR 1067 and *Haystead v Chief Constable of Derbyshire* [2000] 3 All ER 890.

Mens rea

The mens rea requirements for battery are the same as the mens rea requirements for common assault. See earlier discussion for details.

Racially and religiously aggravated assault

S.29 of the Crime and Disorder Act 1998 created a new offence of racially aggravated assault. This is proved where D, at the time of committing the offence, or immediately before or after committing it, showed V hostility based on V's membership (or presumed membership) of a racial group, or where D's offence is wholly or partly motivated by hostility towards members of a racial group based on their membership of that group. S.39 of the Anti-Terrorism, Crime and Security Act 2001 set up a parallel offence of religiously aggravated assault, which mirrors the actus reus of racially aggravated assault.

Study exercise 6.2

In *Rogers* [2007] 2 AC 62, D used the phrase 'bloody foreigners' and this was enough to convict him of a racially aggravated offence. Was this a fair outcome?

Harassment and stalking offences

The Protection from Harassment Act 1997 created two new offences of harassment. Under s.2 of the Act, there must be a 'course of conduct' amounting to 'harassment'. D must know, or should know, that their conduct amounts to harassment, so that a reasonable person would agree that the conduct amounted to harassment, even if D did not (s.1). *Lau v DPP* [2000] Crim LR 580 shows that there needs to be at least two incidents to count as a 'course of conduct' with a link between them. In *Kelly v DPP* [2003] Crim LR 45, D made three phone calls in five minutes to V, leaving an answer phone message each time. V listened to the messages one after the other, and this was enough to be a 'course of conduct'. *Lau* showed that the incidents do not have to be close together like this. However, as there has to be a link between them, the longer the gap in time is between the incidents, the less likely it will be that they will amount to a course of conduct. *Hills* [2001] Crim LR 318 shows that a course of conduct does not have to be the same kind of incident each time, although repetition of behaviour is a factor to be taken into account. *DPP v Hardy* [2008] EWHC 2874 (Admin) is an example of how initially legal behaviour can become harassment through the manner and frequency of its repetition. However, *O'Neill* [2016] EWCA Crim 92 limits the scope of the offence by stating that harassment must involve oppressive conduct, not just alarm or distress.

The more serious harassment offence is causing fear of violence on at least two occasions (s.4 of the 1997 Act). There has to be a course of conduct involving at least two occasions where V experiences fear of violence, where

D knows or ought to know that it will cause V to fear violence against them. D ought to know this if, on any occasion, a reasonable person in possession of the same information would think that the course of conduct would cause V to fear violence on that occasion. *Henley* [2000] Crim LR 582 confirms that for the s.4 offence, the fear of violence must occur on at least two occasions and must be caused by a course of conduct that must also involve at least two incidents. This case also shows that the mens rea for the s.4 offence is that D knew or ought to have known that the course of conduct would cause fear to V on each occasion. *Henley* also shows that the s.4 fear of violence does not have the same requirements as common assault, because for s.4 there is no need for the violence to be immediate. *Caurti v DPP* [2002] Crim LR 131 shows that all of the incidents must target the same person for the s.4 offence, and that V must fear violence against himself or herself, not just violence against someone else. *Widdows* [2011] EWCA Crim 1500 emphasises that the s.4 offence is designed for cases of intimidating stalking or abuse on racial or religious grounds, not for rare cases of harassing behaviour in the context of a relationship which both parties wanted to continue.

Under s.111 of the Protection of Freedoms Act 2012, three new criminal offences of stalking became part of the law. The Act added s.2A and s.4A(1)(b)(i) into the 1997 Act, recognising stalking as a specific form of the existing offences of harassment which can be committed electronically, through social media and email, as well as through personal contact. The 2012 Act also created a new offence of stalking involving serious alarm or distress, under what is now s.4A(1)(b)(ii).

S.76 of the Serious Crime Act 2015 created a new offence of coercive or controlling behaviour in an intimate or family relationship. To be guilty of the offence, D must repeatedly or continuously engage in coercive or controlling behaviour towards V where D and V are personally connected in an intimate or family relationship. The behaviour must have a serious effect on V. This means that either V fears violence against themselves on at least two occasions, or that the behaviour has a substantial adverse effect on V's day-to-day activities (e.g. reduced ability to socialise, detrimental impact on physical or mental health, or changes to work or home routines). In terms of mens rea, D must know or should know that the behaviour will have a serious effect on V.

Study exercise 6.3

Read Hill (2016) on the apparent under-use of the new coercive and controlling behaviour offence by police. Why do you think the police do not use this offence more often in response to domestic violence?

Assault occasioning actual bodily harm

Actus reus

This offence (called 'ABH' hereafter in this chapter), is defined in s.47 of the OAPA. However, the statutory definition does not explain what the actus reus of the offence actually is, and case law has had to provide a more detailed explanation of the scope of the offence. There are three requirements for the proof of the actus reus of ABH. The first is that the actus reus of either common assault or battery has occurred. Secondly, D must cause the ABH to occur. Both factual and legal causation are required in this context, so, for example, if V suffers ABH in escaping from D, the escape must be reasonably foreseeable (*Roberts* (1971) 56 Cr App Rep 95).

Thirdly, 'actual bodily harm' itself has to be caused to V. *Miller* [1954] 2 QB 282 defines ABH as 'any hurt or injury calculated to interfere with health and comfort of V'. ABH does not require physical pain to be caused – in *DPP v Smith* [2006] 1 WLR 1571, for example, D's cutting off of some of V's hair counted as ABH. *T v DPP* [2003] Crim LR 622 again gives ABH a broad and loosely defined scope in stating that it includes any harm that is more than 'transient or trifling' (a momentary loss of consciousness in this case). *Chan-Fook* [1994] 2 All ER 552 and *Ireland; Burstow* show that psychiatric injury can count as ABH, as long as it is in the form of a medically recognised psychiatric condition, rather than simply nervousness, fear, or anxiety. *Constanza* [1997] 2 Cr App Rep 492 states that ABH can be committed by words alone, as well as actions. Finally, *Santana-Bermudez* [2004] Crim LR 417 shows that ABH can be committed by omission.

Mens rea

The mens rea required for ABH is the mens rea for either common assault or battery (i.e. either intention or subjective recklessness) (*Savage; Parmenter* [1991] 4 All ER 698).

Study exercise 6.4

How would you define the actus reus and mens rea for ABH?

Wounding and inflicting grievous bodily harm

Actus reus

S.20 of OAPA defines these offences. There are two separate offences here, both covered by the same section of the statute. The actus reus for wounding is any break in the continuity of V's skin (*Moriarty v Brookes* (1834) 6 C & P 684). A minor external cut that draws blood is enough to meet the actus reus requirements here in theory, if it is more than a scratch (*McLoughlin* (1838) 8 C & P 635). However, internal bleeding does not count as a wound (e.g. *JCC v Eisenhower* (1984) 78 Cr App Rep 48), and neither do broken bones, where the skin is not broken (*Wood* (1830) 1 Mood CC 278).

Inflicting grievous bodily harm ('GBH' hereafter) is the other offence under s.20. GBH, like ABH, is widely defined. The actus reus of GBH is inflicting 'really serious harm' (*DPP v Smith* [1961] AC 290), and the court has to decide whether V's injuries are serious enough to be classified as GBH on the facts, taking into account current social standards (*Golding* [2014] EWCA Crim 889). They must also assess the overall extent of V's injuries rather than individual injuries one by one (*Birmingham* [2002] EWCA Crim 2608) and the impact of the injuries on V in particular, taking into account V's age and state of health (*Bollom* [2004] 2 Cr App Rep 6). GBH can also include very serious psychiatric injury (*Ireland; Burstow*) and broken bones (*Wood; Lewis* [1970] Crim LR 647).

Ireland; Burstow states that there is no difference between 'inflicting' and 'causing', and that, for s.20 GBH, there was no need for violence to be directly or indirectly applied to V's body. Nor was there any need for an assault or battery to prove GBH. *Savage; Parmenter* had decided previously that s.20 wounding also did not have to involve an assault or battery. Causation of GBH or wounding is required (*Marjoram* [2000] Crim LR 372), just as it is for other non-fatal assault offences. *Lewis* shows how the reasonably foreseeable escape principle applies to GBH.

Mens rea

The mens rea requirements are the same for both s.20 offences, namely, intention or subjective recklessness (*Savage; Parmenter*). D only has to intend or foresee the risk of 'some' bodily harm, not necessarily GBH or wounding. D also only has to foresee the risk that some harm 'might' happen, not that it 'would' happen (*Mowatt* [1968] 1 QB 421) and does not have to foresee an obvious and significant risk of harm (*Brady* [2007] Crim LR 564).

Study exercise 6.5

The maximum sentences for s.20 GBH and s.47 ABH are the same (five years' imprisonment). Is this fair?

Wounding or causing grievous bodily harm with intent to inflict grievous bodily harm, and causing grievous bodily harm with intent to resist arrest

Actus reus

S.18 of OAPA covers all three of these offences. The meanings of 'wounding' and 'GBH' are the same as they are for s.20 GBH. As with the other non-fatal assaults, proof of causation of the harm is required.

Mens rea

Unlike s.20 GBH, s.18 GBH cannot be committed recklessly (*Belfon* [1976] 3 All ER 46). D must intend to commit GBH. An intention to wound is not enough (*Taylor* [2009] EWCA Crim 544). D must also have a pre-existing direct or oblique intent to inflict GBH or to wound. As a result, for the s.18 offences of inflicting GBH or wounding with intent to inflict GBH, intention means the same as it does for murder (*Bryson* [1985] Crim LR 699). For the offence of inflicting GBH with intent to resist arrest, the mens rea requirements are different. The intent to resist arrest must be present, but D does not have to have intent to inflict GBH. Subjective recklessness as to whether GBH occurs to V is enough for a conviction (*Morrison* [1989] 89 Cr App Rep 17).

Study exercise 6.6

Read the account of the conviction of Arthur Collins for GBH by throwing acid in Gayle (2017). Do you agree with the sentence given in this case? Give reasons for your answer.

Consent as a defence to non-fatal assaults

Introduction

In some circumstances, V can consent to the assault committed against them, and this then acts as a defence to the assault charge for D. Assaults can occur in a very wide range of social circumstances, and this has led to a great deal of inconsistency in terms of what criminal law will or will not allow people to consent to before criminalising their conduct. In effect, there is a two-stage test to find out whether the defence of consent applies. The first stage asks whether there is express or implied consent. The second stage asks whether the law will allow someone to consent to physical harm in a particular situation.

Express or implied consent?

The starting point for criminal law is to ask whether or not there actually has been express or implied consent by V to an assault. As mentioned earlier, any non-consensual contact with someone else's body is technically enough actus reus for a battery. However, the law recognises that there has to be implied consent from 'victims' for everyday contact with others – for example, contact with other people while brushing past someone on a busy street – so in situations like this the law will not take action (*Collins v Wilcock* [1984] 3 All ER 374). In *Macmillan v CPS* [2008] EWHC 1457 (Admin), there was implied consent where a police officer took hold of an intoxicated woman's arm to escort her from a private garden into a public place. In some cases the law will not allow people to consent to bodily contact because, for example, of their age (e.g. *Burrell v Harmer* [1967] Crim LR 169).

Another issue is what happens when V gives consent to an assault against them, but only does so because of fraud by D. The general rule here is that D's fraud can remove consent if the fraud relates to whom D is, or what D is doing to V, but not if the fraud relates to the circumstances surrounding what D is doing. For example, in *Richardson* [1999] QB 444 there was implied consent by Vs to ABH (in the form of dental treatment) where they knew that D was a dentist but did not know that she was disqualified from practice. On the other hand, in *Tabassum* [2000] 2 Cr App Rep 328, the female victims did not impliedly consent to indecent assault where they knew what D was doing to them (touching their breasts) but did not know that he had lied to them about being a medical student. In *Dica* [2004] QB 1257, it was decided that V did not impliedly consent to the risk of GBH through being infected with HIV/AIDS where she had sex with D, not knowing that D was infected with the disease. In *Konzani* [2005] 2 Cr App Rep 14, another case of HIV/AIDS infection, the Court of Appeal emphasised that only informed consent to contracting a potentially fatal disease could be a defence. Taking the risk of potential harm from unprotected sex was not implied consent to the risk of contracting HIV/AIDS. Therefore, D was guilty of s.20 GBH where he knew that he had HIV/AIDS, did not tell V, and recklessly infected V with the disease.

What legal limits are there on consent?

Attorney-General's Reference (No.6 of 1980) [1981] QB 715 decided that the limit of the consent defence is ABH. In other words, D is guilty, even though V has consented, if D intends or causes ABH or any worse level of harm. The exception to this rule is where the law decides that consent to the harm is in the public interest. There have been a wide range of cases, before and after *Attorney-General's Reference (No. 6 of 1980)*, which have attempted to decide the situations in which the law will and will not allow people to consent to harm committed against them. Two general categories of cases involving this decision will be considered here – cases involving sexual activity or violence (or both) and cases involving sports.

Sex and violence cases

Overall, criminal law has tended to disallow the consent defence where consensual harm occurs during sexual activity. In *Donovan* [1934] 2 KB 498, V was not allowed to consent to D caning her, and causing injury to the level of ABH as a result, for sexual pleasure. Similarly, in *Boyea* [1992] Crim LR 574, where D's actions during consensual sex injured V's vagina, V could not consent to the ABH which resulted, because D's act was 'likely' to cause harm. The most famous case in this category is *Brown* [1994] 1 AC 212, where a group of men engaged in consensual but violent homosexual sadomasochism in private, causing injury to one another as a result. The House of Lords decided that Vs could not consent to the intentional infliction of serious harm, and therefore the Ds were guilty of ABH and GBH as a result. The majority in *Brown* thought that violence for sexual pleasure was not in the public interest and that the risk to participants' health could not be justified, even though no injuries required hospital treatment or caused permanent scarring. The minority made the points that there was no permanent injury or damage to health and that everyone involved had consented fully to what happened. Therefore, the law should not criminalise their behaviour. The two Law Lords in the minority prioritised the Ds' individual rights to freedom of expression over the public interest in not having to see the behaviour involved. The majority approach in *Brown* was later applied to heterosexual sadomasochism in *Emmett* (1999) *The Times*, 15th October, where D was convicted of ABH after causing consensual injury to V, his girlfriend, during sex. In contrast, in *Slingsby* [1995] Crim LR 570, D was not guilty of unlawful act manslaughter where the assault he caused to V (to which she consented lawfully during sex) unintentionally caused V's death.

Cases such as *Brown* can be contrasted with other cases involving consensual non-sexual violence. Here, criminal law is more reluctant to intervene and criminalise people's behaviour. For example, in *Jones* (1986) 83 Cr App Rep 375, the Court of Appeal decided that V impliedly consented to reckless 'horseplay' which caused GBH, and therefore the Ds were not guilty of any offence. Similarly, in *Aitken* [1992] 4 All ER 541, the Court of Appeal stated that the Ds were not guilty of GBH where they had poured flammable white spirit over V and set it alight, causing severe burns, because V had impliedly consented to 'horseplay'. Note that there was no express consent from either of the Vs in these two cases. The courts found implied consent from Vs' behaviour before and during the causing of their injuries. Another interesting example of the courts deciding not to get involved in consensual violence (although violence committed for sexual purposes) is *Wilson* [1997] QB 47, where D was not guilty of ABH where he branded his wife's bottom after she had asked him to do so. The Court of Appeal decided that this was similar to tattooing, another physical injury allowed under the public interest. However, in *BM* [2018] EWCA Crim 560, the Court of Appeal said that consent was no defence to charges of GBH where D performed body modifications (such as the removal of an ear) on others.

Sports cases

Barnes [2005] 1 WLR 910 clarified the criteria by which courts had to decide whether a victim had consented to injuries occurring during sporting activity. Lord Woolf CJ stated that courts had to consider a range of issues in making this decision. The criteria included:

- The type of sport being played (i.e. whether it was a contact or non-contact sport),
- The level at which the game was being played (amateur or professional),
- The nature of the act committed by D (accidental or reckless injuries could be legal or illegal, but intentional injuries are always illegal), and
- The level of force used by D in injuring V.

Study exercise 6.7

In *Laskey, Jaggard and Brown v UK* [1997] 2 EHRR 39, the European Court of Human Rights decided that the decision in *Brown* did not breach Article 8 of the European Convention on Human Rights (right to privacy and respect for private life under criminal law) (Moran 1998). Do you agree with this decision? Give reasons for your answer.

Non-fatal assaults and criminal justice

Non-fatal assaults, the police and the CPS

The CSEW estimated 1.4m incidences of violence against adults aged 16 and over in the year to December 2018. There was no significant change in this figure in this or any of the previous four years, after long-term decreases since the mid-1990s (ONS 2019). Non-government sources, like hospital emergency departments and walk-in centres (Sivarajasingam et al. 2019) and NHS data, show a similar picture of long-term reductions in the incidence of violence on the scale of around a third over the previous decade. It is significant, however, that all of the data sources discussed here record both long- and short-term increases in violence involving the use of knives.

However, the statistics only give a limited picture of the extent of, and harm caused by, non-fatal violence in England and Wales, for a number of reasons. Violence does not have a fixed meaning (Stanko 2003), and its meanings in a particular time and place can depend on a number of social and legal factors (Sumner 1997). A key influential factor is media coverage of particular types of criminal behaviour by particular people, which can give rise to exaggerated reactions known as moral panics (Cohen 2002), especially as violent behaviour is seen as being particularly 'newsworthy' by large sections of the media (Chibnall 1977). There is also the issue of the public not reporting to police the majority of violent crimes which occur, and the additional incidents which are reported to the police but not recorded by them. Thirdly, harassment that does not cause physical injury can have a severe psychological impact on its victims. Pathé and Mullen (1997), for example, found that 83% of the people in their study had experienced increased levels of anxiety because of stalking, 55% had experienced intrusive flashbacks and recollections of the stalking, and 24% had suicidal thoughts. Finally, the risk of violence is unevenly distributed through society. Domestic violence is just one example of how the statistics on violence can mask uneven risks of victimisation. There is also evidence to show that victims of violence in the night-time economy (including bars, restaurants, and live entertainment, among other industries) are less likely to see their experience as a crime and less likely to report it to the police, than victims of other types of violence (Brennan 2016).

This does not mean that most violence is completely hidden, however. Stanko (2007) argues, based on a range of research studies, that nearly all acts of violence are either witnessed directly or known about by someone else. Stanko's argument raises questions about when – and how – criminal justice responds to violence. Cretney and Davis (1995) argue that when dealing with violence, the police make a distinction between reporting an offence and making a complaint. Unless a victim makes a complaint, and so shows commitment to making a statement and providing evidence in court, Cretney and Davis argue that the police are reluctant to take any further action. Other factors beyond criminal law itself can influence police decisions not to arrest, interview, and charge suspects. These can include the 'social worth' of the victim (i.e. whether the victim is seen by the police as being a troublemaker or has previous convictions themselves; victims and witnesses of assaults coming from an area with a reputation for high crime levels; high police workload levels; and only minor injuries having been suffered) (McConville et al. 1991). Factors such as victims seeing themselves as being socially marginalised, or not wanting to have their conduct examined by the police, as well as fear of reprisals, were also important in victims deciding not to report incidents (Clarkson et al. 1994: 11–13).

Cretney and Davis (1995, 1997) go on to argue that the police can test the victim's effectiveness and willingness to help in the criminal justice process by asking victims to gather further evidence or deliberately delaying investigation of the case. The police can also encourage a complaint to be made by seeking out witnesses following arrests in a public order incident, or by charging for assault in an attempt to secure a plea-bargain for an alternative public order offence, such as affray or violent disorder, which represented a public challenge to police authority on the streets (McConville et al. 1991). The effectiveness of the victim in taking part in police and court investigations was more important than the seriousness of the offence. Clarkson et al. (1994) also found no direct relationship between seriousness and the likelihood of police response, and found that other factors, such as the assault being committed against another police officer, made investigation more likely than the level of seriousness.

It is useful to examine domestic violence as a specific example of how criminal justice responds to harm that is hidden from public view. The definition of 'domestic violence' has expanded to include psychological and emotional forms of abuse, and to cover all genders and sexualities. However, this expansion of the scope of harm has been questioned and contested (Dutton 2016). What is clear is that the extensive social harm caused by domestic violence is well documented (e.g. Stanko 1990). In the year ending March 2018, the Crime Survey for England and Wales estimated that 2 million adults experienced domestic abuse in the previous year, with almost twice as many female victims as male (ONS 2018). Even the CSEW figures are likely to be a significant underestimate of how much domestic violence really occurs in England and Wales. Stanko (2001) counted all of the telephone calls made to the police in the UK about domestic violence on one day and found that even in this short period of time, injuries reported included bleeding caused by kicks to the stomach of a pregnant woman, a slashed throat, stabbings, and severe psychological trauma.

Early research showed that police were very reluctant to intervene in cases of domestic violence (e.g. Edwards 1989). Over time, however, public opinion began to recognise how serious a problem domestic violence is and began to demand that criminal justice did more to respond to it effectively (Dobash and Dobash 1992). The government responded by directing the police to develop new proactive policing to tackle domestic violence, and to form multi-agency partnerships with other agencies in doing this. Evidence on changes in police practice is mixed. Fifty percent of domestic abuse incidents recorded by police in the year to March 2018 were not subsequently recorded as a crime, although this was a 7% increase in the number of recorded incidents compared with the previous year (ONS 2018). The police then made 225,714 arrests for domestic violence over the same time period, or 38 arrests per 100 recorded crimes, but were more likely to assign evidential difficulty outcomes for domestic violence cases (71% of cases) than non-domestic cases of violence (50%) and took longer to assign an outcome in domestic violence cases (ibid.).

Hoyle's (1998) study gave some indications as to why the police seem to find it harder to process and resolve domestic violence cases. She found that although victims sometimes withdrew their statements to the police, and that there was some evidence of the police not wanting to get involved with domestic disputes, only a third of victims of domestic violence in her study actually wanted the police to arrest their attackers. This was mainly because they did not want to end their relationship with the attacker or feared more violence if the attacker was arrested. As a result, Hoyle argued that the police response to domestic violence was about negotiating a satisfactory outcome for the people involved, rather than sexist denial of risk to victims or power-based assertion of control. More recent evidence on police responses to harassment and stalking found that police often did not record such offences, recorded them incorrectly, and failed to assess risk properly, viewing incidents as isolated when they were actually part of a behavioural pattern (HM Inspectorate of Constabulary and HM Crown Prosecution Services Inspectorate 2017).

Violence against people based on their ethnic, cultural, or religious group has been a feature of society in England and Wales for centuries (e.g. Fryer 1984). However, it was not until 1978 that the Metropolitan Police began to record crimes as being 'racist', and not until 1982 that the racist motivation of these crimes was emphasised in police records (Ray et al. 2003: 112). Between 2015 and 2018, there were around 184,000 incidences of hate crimes recorded by the Crime Survey for England and Wales per year, showing a moderate reduction from previous years. The concept of hate crime includes crimes motivated by a victim's religion, gender orientation, sexual orientation, and disability, as well as by their ethnic background. Police recorded that hate crime rates increased over the same period (Home Office 2018). Of these, 45% involved violence, compared with 21% of CSEW crime overall – but only 43% of incidents of racist violence were reported to the police (ibid.). Evidence on the reality of criminal justice's responses to racist violence may help to explain why the attrition rate between the occurrence of racist violence and its recording remains high (Burney 2003). Bowling and Phillips (2002) found that the more serious the incident was, the more likely its seriousness would take priority in how criminal justice responded to it, and the more likely the racist nature of the incident would be played down or ignored by police. Hall (2013: ch.4) argues that racist victimisation is better understood as a continuous process connecting minor abuse and serious violence, where minor and major incidents combined to form a 'framework of fear' reducing quality of life for some victims.

Bowling (1999) conducted research into the police's response to violent racist incidents in an area of high victimisation (East London). He found that there was a low rate of satisfaction with police response to racial incidents, with only 5% feeling very satisfied with the way in which the police handled racial harassment in the local area, and less than a third of respondents feeling satisfied at all. Bowling also heard frequent complaints that the police did not do enough to respond to violent racism, showed lack of interest, and failed to keep victims informed about progress made in their cases. In addition, Bowling's interviews with police officers revealed some evidence of racial prejudice on their part. Bowling's observation of the police at work found that these attitudes were reflected in their behaviour towards ethnic minorities, both as victims and suspects of crime. Bowling concluded that whatever changes there had been to levels of violent racism had very little to do with changes in police policy and practice, and that there were significant limits on the extent to which the police's attitudes could be changed due to the features of 'cop culture' (Reiner 2010).

In terms of CPS attitudes towards violence, Clarkson et al. (1994) found extensive levels of plea-bargaining to lesser offences, with as many as a third of cases being 'defined down' through agreement between the prosecution and defence before the start of a trial, thereby distorting the link between harm caused and charges brought. A similar picture is evident when focusing on domestic violence. There were 110,562 referrals of domestic abuse cases from police to CPS in the year ending March 2018, but the CPS only brought charges in 70% of cases, a fall of 2% compared with the previous year (ONS 2018). Barnish (2004) found that the majority of domestic violence cases reaching court were prosecuted as common assault, despite 90% of cases resulting in physical injury, which would qualify as ABH on the current legal definition. One-third of the cases starting out as ABH were reduced to common assault. Cook et al.'s (2004) evaluation of specialist domestic violence courts, designed to provide more efficient and effective justice in these cases, found that 55% of cases did not proceed at all. Only 32% of court cases resulted in a conviction, despite the ease with which most domestic violence perpetrators can be linked to particular offences (Hanmer and Griffiths 2001).

Burney (2003: 31) suggested that the CPS downgrades racially aggravated offences to 'ordinary' offences of the same time in a significant minority of cases and accepts guilty pleas to the lesser offences too often. On the other hand, the vagueness of the legislation meant that other offences were wrongly prosecuted as 'racial' when the motivation behind the offence was some other factor (Burney and Rose 2002). This was partly due to the legislation itself and the difficulty of proving motivation of offenders by hostility, as the 1998 Crime and Disorder Act requires. Hall (2013) argues that this is not only difficult to prove but also raises questions about whether it is ethical to try to punish defendants' beliefs and character rather than just a specific criminal offence. Burney (2003) also found that the police and CPS did not support witnesses well in racially aggravated cases, leading to a high rate of case collapse due to witnesses withdrawing statements, and confusion from magistrates and judges about how to sentence aggravated offences.

Non-fatal assaults, the court process and punishment

Sentencing data show that in 2018, 26,782 people received a sentence for violence against the person, with 43.4% receiving an immediate custodial sentence (Ministry of Justice 2019). There is a slight increase in immediate custody rates in recent years. In 2015, the rate stood at 40.4%, and there has been a slight increase in the use of community sentences and a slight decrease in the use of fines and conditional discharges over the same period (ibid.).

Jones (2000: 140–1) reviewed sentencing practice for the different non-fatal assaults and found that while s.18 GBH offences received the most severe sentences – between three and eight years' imprisonment on average – the normal sentence range for s.47 ABH and s.20 GBH was the same in each case (only a minority of custodial sentences, and sentences of up to three years). This reflects confusion in the courts about the framework of violent offences that has been part of criminal law since 1861. Genders (1999) found similar confusion between the different offences in the courts. Only 19% of cases in her study charged as s.18 GBH ended in a conviction for the same offence. Genders found that the main reason for this was not police or CPS action but rather 're-labelling' in the courts, which accounted for 60% of the changes. She also found that the severity of the actus reus was a significant factor in deciding whether someone would be convicted with s.18 GBH rather than s.20 GBH, even though the standard of harm is supposed to be the same for both offences. The re-labelled cases had more previous convictions, were more likely to involve group violence, and were more likely to involve perpetrators who had been drinking before committing the violence. These factors suggested over-optimistic charging by CPS staff, based on moral judgments about the blameworthiness of different defendants, which did not reflect the difficulties of proving intent for the s.18 offence.

Fielding's (2006) study of how the courts deal with cases of violence focussed on the language (verbal and non-verbal) which is used in courts during hearings. Fielding did not find evidence that the overlaps between the legal categories of assault in terms of actus reus and mens rea were seen as problematic for defendants, victims, and witnesses. These groups did not show much concern about delays in the court process either. However, defendants, witnesses, and victims were frustrated by legal language used in court (which many found difficult to understand), as well as legal procedures on evidence, which they felt did not allow them to tell their story and put their views across effectively in court. Ethnic minority respondents were most likely to question court processes and report difficulties with them, particularly in terms of the role played by the police. Finally, lack of resources – such as evidence on a witness's line of sight being argued over in court when more expensive photographic or video evidence could have resolved the issue – often affected the efficiency and fairness of the violent offence hearings, to the point where miscarriages of justice very likely were made.

Jones (2000: ch.10) provides an overview of the literature on the effectiveness of different approaches to punishing violence. Jones shows that most people do not have the opportunity to address and change their offending behaviour until after criminal conviction (ibid: 160). Jones argues that cognitive-behavioural approaches to treating violent offenders have largely replaced psychoanalytical approaches, which are based around psychiatrists counselling individual offenders. He claims that there were two main reasons for this change. Firstly, psychoanalytical programmes could not be evaluated exactly enough to produce the clear evidence on re-offending rates which politicians want. Secondly, cognitive-behavioural programmes were based around the idea of blaming offenders for their voluntary conduct, rather than implying that offenders were not fully responsible for their actions, as psycho-analytical work tended to do. Jones goes on to say that cognitive-behavioural programmes have been shown to work best for minor offenders rather than serious ones (ibid: 165–6) and points to alternative forms of treatment, such as the intensive group therapy used in HMP Grendon Underwood, which has been shown to reduce re-offending even with serious violent offenders.

Burney argues that punishing racist offenders harshly has a very limited effect – not only in the sense of the mixed evidence on how well deterrence works (von Hirsch et al. 1999)but also in the sense that so few perpetrators of racial violence are actually convicted for their behaviour. Hall (2013) supports this view. He argues strongly that it is unrealistic to expect the police to tackle violent racism on their own. While not arguing that any method guarantees to change the community-based attitudes that express themselves in racist violence (Sibbitt 1997), Hall reviews the evidence on community-based approaches to changing behaviour and concludes that, based on experience in the USA, they are capable of making more of a difference than changes in police or sentencing policy. Hall emphasises the role of education in changing racist attitudes at a young age, in terms of changing the teaching curriculum and training teachers to tackle racist behaviour that could lead to violence later. This is a powerful message that there should be more to tackling racist violence than criminal justice alone.

Study exercise 6.8

Read the account of the public health approach taken to responding to knife-related violence in Scotland in Younge and Barr (2017). Name three initiatives that you think would be important in introducing a public health approach to tackling violence. What role(s) would the criminal justice process play in making such an initiative work?

Conclusions: linking discussion to the roadmap theories

The framework for the legal response to non-fatal violence in England dates back to 1861. Horder (1994) and Jefferson (2012) have criticised the non-fatal assault framework, in terms of how the law splits offences up from one another, and the uneven relationship between the blame attached to each offence, the harm caused by each offence, and the punishments available. For example, ABH has the same maximum penalty as s.20 GBH, when they are arguably not only different in terms of seriousness of harm but also different types of offences. Jefferson proposes four new offences of intentionally and recklessly committing serious and non-serious harm, and the Law Commission has also recently set out proposals for simplifying and clarifying the law (Gibson 2016).

In the law on assaults we can see risk management roadmap theories of managing the danger caused to society by harassment which could lead to more physical violence later – for example, *Ireland; Burstow* criminalising psychiatric assault, or the recent wide-ranging harassment and stalking offences. However, these developments do not change the problem of the overall framework of non-fatal violent offences. It could be argued that the best explanation for why the law has not been reformed is the radical roadmap theory. This can be seen in terms of maintenance of the decision-making power of those who are powerful enough to be able to develop the law, while hiding the social and political decisions which are a necessary part of interpreting old-fashioned legal words such as 'inflict' and 'bodily harm'.

In terms of the defence of consent, the law has maximised its own power by reserving the discretion to decide when the defence is available in different contexts. On the one hand, there is a deterministic roadmap approach, interfering with a person's freedom to do what they want to with their bodies. This approach is visible in cases where violence occurs during consensual sex, such as *Brown* (Giles 1994), *Boyea* and *Emmett*, as well as in the recent non-sexual harm case of *BM*. Such an approach fails to consider the experiences of those who choose to be involved in these types of behaviour (Cowan 2011). The law may say that it is trying to protect vulnerable people from harm in making decisions like *Brown* (Edwards 1996), but evidence that it succeeds in this aim is hard to find. The same deterministic approach is evident where D has obtained consent to harm through fraud by passing on a sexually trans-mitted disease to V without telling V they have the disease, after the decisions in *Dica* and *Konzani*. The law has moved towards risk management in this area, spreading fear of HIV/AIDS while failing to acknowledge the social reality of people who are aware of the risk of contracting sexually transmitted diseases but choose not to protect themselves against this risk (Weait 2007). Weait's argument that prosecutions for sexual GBH discriminate against social groups labelled by the powerful as 'dangerous', such as gay and bisexual men and sub-Saharan African immigrants, is evidence for the combination of radical, socially discriminatory, power-based theories and risk management theories in the law in practice.

On the other hand, the law has taken a much more liberal roadmap approach to the issue of consent to injury while playing sports. Perhaps one explanation for the law's approach here is that playing sports has stereotypically been seen as something which is done by men in society (e.g. Williams and Taylor 1994: 215–6) and that it is therefore not appropriate for the law to become involved with 'natural' masculine activities, since it generally approves of them. Gunn and Ormerod (1995) reviewed the evidence for and against boxing being legal and concluded that, given the extensive medical evidence on increased chances of serious brain damage and other injuries for boxers (ibid: 193–6), boxing could not be said to be in the 'public interest'. *Barnes* gives the courts maximum discretion to decide on the presence or absence of consent to the risk of sport-related injury, while making it clear that criminalisation will be the exception rather than the rule. Another example of the more liberal approach is the so-called horseplay cases such as *Aitken* and *Jones*, where the courts implied consent on very little evidence. Arguably, the approach taken in these cases reinforces societal views on how men should behave. Connell (1987) has claimed that there is a 'hegemonic masculinity' in society which expects men to behave in a macho and violent way and that this culture can be linked to the fact that men currently commit the vast majority of violent crime, at least on the basis of available statistics.

Given the chaotic and outdated nature of criminal law in this area, criminal justice agencies have had to make sense of the response to violence largely by themselves. Clarkson et al. (1994) and Cretney and Davis (1995) provide evidence of risk management concerns influencing the police's response to different types of violence in terms of the police taking into account how likely a victim is to assist criminal justice throughout the police and court process when deciding whether or not to investigate a case. Cretney and Davis (1995) found that the CPS routinely reduced initial police assault charges to lesser offences but only did so to make the process of proving legal guilt easier and to increase the chances of conviction. This could be viewed as a risk management-based attitude that considered prosecution and punishment for 'something' to be better than allowing a defendant to go free on the original charge. It is interesting that Fielding (2006) found that attempts by professional court agencies to make their work more efficient, such as the privatisation of prison escort services bringing defendants to court, actually made the court response to violence less efficient in reality.

It is also useful to think in terms of how and why criminal justice does *not* respond to some types of violence as effectively as other types. Stanko (1994) argues that the idea of individuals committing violent acts in public spaces, such as alcohol-related street violence (Hobbs et al. 2005), heavily influences criminal justice's understanding of violence in general. In a risk management roadmap approach, violence which does not fit in with this stereotype is seen as being 'low risk' and is responded to leniently; violence which is public and seen as a threat to public order is responded to more harshly.

Stanko's approach might explain why the rate of custodial sentences given for violence generally has increased in recent years, as the public fear of violence increases. However, it might also explain the problems experienced by criminal justice in dealing effectively with violence against vulnerable victims. Criminal justice has recently tried to compensate for its traditional ignorance of the impact of violence against vulnerable groups, such as victims of domestic violence. However, changes to police and CPS practice in this area have been slow to take effect. This suggests that risk-based perceptions blend together with radical, power-based, socially excluding ideas about who is most deserving of help as a victim of assault – ideas that stereotype and devalue those whom criminal justice does not always view as deserving victims, such as women and ethnic minorities.

Such ideas give a distorted picture of the true social harm caused by violence, in a wide range of contexts. As well as the scenarios discussed in this chapter, there is also the stereotyping of young people as criminals which ignores their frequent violent victimisation (Loader 1996; Brown 2005: ch.5), and criminology's traditional ignorance of the impact of violence which is caused by governments, both during and outside war, around the world (Cohen 2001; Ruggiero 2006). Between them, criminal law and criminal justice seem to offer the worst of both worlds in responding to the reality of social harm caused by violence. The new laws introduced to combat these significant harms have been designed and interpreted too widely, to punish (in some cases) those who do not deserve to be punished – but the criminal justice response has remained too narrow in practice to offer a holistic and fully effective response to reducing violence.

Key points

- The law on violence in England is based around outdated legislation from 1861 and is conceptually vague and confused as a result
- The availability of consent as a defence to violence is inconsistent and based around moralistic and biased assumptions about acceptable behaviour
- Criminal justice has struggled to respond effectively to the full range of harms caused by violence, especially violence against vulnerable social groups
- The radical and risk management roadmap theories best explain the current shape of the legal and criminal justice response to violence, but other roadmap theories are also important, such as the liberal and deterministic theories

Further reading

Chakraborti, N., and Garland, J. (2015), *Hate Crime: Impact, Causes and Responses* (2nd ed.). London: Sage.

Hoyle, C. (1998), *Negotiating Domestic Violence: Police, Criminal Justice and Victims*. Oxford: OUP.

Ormerod, D., and Laird, K. (2018), *Smith, Hogan and Ormerod's Criminal Law* (15th ed.): ch.16. Oxford: OUP.

Ray, L. (2018), *Violence and Society* (2nd ed.). London: Sage.

Stanko, E.A. (2003), 'Introduction: Conceptualising the Meanings of Violence', in Stanko, E.A. (ed.), *The Meanings of Violence*. London: Routledge.

References

Barnish, M. (2004), *Domestic Violence: A Literature Review*. London: HM Inspectorate of Probation.

Bowling, B. (1999), *Violent Racism: Victimisation, Policing and Social Context*. Oxford: Clarendon.

Bowling, B., and Phillips, C. (2002), *Racism, Crime and Justice*. Harlow: Longman.

Brennan, I. (2016), 'Night-Time Economies, Victims and Victimisation', in Corteen, K., Morley, S., Taylor, P., and Turner, J. (eds.), *A Companion to Crime, Harm and Victimisation*. Bristol: Policy Press.

Brown, S. (2005), *Understanding Youth and Crime: Listening to Youth?* (2nd ed.). Maidenhead: Open University Press.

Burney, E. (2003), 'Using the Law on Racially Aggravated Offences', *Criminal Law Review*: 28–36.

Burney, E., and Rose, G. (2002), *Racist Offences: How Is the Law Working?* Home Office Research Study No.244. London: Home Office.

Chakraborti, N., and Garland, J. (2015), *Hate Crime: Impact, Causes and Responses* (2nd ed.). London: Sage.

Chibnall, S. (1977), *Law and Order News*. London: Tavistock.

Clarkson, C.M.V., Cretney, A., Davis, G., and Shepherd, J.P. (1994), 'Assault: The Relationship Between Seriousness, Criminalisation and Punishment', *Criminal Law Review*: 4–20.

Cohen, S. (2001), *States of Denial: Knowing About Atrocities and Suffering*. Cambridge: Blackwell.

Cohen, S. (2002), *Folk Devils and Moral Panics* (3rd ed.). London: Routledge.

Connell, R.W. (1987), *Gender and Power: Society, the Person and Sexual Politics*. Cambridge: Polity Press.

Cook, D., Burton, M., Robinson, A., and Vallely, C. (2004), *Evaluation of Specialist Domestic Violence Courts/Fast Track Systems*. London: Crown Prosecution Service/Department of Constitutional Affairs.

Cowan, S. (2011), 'Criminalizing SM: Disavowing the Erotic, Instantiating Violence', in Duff, R.A., Farmer, L., Marshall, S.E., Renzo, M., and Tadros, V. (eds.), *The Structures of the Criminal Law*. Oxford: OUP.

Cretney, A., and Davis, G. (1995), *Punishing Violence*. London: Routledge.

Cretney, A., and Davis, G. (1997), 'Prosecuting Sexual Assault: Victims Failing Courts, or Courts Failing Victims?' *Howard Journal of Criminal Justice*, **36**(2): 146–57.

Dobash, R.E., and Dobash, R.P. (1992), *Women, Violence and Social Change*. London: Routledge.

Dutton, K. (2016), 'Domestic Violence, Victims and Victimisation', in Corteen, K., Morley, S., Taylor, P., and Turner, J. (eds.), *A Companion to Crime, Harm and Victimisation*. Bristol: Policy Press.

Edwards, S.S.M. (1989), *Policing "Domestic" Violence: Women, the Law and the State*. London: Sage.

Edwards, S.S.M. (1996), *Sex and Gender in the Legal Process*. London: Blackstone Press.

Fielding, N. (2006), *Courting Violence: Offences Against the Person Cases in Court*. Oxford: Clarendon.

Fryer, P. (1984), *Staying Power*. London: Pluto Press.

Gayle, D. (2017), 'Arthur Collins Jailed for "Despicable" Acid Attack in London Nightclub', *The Guardian*, Tuesday 19 December. Available online at: www.theguardian.com/uk-news/2017/dec/19/arthur-collins-jailed-for-acid-attack-in-london-nightclub. Accessed 16 May 2019.

Genders, E. (1999), 'Reform of the Offences Against the Person Act: Lessons from the Law in Action', *Criminal Law Review*: 689–701.

Gibson, M.J.R. (2016), 'Getting Their "Act" Together? Implementing Statutory Reform of Offences Against the Person', *Criminal Law Review*: 597–617.

Giles, M. (1994), '*R v Brown*: Consensual Harm and the Public Interest', *Modern Law Review*, **57**(1): 101–11.

Gunn, M.J., and Ormerod, D. (1995), 'The Legality of Boxing', *Legal Studies*, **15**(2): 181–203.

Hall, N. (2013), *Hate Crime* (2nd ed.). Abingdon: Routledge.

Hanmer, J., and Griffiths, S. (2001), 'Effective Policing', in Taylor-Browne, J. (ed.), *What Works in Reducing Domestic Violence?* London: Whiting and Birch.

Hill, A. (2016), 'Police Failing to Use New Law Against Domestic Abuse', *The Guardian*, Wednesday 31 August. Available online at: www.theguardian.com/society/2016/aug/31/police-failing-to-use-new-law-against-coercive-domestic-abuse. Accessed 16 May 2019.

HM Inspectorate of Constabulary and HM Crown Prosecution Service Inspectorate (2017), *Living in Fear – the Police and CPS Response to Harassment and Stalking*. Available online at: www.justiceinspectorates.gov.uk/hmicfrs/wp-content/uploads/living-in-fear-the-police-and-cps-response-to-harassment-and-stalking.pdf. Accessed 13 May 2019.

Hobbs, D., Hadfield, P., Lister, S., and Winlow, S. (2005), *Bouncers: Violence and Governance in the Night-Time Economy*. Oxford: OUP.

Home Office (2018), *Hate Crime, England and Wales, 2017–18*. Statistical Bulletin No.20/18. Available online at: https://assets.publishing.service.gov.uk/government/uploads/system/uploads/attachment_data/file/748598/hate-crime-1718-hosb2018.pdf. Accessed 16 May 2019.

Horder, J. (1994), 'Rethinking Non-Fatal Offences Against the Person', *Oxford Journal of Legal Studies*, **14**(3): 335–51.

Hoyle, C. (1998), *Negotiating Domestic Violence: Police, Criminal Justice, and Victims*. Oxford: OUP.

Jefferson, M. (2012), 'Offences Against the Person: Into the 21st Century', *Journal of Criminal Law*, **76**(6): 472–92.

Jones, S. (2000), *Understanding Violent Crime*. Buckingham: Open University Press.

Loader, I. (1996), *Youth, Policing and Democracy*. London: Palgrave Macmillan.

McConville, M., Sanders, A., and Leng, R. (1991), *The Case for the Prosecution: Police Suspects and the Construction of Criminality*. London: Routledge.

Ministry of Justice (2019), *Criminal Justice System Statistics Quarterly, September 2018 – Overview Tables*. Available online via: https://assets.publishing.service.gov.uk/government/uploads/system/uploads/attachment_data/file/780613/overview-tables-sept-2018.ods. Accessed 21 March 2019.

Moran, L.J. (1998), 'Laskey v United Kingdom: Learning the Limits of Privacy', *Modern Law Review*, **61**(1): 77–84.

ONS (2018), *Domestic Abuse in England and Wales, Year Ending March 2018*. Available online at: www.ons.gov.uk/peoplepopulationandcommunity/crimeandjustice/bulletins/domesticabuseinenglandandwales/yearendingmarch2018. Accessed 13 May 2019.

ONS (2019), *Crime in England and Wales, Year Ending March 2019*. Available online at: www.ons.gov.uk/peoplepopulationandcommunity/crimeandjustice/bulletins/crimeinenglandandwales/yearendingmarch2019. Accessed 21 March 2019.

Ormerod, D., and Laird, K. (2018), *Smith, Hogan and Ormerod's Criminal Law* (15th ed.). Oxford: OUP.

Pathé, M., and Mullen, P.E. (1997), 'The Impact of Stalkers on Their Victims', *British Journal of Psychiatry*, **170**(1): 12–17.

Ray, L. (2018), *Violence and Society* (2nd ed.). London: Sage.

Ray, L., Smith, D.B., and Wastell, L. (2003), 'Understanding Racist Violence', in Stanko, E.A. (ed.), *The Meanings of Violence*. London: Routledge.

Reiner, R. (2010), *The Politics of the Police* (4th ed.). Oxford: OUP.

Ruggiero, V. (2006), *Understanding Political Violence*. Maidenhead: Open University Press.

Sibbitt, R. (1997), *The Perpetrators of Racial Harassment and Racial Violence*. Home Office Research Study No.176. London: Home Office.

Sivarajasingam, V., Page, N., Green, G., Moore, S., and Shepherd, J. (2019), *Violence in England and Wales in 2018: An Accident and Emergency Perspective*. Cardiff: Cardiff University Crime and Security Research Institute.

Stanko, E.A. (1990), *Everyday Violence*. London: Unwin Hyman.

Stanko, E.A. (1994), 'Challenging the Problem of Men's Individual Violence', in Newburn, T., and Stanko, E.A. (eds.), *Just Boys Doing Business? Men, Masculinities and Crime*. London: Routledge.

Stanko, E.A. (2001), 'The Day to Count: Reflections on a Methodology to Raise Awareness of the Impact of Domestic Violence in the UK', *Criminal Justice*, **1**(2): 215–26.

Stanko, E.A. (2003), 'Introduction: Conceptualising the Meanings of Violence', in Stanko, E.A. (ed.), *The Meanings of Violence*. London: Routledge.

Stanko, E.A. (2007), 'Lessons About Violence', *Criminal Justice Matters*, **66**: 32–3.

Sumner, C. (ed.) (1997), *Violence, Culture and Censure*. London: UCL Press.

von Hirsch, A., Bottoms, A.E., Burney, E., and Wikstrom, P.-O. (1999), *Criminal Deterrence and Sentencing Severity*. Oxford: Hart.

Weait, M. (2007), *Intimacy and Responsibility: The Criminalisation of HIV Transmission*. London: Routledge.

Williams, J., and Taylor, R. (1994), 'Boys Keep Swinging: Masculinity and Football Culture in England', in Newburn, T., and Stanko, E.A. (eds.), *Just Boys Doing Business? Men, Masculinities and Crime*. London: Routledge.

Younge, G., and Barr, C. (2017), 'How Scotland Reduced Knife Deaths Among Young People', *The Guardian*, Sunday 3 December. Available online at: www.theguardian.com/membership/2017/dec/03/how-scotland-reduced-knife-deaths-among-young-people. Accessed 16 May 2019.

Chapter 7

Homicide

Chapter aims

After reading Chapter 7, you should be able to understand:

- The actus reus and mens rea required for murder
- The actus reus and mens rea required for voluntary manslaughter
- The actus reus and mens rea required for the different forms of involuntary manslaughter
- What other forms of homicide are in criminal law
- How homicide law is enforced in criminal justice practice
- How the evidence on the response to homicide in criminal law and criminal justice fits in with the roadmap theories introduced in Chapter 1

Introduction

Chapter 7 discusses the range of offences which involve unlawful killing, or homicide, in criminal law in England and Wales. The law will then be considered within the specific framework of its application in criminal justice practice. The chapter will examine the unlawful killing offences, starting with murder, moving on to voluntary manslaughter, then the different types of involuntary manslaughter, and finally other forms of homicide created and defined by statute law.

Homicide: the law

Murder

The actus reus for murder has a common law definition in criminal law in England, which dates back several hundred years. This definition is the unlawful killing of a human being, caused by another human being, under the Queen's peace (Child and Ormerod 2017: 147). All of the criminal homicide offences have these actus reus requirements. It is the mens rea requirements that separate the individual offences from one another. 'Unlawful killing' simply means any death that the law considers to be unlawful. 'Human being' means any person who is alive. *Attorney-General's Reference (No. 3 of 1994)* [1997] 3 WLR 421 decided that foetuses who are still in their mothers' wombs are not 'human beings' until after they are born – although those who kill an unborn child could still be guilty of the offence of child destruction under the Infant Life (Preservation) Act 1929. 'Causation' shows that both factual and legal causation are required. Finally, 'under the Queen's (or King's) peace' means killings that do not take place during wartime. *Adebolajo* [2014] EWCA Crim 2779 emphasised that 'under the King's/Queen's peace' referred to the status of the victim as a non-participant in war at the time of their death: the fact that the offender regarded themselves as being a soldier was irrelevant.

The mens rea for murder is 'malice aforethought'. This is the intention to either kill or do grievous bodily harm, shown by *Cunningham* [1982] AC 566. Intention here means the same as it does generally in criminal law.

Voluntary manslaughter

The actus reus and mens rea of voluntary manslaughter are exactly the same as those for murder (discussed earlier). Voluntary manslaughter is an offence of murder plus one of four defences which can only be used for murder – diminished responsibility, loss of control, infanticide, and suicide pact. If successfully used, these reduce a charge of murder to a charge of voluntary manslaughter.

Diminished responsibility

The current law on the defence of diminished responsibility is contained in section 52 of the Coroners and Justice Act 2009, which amended the earlier defence definition in section 2 of the Homicide Act 1957. It is the defence's role to prove that the defence applies, on the balance of probabilities. D can use the diminished responsibility defence if they committed murder or were complicit in murder, and, at the time of the murder, they were suffering from an abnormality of mental functioning, which:

- Arose from a recognised medical condition;
- Substantially impaired D's ability to either i) understand the nature of their conduct ii) form a rational judgment or iii) exercise self-control, and;
- Provides a causal explanation for D's role in the killing.

A medically recognised condition, and medical evidence, is required in order for the diminished responsibility defence to be successful (*Bunch* [2013] EWCA Crim 2498). *Dowds* [2012] EWCA Crim 281 shows that criminal law will not accept all recognised medical conditions (acute voluntary intoxication did not qualify as a medically recognised condition here). This does not prevent a jury from finding that although D was voluntarily intoxicated at the time of the killing, another recognised medical condition which D had caused a substantial impairment and caused the killing (*Dietschmann* [2003] 1 AC 1209, *Stewart* [2009] EWCA Crim 593).

Medical evidence is also essential for proving that there is a 'substantial impairment' to D's ability to do one of the things listed previously. The existence of such a substantial impairment (meaning an important or serious degree of impairment according to *Golds* [2016] UKSC 61) is a question for the jury. However, the jury should not ignore expert evidence unless there is a rational reason for doing so (*Brennan* [2014] EWCA Crim 2387). If there is an uncontested expert medical opinion that substantial impairment exists, then the judge must direct the jury to allow the diminished responsibility defence unless the prosecution has laid down criteria for the jury's rejection of the expert evidence (*Golds*). In *Conroy* [2017] EWCA Crim 81, the Court of Appeal stated that in terms of the ability to form a rational judgment, a court should take into consideration the process of thought as well as the outcome, meaning that the jury needs to consider D's relevant circumstances before and after the killing. In *Blackman* [2017] EWCA Crim 190 the Court of Appeal said that an ability to exercise self-control can be present even if no loss of self-control is externally visible.

Study exercise 7.1

Should criminal law automatically exclude anyone who has become voluntarily intoxicated from using the diminished responsibility defence, even if they have a recognised mental condition causing a substantial impairment?

Loss of control

Sections 54 and 55 of the Coroners and Justice Act 2009 define the current defence of loss of control, abolishing the previous defence of provocation under the 1957 Homicide Act (Norrie 2010: 275). Under the 2009 law, a jury can consider allowing the loss of control defence if there is evidence of all three criteria listed next applying (*Dawes* [2013] EWCA Crim 322):

- D's acts and omissions in committing murder or being complicit in the commission of murder resulted from D's loss of self-control;
- The loss of self-control had a qualifying trigger. The trigger can be *either* D's fear of serious violence from V against D or another person, *or* a thing or things done or said to D which constituted circumstances of an extremely grave character, and caused D to have a justifiable sense of being seriously wronged. Exceptions to these triggers (excluding use of the defence) occur where D has provoked the situation leading to the use of the defence, and where things said or done constituted sexual infidelity, if this is the only trigger being relied on by D (*Clinton* [2012] EWCA Crim 2).
- A person of D's gender and age, with a normal degree of tolerance and self-restraint and in the circumstances of D, would have reacted in the same or a similar way. 'Circumstances' here means any factor which does not only apply to D's ability to exercise self-control (*Asmelash* [2013] EWCA Crim 157). In other words, beyond age and gender, D's characteristics can only be considered if D was actually provoked about those characteristics.

Dawes requires trial judges to consider in detail whether there is evidence of either of the qualifying triggers applying. If there is none, the judge should exclude the defence from the jury's consideration. *Gurpinar* [2015] EWCA Crim 178 shows that the judge in a case where the loss of control defence is raised must be sure that there is enough evidence to meet each of the three stages of the defence test, which requires detailed analysis of the evidence. This case also shows that judges must remember that juries might come to a different conclusion on the evidence than the judge themselves. Ultimately, it is up to the jury to decide whether to allow the defence.

Study exercise 7.2

Using books and journal articles that discuss the 2009 definition of the loss of control defence, find three differences between the pre-2009 law and the post-2009 law.

Infanticide

Infanticide is defined by the Infanticide Act 1938 (s.1(1)). It applies only where a mother causes the death of her child who is under one year old, by act or omission (i.e. has the actus reus and mens rea for murder). At the time of the killing, the balance of her mind must be disturbed due to not having recovered from birth, or because of the effects of lactation after birth. If the jury accepts this defence, the offence is punished as voluntary manslaughter. We can classify infanticide as an offence in its own right or as a defence to murder.

Study exercise 7.3

Does the infanticide defence need to be reformed? If so, how?

Suicide pact

S.4 of the Homicide Act 1957 defines the suicide pact defence. It covers cases where D and V have agreed to a suicide pact (i.e. an agreement that both of them will kill themselves while intending to do so), and D kills V with the actus reus and mens rea for murder under that agreement. Where this has happened, D is guilty of voluntary manslaughter, not murder. However, if D does an act capable of assisting or encouraging V to commit suicide or attempt to commit suicide themselves, with the intent of assisting or encouraging V's suicide or attempted suicide, D is guilty of assisting a suicide under the Coroners and Justice Act section 59. There is no defence of euthanasia in criminal law in England. Prosecution for the assisting suicide offence must be authorised by the Director for Public Prosecutions (*R (Pretty) v DPP* [2002] AC 800), who must also publish guidance in terms of factors for and against prosecution (*R (Purdy) v DPP* [2009] 3 WLR 403). The legalisation of euthanasia under any circumstances is seen as something for Parliament to decide upon in the future, and is not a matter for the courts (*R (Nicklinson) v Ministry of Justice* [2014] UKSC 38).

Involuntary manslaughter

Involuntary manslaughter has the same actus reus as murder and voluntary manslaughter (discussed earlier) but does not have the same mens rea. It is one general offence but includes three different types of manslaughter, each with its own actus reus and mens rea requirements.

Subjectively reckless manslaughter

To be guilty of subjectively reckless involuntary manslaughter, D must foresee the risk of V's serious injury or death as highly probable, and go on to run that risk unreasonably. Herring (2019: 160) points out that there is doubt about whether this type of involuntary manslaughter exists as an independent type of involuntary manslaughter, not least because the courts have never referred to it in a reported case (the only recent example was the report of *Lidar* (2000) 4 *Archbold News* 3).

Unlawful act manslaughter

There are four basic requirements which must be met to prove unlawful act manslaughter has occurred, as shown in *Goodfellow* (1986) 83 Cr App Rep 23. Firstly, D must have committed a crime. It should be noted that any crime is enough here – the crime does not have to be a violent one. A person cannot commit the offence by omission, though (*Lowe* [1973] QB 702). Some cases state that any voluntary unlawful act is enough to form the basis of the offence (*DPP v Newbury* [1977] AC 500 and *Mitchell* [1983] QB 741). Other cases state that D has to have the full mens rea for the base crime as well as the actus reus (as stated in *Lamb* [1967] 2 QB 981 and *Arobieke* [1988] Crim LR 314). If D has a defence to the base crime, they cannot be guilty of unlawful act manslaughter because there is no unlawful act (*Jennings* [1990] Crim LR 588). In *Dhaliwal* [2006] 2 Cr App Rep 348, the Court of Appeal decided that where D inflicts physical and/or psychological abuse on V, D can be liable for unlawful manslaughter if the illness causes V to commit suicide, but only where some kind of recognised psychiatric illness is caused.

Secondly, D's unlawful act must cause V's death. The normal rules about proving factual and legal causation apply here. Thirdly, D's unlawful act does not have to be 'directed at' the victim in the form of some kind of attack. As long as causation is present, D is still guilty. The cases of *Mitchell* (discussed earlier) and *Goodfellow* illustrate this principle.

Fourthly, D's unlawful act must be objectively dangerous. This means that the act must be such that all reasonable people would inevitably recognise the risk of some physical harm, although not necessarily serious physical harm (*Church* [1966] 1 QB 59). Whether or not D's act is dangerous is an objective test for the jury to decide. D's act can still be dangerous even if D does not see the risk themselves, as shown by *Ball* [1989] Crim LR 730, and no account is taken here of D's characteristics which might make them less able to foresee risk, such as young age or low IQ (*JF* [2015] EWCA Crim 351). The case of *JM and SM* [2012] EWCA Crim 2293 illustrated the fact that a reasonable person does not have to be able to foresee the exact type of harm or risk suf-fered by V. However, the dangerousness of what D does is judged according to the facts and circumstances that D would have reasonably known about at the time of the offence. So, in *Watson* [1989] 1 WLR 684, D's act was objec-tively dangerous and resulted in his conviction for unlawful act manslaughter (because D could see that V, whose house he was burgling, was old and frail). However, in *Dawson* (1985) 81 Cr App Rep 150, D's act was not objectively dangerous, so there was no unlawful act manslaughter (where D could not reasonably have known that V had a heart condition). The dangerousness of the act cannot be proved by adding together the behaviour of a group of Ds towards V, during the group public order offence of affray, for example (*Carey* [2006] Crim LR 842).

All of the four factors discussed earlier must be present before D can be convicted of unlawful act manslaughter. Dangerousness and causation have to be proved in each case (*Carey*).

Study exercise 7.4

Read the case of *Carey*. Would you have convicted the defendants of unlawful act manslaughter in this case?

Gross negligence manslaughter

The three legal requirements for proving gross negligence manslaughter, which can either be done by act or by omission, are set out in *Adomako* [1995] 1 AC 171. Firstly, there must be a duty of care between D and V. The judge in this type of case can and should give the jury advice on whether a duty of care exists (*Evans* [2009] EWCA Crim 650). To decide this issue, the jury has to use the basic principles of negligence, which come from the civil law rather than criminal law – looking at the foreseeability that D's negli-gence would put V at risk, and the fairness of punishing D for what has hap-pened (*Adomako*). If the gross negligence manslaughter charge comes from D's omission, rather than an act, D must have had a legal responsibility to do what they failed to do. An example would be a landlord failing to check the safety of the gas fire in a tenant's property, resulting in the tenant's death from carbon monoxide poisoning, as happened in *Singh* [1999] Crim LR 582. *Wacker* [2003] QB 1207 shows that there can still be a duty of care between

D and V even where they are involved in a joint unlawful enterprise together. *Evans* stated that where D creates or contributes to a state of affairs that they know (or should know) is threatening V's life, a duty to act by taking reasonable steps to save V's life normally arises.

Secondly, there must be a gross breach of the duty of care between D and V. As *Adomako* shows, this is a question of fact for the jury to decide. The breach must be so bad, or fall so far below what could reasonably be expected of D in the circumstances, taking into account any specialist knowledge or skills that D has, that it deserves criminal punishment. As this is an objective test, it does not matter that D did not foresee the grossness of the breach in duty of care in what they did, as long as a reasonable person at the scene would have. *Misra* [2005] Crim LR 234 states that the grossness of the breach is proved if a reasonable person present at the scene of the offence would have foreseen an obvious and serious risk of death – only a risk of death is enough to prove the offence. *Misra* also decided that the gross negligence manslaughter offence did not breach Article 7 of the ECHR (the right to legal certainty).

Thirdly, the gross breach of the duty of care must have caused V's death. The normal principles of proving factual and legal causation apply again here.

Study exercise 7.5

Read the case of *Rudling* [2016] EWCA Crim 741. Would you have convicted the doctor of gross negligence manslaughter in this case? Give reasons for your answer.

Other forms of homicide

There are other types of homicide, which statute law has created. The first type – infanticide – has already been discussed because it is both a defence to murder under the Infanticide Act 1938 s.1(2) and a specific offence under s.1(1) of the same Act.

The next category is vehicular homicide. The Road Traffic Act 1988 ss.2 and 2A define the offence of causing death by dangerous driving. This offence is committed where D drives in a way that falls far below what would be expected of a competent and careful driver. It must be obvious to a competent and careful driver that driving in that way would be dangerous (s.2A(1)), or obvious to a competent and careful driver that driving the vehicle in its current state would be dangerous (s.2A(2)). S.2(A)(3) defines 'dangerous' as a danger of injury or serious damage to property. This offence depends on the objective standard of D's driving (or the condition of D's vehicle), rather than D's own mens rea – although circumstances which D actually knew about will be taken into account as well as circumstances which D should have known about when considering how low the standard of driving was.

The Road Traffic Act 1991 s.3 creates an offence of causing death by careless driving while under the influence of drink or drugs, so that D's alcohol level is over the legal limit for driving or D is unfit to drive due to intake of drugs, and D's driving is objectively careless on the facts.

S.20(1) of the Road Safety Act 2006 creates new offences of causing death by careless driving, and causing death while driving without insurance or while driving without a licence. The court judges the standard of driving objectively on the facts – no mens rea is required from D. There has been some uncertainty in the law about whether D is guilty of causing death while driving without a licence or without insurance if they are involved in a collision that was not their fault and were driving well at the time of the collision. *Williams* [2011] 1 WLR 588 stated that D was still guilty in this situation. However, *Hughes* [2013] 1 WLR 2461 reversed this decision and stated that D had to be at least partly at fault for the collision in order to be guilty. All of these offences also require proof of causation.

The Domestic Violence, Crime and Victims Act 2004 s.5(1) creates the new offence of causing or allowing the death of a child or vulnerable adult. If V dies because of an unlawful act or omission of someone who was a member of the same household as V, or who had frequent contact with V, and D was such a person at the time of that act, then D is guilty of the offence. In addition, at that time there must be a significant risk of serious physical harm being caused to V by the unlawful act of such a person. Finally, either D's act must cause V's death, or i) D was, or should have been, aware of the significant risk of harm, ii) D failed to take such steps as were reasonable to protect V from the risk, or iii) the act occurred in circumstances of the kind that D foresaw or should have foreseen.

The Corporate Manslaughter and Corporate Homicide Act 2007 updated the law on corporate homicide, where V's unlawful killing results from the actions and/or omissions of a company or organisation rather than from an individual's actions. Under s.1 of the Act, an organisation is guilty of this offence if the way in which its activities are managed or organised causes a person's death, and amounts to a gross breach of a relevant duty of care owed by the organisation to V. Section 2 gives guidance on when a judge is likely to find that a duty of care exists – for example, between employer and employee, or between business and customer. Section 2 also shows that an organisation breaches a duty of care by failing to perform according to the standards of a relevant reasonable organisation, where a substantial element of the breach is traceable to how the organisation's activities are managed or organised by its senior management. Sections 3 to 7 show where a duty of care cannot exist – through government policy decisions, some emergency services activities, and some probation and child protection activities. Section 8 gives guidance to juries about which factors to consider when deciding on the existence of a gross breach, such as the seriousness of the failure, the foreseeability of death, and the organisation's collective attitude towards health and safety issues.

Study exercise 7.6

How, if at all, would you change the current definition of corporate manslaughter in the Corporate Manslaughter and Corporate Homicide Act 2007?

Homicide and criminal justice

Murder and criminal justice

As Eisner (2017: 568) points out, homicide is unique among crimes in that its definition has remained relatively stable over time. In the year ending December 2018 in England and Wales, the police recorded 732 homicides, including murder, manslaughter, and infanticide offences, an increase of 6% compared with the previous year, and a continuation of an increasing trend in homicide over the past four years (ONS 2019a). Police statistics include all homicides in the same category. Forty percent of homicides involved a knife or sharp instrument (ibid.). Changes in the law's labelling of killings can easily distort homicide statistics. For example, the 96 deaths that occurred at Hillsborough in 1989 counted as manslaughters in the year ending March 2017, following the verdict of the Hillsborough Inquest in April 2016 (ONS 2019b). The Crime Survey for England and Wales relies on victims reporting the crimes committed against them, and so it cannot collect data on homicide.

It is crucial to think not only about what the homicide statistics include but also about what they leave out in terms of killing, and what this tells us about the ways in which criminal law regulates risk in society by labelling some killings as morally worse than others. There are, in fact, several categories of killing that are not included in the homicide statistics. Firstly, there is the category covering work-related killings. This includes such incidents as deaths in industrial incidents that happened due to breaches of health and safety legislation, which aims to maintain safe working conditions, among various other types. The Health and Safety Executive recorded 144 deaths at work in the UK in 2017–18 but also estimated 12,000 lung disease deaths connected with past exposure to asbestos at work (Health and Safety Executive 2018). None of these deaths is included in the homicide statistics.

Secondly, although driving offences causing death are recognised as forms of criminal killing, killings caused while driving are not included in the homicide statistics either. Thirdly, deaths in custody and during the course of arrest by the police are not included in the homicide statistics. Inquest, an organisation which monitors deaths in custody, state that in 2018, there were 160 deaths in prison which were not self-inflicted, 40 deaths in police custody or following contact with police, and two deaths of immigration detainees (Inquest Casework and Monitoring 2019). It is unclear how many of these deaths were due to unlawful behaviour from police and prison officers, although Inquest suspects that many of them were due to gross negligence or excessive institutional violence by these agencies. Finally, various other deaths are not counted in the homicide statistics because of uncertainty over whether they actually were homicides. These include bodies of homicide victims which are hidden or buried by their killers, missing persons who might have been the victims of homicide, and those who have died and been the subject of an inquest where the jury returned an open verdict (Brookman 2005: 20–2). Therefore, even a crime like homicide, which most would agree is morally wrong, has a socially and politically flexible definition.

Murder, at least in terms of how criminal law and criminal justice define it, is a rare offence. Despite the fact that the law on murder has changed little in recent times (Horder 2012), its scope as an offence remains contested, and this has implications for how often criminal justice has to deal with it. Some writers have argued that it is not fair to include those who kill intending grievous bodily harm within the category of murder (e.g. Mitchell 1999), which would reduce the number of murder cases to be processed by criminal justice. Moore (1997) would narrow the law even further by allowing only direct intent as mens rea for murder and excluding oblique intent. Others have argued for maintaining the current scope by including intention to inflict GBH within the mens rea for murder (e.g. Williams 1989; Horder 1997) and allowing juries to decide on whether to allow oblique intent as the mens rea for murder on moral grounds in individual cases (Duff 1990). A third approach favours increasing the scope of murder by including those who intend to create a risk of death (Pedain 2003), or those who act with 'wicked recklessness' as to death (Goff 1988).

It is perhaps unsurprising that there is so much debate about the scope of the offence of murder when, as D'Cruze et al. (2006) point out, the current legal concept of murder has such a wide scope. It covers everything from serial killings to 'mercy killings' like the case of *Inglis* [2011] 1 WLR 1110, where the defendant killed her son by injecting him with heroin after he had been involved in an accident that had left him in a coma with permanent disfiguring injuries. D'Cruze et al. (2006) also argue that media and political responses to murder make notorious murder cases such as the Moors Murders seem pathologically 'bad' and set apart from the rest of society, therefore appearing eviller.

The reality of the social context of murder, however, is very different from its public and media image. In the year to March 2018, 33% of male-on-female homicides involved a woman killed by her current or former partner, and alcohol and/or illicit drugs affected a third of suspects and a third of victims

(ONS 2019b). Dorling, meanwhile, shows that in the 1990s, the poorest people in society were 182% more likely to be murder victims than the richest (2004: 185). Even more disturbingly, he shows that the murder rate for those men born after 1965 in England and Wales is increasing as they get older, in a way which is not occurring for those men born in 1964 or before (ibid: 189). Dorling explains this effect by pointing to the exclusionary economic policies of the Thatcher government in the 1980s, which had the effect of creating recession and mass unemployment among the very poorest in society. Reiner (2007: 106–7) argues that there is a link between homicide rates and variations in political economy between countries. As such, countries with a neoliberal political economy (characterised by higher unemployment and social exclusion), such as England and Wales, generally have a higher rate of homicide than countries with a more social democratic political economy (characterised by stronger welfare systems and a smaller gap between rich and poor), such as Scandinavian countries.

Murder also poses particular problems for the criminal justice process. As Innes (2003) argues, the police investigating murder often have the problem of filtering out inaccurate or misleading information received from the public due to intensive media coverage of murder cases. Innes has also shown that the police investigate murder cases by 'socially constructing' the events surrounding the crime and then presenting their construction of events as 'facts', hiding the process of subjective interpretation which has produced their version of what has happened. The police investigation is organised in line with a standard 'process structure'. This structure has been shaped not only by criminal law governing the legal requirements of the offence of murder and the circumstances and evidence in each particular case but also by the organisation and values of the police itself. Later research by Brookman and Innes (2013) supports this view. Based on interviews with homicide detectives, Brookman and Innes found a range of measures by which the police evaluated the success of homicide investigations, including positive community impact, compliance with policy, and crime prevention as well as securing a legal conviction.

Court data on charges and convictions for murder illustrate the blurred boundaries between murder and other forms of homicide. Between April 2017 and March 2018, 277 men and women were charged with murder, but only 161 (58.1%) were convicted of murder; (17.7%) were acquitted on all charges (ONS 2019b).

The mandatory life sentence for murder is misleading. As Clarkson (2005: 214–15) points out, very few murderers spend the rest of their lives in prison. Only 63 prisoners were on 'whole life' orders in England and Wales at the end of March 2019, with a further three receiving treatment in secure hospitals (Ministry of Justice 2019). The number of life prisoners serving sentences for murder in England and Wales has increased significantly over time in England and Wales, from 58 in 1965 to 310 in 2002 (Shute 2004: 894). Mitchell and Roberts (2012) found that members of the public were often in favour of fixed-term sentences for murder, as a replacement for the mandatory life sentence. They also found a clear link between lack of public understanding of the reality of the frequency of murder, and of sentencing for murder, and a punitive attitude towards sentencing.

In all murder cases, the judge hearing the case has to set a minimum tariff under s.269 of the Criminal Justice Act 2003, and in line with the principles set out in Schedule 21 of the 2003 Act, as amended. This sets out four starting points for the sentencing of murder (Crewe et al. 2015: 256–7):

- 'Exceptionally serious cases' (e.g. the premeditated killing of two or more people) – whole life order;
- 'Particularly serious cases' (e.g. killing a police officer on duty) – 30 years;
- Use of a knife or other weapon in killing – 25 years (this guideline was introduced in 2010);
- All other cases – 15 years if the offender is aged 18 or older, 12 years if the offender is under age 18.

However, Schedule 21 also states that these starting points are only guidelines and that aggravating or mitigating factors can move a sentence up or down from the starting point which is closest to the circumstances of the case. Therefore, judges have a great deal more discretion over the sentencing of murder cases than the phrase 'mandatory life sentence' suggests. The average prison time served by prisoners given a life sentence for murder has increased in recent years, from 12.5 years in 2006 to 21.1 years by 2013 (Crewe et al. 2015: 260), and the percentage of life prisoners released by the Parole Board declined from 23% to 19% over the same time period (ibid: 261).

Study exercise 7.7

Using the Internet, find out about the facts of the case of the murder of Sophie Lancaster in Bacup on 11th August 2007. How long a minimum term would you have sentenced the two offenders to if you had been the judge in this case? On what reasons and principles would you base your decision? Was the minimum sentence on which you decided higher or lower than the minimum terms imposed by the trial judge in the actual case?

Voluntary manslaughter and criminal justice

Diminished responsibility and criminal justice

Although the 2009 Coroners and Justice Act reformed the diminished responsibility defence, there is still considerable academic debate about how fairly the defence operates. Mackay (2011) points out that the 2009 Act reformed the previous law by removing the vague references to the need for an abnormality of mind causing a substantial impairment of mental responsibility. As shown earlier, the 2009 Act instead requires a defined and provable medical condition that substantially impairs a person's ability to do one of a list of things, and actually caused that person to kill. Mackay (ibid.) therefore questions whether the defence is now too harsh on those who morally deserve to be able to use the defence but who do not meet these criteria.

Gibson (2011) questions the fairness of the post-2009 law on those suffering from genuine addiction and other serious mental illnesses such as schizophrenia, who may find it harder to prove substantial impairment or a causal link between their illness and the killing. This is a problematic issue, made worse by the evidence that judges often give inaccurate directions to juries about the applicability of the diminished responsibility defence (Wake 2010), and by juries' tendency to reject the defence if the prosecution contests medical evidence (Mackay 2010). Gibson (2017) has also argued that the recent decisions in *Conroy* and *Blackman* (discussed earlier) reduce the importance of expert medical, psychological, and psychiatric evidence in diminished responsibility trials. The argument is that these decisions represent an attempt by criminal justice to sideline important scientific evidence from the court process, with an increased risk of miscarriages of justice that likely results.

Mackay and Mitchell (2017) note the long-term trend of decreasing numbers of successful diminished responsibility claims, which the 2009 Act has not changed (ibid: 23). The most common successful diminished responsibility scenario in Mackay and Mitchell's study was a male perpetrator, using a knife to kill, receiving a hospital order as a sentence and having a diagnosis of schizophrenia. Mackay and Mitchell found a greater rate of cases where the diminished responsibility plea was contested and a higher rate of murder convictions in this type of case since the law changed in 2009 (ibid: 35).

Loss of control and criminal justice

The old provocation defence was the subject of fierce academic criticism. Horder (1992), for example, argued that the defence was assessed from a male perspective and based around outdated and sexist notions of challenges to male honour. McColgan (1993) also accused the old defence of sexism, citing cases of women who killed their husbands after years of violent abuse but who could not use the defence, and contrasting these cases with cases involving men who were allowed to use the defence after killing 'nagging' or departing female partners.

The question is whether the post-2009 law makes the law fairer for vulnerable groups whose circumstances create such a level of despair that killing is seen as being the only option. Norrie (2010), Edwards (2011) and Mitchell

(2011) are all sceptical about the removal of the need for a sudden and temporary loss of control in the 2009 law being able to do anything to help women who kill as the result of abuse. Others have been critical of the 2009 Act's failure to exclude all morally repugnant killings from qualifying triggers, such as honour killings (Clough 2016). The Act also does not provide a defence for killings that are more justifiable morally, such as mercy killings of loved ones who are terminally ill, in great pain, and begging to be allowed to die (Keating and Bridgeman 2012; Clough 2015). Herring (2011) also criticises the law for not acknowledging domestic violence as a factor causing a justifiable sense of being seriously wronged for the purposes of the loss of control defence. Baker and Zhao (2012) are similarly critical of the decision in *Clinton* to allow sexual infidelity as a qualifying trigger in some loss of control cases, despite the 2009 Act making it clear that it should not be such a trigger.

There is also evidence that men who kill their wives and use the defence of loss of control receive lighter sentences (less than five years' imprisonment on average) than men who kill in a non-domestic setting (where sentences normally start at five years) (Gibb 2005). Burton's (2003) research showed that the average sentence for men convicted of voluntary manslaughter in this way is between five- and seven-years' imprisonment.

The discussion so far has focussed on the subjective part of the test for loss of control, which requires a specified qualifying trigger. However, many writers have criticised the objective part of the test as well, which only allows age and gender to be considered when assessing the reasonableness of the loss of control. Norrie (2010) argues that this would not help an emotionally immature adult, for example, who might be morally entitled to use the defence but could not do so under the post-2009 law. Norrie also criticises the lack of moral evaluation of a person's conduct in the 2009 law due to the law's restriction of such a moral evaluation of factors about which the killer is provoked. Wells (2000) and Power (2006) have argued that criminal justice needs to reflect cultural differences between individuals in terms of their environment and place in society far more than this to ensure that justice is carried out. On the other hand, Macklem and Gardner (2001) argued that there was no need to take any more human characteristics into account in the loss of control test and that extending the test would effectively be accepting that violence against women was inevitable in society.

Study exercise 7.8

Horder (1992) and Wells (2000) argue that there should not be any loss of control defence to murder at all. Do you agree? Give reasons for your answer.

Infanticide and criminal justice

Infanticide is, as shown earlier, a defence to murder with a much narrower scope than either provocation or diminished responsibility. As a result, criminal justice rarely has to deal with infanticide cases. Mackay (1993) found that women who killed their children often received lenient sentences, either by being allowed to use infanticide as a defence and being given a community sentence, or by not being prosecuted at all. Men who killed their children, however, received an average custodial sentence of four and a half years, were not allowed to use the infanticide defence at all by the law, and have been stereotyped by the courts as being evil and calculated killers (Wilczynski 1997). Wilczynski and Morris (1993) argued that about half of the women convicted of infanticide were not suffering from any mental illness at all, and therefore claim that infanticide is being used to introduce socio-economic factors which may have contributed to the child's death (ibid: 35). They conclude that women who kill very young children are treated more leniently through the usage of the infanticide defence – but argue that this is the result of sexist stereotyping of women who kill as being 'mad' by criminal justice, due to equally sexist assumptions that 'normal' women are passive and caring and would never kill a young child.

Suicide pact and criminal justice

It is interesting to contrast the suicide pact defence, which reduces murder to manslaughter, with the approach of the Suicide Act 1961, which legalised suicide but introduced the offence of assisting the suicide of another, which carries a maximum penalty of 14 years' imprisonment. Where a mentally competent but physically paralysed patient wants to die but needs help from someone else to do so, criminal justice will not guarantee that it will not investigate and prosecute the helper for the offence of assisting a suicide under the Suicide Act 1961, as shown by the cases of *Pretty, Purdy,* and *Nicklinson* (all discussed earlier). Papadopoulou (2017) argued that senior judges are now much more in favour of allowing assisted dying in certain circumstances than previously, on the basis of the judgments in *Nicklinson*. Recent public surveys have also indicated support for legalised euthanasia under certain conditions (such as terminal illness), at levels of between 70% and 80% (Riddell et al. 2014). However, concerns remain over vulnerable social groups, such as the disabled or those with dementia, experiencing coercion to agree to assisted dying if it were made legal.

Involuntary manslaughter and criminal justice

The explanation of the law on the three different forms of involuntary manslaughter earlier in this chapter showed how wide this type of homicide is in criminal law. The boundaries between involuntary manslaughter and other offences are not clear because of the width of the offence. At the 'top end', there is considerable overlap between involuntary manslaughter and murder in terms of what defendants are convicted and punished for, an overlap which can be difficult to understand, especially for the relatives of victims of homicide (Blom-Cooper and Morris 2004). A key explanation for these results is the difficulty of proving intent to kill or do GBH. Brookman (2005: 12) argues that the decision to charge and convict of murder or manslaughter may reflect judgments about defendants' and victims' moral worth, tactical CPS judgments about the chances of securing a conviction, and the success of defences, rather than a clear-cut distinction between different classes of behaviour. Mitchell and Mackay's (2011) sample of 127 involuntary manslaughter convictions is further evidence of how much harmful behaviour and moral culpability this offence covers. Behaviour ranged from one punch or slap causing death, to driving a car deliberately at the victim. As a result, sentencing in their sample ranged from probation orders, right up to 11 cases where the court sentenced offenders to more than 10 years' imprisonment. Mitchell (2008) has argued that those who kill by punching their victim once should be guilty of a separate and lesser offence than manslaughter, to make involuntary manslaughter less broad.

The problems surrounding the offence of gross negligence manslaughter epitomise criminal justice's problems in addressing involuntary manslaughter generally. In Mitchell and Mackay's (2011) study, most cases involved unlawful act manslaughter, and gross negligence manslaughter cases were rare. Herring and Palser (2007) criticised the uncertainty in the definition of gross manslaughter and argued that this was likely to lead to an increase in the number of dropped CPS charges. Quick's (2006) study found that the CPS had wide-ranging power and discretion over the prosecution of gross negligence manslaughter cases involving medical misconduct and that prosecutions (and convictions) for this offence have increased since the mid-1990s. However, Quick also found extensive inconsistency between individual prosecutors in terms of when they felt that a defendant's negligence was 'gross' enough to be punished, and uncovered evidence suggesting racial and geographic bias in prosecutions. Quirk (2013) found an increase in the severity of sentencing for cases of gross negligence manslaughter involving doctors, surgeons, and anaesthetists, without any principled basis for such a trend. Like Quick, Quirk also found some evidence of covert racism in prosecution and sentencing patterns for the offence.

Further problems for gross negligence manslaughter have occurred in relation to corporate manslaughter. The use of corporate liability offences in criminal justice has attracted criticism from writers who think that these offences are not enforced and punished effectively (e.g. Tombs and Whyte 2007; cf. Hawkins 2002). The Corporate Manslaughter and Corporate Homicide Act 2007 introduced a new offence of corporate killing, which requires a gross breach of a duty of care at the senior management level to have been the substantial cause of death. Gobert (2008) sees the Act as being a more effective response to corporate killing than the previous law. However, he also pointed out several problems with the Act. Firstly, the offence does not include individual liability. Secondly, limiting liability to senior management wrongdoing still does not focus enough on systemic or cultural causes of corporate killing. Finally, the requirement for the DPP's consent to all prosecutions is likely to restrict the number of prosecutions.

Data from successful corporate manslaughter convictions since 2008 have shown that Gobert's fears were correct. As of 2017, there had been only 25 convictions for corporate manslaughter, almost all of which involved small companies rather than the large, complex organisations that the 2007 Act claimed to be targeting (Tombs 2016), and all involving one-off incidents rather than cases of industrial disease. The highest fine imposed was £700,000, against Baldwins Crane Hire in 2015 (BBC News 2015). In most cases, prosecutors dropped individual prosecutions of company directors for gross negligence manslaughter in return for the company's guilty plea to corporate manslaughter. Such plea-bargaining leaves a fine as the only punishment, arguably disregarding the interests of the victim's family in seeking justice for their loss, and the interests of society in preventing further corporate harm (Woodley 2013).

Study exercise 7.9

Using Internet search engines, read an account of what happened in the Grenfell Tower fire of 14th June 2017. In your own view, should this be a case of corporate killing under the Corporate Manslaughter and Corporate Homicide Act 2007? Do you think the current law would classify what happened as corporate killing?

Other forms of homicide and criminal justice

Legislative attitudes to causing death on the roads have become harsher in recent years, with the maximum penalties for causing death by dangerous driving and causing death by careless driving while under the influence of alcohol or drugs both being increased from 10 years' imprisonment to 14 years' imprisonment by the Criminal Justice Act 2003.

However, prosecutions for vehicle-related homicide are rare. In 2017, for example, 1,793 people were killed in vehicle-related incidents in the United Kingdom (Department for Transport 2018), but only 225 people were prosecuted for causing death by dangerous driving, and only 25 people were prosecuted for causing death by careless driving while 'under the influence' in England and Wales. The dangerous driving offence had an 84.9% conviction rate and a 91.1% rate of immediate custodial sentencing for those convicted, while the 'under the influence' offence had an 88% conviction rate and a 91% rate of immediate custodial sentencing for those convicted. The average custodial sentence was 56.9 months for the dangerous driving offence, and 67.4 months for the 'under the influence' offence, but nobody received the maximum sentence for either offence in 2017 (Ministry of Justice 2018).

Evidence suggests that the CPS has significant power and discretion over the prosecution of offenders for these offences (Cunningham 2005). The introduction of the causing death by careless driving offence has not led to dangerous driving cases being downgraded (Cunningham 2013). However, there is a tendency for defendants to be tried for vehicular homicide in the Crown Court, but then to plead guilty and receive a sentence that the magistrates' court could have passed in any case (Cammiss and Cunningham 2015). This is evidence that in sentencing terms, criminal justice is still reluctant to take action against those who cause death on the roads, despite the toughening of maximum penalties recently and the introduction of offences that require only negligence as mens rea. Corbett (2003) argues that the lenient criminal justice treatment of vehicle-related killing compared to other types of homicide is due to the central role that cars and car ownership play in society and the level of identification of the people who make decisions in criminal justice with the situations of offenders.

Herring (2007) was critical of the definition and operation of the offence of causing or allowing the death of a child or vulnerable adult. He argued persuasively that those convicted of this offence are likely to be women who are victims of domestic violence themselves and who have not received adequate support from the State. Morrison (2013) argues that there is no need for a 'domestic violence' defence since the law offers enough protection to prevent such victims from wrongful conviction. Conviction rates for this offence are remarkably low – only six people were convicted and sentenced for this offence in 2017 (Ministry of Justice 2018).

Study exercise 7.10

Draw up a list of three reasons why the law should treat all driving-related homicides as either murder or manslaughter, and three reasons why we should have specialist offences instead.

Conclusions: linking discussion to the roadmap theories

This chapter has shown that the legal and criminal justice responses to homicide, the 'ultimate crime' of taking someone else's life unlawfully, are more complicated than they first appear. Criminal law bases liability for murder, manslaughter, and other homicide offences on individual responsibility for the lethal harm caused, with apparently clear actus reus and mens rea labels for each offence. This suggests that the law on homicide centres on the liberal/due process roadmap model. Yet the inclusion of oblique intent as mens rea for murder, as well as the intention to do GBH rather than kill, indicates that the law wants to leave itself the room to make moral choices about who and who not to blame for murder, based on paternalistic or even power-based models (Norrie 2005).

This trend is particularly noticeable in terms of the types of killing which the law does not label as unlawful homicide. For example, the law will not intervene to make the killing of a foetus murder or manslaughter (Wells and Morgan 1991) but gives doctors extensive discretion over whether to continue to treat seriously ill or disabled patients, while only intervening to regulate this discretion in very rare cases (Wells 1989). The law also makes decisions based on patients' quality of life rather than individuals' wishes to allow certain death in cases like *Re A* (Huxtable 2002) but will not allow competent but incapacitated adults to enlist help to kill themselves, even on human rights grounds, in cases like *Pretty, Purdy,* and *Nicklinson.* The law on murder is therefore more selectively interventionist than it appears to be.

In terms of the criminal justice response to murder, again it presents as based on liberal responsibility ideas, with an apparently mandatory sentence of life imprisonment. This view hides the discretion criminal justice agencies have in investigating murder, downgrading cases from murder to manslaughter, and setting the minimum sentence tariff. The evidence discussed previously suggests that criminal justice takes an individualistic, risk-based approach to investigating, prosecuting, sentencing, and punishing murder, even though there is more discretion in this process than there appears to be. This analysis shows how criminal justice's individualist, risk-based approach to responding to murder ignores the social harm done by economic policies at the government level (Dorling 2004).

Similarly, the legal and criminal justice response to manslaughter (both voluntary and involuntary) portrays itself as 'black and white' but hides a series of moral assumptions. The defence of diminished responsibility downplays the deterministic model of allowing expert medical evidence through recent legal decisions maximising legal discretion. It operates in practice in a narrow, risk management model. The results are the exclusion of deserving claims, and the contestation of evidence of genuine mental illness in many cases. The rejection of the deterministic, medical model in practice involves the overlooking of scientific evidence on mental illness based on accepted sources such as the Diagnostic and Statistical Manual of Mental Disorders, published by the American Psychiatric Association (Harper 2014), and the

International Classification of Diseases, published by the World Health Organization (Twinley 2014). The rebranded loss of control defence did little to protect female victims of abuse. Instead, it prioritises male anger in a way that reinforces unequal power relations, ignoring the reality of domestic violence and limiting the moral assessment of the circumstances of those who claim this defence.

The scope of involuntary manslaughter is so wide, and so based around the idea of morally punishing the outcome of death rather than the individual's blameworthiness in causing that death, that it clearly goes against the liberal idea of the law punishing based on individual responsibility and chosen outcomes. The risk management roadmap explains the law's approach more effectively. Yet in areas of social harm where a risk-based approach could more easily be justified – such as vehicular homicide and corporate homicide – the law and criminal justice refuse to label a great deal of blameworthy activity as homicide, and prosecute and convict perpetrators of harm very rarely. Conviction rates for these offences are high, prosecution rates are low, and average sentences are far below the maximum allowed. Again, the liberal and risk-assessment approach presented by the law hides the reality of criminal justice's enforcement – and again, this softer response stems from the social respectability and importance of car ownership and the greater moral sympathy with vehicle offenders that this cultural factor creates.

Key Points

- The legal definition of murder in England dates back to at least the 17th century, while specific defences to murder now have statutory definitions most recently updated in 2009
- Manslaughter is also a common law defence, whose scope has expanded through redefinition in case law, and also through new forms of statutory homicide covering driving and corporate offences
- The criminal justice response to both murder and manslaughter varies considerably depending on the social characteristics of the offence, the defendant and the victim, and is often different from public and media perceptions of it
- The liberal roadmap theory is the one which best explains the response to homicide as it is presented by criminal law and criminal justice themselves – but in reality, the risk management and radical roadmap theories explain the responses more accurately

Further reading

D'Cruze, S., Walklate, S., and Pegg, S. (2006), *Murder*. Cullompton: Willan.

Innes, M. (2003), *Investigating Murder: Detective Work and the Police Response to Criminal Homicide*. Oxford: OUP.

Loveless, J., Allen, M., and Derry, C. (2018), *Complete Criminal Law* (6th ed.): chs.6 and 7. Oxford: OUP.

Mackay, R.D., and Mitchell, B. (2017), 'The New Diminished Responsibility Plea in Operation: Some Initial Findings', *Criminal Law Review*: 18–35.

Reed, A., and Bohlander, M. (eds.), *Loss of Self Control and Diminished Responsibility*. Farnham: Ashgate.

References

Baker, D.J., and Zhao, L.X. (2012), 'Contributory Qualifying and Non-Qualifying Triggers in the Loss of Self-Control Defence: A Wrong Turn on Sexual Infidelity', *Journal of Criminal Law*, **76**(3): 254–75.

BBC News (2015), 'Baldwins Crane Hire Fined Over Death of Lindsay Easton', 22 December. Available online at: www.bbc.co.uk/news/uk-england-lancashire-35158578. Accessed 23 May 2019.

Blom-Cooper, L., and Morris, T. (2004), *With Malice Aforethought: A Study of the Crime and Punishment for Homicide*. Oxford: Hart.

Brookman, F. (2005), *Understanding Homicide*. London: Sage.

Brookman, F., and Innes, M. (2013), 'The Problem of Success: What Is a "Good" Homicide Investigation?' *Policing and Society*, **23**(3): 292–310.

Burton, M. (2003), 'Sentencing Domestic Homicide Upon Provocation: Still "Getting Away with Murder"', *Feminist Legal Studies*, **11**(3): 279–89.

Cammiss, S., and Cunningham, S.K. (2015), 'Swift and Sure Justice? Mode of Trial for Causing Death by Driving Offences', *Criminology and Criminal Justice*, **15**(3): 321–39.

Child, J.J., and Ormerod, D. (2017), *Smith, Hogan and Ormerod's Essentials of Criminal Law* (2nd ed.). Oxford: OUP.

Clarkson, C.M.V. (2005), *Understanding Criminal Law* (4th ed.). London: Sweet and Maxwell.

Clough, A. (2015), 'Mercy Killing: Three's a Crowd?' *Journal of Criminal Law*, **79**(5): 358–72.

Clough, A. (2016), 'Honour Killings, Partial Defences and the Exclusionary Conduct Model', *Journal of Criminal Law*, **80**(3): 177–87.

Corbett, C. (2003), *Car Crime*. Cullompton: Willan.

Crewe, B., Liebling, A., Padfield, N., and Virgo, G. (2015), 'Joint Enterprise: The Implications of an Unfair and Unclear Law', *Criminal Law Review*: 252–69.

Cunningham, S.K. (2005), 'The Unique Nature of Prosecutions in Cases of Fatal Road Traffic Collisions', *Criminal Law Review*: 834–49.

Cunningham, S.K. (2013), 'Has Law Reform Policy Been Driven in the Right Direction? How the New Causing Death by Driving Offences Are Operating in Practice', *Criminal Law Review*: 711–28.

D'Cruze, S., Walklate, S., and Pegg, S. (2006), *Murder*. Cullompton: Willan.

Department for Transport (2018), *Reported Road Casualties in Great Britain: 2017 Annual Report*. Available online at: https://assets.publishing.service.gov.uk/government/uploads/system/uploads/attachment_data/file/744077/reported-road-casualties-annual-report-2017.pdf. Accessed 23 May 2019.

Dorling, D. (2004), 'Prime Suspect: Murder in Britain', in Hillyard, P., Pantazis, C., Tombs, S., and Gordon, D. (eds.), *Beyond Criminology: Taking Harm Seriously*. London: Pluto Press.

Duff, R.A. (1990), *Intention, Agency and Criminal Liability*. Oxford: Blackwell.

Edwards, S.S.M. (2011), 'Loss of Self-Control: When His Anger Is Worth More Than Her Fear', in Reed, A., and Bohlander, M. (eds.), *Loss of Self Control and Diminished Responsibility*. Farnham: Ashgate.

Eisner, M. (2017), 'Interpersonal Violence on the British Isles, 1200–2016', in Liebling, A., Maruna, S., and McAra, L. (eds.), *The Oxford Handbook of Criminology* (6th ed.). Oxford: OUP.

Gibb, F. (2005), 'Jealousy Is No Longer an Excuse for Murder', *The Times*, 28 November.

Gibson, M.J.R. (2011), 'Intoxicants and Diminished Responsibility: The Impact of the Coroners and Justice Act 2009', *Criminal Law Review*: 909–24.

Gibson, M.J.R. (2017), 'Diminished Responsibility in *Golds* and Beyond: Insights and Implications', *Criminal Law Review*: 543–53.

Gobert, J. (2008), 'The Corporate Manslaughter and Corporate Homicide Act 2007 – Thirteen Years in the Making, But Was It Worth the Wait?' *Modern Law Review*, **71**(3): 413–33.

Goff, R. (1988), 'The Mental Element in the Crime of Murder', *Law Quarterly Review*, **104**(1): 30–59.

Harper, C. (2014), 'Diagnostic and Statistical Manual of Mental Disorders', in Taylor, P., Corteen, K., and Morley, S. (eds.), *A Companion to Criminal Justice, Mental Health and Risk*. Bristol: Policy Press.

Hawkins, K. (2002), *Law as Last Resort: Prosecution Decision-Making in a Regulatory Agency*. Oxford: OUP.

Health and Safety Executive (2018), *Health and Safety at Work: Summary Statistics for Great Britain, 2018*. Available online at: www.hse.gov.uk/statistics/overall/hssh1718.pdf. Accessed 21 May 2019.

Herring, J. (2007), 'Familial Homicide, Failure to Protect and Domestic Violence: Who's the Victim?' *Criminal Law Review*: 923–33.

Herring, J. (2011), 'The Serious Wrong of Domestic Abuse and the Loss of Control Defence', in Reed, A., and Bohlander, M. (eds.), *Loss of Self Control and Diminished Responsibility*. Farnham: Ashgate.

Herring, J. (2019), *Criminal Law* (11th ed.). London: Palgrave Macmillan.

Herring, J., and Palser, E. (2007), 'The Duty of Care in Gross Negligence Manslaughter', *Criminal Law Review*: 24–41.

Horder, J. (1992), *Provocation and Responsibility*. Oxford: OUP.

Horder, J. (1997), 'Two Histories and Four Hidden Principles of Mens Rea', *Law Quarterly Review*, **113**(1): 95–119.

Horder, J. (2012), *Homicide and the Politics of Law Reform*. Oxford: OUP.

Huxtable, R. (2002), 'Separation of Conjoined Twins: Where Next for English Law?' *Criminal Law Review*: 459–70.

Innes, M. (2003), *Investigating Murder: Detective Work and the Police Response to Criminal Homicide*. Oxford: OUP.

Inquest Casework and Monitoring (2019), *Statistics and Monitoring: Deaths in Police Custody, Deaths in Prison, Deaths of Immigration Detainees*. Available online at: www.inquest.org.uk/Pages/Category/statistics-and-monitoring. Accessed 17 May 2019.

Keating, H., and Bridgeman, J. (2012), 'Compassionate Killings: The Case for a Partial Defence', *Modern Law Review*, **75**(5): 697–721.

Loveless, J., Allen, M., and Derry, C. (2018), *Complete Criminal Law* (6th ed.). Oxford: OUP.

Mackay, R.D. (1993), 'The Consequences of Killing Very Young Children', *Criminal Law Review*: 21–30.

Mackay, R.D. (2010), 'The Coroners and Justice Act 2009 – Partial Defences to Murder: (2) The New Diminished Responsibility Plea', *Criminal Law Review*: 290–302.

Mackay, R.D. (2011), 'The New Diminished Responsibility Plea: More Than Mere Modernisation?' in Reed, A., and Bohlander, M. (eds.), *Loss of Control and Diminished Responsibility*. Farnham: Ashgate.

Mackay, R.D., and Mitchell, B. (2017), 'The New Diminished Responsibility Plea in Operation: Some Initial Findings', *Criminal Law Review*: 18–35.

Macklem, T., and Gardner, J. (2001), 'Provocation and Pluralism', *Modern Law Review*, **64**(6): 815–30.

McColgan, A. (1993), 'In Defence of Battered Women Who Kill', *Oxford Journal of Legal Studies*, **13**(4): 508–29.

Ministry of Justice (2018), *Criminal Justice System Statistics: Outcomes by Offence, 2007 to 2017 – Pivot Table Analytical Tool for England and Wales*. Available online at: https://assets.publishing.service.gov.uk/government/uploads/system/uploads/attachment_data/file/733981/outcomes-by-offence-tool-2017-update.xlsx. Accessed 2019.

Ministry of Justice (2019), *Offender Management Statistics Bulletin, October-December 2018*. Available online at: https://assets.publishing.service.gov.uk/government/uploads/system/uploads/attachment_data/file/796902/offender-management-statistics-quarterly-q4-2018.pdf. Accessed 17 May 2019.

Mitchell, B. (1999), 'In Defence of the Correspondence Principle', *Criminal Law Review*: 195–205.

Mitchell, B. (2008), 'Minding the Gap in Unlawful and Dangerous Act Manslaughter: A Moral Defence of One-Punch Killers', *Journal of Criminal Law*, **72**(6): 537–47.

Mitchell, B. (2011), 'Loss of Self Control Under the Coroners and Justice Act 2009: Oh No!' in Reed, A., and Bohlander, M. (eds.), *Loss of Self Control and Diminished Responsibility*. Farnham: Ashgate.

Mitchell, B., and Mackay, R.D. (2011), 'Investigating Involuntary Manslaughter: An Empirical Study of 127 Cases', *Oxford Journal of Legal Studies*, **31**(1): 165–91.

Mitchell, B., and Roberts, J.V. (2012), 'Sentencing for Murder: Exploring Public Knowledge and Public Opinion in England and Wales', *British Journal of Criminology*, **52**(1): 141–58.

Moore, M.S. (1997), *Placing Blame: A Theory of the Criminal Law*. Oxford: OUP.

Morrison, S. (2013), 'Should There Be a Domestic Violence Defence to the Offence of Familial Homicide?' *Criminal Law Review*: 826–38.

Norrie, A. (2005), *Law and the Beautiful Soul*. London: GlassHouse.

Norrie, A. (2010), 'The Coroners and Justice Act 2009 – Partial Defences to Murder: (1) Loss of Control', *Criminal Law Review*: 275–89.

ONS (2019a), *Crime in England and Wales, Year Ending March 2019*. Available online at: www.ons.gov.uk/peoplepopulationandcommunity/crimeandjustice/bulletins/crimeinenglandandwales/yearendingmarch2019. Accessed 21 March 2019.

ONS (2019b), *Homicide in England and Wales: Year Ending March 2018*. Available online at: www.ons.gov.uk/peoplepopulationandcommunity/crimeandjustice/articles/homicideinenglandandwales/yearendingmarch2018. Accessed 17 May 2019.

Papadopoulou, N. (2017), 'From *Pretty* to *Nicklinson:* Changing Judicial Attitudes to Assisted Dying', *European Human Rights Law Review*, **3**: 298–307.

Pedain, A. (2003), 'Intention and the Terrorist Example', *Criminal Law Review*: 579–93.

Power, H. (2006), 'Provocation and Culture', *Criminal Law Review*: 871–88.

Quick, O. (2006), 'Prosecuting "Gross" Medical Negligence: Manslaughter, Discretion and the Crown Prosecution Service', *Journal of Law and Society*, **33**(3): 421–50.

Quirk, H. (2013), 'Sentencing White Coat Crime: The Need for Guidance in Medical Manslaughter Cases', *Criminal Law Review*: 871–88.

Reed, A., and Bohlander, M. (eds.) (2011), *Loss of Self Control and Diminished Responsibility*. Farnham: Ashgate.

Reiner, R. (2007), *Law and Order: An Honest Citizen's Guide to Crime and Control*. Cambridge: Polity Press.

Riddell, M., Hope, C., and Bingham, J. (2014), 'Lloyd-Webber: I Wanted to Join Dignitas and Die', *The Telegraph*, 17 July. Available online at: www.telegraph.co.uk/news/politics/10974783/Lloyd-Webber-I-considered-Dignitas-but-am-set-to-oppose-assisted-dying.html. Accessed 23 May 2019.

Shute, S. (2004), 'Punishing Murderers: Release Procedures and the "Tariff", 1953–2004', *Criminal Law Review*: 873–95.

Tombs, S. (2016), 'Corporate Manslaughter', in Corteen, K., Morley, S., Taylor, P., and Turner, J. (eds.), *A Companion to Crime, Harm and Victimisation*. Bristol: Policy Press.

Tombs, S., and Whyte, D. (2007), *Safety Crimes*. Cullompton: Willan.

Twinley, R. (2014), 'Mental Disorder', in Taylor, P., Corteen, K., and Morley, S. (eds.), *A Companion to Criminal Justice, Mental Health and Risk*. Bristol: Policy Press.

Wake, N. (2010), 'Intoxication in the Dock: Specimen Directions for Jurors', *Journal of Criminal Law*, **74**(1): 16–20.

Wells, C. (1989), 'Otherwise Kill Me: Marginal Children and Ethics at the Edge of Existence', in Lee, R.G., and Morgan, D. (eds.), *Birthrights: Law and Ethics at the Beginning of Life*. London: Routledge.

Wells, C. (2000), 'Provocation: The Case for Abolition', in Ashworth, A., and Mitchell, B. (eds.), *Rethinking English Homicide Law*. Oxford: OUP.

Wells, C., and Morgan, D. (1991), 'Whose Foetus Is It?' *Journal of Law and Society*, **18**(4): 431–47.

Wilczynski, A. (1997), 'Mad or Bad? Child-Killers, Gender and the Courts', *British Journal of Criminology*, **37**(3): 419–36.

Wilczynski, A., and Morris, A. (1993), 'Parents Who Kill Their Children', *Criminal Law Review*: 31–6.

Williams, G. (1989), 'The Mens Rea for Murder: Leave It Alone', *Law Quarterly Review*, **105**(3): 387–97.

Woodley, M. (2013), 'Bargaining Over Corporate Manslaughter: What Price a Life?' *Journal of Criminal Law*, **77**(1): 33–40.

Chapter 8

Sexual offences

Chapter aims

After reading Chapter 8, you should be able to understand:

- The framework of sexual offences introduced in the Sexual Offences Act 2003
- The actus reus and mens rea required for these offences
- The special offences used to regulate sexual behaviour involving children, and those in a position of trust
- How perpetrators and victims of sexual offences are responded to in criminal justice practice
- How the evidence on the response to sexual offences in criminal law and criminal justice fits in with the theoretical models introduced in Chapter 1

Introduction

Chapter 8 covers the area of sexual offences in criminal law – an area that underwent a radical overhaul in the Sexual Offences Act 2003. Some pre-2003 case law is still important in interpreting the provisions of the 2003 Act, however, and it is used to explain the statutory law here. It is important to note that the 2003 Act is complex and detailed legislation, and so not all sexual offences defined in it are discussed here. This chapter explains the key provisions in the current law, as well as placing them in the wider social and criminal justice context of attitudes towards sexual behaviour.

Sexual offences: the law

Rape

Actus reus

The actus reus of rape is the penetration of V's vagina, anus, or mouth by D's penis. Men can be the victim of rape if a penis penetrates their mouth or anus. Only men can commit rape (Herring (2019: 132). S.79(3) of the Act includes body parts created by surgical reconstruction within the offence of rape, so that transsexuals can be both offenders and victims for the purposes of rape. S.79(2) defines penetration in such a way that even the slightest degree of penetration is enough and states that penetration is a 'continuing act' from the time of entry to the time of withdrawal. This means that if V withdraws consent and D continues the penetration, the penetration has to be without consent (*Cooper and Schaub* [1994] Crim LR 531), and D can be convicted of rape as a 'continuing act' if the penetration continues beyond the point where consent is withdrawn (*Kaitamaki* [1985] AC 147).

Mens rea

D has to penetrate V's vagina, anus, or mouth intentionally with his penis. Here, intention means the same as it does elsewhere in criminal mens rea. *Watson* [1992] Crim LR 434 suggests that if D has consent to penetrate one of the other person's orifices with his penis, but accidentally penetrates another orifice instead, he will not be guilty of rape.

The second element of mens rea is that D must not reasonably believe that V is consenting. S.1(2) of the Sexual Offences Act says that the reasonableness of D's belief is an objective test, to be decided with regard to all of the circumstances, including any steps D has taken to find out whether V is consenting. This means that the jury has to take into account what has happened before the rape as well as during it (*McFall* [1994] Crim LR 226), as well as any characteristics D has which might reasonably affect his understanding of whether V is consenting. The Court of Appeal in *B* [2013] EWCA Crim 3 stated that where D is suffering from a delusional psychotic illness or personality disorder, their delusional belief that V was consenting to sex could not be seen as a reasonable belief.

Ss.74, 75, and 76 of the 2003 Act deal with proof of lack of consent and the unreasonableness of D's belief in consent. S.74 defines consent as agreeing by choice and having the freedom and capacity to make that choice. The decision of whether or not there is consent is one for the jury, on the facts of each case. *Olugboja* [1982] QB 320 shows that consent to sex and submission to sex are two different things in respect of violent threats, but it is less clear on when submission indicates consent in other contexts and does not take into account that different types of threat might have different psychological effects on different people (Gardner 1996).

S.75 sets up evidential presumptions about the complainant's consent, to make the decision on consent easier for the jury. If it is proved that D penetrated, any one of six specified circumstances are proved to exist, and if D knew they existed, then V is presumed not to have consented unless enough evidence to leave the jury in reasonable doubt is raised to show that V did consent. There must be substantive evidence to rebut a s.75 presumption – a belief that the presumption does not apply is not enough (*Cicerelli* [2011] EWCA Crim 2665). The specified circumstances include:

- Fear of or use of violence against V or another
- V being unconscious or asleep
- V being unable to communicate due to physical disability
- V being unlawfully detained
- V being drugged

D is presumed not to have reasonably believed in V's consent unless enough evidence is raised to show that D did reasonably believe in it. In *Bree* [2007] 2 All ER 676, the Court of Appeal was critical of over-generalising in terms of evidential presumptions. Sir Igor Judge P stated that whether or not V had the capacity to consent to sex while voluntarily intoxicated depended on the facts of each individual case and the states of mind of the individuals involved. Therefore, while it is possible that a person is so intoxicated that they are not capable of giving consent (*Malone* [1998] 2 Cr App Rep 447), it is the jury's job to decide whether someone who was drunk actually had the capacity to consent to sex on the facts of each case. He added that, while the meaning of consent in s.74 was clear, the evidential presumptions in s.75 should not lead to short-cuts in terms of not considering all of the evidence or not giving the jury enough guidance.

S.76 introduces conclusive evidential presumptions regarding lack of consent and the unreasonableness of D's belief in consent. Here, it must be proved that D did the relevant act, and D intentionally deceived V as to the nature or purpose of the relevant act (as happened in *Flattery* (1877) 2 QBD 410 and *Williams* [1923] 1 KB 340). Alternatively, D must have induced V intentionally to consent to the relevant act by impersonating a person known personally to the complainant (as in *Elbekkay* [1995] Crim LR 163). In either case, there is a presumption that V did not consent and that D did not believe in the complainant's consent.

The Court of Appeal interpreted the scope of the s.76 provisions narrowly in *Jheeta* [2008] Crim LR 144. Here, the Court stated that they apply only where D deceives the complainant about the nature or purpose of a particular type of sexual intercourse, and not where D deceives the complainant about the circumstances surrounding sex. This is true even where those circumstances may lead V to consent to having sex with D more often than they would have done otherwise (e.g. *Linekar* [1995] 3 All ER 69, where D promised to pay V for sex, but in fact did not pay, and never intended to pay – here, D's conviction for rape was quashed). Similarly, in *EB* [2007] 1 Cr App Rep 29, the Court of Appeal decided that D not telling V that he had HIV/AIDS before they had sex did not count as a conclusive presumption that V did not consent to sex – s.76 did not say anything about 'implied deception' like this. On the other hand, in *Assange v Swedish Prosecution Authority* [2011] EWHC 2849 (Admin) the Court decided that if someone actively lied about an intention to wear a condom during sex, this could remove consent. Similarly, in *R (on the application of F) v DPP* [2013] EWHC 945 (Admin), the Court said that V's consent to sex would be removed where D knew that consent depended on him not ejaculating, but intended to ejaculate and did so. In both *Assange* and *F*, there was no deception as to the nature of the act under s.76 – instead, the issue was one of removal of choice over whether or not to consent to sex under s.74.

The third element of mens rea in relation to rape, therefore, is required where the prosecution uses the presumptions in ss.75 and 76. For s.75, they have to prove D's knowledge of whichever of the circumstances listed in s.75 applies in the circumstances. For s.76, they have to prove that D intentionally deceived the complainant as to the nature or purpose of the relevant act.

Study exercise 8.1

Read Box's (1983: 120–31) discussion of the legal definition of rape. Do you agree with him that the legal definition of rape should be considerably wider than it currently is?

Sexual assault offences

Actus reus

There are three elements to the actus reus for the three sexual assault offences in the 2003 Act. The first element is the act itself – sexual penetration of V's vagina or anus with a part of D's body or anything else for s.2, sexual touching for s.3, and sexual activity against V's wishes involving penetration of one of V's orifices, or penetration of V's mouth with D's penis, for s.4. The second element, for all three offences, is that the conduct is 'sexual'. 'Sexual' is defined by s.78 as something which a reasonable person would consider that, a) whatever its circumstances or any person's purpose in relation to it, it is because of its nature sexual, or b) because of its nature it may be sexual and because of its circumstances or the purpose of any person in relation to it (or both) it is sexual. In *H* [2005] 1 WLR 2005, the Court of Appeal said that the test in s.78(b) is a two-stage test on the facts. Firstly, would a reasonable person consider that because of its nature the act could be sexual, where the circumstances before or after the act took place and D's purpose are irrelevant? If the answer is 'yes', the second part of the test is whether, because of the circumstances of the act and the purpose of any person in relation to it, the act actually is sexual.

The third element is absence of consent, as defined under s.74 of the Act – the presumptions in ss.75 and 76 apply for all three offences. In *Devonald* [2008] EWCA Crim 527, the Court of Appeal decided that there was deception as to the purpose of the act (in this case, V thought the purpose was to give sexual pleasure, when in fact the purpose was to embarrass V). Since s.76 covers deception as to the nature or purpose of an act, V's awareness of the sexual nature of the act was irrelevant. In *McNally* [2013] EWCA Crim 1051, D's active deception as to her gender removed V's consent to sexual activity. As with *Assange* and *F*, though, and even though there was deception about the nature of the sexual act, the court in *McNally* decided the case under s.74 rather than under s.76.

Mens rea

The mens rea for these offences is intention to either penetrate V, touch V in a sexual way, or cause V to engage in sexual activity (as appropriate), and an absence of a reasonable belief that V is consenting. For all three offences, whether a belief is reasonable is to be determined having regards to all of the circumstances, including any steps D has taken to ascertain whether the complainant is consenting. Sections 75 and 76 apply to all three offences. The latter two provisions are the same as in the statutory definition of rape in the Sexual Offences Act 2003.

Study exercise 8.2

Do you think that *H* defines sexual assault, in terms of the meanings of 'sexual' and 'touching', too widely?

Sexual offences against children

The SOA maintains the age of sexual consent as being 16 (s.9). The Act assumes that children under age 13 are incapable of giving sexual consent, although the Act itself does not actually say this. None of the sexual offences against children needs proof that V did not consent, which makes them different from the adult sexual offences discussed previously. However, the categories of sexual offences against children are the same as for adults. The child offences fall into two categories: offences where V is under 13 years old, and offences where V is over age 13 but under age 16. For these offences, the terms 'sexual', 'penetration', and 'sexual touching' mean the same as they do for the adult sexual offences discussed previously.

Offences against children under 13 years old

S.5 creates the offence of rape of a child under age 13. The actus reus is D's penetration of V's vagina, anus, or mouth where V is under the age of 13. The mens rea is intentional penetration. V's consent is irrelevant here. *G* [2009] 1 AC 92 emphasised that as long as penetration is proved, D is guilty of rape, even though D has a reasonable belief that V is over age 13, s.5 itself does not actually say that the offence is strict liability, and liability could overlap with the offence under s.13 (see the following). As a result, there was no breach of either Article 6 (right to a fair trial) or Article 8 (right to privacy) in *G*.

S.6 creates an offence of assault of a child under age 13 by penetration, where the actus reus is D's sexual penetration of V who is under age 13, with a part of the body or anything else, of V's vagina or anus, and the mens rea is that the penetration is intentional. S.7 creates an offence of sexual assault of a child under age 13, where the actus reus is D's sexual touching of V who is under age 13, and the mens rea is that the touching is intentional. S.8 creates an offence of causing or inciting a child under age 13 to engage in sexual activity. Here, the actus reus is causing or inciting a child under age 13 to engage in sexual activity. For the offences in ss.6–8 of the SOA, there is no need to prove V's lack of consent for this offence, so D's belief in consent is irrelevant.

Offences against children under 16 years old

The offences of sexual activity with a child (s.9) and causing or inciting a child to engage in sexual activity (s.10) have the same actus reus and mens rea requirements as the offences against children under age 13 in ss.7 and 8, discussed in the previous subsection. The only difference in the ss.9 and 10 offences is that in mens rea terms, the prosecution has to prove that either D did not believe that V was over 16, or that D did believe this but the belief was not a reasonable one.

S.11 creates an offence of engaging in a sexual activity in the presence of a child. The actus reus is D (an adult aged 18 or over) engaging in a sexual activity, which they undertake for the purposes of sexual gratification where V (a child under the age of 16) is present or is in a place from which D can be observed. The mens rea is that D intentionally engages in a sexual activity; D knows or believes that V is aware, or intends that V should be aware that D is engaging in the sexual activity; and that D did not believe that V was over age 16, or that D did believe this, but the belief was not a reasonable one, or that V is under age 13 (in which case D's belief is irrelevant anyway).

S.12 creates an offence of causing a child to watch a sexual act. The actus reus is D (an adult aged 18 or over) causing V (a child under the age of 16) to watch a third person engaging in sexual activity, or to look at an image (still or moving) of any person engaging in a sexual activity, for the purposes of obtaining sexual gratification. The mens rea is that D intentionally causes V to watch the sexual activity; and that D did not believe that V was over 16, or that D did believe this but the belief was not a reasonable one, or that V is under age 13 (in which case D's belief is irrelevant anyway). In *Abdullahi* [2007] 1 WLR 225, the Court of Appeal confirmed that the sexual gratification did not have to happen at or soon after the same time as causing V to view the sexual activity – the offence could cover a more long-term plan to obtain gratification later.

S.13 states that it is an offence for D (a child under the age of 18) to do anything which would be an offence under ss.9–12 if D was an adult. S.14 creates an offence of grooming (i.e. arranging or facilitating the commission of a child sex offence under ss.9–13. The actus reus is D arranging or facilitating something that amounts to an offence under these subsections. The mens rea is that D intentionally arranges or facilitates the thing that is an offence, and that D intends to commit the offence, intends for someone else to commit the offence, or believes that someone else will commit the offence, in any part of the world. Under s.14(2), D has a defence to this offence if they arrange or facilitate something that they believe another person will do, but that D does not intend to do or intend another person to do, and an offence under ss.9–13 would be an offence against a child, whom D is protecting by acting. S.14(3) lists a range of circumstances under which D is taken to be protecting a child by acting as they do, as long as they are not also acting for the purpose of sexual gratification, or for the purpose of causing or encouraging the activity which constitutes the offence under ss.9–13, or the child's participation in that offence. This defence covers police officers using a child as a decoy to trap a child sex offender, and health workers providing contraception advice, or contraception and advice on sexually transmitted diseases to children.

S.15 creates an offence of meeting with a child following sexual grooming. The actus reus is D (an adult over age 18) meeting or communicating with V on at least two previous occasions, and then meeting V or travelling to meet V in any part of the world, where V is under age 16. The mens rea is D intentionally meeting V, or having the intention to meet V by travelling; plus intention to do anything in respect of V, during or after the meeting in any part of the world, which if done will involve D committing a relevant sexual offence; plus a lack of a reasonable belief on D's part that V is age 16 or over. This is a preparatory offence designed to prevent offenders from using developed relationships as a gateway to sexual offending (*G* [2010] EWCA Crim 1693).

A further offence of sexual communication (s.15A) became part of the SOA in 2017. Here, D must intentionally communicate with V in a sexual way (i.e. relating to sexual activity, or to be reasonably considered as sexual), or in a way intended to encourage V to make a sexual communication to D or another. V must be under age 16, and D must have no reasonable belief that V is age 16 or over.

Study exercise 8.3

'The decision in *G* [2009] breached Article 6(2) of the ECHR (presumption of innocence until proven guilty), because it punished D where he was not morally at fault'. Do you agree with this statement?

Sexual offences involving abuse of a position of trust

These offences are contained in ss.16–24 of the Sexual Offences Act. They are the same offences as in ss.9–12, with the extra requirements that D is 18 years old or over, is in a position of trust in relation to V, and that V is 18 years old or under. For each offence, D has a defence where V is under 18 years old but D reasonably believes that V is 18 or over, but D has no 'mistaken age' defence if V is under 13. Where D points to evidence that raises an issue about whether they knew or should reasonably have known that they were in a position of trust, the prosecution has to prove that D did in fact know or should reasonably have known that they were in a position of trust. Section 21 of the SOA defines those in a position of trust. The section covers care workers and probation officers but does not mention others in positions of social power over the young, such as celebrities, doctors, and those in religious office.

Offences abolished by the Sexual Offences Act 2003, and post-2003 offences

The Sexual Offences Act 2003 did not only create new sexual offences and amend existing ones. It also abolished several pre-existing sexual offences under Schedule 7 of the 2003 Act. The most important were the offences of buggery (anal sexual intercourse), gross indecency between men, and solicitation by men for immoral purposes.

New sexual offences have been added to criminal law since the 2003 Act. Under section 33 of the Criminal Justice and Courts Act 2015, there is a new offence of disclosing private sexual photographs or films without the consent of an individual who appears in them, and with intent to cause that individual distress (informally known as 'revenge porn'). Most recently, the Voyeurism (Offences) Act 2019 adds new offences to the 2003 Act, relating to 'upskirting'. The offences involve an individual operating equipment or recording an image beneath another person's clothing, without consent, and with the motive of either obtaining sexual gratification or causing humiliation, distress, or alarm to the complainant. This adds to the offence of voyeurism, involving the filming, recording, or observing of private acts for sexual gratification without consent, in the 2003 Act.

Study exercise 8.4

Why do you think the post-2003 offences were added? Why do you think they were not part of the 2003 Act in the first place?

The second section of this chapter considers sexual offences in their criminal justice context.

Sexual offences and criminal justice

Sexual offences, the police, and the CPS

The number of sexual offences reported by the public has increased steadily over the past 20 years, as has the number recorded by the police. The police recorded 121,187 sexual offences in England and Wales in 2016–17, the highest level of recording since 2002 (ONS 2018a: 7). This increase is thought to be driven by improvements in police recording practices, as well as by a greater willingness of victims to come forward to report such crimes, including victims of non-recent offences. One high-profile example of this trend is the victims of the TV personality Jimmy Savile who reported their experiences in response to the Operation Yewtree investigation, which took place after Savile's death.

The increase in police recording of sexual offences should not disguise the fact that most known sexual offences are still not reported to the police at all. The Crime Survey for England and Wales found in 2017 that 83% of sexual offence victims did not report their crime to the police (ONS 2018a: 3). The CSEW also estimated that 12.1% of adults aged 16 to 59 (4 million people) have experienced sexual assault since the age of 16 (ibid: 5) and that 2% of adults (646,000) had experienced it in the previous year. Such a finding fits in with academic research into the prevalence of sexual assault. In Kelly's (1988) study, all of the 60 female interviewees had experienced the threat of violence; 56 (93%) had experienced sexual harassment; 50 (83%) experienced pressure to have sex; 42 (70%) had experienced sexual assault; and 30 (50%) had experienced rape or other sexual abuse. Uncovering the range of behaviours that women experienced as being sexually abusive, some of which would not be defined as rape or any other type of crime, led Kelly to argue that legally defined rape was just the most extreme end of a 'continuum', or range, of violence against women, and that rape should not be seen as separate from this range of violence.

Despite police efforts to address the historical issues of police environments and questioning being experienced as hostile and traumatic by the victims of sexual assault (Jordan 2011), attrition rates in rape cases remain extremely high (Kelly et al. 2005). Sexual offences are still significantly under-recorded by police compared to other types of offence (HM Inspectorate of Constabulary 2014). There is evidence that the police and the CPS are less likely to prosecute where there is a previous false allegation by the victim, where there were inconsistencies in the victim's recollection of a rape, and where the suspect is white with no previous police record (Hohl and Stanko 2015). There is also considerable evidence to suggest that one of the main reasons why rape victims do not report their crime to the police is because they feel that they will not be believed (Kelly 2010; Horvath et al. 2011). Jordan (2001) found a clash of cultures between police and rape victims in terms of their aims. Police culture in her study was about crime-fighting, not making things better for victims. This had the effect of alienating victims and sidelining their needs in practice. Finally, McMillan (2018) found wide variations in police estimations of the extent of false rape accusations, which she linked to a masculine police organisational culture, and in turn to negative attitudes towards rape victims in wider society (Walklate 2008).

Police attitudes towards defendants in sexual offence cases also risk wrongful convictions. Corteen and Steele (2018) point to a police tendency to presume guilt in sex offence cases, leading to incomplete investigations, non-disclosure of evidence, and pressure to believe the complainant, however doubtful the evidence of guilt may be (Naughton 2010). The recent social media '#MeToo' campaign has done much valuable work to highlight the social harm caused by historical sexual abuse. However, if the result is wrongful convictions stemming from a lack of objectivity in police investigation, then criminal justice is letting both complainants and defendants down (Corteen and Steele 2018). There is also recent evidence to show a widening gap between allegations of rape (58,000 in 2018–19) and convictions (1,925 in 2018–19). Such data in turn suggest that there is an emerging trend in CPS practice of screening out cases that a jury is perceived as being unlikely to convict, rather than building up evidence in support of prosecution (Crown Prosecution Service 2019).

Adler's (2000) review of the literature on the response of criminal justice to male victims of sexual assault did not reveal that male victims experienced very similar feelings to female victims – such as fear, embarrassment, and shame. But Adler's review did show that male victims had additional trauma relating to the fear of being labelled as a homosexual if they reported the assault to the police, discouraging many from reporting. Adler concludes that if the criminal justice response to female victims of rape has been slow to develop and improve, the response to male victims has been even more limited, and distorted by sexual stereotyping of men who are sexually assaulted as either 'weak' or homosexual. These limitations are visible in the very narrow range of treatment services for male victims, both in connection with criminal justice and independently of it in the health sector (Mezey and King 2000).

Focusing now on sexual offences against children, data from the Home Office Data Hub suggest that children aged between five and 19 were disproportionately likely to be the victims of sexual offences recorded by police (ONS 2018a). The police recorded 64,667 sexual offences against children in 2016–17, a higher rate than ever before, with 21% of these being committed against children under age 11, and 4% being committed against children under age four (Dearden 2018). As with other offences discussed in this book, however, it seems likely that only a tiny percentage of child sex abuse cases ever reaches the criminal justice process. Radford et al. (2011) estimated that one in 20 children in the UK had suffered sexual abuse, with one in three children abused by an adult not telling anyone about the crime, and over 90% abused by someone they knew.

The context of police responses to child sexual abuse is the shame and fear of reprisals that can prevent victims from reporting the offences against them. The police response to child sexual abuse has undoubtedly become more effective and thorough since the 1980s (Thomas 2015). However, Hughes et al. (1996) found evidence that women were over-represented within the CPUs, leading to suggestions of sexist stereotyping of work with children who had been victimised as women's work and not 'proper policing'. Thomas (2015) has also pointed to high-profile failures to share police intelligence with other forces, which was named as a factor in the failure to prevent Ian Huntley, a convicted sex offender, from killing Holly Wells and Jessica Chapman in Soham in 2002.

Study exercise 8.5

Mackinnon (1983) argues that it is difficult for women to tell the difference between rape and 'normal' sex because society is systematically controlled by men and biased against women. Do you agree with this view? How well do you think Mackinnon's arguments explain what we know about how much rape is reported to police and recorded by them?

Sexual offences, the court process, and punishment

The nature of rape as a criminal offence means that there is often a heavy reliance upon the evidence of the victim as a witness to the offence in court. This is particularly true given the importance of proving lack of consent in rape cases, since consent is really about the victim's state of mind. However, a range of studies have shown that rape victims giving evidence in court have often felt as if they were the ones on trial. Research has shown that the cross-examination of rape victims by defence barristers was regularly experienced by victims as upsetting and traumatic, involving continual questioning on the details of the rape, the victim's sexual history with the defendant and others, and the 'respectability' of the victim's behaviour (Adler 1987; Burman 2009).

Temkin (2002) also showed that judges did not do enough to prevent such aggressive tactics in court, despite their powers (introduced as part of the Youth Justice and Criminal Evidence Act 1999 s.41) to prohibit sexual history evidence where it was not relevant to the case. Kelly et al. (2006) studied a sample of over 400 rape cases that reached court. They found that an application was made to the judge to allow sexual history evidence in a third of cases, and that two-thirds of applications were allowed. References to sexual history evidence outside the s.41 exceptions occurred without application – something that is now illegal – in three-quarters of cases, there was a significant relationship between reference to it and acquittals. The rules about making applications to allow sexual history evidence before the trial and in writing were usually broken. Such an approach increases the risk of miscarriages of justice for defendants through false accusations, a phenomenon which is difficult to measure accurately (Rumney and McCartan 2017), but which is generally accepted to exist in a minority of court cases (Kelly et al. 2005; Burton 2013). The approach also makes the court process more difficult, and psychologically harmful, for victims.

Temkin (2000) revealed extensive hostility and prejudice towards rape victims from barristers who had conducted rape cases for both the prosecution and the defence, sometimes blaming them for the rape they had suffered, while Carline and Gunby's (2011) study found resistance to further reform among barristers of the law on rape. Lees (1997) argued that the rape trial acted as a social control on women, by warning them about the consequences of being sexually active, and punishing women who broke sexist stereotypes of female respectability and passiveness by giving evidence against those who had sexually attacked them in court.

Rumney (2001) conducted a study into how the court process handles male rape. He found evidence that male victims of rape were stereotyped in very similar ways to female victims when giving evidence in court. The defence's accounts of 'normal' behaviour for victims during and after the rape did not match research evidence on how victims actually did tend to behave. For example, male victims who had not tried to fight off their attacker or run away after the attack were characterised as having consented to sex, even where they had in reality 'frozen' due to fear. Male victims were sometimes accused of falsely reporting rape or being unreliable witnesses, in the same way that research suggests that female victims tend to be.

The continuing flaws in the treatment of the victims of sexual offending in the court process are highlighted by the widening 'justice gap' in rape cases in England and Wales. While reporting and recording rates have gone up, the conviction rate for rape, as a percentage of proceedings at court, was 36% in 2017, down 5% compared with 2012 (ONS 2018a).

Study exercise 8.6

Should sexual history evidence ever be allowed in a rape trial? Explain your answer with reference to the current rules under s.41 of the Youth Justice and Criminal Evidence Act 1999.

Rape carries a maximum sentence of life imprisonment. However, sentences can vary widely in practice. The Court of Appeal issued new sentencing guidelines for rape in *Millberry* [2003] 2 All ER 939. These new guidelines, designed with help from the Sentencing Advisory Panel, have a sentencing starting point of five years' imprisonment. There are then seven named aggravating factors. If at least one of these applies, the starting point goes up to eight years' imprisonment. For serial rapists, the starting point is 15 years' imprisonment. *Millberry* made it clear that the starting point for sentencing should be the same whether it was stranger rape, acquaintance rape, or marital rape; whether the victim is male or female; and whether the rape is vaginal or anal.

We can contrast this with data showing that sentencing for rape, and for other types of sexual offences, has increased in severity in recent years. The average custodial sentence length for rape has increased from 104 months for the rape of a female, and 101 months for rape of a male, in 2012, to 118 and 113 months respectively in 2017 (ONS 2018b). The trend towards increasing punishment and risk assessment is clear, and the doubts over whether sex offenders can ever be completely cured mean that some sex offenders, especially more minor sex offenders, receive little or no treatment in prison (Henham 1998). This is so although Sex Offender Treatment Programmes are in place throughout the prison estate and have achieved moderately encouraging results (Thomas 2015: ch.6).

The sentencing response to child sex offenders in England and Wales has become significantly tougher in recent years, in line with growing public concern about this type of behaviour, influenced in turn by the selective and sensationalist reporting practices of the media (Soothill and Walby 1991). Successive pieces of legislation – the Criminal Justice Act 1991, the Crime (Sentences) Act 1997, and the Crime and Disorder Act 1998 – made available sentences for child sex offenders tougher and tougher, reflecting the new perception of paedophiles as being one of the leading dangers to society. It is noticeable when looking at sentencing data that although sentences for sexual activity with children have increased overall, average sentences are considerably lower than for rape, increasing from 34.3 months in 2012 to 44.8 months in 2017 (ONS 2018b).

The increasing number of civil measures aimed at child sexual offenders has been an important recent trend. The most high-profile development in this context has been the introduction of sex offender notification requirements, commonly referred to as the 'Sex Offenders' Register', in Part I of the Sex Offenders Act 1997. Under the 1997 Act as amended by the Sexual Offences Act 2003 s.83, convicted sex offenders are required to give their name, National Insurance number, and address to police within three days of conviction. They are also required to notify the police of any changes to these details within three days of changes occurring (s.84) and submit an annual report to police confirming these details for as long as they are on the Register (s.85). Failure to comply with these requirements is a criminal offence, punishable with a maximum of six months' imprisonment in the magistrates' courts, and five years' imprisonment in the Crown Court (s.91). How long offenders have to remain on the Register depends on the sentence that they received in court for their offence, but if they receive an initial sentence of 30 months' imprisonment or more, they must stay on the Register for life (s.82).

A key issue in relation to the Register is what access (if any) the public should have to the details contained in it. The Criminal Justice and Court Services Act 2000 introduced Multi-Agency Public Protection Panels (MAPPPs) whose job it would be to assess the level of risk posed by sex offenders in the community, and to decide whether certain individuals could access a sex offender's name and address in the interests of the public. The MAPPPs include representation from the police, probation, social services, and the public. Kemshall et al. (2005) found that the MAPPPs' division of supervision of offenders into three levels according to the level of risk was effective and that supervision was more effective with a trained co-ordinator (which only two-thirds of MAPPPs had). However, they also found that training for

MAPPP members and the keeping of administrative records were inconsistent and that some over-allocation of offenders into a higher risk category than was necessary was occurring.

In 2000, following the murder of eight-year-old Sarah Payne by the convicted sex offender Roy Whiting, the *News of the World* newspaper launched a campaign to allow the public unrestricted access to the Register by publishing the names and addresses of convicted sex offenders. In February 2008, the government announced plans to launch a pilot scheme in four areas of England and Wales that would allow families to access the Register to check on people who had contact with their children. All police forces in England and Wales were taking part in the scheme by early 2011 (Jones and Newburn 2013). This scheme stops short of the full unrestricted access campaigned for by the *News of the World*, which has been introduced in the USA – although evidence from there suggests that unlimited access does not make supervision of sex offenders more effective or improve safety for either offenders or the public (Thomas 2003).

Some writers have been highly critical of the concept of the Sex Offenders Register itself and of attempts to increase public access to its contents. Soothill and Francis (1997) pointed out that the Register includes not only non-consensual child sex offenders but also anyone convicted of a wide variety of sexual offences, even convicted by caution at the police station rather than in court. They conclude that the Register is 'criminal apartheid' designed to demonise sex offenders. Ironically, such exclusion can make offenders go 'underground', out of the reach of supervision. This, in turn, can make them more likely to offend, as well as making vigilante-style violence against sex offenders – or even people who are wrongly suspected of being sex offenders – more likely (Silverman and Wilson 2002).

Compliance rates with the Register's requirements have consistently run at around 95%, indicating effectiveness on its own terms – but Plotnikoff and Woolfson (2000) found no conclusive proof that it has actually made communities any safer from the perceived dangerousness of child sex offenders. It is arguable that the focus on 'stranger danger' that the Register implies ignores evidence that the majority of child sex offences are committed by someone whom the child knows (Radford et al. 2011). There is the danger that the Register has become so punitive, in terms of making notification increasingly difficult and increased police powers to track down those who have not complied, that it is now a punishment in its own right, rather than the administrative measure to improve community safety that it is supposed to be (Thomas 2008).

Finally, the selective media treatment of different types of child sex offenders is vital to understanding public and criminal justice responses to this behaviour. Boyle (2018) shows that society and criminal justice ignored and downplayed the initial allegations of sexual abuse by the TV celebrity Jimmy Savile, both before and initially after Savile's death, because the victims were young females. Such an approach clearly displays sexism and ignores the links between sexual violence against children and sexual violence against adult women. The scandal caused by the revelations about Savile's long-standing predatory sexual behaviour moved from 'latent' to 'active', being further amplified by the BBC's denial of responsibility for Savile's behaviour and its institutional cover-up, which in turn triggered the scandal's amplification by the media (Greer and McLaughlin 2013). Powerful social institutions can use the media to cover up their harmful behaviour – Mancini and Shields' (2014) research in the USA found that Catholics who had greater exposure to media coverage of the sexual abuse scandal within the Catholic Church had increased confidence in the Church's ability to prevent sexual abuse in the future.

Study exercise 8.7

Should we have a law allowing unrestricted access to sex offenders' personal details by any member of the public? What measures could be enacted to deal with the risks that passing such legislation might create?

Conclusions: linking discussion to the roadmap theories

Both criminal law regulating sexual offences, and the criminal justice enforcement of that law, have undergone radical change in recent years. The Sexual Offences Act 2003 redefined a range of major sexual offences, including rape, sexual assault, and most of the sexual offences against children. Arguably, the 2003 Act reflected liberal theoretical ideas about what role criminal law should play in society. As well as abolishing offences criminalising sexual behaviour between consenting adult men, the Act also extended the offence of rape to include non-consensual oral penetration as well as the anal and vaginal types, and marked out sexual assault by penetration with something other than a penis as an offence which is just as socially harmful as rape itself. Equally significantly, consent, the element that if absent turns lawful sex into rape, was defined for the first time. Again, the definition was liberal, framing consent in terms of being able to make a free and informed choice about whether or not to have sex.

However, the new law is not really about liberal ideas. The definition of consent may be liberal on the surface, but it is vague, and as a result juries will be able to include their own ideas about what 'freedom' and 'choice' mean (Temkin and Ashworth 2004: 336). These ideas may reflect risk-based criminality (by being too harsh on defendants) or patriarchal values (by being too lenient on defendants) rather than liberalism. The need for a reasonable belief in consent also moves the law away from liberal ideas about punishing only based on what the defendant actually thought or saw themselves. There is also room for sexist stereotyping in asking the jury to assess the reasonableness of belief in consent in 'all the circumstances' without defining which circumstances should be considered (ibid: 342).

The 2003 Act also includes situations where there is a conclusive presumption, or a rebuttable presumption, that consent was not given. These provisions move beyond liberalism and due process to reflect the risks or immorality of certain types of conduct (McEwan 2005: 18), but if the presumptions are supposed to reflect morality or risk, their ordering does not make sense. Deceit as to identity carries a conclusive presumption of non-consent, which may not reflect what actually happened in the sense that the victim might still have consented despite the deceit (ibid: 21). Consent through threats or involuntarily intoxicating the victim carries only a rebuttable presumption even though they look morally 'worse' than some forms of deceit (Temkin and Ashworth 2004: 337). Consent where the victim has voluntarily become drunk does not carry any presumption at all. These provisions are clearly aimed at reflecting morality, the defendant's blameworthiness, and risk rather than liberal independence (McEwan 2005: 19), but they are so confusing and discretionary that they are unlikely to end the sexist stereotyping of rape victims and low conviction rates that they were designed to tackle. The conclusion must be that in trying to respond to the social harm caused by sexual abuse generally, the law has gone too far in imposing risk management values.

Criminal justice has traditionally faced accusations that it has failed to take the harm caused by sexual offences seriously. Historical evidence showed the police treating victims unfairly and intrusively, the CPS being too willing to drop cases, and the courts sentencing offenders too leniently, in a way that seemed to reinforce radical, power-based understandings of criminal justice. Evidence from HM Inspectorate of the Constabulary (2014) would suggest that attitudes have been changed in some cases, but victims' welfare is still not the consistent priority, as Jordan (2011) argued.

A similar story can be told with developments in the courts' handling of sex offence cases. Legislation such as s.41 of the Youth Justice and Criminal Evidence Act 1999 is aimed at making things easier for victims giving evidence in court, by excluding intrusive cross-examination about their sexual behaviour in the past under certain circumstances. However, the legislation has not improved the court experience for victims. Temkin and Krahé (2008) found that despite s.41, myths and stereotypes about what is and is not 'real rape' persist in the criminal justice process. In this situation, the power of courts to exercise discretion and impose their own views on what is and is not acceptable sexual behaviour still takes priority over efficiency and the interests of victims.

The sentencing and punishment of sex offenders has seen several moves towards risk-management roadmap ideas. Sentencing has become harsher over time. The Sex Offenders Register, marketed as an administrative tool to make the public safer from sex offenders in the community, has become so difficult to comply with that it is effectively a punishment in itself, and public access to its information risks social exclusion for offenders as well as vigilantism (Silverman and Wilson 2002). However, its ability to make communities safer is unproven. By contrast, there is evidence that the risk posed by offenders would be more effectively managed by a restorative approach (such as the 'Circles of Support' initiative in Canada) than by the current retributive focus (McAlinden 2006). The current approach makes social inclusion for offenders more difficult to achieve, while doing little to actually make the public safer, and increasing the public's media-fuelled fear of a relatively unlikely type of offending (attack by a predatory stranger) while diverting their attention away from a more likely type (sex attack by someone the victim knows and trusts). At the same time, the problem of male-victim rape and sexual assault remains largely hidden from public and criminological discussion.

Perhaps, given the attitudes of some sections of the public towards rape and other sexual assaults, it is not fair to expect the criminal justice process to make much progress. In a survey of 2000 members of the public, Temkin and Krahé (2008) uncovered widespread prejudice against the victims of rape. Many thought that sex without consent where the victim had been drinking or where the victim and defendant had a relationship previously was not 'real rape', even though this type of rape is far more common than attack by a stranger. The selective media coverage of rape, based around serial rapists and stranger attacks (Soothill 1991), is also significant in understanding public attitudes.

Key points

- The law on sexual offending in England changed radically as a result of the Sexual Offences Act 2003
- Criminal justice's response to sexual offending has traditionally been characterised by discrimination against victims, and this still takes place in spite of recent reforms in policy and practice, but criminal justice can and does discriminate against those accused of sexual offending as well
- Recent policy initiatives on responding to sexual offences have focussed on risk management of offenders in an attempt to improve victim and public satisfaction
- The radical and risk management roadmap theories best explain the inequality in the law and criminal justice response to the victims of sexual offences, and the attempts to mask this inequality through increased punishment of offenders

Further reading

Jordan, J. (2011), 'Here We Go Round the Review-Go-Round: Rape Investigation and Prosecution – Are Things Getting Worse, Not Better?' *Journal of Sexual Aggression*, **17**(3): 234–49.

McMillan, L. (2018), 'Police Officers' Perceptions of False Allegations of Rape', *Journal of Gender Studies*, **27**(1): 9–21.

Temkin, J., and Ashworth, A. (2004), 'The Sexual Offences Act 2003: (1) Rape, Sexual Assaults and the Problems of Consent', *Criminal Law Review*. 328–46.

Temkin, J., and Krahé, B. (2008), *Sexual Assault and the Justice Gap: A Question of Attitude*. Oxford: Hart.

Thomas, T. (2015), *Sex Crime: Sex Offending and Society* (3rd ed.). Abingdon: Routledge.

References

Adler, Z. (1987), *Rape on Trial*. London: Routledge.

Adler, Z. (2000), 'Male Victims of Sexual Assault – Legal Issues', in Mezey, G., and King, M. (eds.), *Male Victims of Sexual Assault* (2nd ed.). Oxford: OUP.

Box, S. (1983), *Power, Crime and Mystification*. London: Tavistock.

Boyle, K. (2018), 'Hiding in Plain Sight: Gender, Sexism and Press Coverage of the Jimmy Savile Case', *Journalism Studies*, **19**(11): 1562–78.

Burman, M. (2009), 'Evidencing Sexual Assault: Women in the Witness Box', *Probation Journal*, **56**(1): 1–20.

Burton, M. (2013), 'How Different Are "False" Accusations of Rape from False Complaints of GBH?' *Criminal Law Review*. 203–13.

Carline, A., and Gunby, C. (2011), ' "How an Ordinary Jury Makes Sense of It Is a Mystery": Barristers' Perspectives on Rape, Consent and the Sexual Offences Act 2003', *Liverpool Law Review*, **32**(3): 237–50.

Corteen, K., and Steele, R. (2018), 'A Criminal Injustice System? Sex Offender Suspects and Defendants', *Liverpool Law Review*, **39**(3): 265–77.

Crown Prosecution Service (2019), *Violence Against Women and Girls Report, 2018–19*. Available online at: www.cps.gov.uk/sites/default/files/documents/publications/cps-vawg-report-2019.pdf. Accessed 12 September 2019.

Dearden, L. (2018), 'Children "Abused Every Eight Minutes" in England and Wales as Recorded Sex Offences Hit Record High', *The Independent*, Tuesday 20 February. Available online at: www.independent.co.uk/news/uk/crime/child-abuse-sexual-offences-england-wales-record-all-time-high-eight-minutes-paedophilia-a8218576.html. Accessed 9 May 2019.

Gardner, S. (1996), 'Appreciating *Olugboja*', *Legal Studies*, **16**(3): 275–97.

Greer, C., and McLaughlin, E. (2013), 'The Sir Jimmy Savile Scandal: Child Sexual Abuse and Institutional Denial at the BBC', *Crime, Media, Culture*, **9**(3): 243–63.

Henham, R. (1998), 'Sentencing Sex Offenders: Some Implications of Recent Criminal Justice Policy', *Howard Journal of Criminal Justice*, **37**(1): 70–81.

Herring, J. (2019), *Criminal Law* (11th ed.). London: Palgrave Macmillan.

HM Inspectorate of Constabulary (2014), *Crime Recording: Making the Victim Count*. Available online at: www.justiceinspectorates.gov.uk/hmicfrs/wp-content/uploads/crime-recording-making-the-victim-count.pdf. Accessed 25 April 2019.

Hohl, K., and Stanko, E.A. (2015), 'Complaints of Rape and the Criminal Justice System: Fresh Evidence on the Attrition Problem in England and Wales', *European Journal of Criminology*, **12**(3): 324–41.

Horvath, M.A.H., Tong, S., and Williams, E. (2011), 'Critical Issues in Rape Investigation: An Overview of Reform in England and Wales', *Journal of Criminal Justice Research*, **1**: 1–18.

Hughes, B., Parker, H., and Gallagher, B. (1996), *Policing Child Sexual Abuse: The View from Police Practitioners*. London: Home Office Police Research Group.

Jones, T., and Newburn, T. (2013), 'Policy Convergence, Politics and Comparative Penal Reform: Sex Offender Notification Schemes in the USA and UK', *Punishment and Society*, **15**(5): 439–67.

Jordan, J. (2001), 'Worlds Apart? Women, Rape and the Police Reporting Process', *British Journal of Criminology*, **41**(4): 679–707.

Jordan, J. (2011), 'Here We Go Round the Review-Go-Round: Rape Investigation and Prosecution – Are Things Getting Worse, Not Better?' *Journal of Sexual Aggression*, **17**(3): 234–49.

Kelly, L. (1988), *Surviving Sexual Violence*. Cambridge: Polity Press.

Kelly, L. (2010), 'The (In) Credible Words of Women: False Allegations in European Rape Research', *Violence Against Women*, **16**: 1345–55.

Kelly, L., Lovett, J., and Regan, L. (2005), *A Gap or Chasm?* Home Office Research Study No.293. London: Home Office.

Kelly, L., Temkin, J., and Griffiths, S. (2006), *Section 41: An Evaluation of New Legislation Limiting Sexual History in Rape Trials*. Home Office Online Report No. 20/06.

Kemshall, H., Mackenzie, G., Wood, J., Bailey, R., and Yates, J. (2005), *Strengthening Multi-Agency Public Protection Arrangements (MAPPAs)*. Home Office Development and Practice Report No.45. London: Home Office.

Lees, S. (1997), *Ruling Passions: Sexual Violence, Reputation and the Law*. Buckingham: Open University Press.

Mackinnon, C.A. (1983), 'Feminism, Marxism, Method and the State: Toward Feminist Jurisprudence', *Signs*, **8**(4): 635–58.

Mancini, C., and Shields, R.T. (2014), 'Notes on a (Sex Crime) Scandal: The Impact of Media Coverage of Sexual Abuse in the Catholic Church on Public Opinion', *Journal of Criminal Justice*, **42**(2): 221–32.

McAlinden, A-M. (2006), 'Managing Risk: From Regulation to the Reintegration of Sexual Offenders', *Criminology and Criminal Justice*, **6**(3): 197–218.

McEwan, J.A. (2005), 'Proving Consent in Sexual Cases: Legislative Change and Cultural Evolution', *International Journal of Evidence and Proof*, **9**(1): 1–28.

McMillan, L. (2018), 'Police Officers' Perceptions of False Allegations of Rape', *Journal of Gender Studies*, **27**(1): 9–21.

Mezey, G., and King, M. (2000), 'Treatment of Male Victims of Sexual Assault', in Mezey, G., and King, M. (eds.), *Male Victims of Sexual Assault* (2nd ed.). Oxford: OUP.

Naughton, M. (2010), *Claims of Innocence: An Introduction to Wrongful Convictions and How They Might Be Challenged*. Bristol: University of Bristol.

ONS (2018a), *Sexual Offences in England and Wales, Year Ending March 2017*. Available online at: www.ons.gov.uk/peoplepopulationandcommunity/crimeandjustice/articles/sexualoffencesinenglandandwales/yearendingmarch2017. Accessed 3 May 2019.

ONS (2018b), *Sexual Offending: Victimisation and the Path Through the Criminal Justice System*. Available online at: www.ons.gov.uk/peoplepopulationandcommunity/crimeandjustice/articles/sexualoffendingvictimisationandthepaththroughthecriminaljusticesystem/2018-12-13#sentencing. Accessed 9 May 2019.

Plotnikoff, J., and Woolfson, R. (2000), *Where Are They Now? An Evaluation of Sex Offender Registration in England and Wales*. Police Research Series Paper No.126. London: Home Office.

Radford, L., Corral, S., Bradley, C., Fisher, H., Bassett, C., Howat, N., and Collishaw, S. (2011), *Child Abuse and Neglect in the UK Today*. London: NSPCC.

Rumney, P.N.S. (2001), 'Male Rape in the Courtroom: Issues and Concerns', *Criminal Law Review*: 205–13.

Rumney, P.N.S., and McCartan, K.F. (2017), 'Purported False Allegations of Rape, Child Abuse and Non-Sexual Violence: Nature, Characteristics and Implications', *Journal of Criminal Law*, **81**(6): 497–520.

Silverman, J., and Wilson, D. (2002), *Innocence Betrayed: Paedophilia, the Media and Society*. Cambridge: Polity Press.

Soothill, K. (1991), 'The Changing Face of Rape?' *British Journal of Criminology*, **31**(4): 383–92.

Soothill, K., and Francis, B. (1997), 'Sexual Reconvictions and the Sex Offenders Act 1997 – Part One', *New Law Journal*, **147** (5 September): 1285–6.

Soothill, K., and Walby, S. (1991), *Sex Crime in the News*. London: Routledge.

Temkin, J. (2000), 'Prosecuting and Defending Rape: Perspectives from the Bar', *Journal of Law and Society*, **27**(2): 219–48.

Temkin, J. (2002), *Rape and the Legal Process* (2nd ed.). Oxford: OUP.

Temkin, J., and Ashworth, A. (2004), 'The Sexual Offences Act 2003: (1) Rape, Sexual Assaults and the Problems of Consent', *Criminal Law Review*: 328–46.

Temkin, J., and Krahé, B. (2008), *Sexual Assault and the Justice Gap*. Oxford: Hart.

Thomas, T. (2003), 'Sex Offender Community Notification: Experiences from America', *Howard Journal of Criminal Justice*, **42**(3): 217–28.

Thomas, T. (2008), 'The Sex Offender "Register": A Case Study in Function Creep', *Howard Journal of Criminal Justice*, **47**(3): 227–37.

Thomas, T. (2015), *Sex Crime: Sex Offending and Society* (3rd ed.). Abingdon: Routledge.

Walklate, S. (2008), 'What Is to Be Done About Violence Against Women? Gender, Violence, Cosmopolitanism and the Law', *British Journal of Criminology*, **48**(1): 39–54.

Offences against society

Chapter aims

After reading Chapter 9, you should be able to understand:

- The framework of public order offences defined in the Public Order Act 1986 and the common law in terms of actus reus and mens rea requirements
- The civil law orders regulating antisocial behaviour and how these operate
- The framework of offences relating to the possession and supply of prohibited drugs, in the Misuse of Drugs Act 1971 and the Psycho-active Substances Act 2016

- The framework of offences relating to the possession of different types of offensive weapons
- How the different stages of criminal justice respond to these types of offences
- How the evidence on the responses to offences against society in criminal law and criminal justice fits in with the theoretical models introduced in Chapter 1

Introduction

Chapter 9 deals with a group of criminal law offences that involve the regulation of behaviour that criminal law views as being harmful to society, rather than necessarily harmful to an individual in terms of damaging their physical or mental health or property. This is particularly true of public order offences (Smith 1987: 1–3) but is also true of a range of other offences that aim to reduce threats to public order and safety. In this context, the chapter discusses civil behaviour orders, as well as drugs offences and weapons offences, before analysing the criminal justice response to each of these offence types, and linking back to the roadmap theories in Chapter 1.

Offences against society: the law

Public order offences

Breach of the peace

Breach of the peace is not a substantive criminal offence in England, but it does give the police the power to arrest when a breach occurs in their presence or when a breach is reasonably anticipated (Channing 2017). This common law power is retained in s.40 (4) of the Public Order Act 1986. A breach of the peace occurs when harm occurs, or is likely to occur, to a person or to a person's property in their presence. It can also occur where a person fears such harm through assault, affray, riot, unlawful assembly or another disturbance (*Howell* [1982] QB 416). Breaches of the peace can occur on private land as well as in public spaces (*McConnell v CC Greater Manchester Police* [1990] 1 WLR 364). Any member of the public has the right to take reasonable steps, including detention, against someone who is breaching the peace or threatening to do so (*Albert v Lavin* [1982] AC 546). What the police cannot do is take action short of arrest to prevent a breach of the peace which is not sufficiently imminent to justify arrest (*R (Laporte) v CC Gloucestershire Police* [2007] 2 WLR 46). Although breach of the peace is not a substantive crime, it can lead to magistrates issuing a binding over to be of good behaviour, or to keep the peace, under s.1(7) of the Justices of the Peace Act 1968 and s.115 of the Magistrates' Court Act 1980.

Offences relating to trespass and unlawful assembly

S.11 of the Public Order Act 1986 makes it an offence not to give the police written advance notice of a public procession, and an offence not to comply with the terms of the written notice in terms of the specified date, time, or route of the procession. The police can impose conditions on the timing and route of public processions (under s.12) and assemblies (under s.14), either before or during the activity if they reasonably believe that the activity may result in public disorder, serious property damage, disruption to community life, or intimidation of others acting lawfully. Failure to comply with such conditions gives rise to an offence. In *Austin (FC) and another v Commissioner of Police of the Metropolis* [2009] UKHL 5, the House of Lords decided that the police tactic of 'kettling', or restricting the movement of protestors without food, water, or toilet facilities, did not deprive protestors of their right to liberty under s.5(1) of the ECHR.

The Criminal Justice and Public Order Act 1994, alongside giving police powers of entry, search, seizure, and dispersal in relation to outdoor raves, also created the offence of aggravated trespass. The offence occurs under s.68 of the Act, when someone trespasses on private land with the intention of intimidating people and discouraging them from taking part in a lawful activity, obstructing a lawful activity, or disrupting a lawful activity. S.69 makes it an offence not to leave private land when told to do so by police, or to return to private land within seven days if told to leave. S.70 amends s.14 of the Public Order Act 1986 to make it an offence to organise, take part in, or incite another to take part in a trespassory assembly that the police have banned.

Offences of disorderly behaviour

Section 4 of the 1986 Act makes it an offence to use threatening, abusive, or insulting words or behaviour, or to distribute to another person any writing or images that are threatening, abusive, or insulting, in either public or private (unless D and V are both in a dwelling). The mens rea is intent to cause V to believe that immediate unlawful violence will be used against them by someone else, or intent to provoke the immediate use of unlawful violence, or whereby V is likely to believe that violence will be used or provoked. Section 4A of the 1986 Act has the same actus reus as the s.4 offence but a different mens rea. For the section 4A offence, the mens rea is an intention to cause V harassment, alarm, or distress. Both the s.4 and the s.4A offences can be charged as racially or religiously aggravated offences under the Crime and Disorder Act 1998 ss.31(1)(a) and 31(1)(b), as amended by the Anti-Terrorism, Crime and Security Act 2001.

S.5 of the 1986 Act (as amended by s.57 of the Crime and Courts Act 2013) creates an offence of causing harassment, alarm, or distress. The offence can occur in a public or private place (unless both D and V are in a private dwelling), with the same types of conduct as the S.4 offence. It must also occur within the actual hearing or sight of a person who is likely to experience harassment, alarm, or distress through D's conduct (*Holloway v DPP* [2004] EWHC 2621 (Admin)). In *Hammond v DPP* [2004] EWHC 69, a sign saying 'stop immorality', 'stop homosexuality', and 'stop lesbianism' was held to be insulting. The mens rea for the s.5 offence is an intention that the words or behaviour will be threatening or abusive, an awareness that they may be threatening or abusive, an intention that the words or behaviour will be disorderly, or an awareness that they may be disorderly.

Finally, under s.91 of the Criminal Justice Act 1967, there is also an offence of drunken behaviour. This offence simply requires disorderly behaviour in a public place while drunk. This offence is summary only, and the maximum penalty is a fine.

Affray

Under s.3 of the Public Order Act 1986, the actus reus for affray is the use of violence, or threat of the use of violence, towards another person. Conduct must be such as to cause a person of reasonable firmness, present at the scene, to fear for their personal safety. However, no reasonable person has to be, or be likely to be, present at the scene of the offence – this is a hypothetical test (*Sanchez* [1996] Crim LR 572). If more than one person is involved in the affray, prosecutors need to consider the conduct of both or all of them for the purposes of proving the offence. Threats made by words alone are not enough to prove affray. Affrays can occur in private or public places. The mens rea, under s.6(2) of the 1986 Act, is an intention to use or threaten violence, or an awareness that conduct may be violent or may threaten violence. Affray is a triable either way offence. The maximum sentence for affray in the Crown Court is three years' imprisonment. In *I and others v DPP* [2002] 1 AC 285, the House of Lords stated that the carrying of dangerous weapons (petrol bombs in this case) by a group of people without waving them or brandishing them was enough to prove a threat of unlawful violence. However, the court also stated that a person threatened with violence must be present at the scene in order to prove that affray has occurred.

Violent disorder

Under s.2 of the Public Order Act 1986, the actus reus for violent disorder requires three or more people present together, to use (or threaten to use) unlawful violence for a common purpose. It is possible to infer common purpose from the group's conduct. 'Violence' for the purposes of violent disorder and riot (discussed next) is basically defined in s.8 as any violent behaviour against a person or property, and including any behaviour capable of damage or harm, not only behaviour which does cause or intends to cause these things. The group does not have to use or threaten violence all at the same time. Not all three people need to be charged and prosecuted for violent disorder, as long as the person on trial was one of the group (*Mahroof* (1988) 88 Cr App Rep 317). Their conduct, taken together, must be such as to cause a person of reasonable firmness, present at the scene, to fear for their personal safety. However, no reasonable person has to be, or be likely to be, present at the scene of the offence. Violent disorder can occur in private or public places. The mens rea, under s.6(2) of the 1986 Act, is an intention to use or threaten violence, or an awareness that conduct may be violent or may threaten violence. Violent disorder is a triable either way offence. The maximum sentence for violent disorder in the Crown Court is five years' imprisonment.

Riot

Under s.1 of the Public Order Act 1986, the actus reus of the offence of riot requires 12 or more people present together, to use (or threaten to use) unlawful violence for a common purpose. It is possible to infer common purpose from the group's conduct. The group does not have to use or threaten violence all at the same time. Their conduct, taken together, must be such as to cause a person of reasonable firmness, present at the scene, to fear for their personal safety. However, no reasonable person has to be, or be likely to be, present at the scene of the offence. Riots can occur in private or public places. The mens rea, under s.6(1) of the 1986 Act, is an intention to use violence, or an awareness that conduct may be violent. Riot is triable only in the Crown Court, where the maximum sentence for it is 10 years' imprisonment. *Jefferson* [1994] 1 All ER 270 confirmed that secondary offenders (see Chapter 4 for further discussion on this issue) can also commit the offence of riot through assisting or encouraging main offenders.

As well as the public order offences discussed here, you should also refer back to the discussion of stalking and harassment offences in Chapter 6. The kind of behaviour criminalised by those offences overlaps with the kind of behaviour criminalised by public order offences, especially the offences in ss.4, 4A, and 5 of the Public Order Act 1986.

Study exercise 9.1

Read the case of *Blackshaw* [2011] EWCA Crim 2312. Do you agree with the sentence that Blackshaw received? If not, how would you have sentenced this case?

Antisocial behaviour offences

Part 2 of the Antisocial Behaviour, Crime and Policing Act 2014 introduces Criminal Behaviour Orders, which replace Antisocial Behaviour Orders (introduced in the Crime and Disorder Act 1998), as a response to antisocial behaviour. A court can give only Criminal Behaviour Orders (hereafter CBOs) after a criminal conviction. To give a CBO, the court must be satisfied beyond reasonable doubt that the offender has engaged in behaviour that caused, or was likely to cause, harassment, alarm, or distress to any person (this is the only definition of antisocial behaviour used in the law and mirrors the definition in the 1998 Act) (Jarvis 2015). In addition, the court must believe that making the order will help in preventing the offender from engaging in such behaviour. CBOs include prohibitions against certain types of behaviour but can also include requirements that aim to address the causes of the antisocial behaviour. There is no need for a causal link between the behaviour that led to the criminal conviction and the behaviour that has led to the application for a CBO. In deciding whether to make a CBO, a court may take account of conduct occurring up to one year before the commencement day. The court must specify the length of the CBO. If the offender is under age 18, the CBO must last for between one and three years. If the offender is over age 18, the CBO must last for a fixed period of two years or more, or must be indefinite until further review. If an offender breaches any CBO condition or requirement, proof of the breach is a criminal offence punishable by a maximum of six months' imprisonment in the magistrates' court, or a maximum of five years' imprisonment in the Crown Court.

Other responses to note, which do not require a criminal conviction, are civil injunctions and community prevention notices (hereafter 'CPNs') that prevent various types of antisocial behaviour. Civil injunctions and CPNs have no maximum time limit. For adults, a breach of a civil injunction can receive a sentence of up to two years' imprisonment in the Crown Court, and breach of a CPN is punishable by a maximum fine of £2,500.

Study exercise 9.2

Compare criminal law's definition of antisocial behaviour with the definitions of public order offences discussed earlier. Given the range of public order offences available, what rationale (if any) do you think there is for having antisocial behaviour offences in criminal law as well?

Drugs offences

The main offences aimed at regulating the use of controlled drugs appear in the Misuse of Drugs Act 1971. The discussion will now explain each of the key offence types in turn.

Possession offences

Under s.5(1) of the 1971 Act, it is an offence to possess a drug if that drug is specified as being Class A, B, or C in Schedule 2 of the 1971 Act. Table 9.1 shows the classification of commonly used drugs in England under Schedule 2 of the Act. Note that there are many other drugs included in the three categories of controlled drugs apart from the ones listed in Table 9.1.

Under *Warner v MPC* [1969] 2 AC 256, D possesses a controlled drug if they are in physical possession or control of the drug and have knowledge of possession. It is not necessary for D to know that what they possess is a controlled drug. However, it is a defence to possession charges (and other drug-related offences) if D neither knew, suspected, or had reason to suspect that the substance that they possessed was a controlled drug (s.28 of the 1971 Act). D only has an evidential burden in relation to calling evidence that they did not have knowledge, belief, or suspicion in relation to what they possessed was – it is the prosecution's role to prove that D had such knowledge, belief, or suspicion (*Lambert* [2002] 2 AC 545). D can still possess a drug if they control it, even if the drug was in the custody of someone else.

Supply and production offences

Under s.5(3) of the 1971 Act, it is an offence to possess a controlled drug with intent to supply that drug to another person. For this offence, the prosecution must prove possession (discussed earlier) and must also prove an intention to supply. A number of factors can be used to infer intention to supply if D does not admit to it. These factors include:

• Possession of a quantity of drugs inconsistent with personal use;
• Possession of uncut or pure drugs suggesting proximity to manufacturers or importers;

Table 9.1 The classification of controlled drugs in England

Class A	Class B	Class C
Diamorphine (heroin)	Amphetamine	Tranquiliser drugs
Cocaine/crack cocaine	Cannabis/cannabis resin	Gamma Hydroxybutyrate (GHB)
Psilocin (magic mushrooms)	Codeine	Anabolic steroids
Ecstasy	Ketamine	Khat
LSD	Synthetic cannabinoids (e.g. Spice)	
Methamphetamine (crystal meth)	Barbiturates	

- Possession of a variety of different drugs;
- Evidence of preparation of drugs for sale (e.g. cutting equipment, weighing scales, drugs divided into portions and wrapped up), or;
- Information relating to supply (e.g. records of phone numbers and quantities of drugs).

D's possession of large amounts of money could be evidence of past supply but cannot be evidence of future intent to supply by itself (*Batt* [1994] Crim LR 592) and is only admissible as evidence if it is of probative significance to an issue in the case (*Morris* (1995) 2 Cr App Rep 69).

Under s.4 of the 1971 Act, it is an offence to produce a controlled drug, to supply a controlled drug to another person, or to offer to supply a controlled drug to another person. The prosecution needs to prove production of a controlled drug, a link between D and the drug's production, and D's knowledge of the production of a controlled drug. An offence of production is committed when D has some identifiable participation in the process of producing a controlled drug by manufacture, cultivation, or any other method. Under *Maginnis* [1987] 1 All ER 907, supplying means more than transfer of physical control over the controlled drugs. It also includes the recipient of the drugs being able to apply the drugs handed over to purposes that they desire. This means that returning drugs to the original supplier would count as a supply offence. The Drugs Act 2005 inserted s.4A into the 1971 Act. S.4A makes the supply of controlled drugs on, or near, school premises, and the use of a courier under the age of 18 to supply drugs, aggravating factors. Under s.37(1) of the 1971 Act, supplying includes distribution and does not require proof of reward or profit from the act of supply. Injecting someone with a controlled drug is not supplying that drug to him or her (*Harris* [1968] 1 WLR 769).

Importation and exportation offences

S.3 of the 1971 Act prohibits the importation and exportation of controlled drugs. The actual offence of knowingly acquiring possession of prohibited goods, and knowingly being involved in carrying, removing, depositing, harbouring, keeping, or concealing or in any manner dealing with any such goods, with intent to evade (or attempt to evade) prohibition of the goods, is in s.170 of the Customs and Excise Management Act 1979.

Table 9.2 shows the maximum sentences in the Crown Court for possession, possession with intent to supply, production, supply, and importation/exportation of controlled drugs, under Schedule 4 of the 1971 Act.

Offences against the Psychoactive Substances Act 2016

The Psychoactive Substances Act 2016 makes it an offence to produce, supply, offer to supply, possess with intent to supply, import and export psychoactive

Table 9.2 Maximum sentences for drugs offences in England in the Crown Court

Offence Type	Class A	Class B	Class C
Possession	Seven years' imprisonment and/or fine	Five years' imprisonment and/or fine	Two years' imprisonment and/or fine
Possession with intent to supply, supply, production, importation and exportation	Life imprisonment and/or fine	14 years' imprisonment and/or fine	14 years' imprisonment and/or fine

substances and to possess a psychoactive substance in a custodial institution. The maximum sentence for all of these offences apart from possessing a psychoactive substance in a custodial institution is seven years' imprisonment. For the possession of a psychoactive substance in a custodial institution offence, the maximum sentence is two years' imprisonment.

Under s.2 of the 2016 Act, a psychoactive substance is any substance capable of producing a psychoactive effect in someone who consumes it, and a psychoactive effect is the stimulation or depression of the person's central nervous system, which affects the person's mental functioning or emotional state. The 2016 Act therefore regulates 'legal highs' such as nitrous oxide.

Study exercise 9.3

Read Nutt et al. (2010). Do you agree with how the authors of this article approach the issue of classifying illegal drugs? What implications do you think their findings have for the ways in which alcohol use is currently regulated in England?

Weapons offences

It is an offence to possess an offensive weapon without lawful authority or excuse, under s.1(1) of the Prevention of Crime Act 1953. S.1(4) of the 1953 Act defines an offensive weapon as any article made or adapted for use for causing injury to the person, or intended by the person having it with them for such use by them. Under *Jura* [1954] 1 QB 503, if D uses an article offensively in a public place, the offensive use of the article is not conclusive of the question as to whether D had it with them as an offensive weapon. Having an article innocently will convert into having the article guiltily if an intent to use the article offensively forms before the actual occasion to use violence has arisen. It is a defence to this offence if D can prove lawful authority or a reasonable excuse for possessing the weapon. In *Williamson* (1978) 67 Cr App Rep 35, the Court of Appeal identified three types of offensive weapons. The first type are offensive weapons designed for causing injury to the person. The second type are weapons that are not designed for causing injury but that are adapted for that purpose. The third type are weapons not designed or adapted for causing injury but intended by the person who has the weapon for the purpose of causing personal injury to someone. The question of whether an article is an offensive weapon is one of fact for the magistrates or jury.

Section 139 of the Criminal Justice Act 1988 makes it an offence to have an article with a blade or point in a public place. It is a defence to prove lawful authority or reasonable excuse. It is also a defence to show that D possessed the article for use at work, that D had the article for religious reasons, or that D had the article as part of a national costume. *Brooker v DPP* [2005] EWHC 1132 stated that a butter knife without any blade or point is a bladed article, but *Davies* [1998] Crim LR 564 showed that a screwdriver is not a bladed article. Section 139A, inserted by the Offensive Weapons Act 1996, makes it a specific offence to have an article with a blade or point on school premises. S.28 of the Criminal Justice and Courts Act 2015 introduced a minimum sentence of six months' imprisonment for a second conviction for any of the three offences discussed in this section, for anyone age 16 or over.

Section 1A of the 1953 Act, inserted by s.142(1) of the Legal Aid, Sentencing and Punishment of Offenders Act 2012, makes it an offence to threaten another person unlawfully and intentionally with an offensive weapon in a public place, in such a way that there is an immediate risk of serious physical harm to that other person. 'Serious physical harm' in this offence means grievous bodily harm (see Chapter 6). There is no defence of lawful authority or reasonable excuse to this offence. Similarly, there is s.139AA of the 1988 Act, inserted by s.142(2) of the Legal Aid, Sentencing and Punishment of Offenders Act 2012. This makes it an offence to threaten another person unlawfully and intentionally with an offensive weapon or bladed article in a public place or on school premises, in such a way that there is an immediate risk of serious physical harm to that other person. The minimum sentence for both of the offences discussed in this paragraph is six months' imprisonment for those aged 16 or over.

Finally, s.19 of the Firearms Act 1968, as amended by s.37 of the Antisocial Behaviour Act 2003, makes it a specific offence to carry a firearm in a public place. The definition of 'firearm' includes a loaded shotgun, a loaded or unloaded air weapon, any other loaded or unloaded firearm together with suitable ammunition, or any imitation firearm. The maximum sentence for this offence in the Crown Court is seven years' imprisonment or 12 months' imprisonment if the weapon is an imitation firearm.

Study exercise 9.4

Which of the weapons possession offences discussed earlier (if any) would you remove from criminal law? Give reasons for your answer.

Offences against society and criminal justice

Public order offences and criminal justice

Criminal justice statistics do not differentiate between the different types of public order offences. In 2018, the police recorded 438,236 public order offences, an increase of 19% from the previous year (ONS 2019). It is almost impossible to say whether this change reflects differences in police recording practices (the reclassification of antisocial behaviour as public order offences, for example) or a genuine increase in offending. We can say that for public order offences generally, in 2018, the conviction rate was 94.1%, the highest for any offence group, and while the custody rate was comparable to other offence types at 29%, the average custodial sentence length was 6.7 months, lower than for any other offence group (Ministry of Justice 2019a). The last of these statistics perhaps reflects the very wide range of behaviour covered by the category of public order offences.

Lowerson (2018) argues that the definition of riot is vague and was hastily drafted in response to the threat to public order posed by the Miners' Strike of 1984–5. As such, the CPS and courts rarely prosecute or convict for riot, particularly in relation to football-related disorder. Lowerson goes on to argue that one of the main reasons for riot's rare usage by criminal justice is the offence's requirement that 12 people are involved in the offence. We can contrast this with the old common law definition of riot, which only required the involvement of three people (*Field v Receiver of Metropolitan Police* [1907] 2 KB 859). Lowerson also criticises the offences of riot and violent disorder for removing the need for a reasonable person who fears for their safety to be present at the scene of the offence. For Lowerson, this is an issue not only in terms of making the offences unfairly wide, but also in terms of making them harder to prosecute and convict.

Lightowlers and Quirk (2015) show how harshly the criminal justice process responded to those who took part in the English riots of summer 2011. Lightowlers and Quirk, using data from the North-West of England, argue that the criminal justice response was progressively harsher than normal all the way through the process. This was true in terms of the charge (where behaviour was far more likely to be charged as burglary than theft – also interestingly, very few people were charged with the riot offence itself). It was also true of court processes (where rates of remand to custody and sending of triable either way cases to the Crown Court rose sharply), and sentencing (where sentencing guidelines were ignored by courts, and custody rates and sentence lengths increased noticeably for those involved in the riots). Such a criminal justice approach focuses on individual responsibility for public order-related crime. However, it ignores the empirical evidence presented by Lightowlers (2015) that points to a connection between social and economic exclusion and inequality and the likelihood of engaging in public order-related behaviour, of charges for such behaviour, and sentences for such behaviour in court. This represents evidence of criminal justice ignoring the social context of offending and causing further feelings of injustice through harsh responses – Lewis et al. (2011) found that rioters saw police violence and injustice as a key trigger for rioting. Such a view receives further support from research by Briggs (2012), Treadwell et al. (2013), and Winlow et al. (2015). This body of research argues that criminal justice disregards the effects of a neoliberal socio-economic approach that systematically excludes the poorest in society from opportunities to succeed in life, harshly punishing those who are seen as offenders, while at the same time encouraging the excluded to become individually selfish, and to define success through acquisition and consumption of material goods. Newburn's (2016) comparative analysis of riots in different countries found interesting differences not only in the nature of riots (far more based on theft and burglary in England than in France or Sweden) but also in the response to them (a far harsher and longer-lasting criminal justice response in England than in France or Sweden).

Greer and McLaughlin (2010) examine media coverage of the protests at the G20 summit in London in 2009. They note the shift towards 'citizen journalists' recording news events at the scene of the protests and the police's response to those protests. They also argue that individuals have an increased ability to produce and use information that challenges the State's version of public order-related events using technology such as smartphones. There is also a marketplace that can profit from anti-establishment news (social media sites such as Facebook, Twitter, Snapchat, and Instagram, for example). Together, these factors can change media and public views about who is to blame for public order-related violence.

So far, the discussion in this section has focussed on the more serious public order offences, such as riot and violent disorder. Given the wide scope of police powers to regulate lower-level public order offences such as those under sections 4 and 5 of the 1986 Public Order Act, it is perhaps not surprising that section 5 powers are used widely by police, often in situations where neither the police nor the public are actually alarmed or distressed by behaviour, or where there is no real purpose for arrest (Brown and Ellis 1994). Although the usage of Penalty Notices for Disorder has declined noticeably over the past decade, they are still used more commonly for section 5 and drunk and disorderly offences than for any other offence except theft (Ministry of Justice

2019a: table Q2.1). In 2017, there was a 70.9% conviction rate for the section 4A offence, with a fine (37%) being the most popular sentence; for the section 4 offence, there was a 79.6% conviction rate, with a community order (37%) being the most popular sentence; and for the section 5 offence, there was a 82.6% conviction rate, with a fine (56.6%) being the most popular sentence. While the number of section 4A cases has only declined slightly between 2007 and 2017, the numbers of section 4 and section 5 cases have declined sharply over the same time (Ministry of Justice 2018).

Study exercise 9.5

Read the account of Angie Zelter's conviction for a public order offence because of her involvement in the Extinction Rebellion protests of April 2019 in Taylor (2019). Taking into account what Angie Zelter did and why she did it, would you have convicted her of a public order offence? Explain your answer.

Antisocial behaviour offences and criminal justice

It is useful to examine the historical enforcement of antisocial behaviour legislation in England and Wales before moving on to the current framework. This is true because the new framework of civil injunctions and Criminal Behaviour Orders following conviction retains the open-ended definition of antisocial behaviour, the restrictive conditions, and the criminal punishment on breach that the previous antisocial behaviour order, or ASBO, had.

The ASBO received heavy academic criticism following its introduction in the 1998 Crime and Disorder Act. Macdonald (2006) pointed to the usage of ASBOs to regulate and punish behaviour that would never be considered criminal in its own right, such as attempted suicide. Bakalis (2003) criticised the uncertainty over whether ASBOs were a civil or criminal law measure. Burney (2009: ch.5), on the other hand, criticised the 1998 Act's definition of antisocial behaviour as individualising, exclusionary, and ignorant of the social causes of antisocial behaviour – a criticism which can also be made about the Criminal Behaviour Orders which replaced the ASBO, since the definition has remained the same. Burney (ibid: ch.10) further argues that using the law to replace welfare measures as a tool for responding to antisocial behaviour in this way has little chance of reducing and preventing it. This is especially true given the compelling evidence of the inconsistent enforcement of ASBOs in different areas of the UK (Millie 2009: ch.2), and of the disproportionate impact of ASBOs in terms of criminalising young people's behaviour that was previously considered normal (Goldsmith 2008; McIntosh

2008). Other evidence pointed to a lack of criminal justice understanding of the impact of ASBOs on young people with learning disabilities (Fyson and Yates 2011) or from Black, Asian and Minority Ethnic (BAME) backgrounds (Prior and Spalek 2008). Research done by Matthews et al. (2007) showed that while some criminal justice practitioners in their study saw potential in ASBOs to protect communities from harm, others saw ASBOs as punitive, targeted at vulnerable populations, and characterised by the imposition of conditions that were inappropriate or unenforceable.

Government data show that the number of breaches of criminal behaviour orders has increased rapidly since the introduction of the orders in 2014. In 2015, 889 people were prosecuted in England and Wales for breaching criminal behaviour orders, but, by 2017, the number had risen to 3,142, with an 88.8% conviction rate, and a 33.3% rate of immediate custody that has remained consistent since the orders' introduction (Ministry of Justice 2018).

Study exercise 9.6

How, if at all, do you think criminal behaviour orders are a more effective response to antisocial behaviour than the previous antisocial behaviour orders were?

Drugs offences and criminal justice

Evidence shows that the nature, extent, and economics of drug use in Britain is considerable. Bean (2014: 155) cites data suggesting that the size of the drugs market in Britain could be anywhere between £4bn and £8n per year, with around 300 major drug importers, 3,000 drug wholesalers, and 70,000 street dealers. This has led to some academicians arguing that drug use has become normalised in the sense of being accepted as normal behaviour not worthy of reporting or sanction, particularly among young people (Parker et al. 1998). This is a point that, if true, shows the limits of what criminal justice can do to address and reduce drug use. The Home Office (2018) estimated that in 2017–18, around one in 11 adults aged 16 to 59 (around 3 million people) took a drug in the previous year, a rate that has remained relatively stable over the previous decade. Drug use was more common among 16 to 24-year-olds, who were also most likely to be frequent users, defined as drug use more than once a month. Cannabis was the most commonly used drug, followed by powder cocaine (ibid: ch.2). Frequent drug use is much more likely among those who participate in the night-time economy by visiting bars and night-clubs, and more likely among people with low levels of happiness (ibid: ch.3). There is clearly a high reported rate of drug use in English society compared with the number of people receiving a criminal justice intervention for drug use, and a high rate of people who think it would be easy to obtain drugs within 24 hours if they wanted them (37% in the 2017/18 CSEW – ibid: 31). Stevens (2011) points to the link between socio-economic deprivation and inequality on the one hand and the likelihood of drug addiction on the other.

Turning to statistics about criminal justice responses to drug use, in 2018, 14,653 people (29.6% of those proceeded against by criminal justice agencies for this type of offence) received a caution for drugs-related offences – a noticeable decrease from the 46,419 (47.7%) people cautioned in 2008 (Ministry of Justice 2019a: table Q2.2). However, there was also a decrease in the number of people proceeded against in magistrates' courts for drugs offences over the same period, from 55,195 in 2008 to 38,763 in 2018 (ibid. table Q3.2). Guilty plea rates and conviction rates for drugs offences are among the highest for any offence group, standing at 82% and over 90% respectively in 2016 (Ministry of Justice 2018: 18). Usage of fines and community sentences for drugs offences has declined in recent years (ibid: 23, 25). By contrast, the custody rate for drugs offences has increased over the past decade, from 18.4% in 2008 to 22.4% in 2018 (Ministry of Justice 2019a: table Q5.2b). In addition, the average length of custodial sentence for drugs offences has increased from 32.7 months to 36.1 months over the same period (ibid: table Q5.2c). This is evidence that the criminal justice approach to drugs offences is becoming harsher, even though the number of people sentenced in court for drugs offences was lower in 2018 (33,934) than at any time over the previous decade (ibid: table Q5.3). The introduction of the Psychoactive Substances Act 2016, which effectively presumed that substances were illegal unless the Act clearly stated that they were not, is further evidence of the continued toughening of criminal justice responses to drug use.

What is far less clear is the nature and extent of the link between drug use and crime that could justify intervention from criminal law and criminal justice. Stevens (2007) argues that claims about drug use causing crime are exaggerated, not only because the overlap between drug users and offenders is overestimated but also because of false assumptions that the same overlap is also present among much larger groups of unknown drug users and offenders. Stevens goes on to argue that this flawed knowledge has had undue influence on drugs-related criminal justice policy, because such knowledge is useful to powerful groups in terms of maintaining their own social power. Similarly, Seddon (2006) argues that the links between crime and drugs are localised, influenced by the availability of different drugs and their market value (see also Bennett and Holloway 2009). Seddon shows how criminal justice drug policy discourse often ignores the role of poverty and social exclusion in drug use. He also shows how a historical analysis of the response to heroin use, for example, reveals no particular policy connection with crime or other social problems until as late as the early 1980s, when heroin use became more common among young, unemployed people (Seddon 2017: 706–7). Nor should we overlook the role of large pharmaceutical companies in drug manufacture for profit, and the role of political events (such as the opening of new drug supply lines from the Golden Crescent region of Asia to increase availability in the case of heroin) in the availability and usage of illegal drugs (ibid.).

Bean (2014: 68) identifies four principles relating to drugs treatment within criminal justice. These are:

- Treatment should not be a substitute for punishment or legal sanctions;
- Treatment should be available to all and tailored to individual needs;
- Supervision of those being treated should continue throughout treatment, and;
- Offenders should remain accountable to criminal justice whether they are treated in prison or in the community.

Having reviewed the evidence, Bean (ibid: ch.4) notes the improvement in the effectiveness of criminal justice drugs treatment, in both the Drug Rehabilitation Requirement that can form part of a community order sentence, and in prison. However, he also points to the complexity of the management of community-based treatment, the higher reconviction rate for prisoners who used drugs before imprisonment, and the problem of drug use and trafficking in prisons (ibid:. 116). Overall, he doubts that criminal justice treatment meets these four principles consistently, given the lack of concrete evaluation of effectiveness of various criminal justice interventions, and limitations in the financial resources available for meaningful treatment. Bean also identifies confusion in what criminal justice drug testing and treatment is trying to achieve in terms of the choice between harm reduction and abstinence. Werb et al. (2016)'s review of international literature supports Bean's uncertainty about the effectiveness of compulsory drug treatment. Their review found no conclusive evidence of the effectiveness of compulsory drug treatment, with some studies suggesting that it caused additional harm to participants.

Stevens (2017: 831–2) puts forward ideas about drug policy that is driven by a medico-penal 'constellation' of public health professionals, the medical establishment, politicians, civil servants and criminal justice agencies rather than by academic evidence. Stevens points to the partial privatisation of criminal justice agencies' response to service users who use drugs, and the onset of payment by results, as a cause of harm among drug users who, for example, feel pressured into leaving treatment programmes too soon to meet targets. Such an emphasis on a particular definition of individualised 'recovery' as a target of criminal justice intervention contrasts with Wakeman's (2016) account of heroin use providing social and economic support in disadvantaged communities. Pierce et al. (2018) found uncertain evidence that initiating drug treatment on heroin users reduced the risk of fatal overdose, and found no evidence that such treatment reduced the risk of future property crime.

Overall, there is considerable evidence in favour of the normalisation of drugs in English society. There is also considerable evidence that public and criminal justice discourse about the 'drug problem' is based around particular understandings of terms like 'misuse', 'dependency', and 'addiction' that are often contested and ambiguous (Sturgeon-Adams 2013), which in turn confuses the purpose of treatment. Sensationalist media reporting of unusual drug-harm cases as being normal (Taylor 2008), and the exchange of user-generated information via online social media (Forsyth 2012), exaggerate the harm caused by illegal drugs. This can then play a part in the toughening of criminal justice's response, such as the prohibition of 'legal highs' in the Psychoactive Substances Act 2016 after media focus on young, middle-class people whose deaths were related to these substances and ignorance of more common heroin-related deaths (Stevens 2017: 835–40). This is the case despite considerable debate about how to measure the harm caused by illegal drugs (Rolles and Measham 2011), and evidence of the extensive harm caused by legalised substances such as alcohol (Nutt et al. 2010). Taylor et al. (2016) argue that selective regulation, decriminalisation, and legalisation of drugs in particular circumstances (such as the recent legalisation of cannabis for medicinal use) only reinforces the flaws inherent in the current socially exclusionary response associated with drug prohibition. Instead, Taylor et al. argue for an abolitionary response to drugs, starting with legalisation of all drugs possession for personal use, and policy firmly based on scientific evidence on the actual harm caused by different types of drugs.

Study exercise 9.7

Which currently illegal substances would you decriminalise (if any), and why?

Weapons offences and criminal justice

The possession of offensive weapons is often linked together by criminal justice with the violence that results from usage of these weapons, and the outcomes of non-fatal and fatal assaults using weapons are discussed in Chapters 6 and 7. The police have recorded increases in offences of attempted murder, threats to kill, rape, robbery, sexual assault, and homicide involving the use of a knife over the past five years. The result is that the number of knife-related offences of these types (excluding unreliable data from Greater Manchester Police) stood at 43,516 in the year to March 2019, 42% higher than in March 2011, the earliest date for comparable data (ONS 2019). Police rates of recording offences of knife possession rose by 21% in the year to March 2019 to 22,169, the highest number since specific data were made available in 2009 (ibid.). Padfield (2019) notes the recent increase in legislation and police stop and search powers in relation to weapons possession. In this context, it is unsurprising that the number of knife and offensive weapon offences has increased by 34% between 2015 and 2019, or that the rate of immediate custody has risen from 22% in 2009 to 37% in the year to March 2019. The average custodial sentence length has also risen from 5.5 months to 8.1 months over the past decade (Ministry of Justice 2019b).

There is clear evidence of the social harm caused by weapons possession, especially in urban areas (ONS 2019), but whether criminal justice actions such as more police powers and tougher sentencing are enough to address this harm is extremely doubtful (Padfield 2019). Roberts (2019) argues for a more community-driven and progressive approach, involving criminal justice partnerships sharing resources and information with a range of other agencies in the health and education sectors. The Violence Reduction Unit operating in Scotland has taken a similar approach to violent crime, with significant success, since 2005. Such an approach focuses on the physical, social, and psychological health of communities as a means of combating the kind of social exclusion, isolation, and fear in individuals that can and does lead to weapon possession and subsequent violence. Roberts' (ibid.) interviews with those directly affected by violent knife and gun crime also shows how government austerity policies, and cuts to police resources, youth services, health services, and accommodation resources in particular, make such a 'public health' approach far more difficult to achieve.

Study exercise 9.8

'Tougher prison sentences are a useful way of deterring people from carrying weapons'. Debate arguments in favour of and against this statement.

Conclusions: linking discussion to the roadmap theories

The offences discussed in this chapter cover a wide range of ground. The argument here, though, is that they share a feature. This is that they are 'pre-crime' offences (Zedner 2007) aimed at establishing a sense of security from threats (Wells and Quick 2010: 144), rather than being aimed at responding to direct harm to the person or to property. They attempt to reduce the risk of crime occurring by criminalising behaviour (such as weapons or drugs possession) or circumstances (such as groups of people behaving in a disorderly way) that are seen as triggering off other, more serious harm in some way.

Wells and Quick (2010: 225–9) identify several key themes in relation to these offences against society. They identify historical continuities in the identification of public disorder as being connected with socially marginalised groups: the poor, ethnic minorities, and the young (Pearson 1983). They point out how flexible the concept of public order offences is in criminal law and criminal justice, and how political the concept is. The close connection of the redefinition of public order offences in the Public Order Act 1986 with the events of the Miners' Strike of 1984–5 supports this view, as does the powerful influence of social elites in deciding on the responses to drug use and supply. They further illustrate how much the boundaries of this area of criminal law are defined by what the State sees as being a threat to its own authority. Wells and Quick also point out that socially harmful offences such as domestic violence and child abuse are not defined as being a public order threat by criminal law, despite the social damage that they cause. Next, Wells and Quick point to the influential role of the media in constructing moral panics in relation to particular kinds of public disorder. This argument is supported by the recent extension of the laws on illegal drug use and possession in the Psychoactive Substances Act 2016, following a chain of moral panics relating to high-profile deaths linked with drug use. The argument is also supported by the increasingly tough criminal law and criminal justice responses to knife and gun possession in recent times. Such a response claims to be responding to the genuine social harm caused by violence and property offences because of weapon possession and drug use and supply, but it is in fact undermined by socio-economic policies that create the social exclusion, isolation, and fear that so often lead to crime.

The very nature of these offences against society, and of many other offences of a similar kind that are outside the scope of this book, are connected with the idea of preventing the risk of criminal behaviour. However, the State's ideas about what is risky, together with the media's ideas on the same topic, are clearly dominant in criminal law and criminal justice responses to offences against society. For this reason, while liberal due process plays a part in criminal law and criminal justice response to offences against society in terms of offering basic safeguards to those accused of such offences by police and the courts, the radical and risk management models offer the most convincing explanation of what criminal law and criminal justice practice is really like. The combination of increasing numbers of criminal law offences on the one hand, and wide discretion and punitiveness with insufficient consideration of social causes of crime on the other, shows the strong explanatory power of these two models.

Key points

- The law on public order offences is defined by the Public Order Act 1986, which defines these offences broadly
- The law on drugs offences is primarily defined by the Misuse of Drugs Act 1971, but the capacity to regulate substance use has been widened considerably by the Psychoactive Substances Act 2016
- The law on weapons offences has been expanded by the addition of a range of recent criminal offences prioritising the regulation of risk
- Criminal justice's response to all of these offence types is based around responding to the risk of such behaviour triggering further criminal offences
- Criminal justice has become more punitive in terms of the response to these offence types over the past decade
- The radical and risk management roadmap theories best explain the focus on crime prevention inherent in offences against society, the State's great influence over the definition of what is and is not 'risky' or 'disorderly' behaviour, and the disproportionate effects of the criminal justice response on socially excluded groups

Further reading

Bean, P. (2014), *Drugs and Crime* (4th ed.). Abingdon: Routledge.
Roberts, S. (2019), 'The London Killings of 2018: The Story Behind the Numbers and Some Proposed Solutions', *Crime Prevention and Community Safety*, **21**(2): 94–115.
Stevens, A. (2017), 'Principles, Pragmatism and Prohibition: Explaining Continuity and Change in British Drug Policy', in Liebling, A., Maruna, S., and McAra, L. (eds.), *The Oxford Handbook of Criminology* (6th ed.). Oxford: OUP.
Wells, C., and Quick, O. (2010), *Lacey, Wells and Quick's Reconstructing Criminal Law: Text and Materials* (4th ed.): chs.4–7. Cambridge: CUP.
Winlow, S., Hall, S., Treadwell, J., and Briggs, D. (2015), *Riots and Political Protest: Notes from the Post-Political Present*. Abingdon: Routledge.

References

Bakalis, C. (2003), 'Anti-Social Behaviour Orders – Criminal Penalties or Civil Injunctions?' *Cambridge Law Journal*, **62**(3): 583–6.
Bean, P. (2014), *Drugs and Crime* (4th ed.). Abingdon: Routledge.
Bennett, T., and Holloway, K. (2009), 'The Causal Connection Between Drug Misuse and Crime', *British Journal of Criminology*, **49**(4): 513–31.

Briggs, D. (ed.) (2012), *The English Riots of 2011: A Summer of Discontent*. Hook: Waterside Press.

Brown, D., and Ellis, T. (1994), *Policing Low Level Disorder: Police Use of Section 5 of the Public Order Act 1986*. Home Office Research Study No.135. London: Home Office.

Burney, E. (2009), *Making People Behave: Antisocial Behaviour, Politics and Policy* (2nd ed.). Abingdon: Routledge.

Channing, I. (2017), 'Breach of the Peace', in Turner, J., Taylor, P., Morley, S., and Corteen, K. (eds.), *A Companion to the History of Crime and Criminal Justice*. Bristol: Policy Press.

Forsyth, A. (2012), 'Virtually a Drug Scare: Mephedrone and the Impact of the Internet on Drug News Transmission', *International Journal of Drug Policy*, **23**(3): 198–209.

Fyson, R., and Yates, J. (2011), 'Anti-Social Behaviour Orders and Young People with Learning Disabilities', *Critical Social Policy*, **31**(1): 102–25.

Goldsmith, C. (2008), 'Cameras, Cops and Contracts: What Anti-Social Behaviour Management Feels Like to Young People', in Squires, P. (ed.), *ASBO Nation: The Criminalisation of Nuisance*. Bristol: Policy Press.

Greer, C., and McLaughlin, E. (2010), 'We Predict a Riot? Public Order Policing, New Media Environments and the Rise of the Citizen Journalist', *British Journal of Criminology*, **50**(6): 1041–59.

Home Office (2018), *Drug Misuse: Findings from the 2017/18 Crime Survey for England and Wales*. Statistical Bulletin No.14/18. Available online at: https://assets.publishing.service. gov.uk/government/uploads/system/uploads/attachment_data/file/729249/drug-misuse-2018-hosb1418.pdf. Accessed 28 June 2019.

Jarvis, P. (2015), 'The New Criminal Behaviour Order', *Criminal Law Review*: 278–83.

Lewis, P., Newburn, T., Taylor, M., McGillivray, C., Greenhill, A., Frayman, H., and Proctor, R. (2011), *Reading the Riots: Investigating England's Summer of Disorder*. Available online at: www.theguardian.com/uk/series/reading-the-riots. Accessed 16 July 2019.

Lightowlers, C.L. (2015), 'Let's Get Real About the "Riots": Exploring the Relation Between Deprivation and the English Summer Disturbances of 2011', *Critical Social Policy*, **35**(1): 89–109.

Lightowlers, C.L., and Quirk, H. (2015), 'The 2011 English "Riots": Prosecutorial Zeal and Judicial Abandon', *British Journal of Criminology*, **55**(1): 65–85.

Lowerson, A.J. (2018), 'Managing the Unmanageable: The Offence of Riot in England and Wales', *Journal of Criminal Law*, **82**(1): 35–47.

Macdonald, S. (2006), 'A Suicidal Woman, Roaming Pigs and a Noisy Trampolinist: Refining the ASBO's Definition of "Anti-Social Behaviour"', *Modern Law Review*, **69**(2): 183–214.

Matthews, R., Easton, H., Briggs, D., and Pease, K. (2007), *Assessing the Use and Impact of Antisocial Behaviour Orders*. Bristol: Policy Press.

McIntosh, B. (2008), 'ASBO Youth: Rhetoric and Realities', in Squires, P. (ed.), *ASBO Nation: The Criminalisation of Nuisance*. Bristol: Policy Press.

Millie, A. (2009), *Anti-Social Behaviour*. Maidenhead: Open University Press.

Ministry of Justice (2018), *Criminal Justice System Statistics: Outcomes by Offence, 2007 to 2017 – Pivot Table Analytical Tool for England and Wales*. Available online at: https:// assets.publishing.service.gov.uk/government/uploads/system/uploads/attachment_data/ file/733981/outcomes-by-offence-tool-2017-update.xlsx. Accessed 18 July 2019.

Ministry of Justice (2019a), *Criminal Justice System Statistics Quarterly, September 2018 – Overview Tables*. Available online at: https://assets.publishing.service.gov.uk/government/ uploads/system/uploads/attachment_data/file/780613/overview-tables-sept-2018.ods. Accessed 21 March 2019.

Ministry of Justice (2019b), *Knife and Offensive Weapon Sentencing Statistics, England and Wales – Year Ending March 2019*. Available online at: https://assets.publishing.service. gov.uk/government/uploads/system/uploads/attachment_data/file/808496/Knife_and_ Offensive_Weapon_Sentencing_Pub_Q1_2019.pdf. Accessed 18 July 2019.

Newburn, T. (2016), 'The 2011 England Riots in European Context: A Framework for Understanding the "Life-Cycle" of Riots', *European Journal of Criminology*, **13**(5): 540–55.

Nutt, D.J., King, L.A., and Phillips, L.D. (2010), 'Drug Harms in the UK: A Multicriteria Decision Analysis', *The Lancet*, **376**(9752): 1558–65.

ONS (2019), *Crime in England and Wales, Year Ending March 2019*. Available online at: www. ons.gov.uk/peoplepopulationandcommunity/crimeandjustice/bulletins/crimeinenglandand wales/yearendingmarch2019. Accessed 21 March 2019.

Padfield, N. (2019), 'Offensive Weapons and Knife Crime (Editorial)', *Criminal Law Review*: 461–2.

Parker, H., Aldridge, J., and Measham, F. (1998), *Illicit Leisure: The Normalization of Adolescent Recreational Drug Use*. London: Routledge.

Pearson, G. (1983), *Hooligan: A History of Respectable Fears*. Basingstoke: Palgrave Macmillan.

Pierce, M., Bird, S.M., Hickman, M., Marsden, J., Dunn, G., Seddon, T., and Millar, T. (2018), 'Effect of Initiating Drug Treatment on the Risk of Drug-Related Poisoning Death and Acquisitive Crime Among Offending Heroin Users', *International Journal of Drug Policy*, **51**(1): 42–51.

Prior, D., and Spalek, B. (2008), 'Anti-Social Behaviour and Minority Ethnic Populations', in Squires, P. (ed.), *ASBO Nation: The Criminalisation of Nuisance*. Bristol: Policy Press.

Roberts, S. (2019), 'The London Killings of 2018: The Story Behind the Numbers and Some Proposed Solutions', *Crime Prevention and Community Safety*, **21**(2): 94–115.

Rolles, S., and Measham, F. (2011), 'Questioning the Method and Utility of Ranking Drug Harms in Drug Policy', *International Journal of Drug Policy*, **22**(4): 243–6.

Seddon, T. (2006), 'Drugs, Crime and Social Exclusion', *British Journal of Criminology* **46**(4): 680–703.

Seddon, T. (2017), 'Drugs: Consumption, Addiction, and Treatment', in Liebling, A., Maruna, S., and McAra, L. (eds.), *The Oxford Handbook of Criminology* (6th ed.). Oxford: OUP.

Smith, A.T.H. (1987), *Offences against Public Order*. London: Sweet and Maxwell.

Stevens, A. (2007), 'When Two Dark Figures Collide: Evidence and Discourse on Drug-Related Crime', *Critical Social Policy*, **27**(1): 77–99.

Stevens, A. (2011), *Drugs, Crime and Public Health: The Political Economy of Drug Policy*. Abingdon: Routledge.

Stevens, A. (2017), 'Principles, Pragmatism and Prohibition: Explaining Continuity and Change in British Drug Policy', in Liebling, A., Maruna, S., and McAra, L. (eds.), *The Oxford Handbook of Criminology* (6th ed.). Oxford: OUP.

Sturgeon-Adams, L. (2013), 'Talking About Drugs: Towards a More Reasoned Debate', *British Journal of Community Justice*, **11**(1): 35–46.

Taylor, M. (2019), 'Extinction Rebellion Protester Convicted of Public Order Offence', *The Guardian*, Tuesday 25 June. Available online at: www.theguardian.com/world/2019/jun/25/ extinction-rebellion-first-protester-convicted-public-order-offence. Accessed 19 July 2019.

Taylor, S. (2008), 'Outside the Outsiders: Media Representations of Drug Use', *Probation Journal*, **55**(4): 369–87.

Taylor, S., Buchanan, J., and Ayres, T. (2016), 'Prohibition, Privilege and the Drug Apartheid: The Failure of Drug Policy Reform to Address the Underlying Fallacies of Drug Prohibition', *Criminology and Criminal Justice*, **16**(4): 452–69.

Treadwell, J., Briggs, D., Winlow, S., and Hall, S. (2013), 'Shopocalypse Now: Consumer Culture and the English Riots of 2011', *British Journal of Criminology*, **53**(1): 1–17.

Wakeman, S. (2016), 'The Moral Economy of Heroin in "Austerity Britain"', *Critical Criminology*, **24**(3): 363–77.

Wells, C., and Quick, O. (2010), *Lacey, Wells and Quick's Reconstructing Criminal Law: Text and Materials* (4th ed.). Cambridge: CUP.

Werb, D., Kamarulzaman, A., Meacham, M.C., Rafful, C., Fischer, B., Strathdee, S.A., and Wood, E. (2016), 'The Effectiveness of Compulsory Drug Treatment: A Systematic Review', *International Journal of Drug Policy*, **28**(1): 1–9.

Winlow, S., Hall, S., Treadwell, J., and Briggs, D. (2015), *Riots and Political Protest: Notes from the Post-Political Present*. Abingdon: Routledge.

Zedner, L. (2007), 'Pre-Crime and Post-Criminology?' *Theoretical Criminology*, **11**(2): 261–81.

Chapter 10

Criminal defences and responsibility for crime

Chapter aims

After reading Chapter 10, you should be able to understand:

- Which general criminal defences are available in criminal law and how they work
- How criminal sentencing reflects responsibility for crime in different ways
- The difference between retributive and reductivist approaches to sentencing, and the strengths and weaknesses of each approach
- How these approaches have been used in recent sentencing legislation
- How these approaches have influenced sentencing in practice
- How the evidence on defences in criminal law and sentencing in criminal justice fits in with the roadmap theories introduced in Chapter 1

Introduction

Chapter 10 follows on from previous discussion of the foundations of criminal liability in Chapters 3 to 5 by looking at defences in criminal law. This chapter considers the range of general criminal defences in the law and how they work, as well as their context in criminal justice. In the criminal justice section of the chapter, the discussion will examine the links between the role and aims of defences in criminal law and the role and aims of sentencing and punishment in criminal justice. The focus here will be on how criminal defences and criminal punishment both make decisions based on perceived levels of individual responsibility for criminal behaviour in varying social situations.

Criminal defences: the law

Making sense of criminal defences

Defences are ways in which people can avoid criminal liability, even though they have the actus reus and mens rea for the offence with which they have been charged. There are different types of defence in criminal law. Some are specific to certain offences (such as murder – see Chapter 7's discussion of voluntary manslaughter for more details), but this chapter deals with general defences. The legal team for the defence has to raise evidence that a particular criminal defence applies in each case. Then, for most of the common law defences discussed in this chapter, the prosecution has to prove beyond reasonable doubt that the defence does not apply; otherwise, the defendant has to be acquitted. D must know the facts which justify them being able to use the defence at the time of the crime which they claim is covered by the defence; otherwise, they cannot use it (*Dadson* (1850) 4 Cox CC 350).

General defences are sometimes split up as either excusatory (based on an excuse or internal characteristic which is special to D) or justificatory (based on an external factor or situation which D has to face, which makes D behave in a way for which criminal law does not blame them) (e.g. Fletcher 1978; Wilson 2017: 196–7). However, there is considerable overlap between internal and external requirements across different defences, so this classification is not used in the discussion that follows.

General criminal defences

Insanity (insane automatism)

The legal definition of the requirements of the insanity defence is in *M'Naghten* (1843) 10 Cl & Fin 200. Firstly, D must have been suffering from a 'defect of reason'. This means that at the time of the offence, D must have been unable to use their ability to think and use the brain to make decisions, rather than just failing to use the power to reason because they were absent-minded or distracted temporarily, for example. The defect of reason can be temporary as well as permanent (*Clarke* [1972] 1 All ER 219).

Secondly, this defect of reason must have been caused by a 'disease of the mind'. *Quick* [1973] QB 910 shows that the disease must be an 'internal' factor. It must be something that is only 'inside D's head'. *Sullivan* [1984] AC 156 shows that the disease can have an 'organic' or a 'functional' cause, so it can be something physical, like brain damage or some other medical condition like epilepsy, or psychological, like a nervous condition. *Sullivan* also says that the condition causing the disease of the mind can be temporary as well as permanent. *Burgess* [1991] 2 QB 92 stated that there did not have to be any danger of the disease recurring – the condition could be a 'one off' and still count for the purposes of insanity. Examples of the insanity defence being used successfully due to the presence of 'diseases of the mind' which were decided to be relevant, include *Kemp* [1957] 1 QB 399 (where the disease was arteriosclerosis); *Sullivan* (epilepsy); *Hennessy* [1989] 2 All ER 9 (hyperglycaemia, or high blood sugar levels caused by diabetes); and *Burgess* (sleepwalking). *Coley, McGhee and Harris* [2013] EWCA Crim 223 shows that 'toxic psychosis' caused by voluntary intoxication (heavy use of cannabis in this case) cannot be a disease of the mind for the purposes of the insanity defence.

Thirdly, the defect of reason caused by a disease of the mind must have had such an effect on D that *either* D did not know what they were doing, *or*, if D did know what they were doing, that D did not know what they were doing was wrong. In terms of proving that D did not know what they were doing, D has to show that at the time of the offence they did not understand the physical consequences of what they were doing, or the circumstances surrounding it (*Codere* (1916) 12 Cr App Rep 21). If D is trying to prove that they did not know what they were doing was wrong, this means that D did not know what they were doing was *legally* wrong (i.e. that it was a crime), as opposed to *morally* wrong (*Windle* [1952] 2 QB 826).

The insanity defence works differently from other common law defences because the defence has to prove that D is legally insane on the balance of probabilities (after the judge has decided whether D's defence meets the insanity criteria – *Roach* [2001] EWCA Crim 2698), rather than just raising evidence of the defence which the prosecution then has to disprove. However, the defence only has to prove insanity if the prosecution has already proved beyond reasonable doubt that D committed the actus reus of the offence with which they have been charged. If the prosecution cannot prove the actus reus in this way, then D has to be acquitted anyway (*Attorney-General's Reference (No.3 of 1998)* [2000] QB 401). Finally, in *Oye* [2013] EWCA Crim 1725, the Court of Appeal decided that where D claims more than one defence, including insanity, the insanity defence should be applied ahead of any others.

Study exercise 10.1

Do you think that a) sleepwalkers, b) hyperglycaemic diabetics, and c) epileptics should be labelled by criminal law as 'insane'? If not, what sort of defence should these groups have access to if they commit a crime due to their medical condition?

Infancy

The infancy defence excuses criminal conduct because D is below the age of criminal responsibility for England and Wales. The minimum age of criminal responsibility in England and Wales is currently 10 (Children and Young Persons Act 1933 s.50). For children aged between 10 and 13, the principle in the law called doli incapax, which set up a rebuttable presumption that a child did not know that they were committing the crime with which they had been charged, has now been abolished by the Crime and Disorder Act 1998 s.34. In *JTB* [2009] UKHL 20, the House of Lords stated that the abolition of the presumption was intended to abolish the concept of doli incapax completely, not just reverse the presumption so that the defence could still be used. *DM* [2016] EWCA Crim 674 did confirm that doli incapax could still be used for cases dating from before 1998, however.

Study exercise 10.2

Find out what the minimum age of criminal responsibility is in other European countries. Why do you think different countries have different minimum ages? What do you think the minimum age of criminal responsibility should be and why?

Automatism (non-insane automatism)

Bratty v Attorney-General for Northern Ireland [1963] AC 386 defines automatism as an act which is done physically but without any mental control, or which is done during a loss of consciousness. *Coley et al.* [2013] defines the defence as 'movements or actions at material time (which were) totally involuntary. . . (characterised by) complete destruction of voluntary control', but also emphasises that irrational or disinhibited behaviour cannot form the basis of an automatism defence.

Under *Quick*, the factor causing automatism must be external to the defendant (in contrast to insanity mentioned earlier), and must not be voluntarily self-induced or caused by doing, or not doing, something which D should have foreseen would lead to the condition. Examples of automatism are given in *Hill v Baxter* [1958] 1 QB 277, *T* [1990] Crim LR 256 (where the condition was post-traumatic stress disorder triggered by D being raped several days before her offence), *Quick*, and *Bailey* [1983] 2 All ER 503. Where D has recklessly caused the automatic action in some way, though, self-induced automatism is a defence to 'specific intent' offences if the automatism was caused by voluntary intoxication, but not a defence to 'basic intent' offences (following is a discussion of 'specific intent' and 'basic intent' in the context of voluntary intoxication). If the automatism was due to something else other than voluntary intoxication, it was a defence even for basic intent offences – *unless* D was subjectively reckless (i.e. D saw the risk that whatever they did or did not do would make them behave aggressively or uncontrollably and went ahead anyway) (*Bailey*).

Study exercise 10.3

Should people who have successfully used the defence of automatism always be allowed to go free without any intervention in their lives to control their behaviour? Explain your answer.

Voluntary intoxication

The voluntary intoxication defence deals with situations where D has voluntarily taken alcohol or drugs and has later committed a crime while under the influence of them. Mostly, voluntary intoxication is not a defence to any crime. Under *Sheehan and Moore* [1975] 2 All ER 960, drunken intent is still intent. So, as long as D actually formed the mens rea needed for the offence with which they have been charged, they will be guilty no matter how intoxicated they were. It is the magistrates' or jury's job to decide, based on all of the relevant evidence, whether D actually did form the intent needed. Under *Attorney-General for Northern Ireland v Gallagher* [1963] AC 349, the only time voluntary intoxication can ever be a defence is where D was so intoxicated that they had no mens rea at all. This case also shows that if D uses intoxication for 'Dutch courage', then their intoxication is no defence to any crime they commit as a result.

DPP v Majewski [1977] AC 443 gives further explanation about what happens in situations where D has no mens rea at all due to voluntary intoxication, where the House of Lords distinguished between specific intent and basic intent offences. Voluntary intoxication can be a defence to specific intent crimes but not basic intent ones. In *Heard* [2007] 3 All ER 306, the Court of Appeal changed the scope of specific intent offences, by saying that a specific intent offence was one where to satisfy the mens rea requirements, D needed ulterior intent or ulterior recklessness about the consequences of their actions, rather than just intent in the normal sense of planning or desiring to do something.

Lipman [1970] 1 QB 152 applies the rules on voluntary intoxication to crimes committed under the influence of drugs. In this case, D was not guilty of murder, a specific intent offence, because he had not formed an intent to kill or do GBH. However, because D had killed V by doing an unlawful and dangerous act (assault), and this was the basis of liability for manslaughter, a basic intent offence, it did not matter that D did not have mens rea. He only lacked mens rea because of his intoxication, and so he was guilty of manslaughter. If, on the other hand, the drugs which have intoxicated D are not known to cause aggression or violence in the people who take them, then *Bailey* and *Hardie* [1985] 1 WLR 64 show that D can use voluntary intoxication as a defence. The exception to this rule is where D saw the risk of behaving dangerously when they took the drugs – (i.e. D was subjectively reckless as to the risk of dangerous behaviour). In this situation, D cannot use the voluntary intoxication defence due to their recklessness in intoxicating themselves.

Study exercise 10.4

Should we replace the current voluntary intoxication defence with a new offence of 'criminal intoxication' which carries a lesser sentence than the one for the full offence with which D has been charged?

Involuntary intoxication

The involuntary intoxication defence deals with situations where D has unknowingly taken alcohol or drugs and has later committed a crime while under the influence of them. Situations where this could happen include D taking a medically prescribed drug without realising what the side effects would be, or D drinking a soft drink which, unknown to them, has been spiked with alcohol or drugs.

Involuntary intoxication, like voluntary intoxication, is only a defence where D has not formed the mens rea at all. Unlike voluntary intoxication, though, it can apply to either basic or specific intent offences. The scope of the defence is very narrow, however. In *Allen* [1988] Crim LR 698, D's drinking of alcohol which was stronger than D thought it was did not entitle D to use the involuntary intoxication defence. In *Kingston* [1995] 2 AC 355, the House of Lords confirmed that as long as D has the required mens rea, they are guilty, even if their intoxication was involuntary. Therefore, even though it was only the drugs which had been used to spike D's drink that caused D to form the intent to commit the offence in *Kingston*, D's conviction stood.

Study exercise 10.5

Do you think the House of Lords' decision in *Kingston* was fair to the defendant? Explain your answer.

Self-defence

Common law self-defence (private defence) allows the use of defensive force to prevent unjustified harm to the person using the force, their property, or another person. Under Criminal law Act 1967 s.3, defensive force can also be used to prevent crime, or to make (or help others to make) a lawful arrest of offenders or suspected offenders (public defence). This form of self-defence can only apply while the crime to which they are responding is continuing (*Morris* [2013] EWCA Crim 436).

Under *Williams* [1987] 3 All ER 411, the force D uses must be 'necessary'. The necessity of the force used is judged on the facts of the situation as D believed them to be. This means that D is allowed to make an honest mistake about the facts which lead to the force being used (even if the mistake is not reasonable). However, D cannot rely on any mistake made due to voluntary intoxication (*O'Grady* [1987] QB 995, *Hatton* [2006] Crim LR 353) or due to mental illness (*Oye*).

D's response also must be 'reasonable & proportionate' to the threat as it was, or as D honestly believed it to be (*Palmer v R* [1971] 1 All ER 1077). The response does not have to be exactly proportionate to the threat – the jury or magistrates should take a liberal approach, including consideration of the time available to D for reflection on the situation. Under *Owino* [1996] 2 Cr App Rep 128, the force used must be 'objectively reasonable' in the circumstances as D honestly believed them to be. Therefore, it is not enough that D believed subjectively that the force used was reasonable in the circumstances as they believed them to be. The force must be 'objectively' reasonable in those circumstances. In *Oye* (discussed earlier), D had an honest belief that he was being attacked by evil spirits when he attacked officers at a police station, and there was clear evidence that D was mentally ill at the time. However, the Court of Appeal decided that D's reaction to the perceived threat was disproportionate, and so D was not allowed to use self-defence.

There has been some uncertainty in the law regarding how the level of danger which D is in should be assessed. *Shaw v R* [2001] 1 WLR 1519 stated that the facts and level of danger must both be assessed subjectively (i.e. as D believed them to be), including any honest mistakes. However, in *Martin* [2003] QB 1, although the facts D was facing had to be assessed subjectively, the level of danger D was facing had to be assessed objectively.

The threatened harm which D is facing, or which D honestly believes they are facing, must be 'imminent' (i.e. about to happen). However, D can 'get in there first' and use necessary, reasonable, and proportionate force against an attack which is about to happen imminently, before it actually does (e.g. *Attorney-General's Reference (No. 2 of 1983)* [1984] QB 456). D is also under no duty to retreat from the situation (i.e. to show unwillingness to fight), 'back away' from the threat and seek help, although if D does so, it would be seen as evidence that their actions were necessary and reasonable (*Bird* [1985] 1 WLR 816). *Harvey* [2009] EWCA Crim 469 shows that D can still use self-defence even if D was the one who initially launched the attack, if the violence from the original victim was disproportionate to the force used by D, unless D planned the situation (*Rashford* [2005] EWCA Crim 3377), or V was provoked and was defending themselves reasonably against D's force.

S.76 of the Criminal Justice and Immigration Act 2008 restates the principles of self-defence explained earlier, with the aim of 'clarifying their operation' (s.76(9)) rather than changing the existing law (*Keane* [2010] EWCA Crim 2514). All of the common law principles explained earlier are included in the statutory law, and s.148 of the Legal Aid, Sentencing and Punishment of Offenders Act 2012 makes it clear that this form of defence applies to defence of property as well. One notable feature is s.76(7), which emphasises that 'a person acting for a legitimate purpose may not be able to weigh to a nicety the exact measure of any necessary action', to encourage courts to give the benefit of the doubt to Ds who use slightly too much force in self-defence. S.43 of the Crime and Courts Act 2013 emphasises this approach by stating that house owners can now use disproportionate force on intruders in self-defence, as long as they believed that the force used was reasonable, and as long as the force used was not 'grossly disproportionate'. However, self-defence claims involving disproportionate force will not automatically be allowed, and the question of whether force is reasonable in an intruder case is separate from the question of whether force is proportionate (*R (Collins) v Secretary of State for Justice* [2016] EWHC 33 (Admin)).

Study exercise 10.6

Read an account of the *Martin* case using a newspaper archive website. Do you think he should have been allowed to use self-defence? Why?

Duress through threats (duress per minas)

This defence can be used where someone is threatened with harm unless they commit a crime. *Hudson & Taylor* [1971] 2 QB 202 shows that only threats to kill or do GBH (serious injury) are enough to allow a defence of duress. For example, in *Quayle* [2005] 2 Cr App Rep 527, the threat of severe physical pain (possibly leading to psychological injury was not enough; and *M'Growther* (1746) Fost 13 shows that threats to damage property also cannot be used as a basis for duress through threats. However, if the threats made to D involve non-relevant threats and threats to kill or do GBH together, then the relevant threats can still be considered (*Valderrama-Vega* [1985] Crim LR 220). *Safi* [2004] 1 Cr App Rep 14 shows that the threat of death or GBH does not actually have to exist, as long as D reasonably believes that it exists. There is some uncertainty in the law about how specific the threats made to D have to be. *Cole* [1994] Crim LR 582 stated that duress could only be used where the person making the threats specified exactly not only which offence to commit, but also which victim to target. However, in *Ali* [1995] Crim LR 303, the Court of Appeal thought that as long as the person making threats nominates a particular crime, duress can still be used where no particular victim was nominated.

The next issue is who can receive the threats of death or GBH. *Wright* [2000] Crim LR 510 states that the threats do not have to be made to D in order for D to use the duress through threats defence. The threats can also be made to those for whom D reasonably considers themselves to be responsible – for example, a close family member or a partner.

The third issue is how soon the threat of death or GBH must be capable of being carried out. In *Hasan* [2005] 2 WLR 709, the House of Lords emphasised the importance of immediacy, rather than imminence in the sense of being able to be carried out soon but not necessarily straight away. The offence must be carried out immediately or almost immediately after the threat was made for the duress through threats defence to be allowed. Under *Hasan*, a delay of a day between the threat and the crime would be too long.

The fourth issue is what happens if D could be held responsible for getting into the situation which resulted in them being threatened. Where D has voluntarily joined a criminal gang, the scope for using duress through threats is severely limited. *Hasan* stated that if D has voluntarily joined a violent criminal association and D saw, or should have seen, the risk of being put under duress by threats of violence against them, D cannot later use duress through threats as a defence. The association D joins does not have to be violent at the time of joining, as long as D foresees the risk of violence, or should have foreseen it (*Ali* [2008] EWCA Crim 716), and the threats of violence are later made. D also does not have to foresee the exact type of crime they will be forced to commit, as long as D, when they began to associate voluntarily with the group, knew that by doing so they were likely to be pressured by threats of violence to commit *any* crime.

The fifth issue is how the impact of the threat on D is assessed. The rules for this are found in *Graham* [1982] 1 All ER 801, which lays down a mixed subjective and objective test in three parts – a) whether D 'reasonably' believed they had to do what they did because of the threat; b) whether the belief was a 'good cause' for D's fear; and c) whether a 'sober person of reasonable firmness' would have reacted in the same way as D did. If the answer to all three of these questions is yes, then D is allowed to use the duress through threats defence. The more serious the crime, the more resistance is expected from D in terms of not committing it. *Bowen* [1996] 4 All ER 837 lists the characteristics that can be included in assessing the reasonableness of D's response to the threat – in other words, which of D's characteristics can be taken into account as being things which reduced D's ability to resist the threat. The following characteristics are relevant here: D's age and (maybe) gender, pregnancy, serious physical disability, or a recognised mental illness or psychiatric condition. However, characteristics which are present due to D's self-induced alcohol or drug abuse cannot be taken into account and neither can suggestibility, vulnerability, nervousness, neuroticism, or evidence of sexual abuse in childhood which does not amount to a recognised psychiatric disorder.

The final issue is the range of crimes for which duress through threats can be used. It is a general defence, so it applies to most crimes, even strict liability offences where no mens rea is required for one or more parts of the actus reus (e.g. *Eden DC v Braid* [1999] RTR 329). However, *Howe* [1987] AC 417 shows that it is not a defence to murder, whether D is being charged as a principal offender or as a secondary offender. In addition, *Gotts* [1992] 2 AC 412 shows that duress through threats is not a defence to attempted murder either.

Study exercise 10.7

Should duress be a defence to murder and attempted murder? Why do you think the law decided that duress should not be an available defence for these crimes?

Duress of circumstances

Duress of circumstances is available when D commits crime to avoid 'objective dangers' threatening themselves or others. The threat has to be one of death or GBH, as with the duress through threats defence (*Pipe v DPP* [2012] EWHC 1821 (Admin)). The threat does not have to come from a person – it could come from a natural source, such as a fire – but it can come indirectly from a person, as it did in *Pommell* [1995] 2 Cr App Rep 607. For duress of circumstances, the threat does not have to be verbal and direct as a threat relating to duress through threats has to be. The threatening circumstances also do not have to involve committing a crime, as is the case with duress through threats, as *Willer* (1986) 83 Cr App Rep 225 and *Conway* [1989] QB 290 illustrate. The threats do have to be external and able to be examined objectively by a court, however (*Rodger and Rose* [1998] 1 Cr App Rep 143).

The test for assessing the impact of the threat in terms of the duress of circumstances defence was set out in *Martin* [1989] 1 All ER 652. The questions to be asked are – a) whether D was forced to act because of what happened, or what D reasonably believed to be happening (*Cairns* [1999] 2 Cr App Rep 137); b) whether D had good cause to fear death or serious injury, either to D themselves or to someone else; and c) whether a sober person of reasonable firmness, sharing D's characteristics, would have responded by acting in the same way that D did. If the answer to these questions is yes, a defence of duress of circumstances should be made available to the jury or magistrates to decide on the facts. Where D has started to commit the offence, but then the threat which they are responding to ends, D must stop committing the offence as soon as they reasonably can in the circumstances, according to *Pommell.*

The other principles of duress through circumstances are similar to the principles of duress through threats discussed earlier. *Abdul-Hussain* [1999] Crim LR 570 shows that there must be a close and direct link between the threatening circumstances and the offence being committed; *Hasan* states that the offence has to follow the threat more or less immediately; and *Pommell* emphasises that the defence could apply to any crime, subject to the exceptions to the availability of duress through threats set up in *Howe* and *Gotts.*

Necessity

The defence of necessity is similar to duress of circumstances, but wider in its scope, because it does not have to link to a particular identifiable threat in the same way as duress of circumstances does. The idea behind necessity is that, in a crisis situation, D commits a crime because doing so is the 'lesser of two evils'. Committing the crime, in other words, means that D prevents something that is worse than the crime from happening.

The existence of the necessity defence in criminal law in England and Wales is controversial. It was not allowed for murder in *Dudley and Stephens* (1884) 14 QBD 273, which is discussed further in Chapter 2. However, necessity has re-appeared, either in arguments made by the defence in court or in court judgments, in various cases since then that have not involved murder. For example, in *Re A (Conjoined Twins)* [2001] 3 All ER 1, Brooke LJ set out three requirements for the use of necessity. Firstly, the act must be needed to avoid inevitable and irreparable evil. Secondly, no more should be done than is reasonably necessary for the purpose to be achieved. Thirdly and finally, the evil inflicted must not be disproportionate to the evil avoided. However, since *Re A* the necessity defence has not been allowed in *Shayler* [2001] 1 WLR

2206, in *Quayle* [2005] 2 Cr App Rep 527, or in *Jones & Milling* [2007] 1 AC 136. It is therefore still uncertain whether the necessity defence actually exists in criminal law.

Study exercise 10.8

Why do you think the courts will not allow a general defence of necessity to be used?

The second part of Chapter 10 considers how defences relate to responsibility for criminal justice, using criminal sentencing and punishment as a case study.

Criminal defences, responsibility for crime, and criminal justice

The operation of criminal defences in criminal justice

Before moving on to sentencing and punishment issues, it is important to consider how criminal justice handles cases where there is no need for sentencing because the suspect has successfully used one of the criminal defences discussed earlier in this chapter.

Research data on the usage of defences in England are rare for most of the defences available. One key exception is the work of Mackay in showing how criminal justice handles the defence of insanity. Mackay (2012) found evidence of 359 cases where the suspect successfully used the insanity defence between 1991 and 2011, at an average of only 17.59 cases per year, despite an increase in usage towards the end of that period. Ninety percent of successful applicants were male, with the majority aged between 20 and 40. Only 1.8% of successful cases involved a charge of murder, with another 20% involving grievous bodily harm. Mackay also found increased use of community orders as a response to the insanity defence, with 51.8% of cases resulting in this outcome, compared with a reduced 28% of cases resulting in hospital orders. These data show how rarely the insanity defence is successfully used in criminal justice practice. In some cases this will be the result of suspects preferring to plead guilty rather than receiving the stigma of being labelled 'insane' in court (Child and Sullivan 2014). However, in many other cases, this is the result of the narrow scope of the defence in criminal law itself. The definition of the insanity defence not only allows the law to ignore the significant over-representation of people with recognised mental illnesses in criminal justice, and deny even some people suffering from psychosis any excuse for their criminal behaviour (Child and Sullivan 2014), but conversely allows people who are seen as being socially dangerous (such as epileptics and sleepwalkers as in *Sullivan* and *Burgess*, respectively) to be unfairly labelled as 'mad'. Under s.24 of the Domestic Violence, Crime and Victims Act 2004, where D is found not guilty by reason of insanity, the judge must make one of three orders. The options are a hospital order (with or without a restriction order limiting the ability of D to be released from hospital) under s.37 of the Mental Health Act 1983, a supervision order, or an absolute discharge. However, where D has been charged with murder and found to be insane, the judge must make a hospital order and attach a restriction order without a time limit. However, those who are allowed to use the automatism defence receive no further intervention in their lives.

In terms of infancy, the abolition of doli incapax in 1998 ignores the extensive psychological evidence that children's brains – and therefore their ability to reason and see consequences – are still developing at the age of 10 and continue to do so throughout most of the teenage years on average (Haines and Case 2015). Given the apparent links between alcohol abuse and crime (e.g. Finney 2004), criminal law could argue that it is justified in severely limiting the ability of offenders to excuse their behaviour through the voluntary intoxication defence. However, the government has also increased the availability of alcohol by extending licensing hours, removed obstacles to new pubs and bars opening even in areas already overcrowded with licensed premises (both via the Licensing Act 2003), as well as allowing the alcohol industry to regulate itself rather than being regulated by the government – all in the knowledge of the massive social harm caused by binge-drinking (Hadfield 2006). It could therefore be argued that the law's approach to intoxication is somewhat hypocritical, allowing the powerful in society to profit from alcohol consumption but not allowing the less powerful to use it as an excuse for crime. The intoxication defence looks even more unfair when involuntary intoxication is considered. Here, it is difficult to argue that an offender should be held responsible for their actions when they have become intoxicated through no fault of their own, unless they have absolutely no mens rea at all. It is perhaps significant that the case where this principle was confirmed – *Kingston* – involved paedophilia at a time when sexual offences were being re-politicised in England and Wales.

While there is not always empirical evidence to prove declining usage of defences like duress and intoxication, as there is with Mackay's work on insanity, the argument here is that just as sentencing has focussed increasingly on individual responsibility and risk, so has the applicability of criminal defences in criminal justice practice.

Sentencing processes, responsibility for crime, and criminal justice

As Norrie (2014) points out, criminal defences limit the central liberal principle of criminal law, which is that people are held responsible for the crimes they commit. The aim of this section is to introduce the key approaches to criminal justice sentencing and the recent legislation which has influenced sentencing in England and Wales, and then to compare these sentencing principles and policies with how sentencing is carried out by the courts in practice. In this way, the discussion will examine whether or not the nature and scope of criminal defences can be explained by approaches to sentencing theory, policy, and practice – in other words, whether the justifications given for sentencing people match up with the justifications for *not* sentencing them, in the form of defences.

To understand how sentencing works in criminal courts, it is necessary to consider the key theories of sentencing briefly. These can be broken down into two groups: retributivism and reductivism. Retributivism justifies punishment through sentencing on the ground that it is deserved by the offender. On this view, punishment is justified because people have made the choice to commit crime (Cavadino et al. 2013: ch.2). However, criminal sentencing and punishment can also use incapacitation as a ground for sentencing violent and sexual offenders to punishments that are longer than proportionate, and can allow other sentencing aims such as rehabilitation to be taken into account in certain circumstances. These aims are collectively known as reductivism.

Whereas retributivism 'looks back' to the type of offence committed, reductivism 'looks forward'. It justifies punishment through sentencing on the ground that it helps to reduce the incidence of crime (Easton and Piper 2016: ch.4) through deterrence (making punishment so unpleasant that offenders or others avoid crime so as to avoid being punished), rehabilitation (preventing crime through reforming or curing the offender), and incapacitation (physically preventing the commission of crime through punishment).

A third theory, reparation, or restorative justice, is different from both retribution and reductivism as a sentencing strategy. The aims of reparation are varied and sometimes vague. Even so, a few key principles can be identified. Firstly, reparation focuses on the offender making amends in some way to the victim of the offence for the harm which the victim has suffered. It aims to bring the offender and victim together to work out how to resolve the conflict caused by the crime (Johnstone 2011). It therefore 'looks back' to the harm caused by crime but also 'looks forward' to how that harm can be repaired, and how the offender can be reintegrated into society after being 'shamed' for committing the offence (Braithwaite 1989).

The discussion begins by critically discussing the development of sentencing policy in England in the 21st century.

Sentencing legislation: a critical overview

The Criminal Justice Act 2003 introduced a new set of criminal sentencing principles. There are some elements of retribution and proportionality in this Act, which have been carried over from the previous sentencing principles in the Criminal Justice Act 1991. For example, under ss.142, 152, and 153, there are custody and community sentence thresholds, so that before a court can pass a custodial sentence it must be satisfied that the offence is 'so serious' that only prison can be justified, and before it can pass a community sentence it must be satisfied. The sentence must also be proportionate to the offence (Easton and Piper 2016: ch.2). But the Act (s.142) also states that the court must have regard to five different sentencing aims – punishment or retribution, reduction of crime or deterrence, the reform and rehabilitation of offenders, the protection of the public or incapacitation, and reparation by offenders. These sentencing aims conflict with each other, so it is no wonder that Cavadino et al. (2013), among other writers, describe this sentencing framework as ambiguous and incoherent.

Four other key changes introduced by the 2003 Act should also be noted. Firstly, community orders (s.177) replaced the previous range of community sentence options with one generic community sentence which had to include at least one of a menu of 12 requirement options (Mair 2017: 286). Secondly, suspended sentence orders (ss.189–94) replaced the earlier suspended sentence with a new scheme. Under the new suspended sentence order, courts could impose a fixed prison sentence of between 28 and 51 weeks and suspend that sentence for between six months and two years. Courts can include one or more of the 13 community order requirements as part of the suspended sentence order package, or alternatively, since the Legal Aid, Sentencing and Punishment of Offenders Act 2012, not include any requirements at all (ibid: 289–90). Thirdly, the Act introduced a new Sentencing Guidelines Council, now called the Sentencing Council, whose job it is to improve consistency in sentencing by setting guidelines for particular offences and types of offences. Finally, the 2003 Act also introduced indeterminate sentences for public protection (IPPs), which, as their name suggests, had no fixed term for sentencing. The Legal Aid, Sentencing and Punishment of Offenders Act 2012 abolished IPPs, replacing them with extended determinate sentences for violent and sexual offences, whereby a risk assessment takes place after a recommended tariff of imprisonment has been completed. If the person involved is still considered dangerous following this assessment, they can be imprisoned for up to a further eight years (Case et al. 2017: 580–1). In 2017, there were still 3,300 people in prison on IPPs, with a high rate of self-harm and suicide among those involved (Weaver 2017).

Table 10.1 gives an outline of which sentences are currently available for adults aged 18 and over in England and Wales.

Looking at recent sentencing legislation in England and Wales since 1998, there seems to have been a retreat from principles of proportionality and just deserts and a move towards the exclusion, based on incapacitation and deterrence, of those considered to be a 'danger to society' (Faulkner 2006: Chapter 9). The current sentencing framework in the 2003 Act allows a range of sentencing principles to be taken into account, some of which contradict

Table 10.1 Currently available sentences for adults in England and Wales

FINANCIAL AND ADMONITORY PENALTIES

Fine
Compensation order
Confiscation order
Conditional discharge
Bind-over
Absolute discharge

COMMUNITY PENALTIES

Community order (max length three years) including one or more of:
* Exclusion requirement (up to 24 months)
* Electronic monitoring requirement (two–16 hours per day, up to 12 months)
* Residence requirement (up to 36 months, or up to 24 months on the SSO)
* Mental health treatment requirement (up to 36 months, or up to 24 months on the SSO – service user's consent required)
* Drug rehabilitation requirement (between six and 36 months, or between six and 24 months on the SSO – service user's consent required)
* Alcohol treatment requirement (between six and 36 months, or between six and 24 months on the SSO – service user's consent required)
* Unpaid work requirement (40 to 300 hours, completed within 12 months)
* Programme requirement
* Rehabilitation activity (up to 36 months, or up to 24 months on the SSO)
* Prohibited activity requirement (up to 36 months, or up to 24 months on the SSO)
* Alcohol abstinence and monitoring requirement (up to 120 days)
* Activity requirement
* Prohibited activity requirement
* Foreign travel requirement (up to 12 months)
* Attendance centre requirement (12–36 hours, only for those aged 18 to 25)

CUSTODIAL PENALTIES

Indeterminate immediate prison – mandatory life sentence
Determinate immediate prison (with or without extension for 'dangerousness')
Suspended sentence order (prison 28–51 weeks, suspended for six months–
   two years)

Source: Adapted from Newburn (2017: ch.28) and Mair (2017: 291)

others. As a result, it is difficult to say which sentencing principles now drive sentencing in England and Wales. Norrie (2014) argues that this outcome is inevitable, because no one sentencing theory can explain sentencing generally, and in fact they all conflict with one another. However, on the other hand, Norrie argues that all of the sentencing theories are concerned with the same process of removing social factors from sentencing – by either blaming individuals for crime or trying to control and cure their criminal behaviour. This is what links the approaches to criminal law defences and criminal justice sentencing together – both focus on an individual's behaviour primarily, with external and social influences on that behaviour either relegated to a secondary role of importance or not considered in any meaningful way.

The next subsection turns to the evidence on trends in sentencing and punishment in practice, to look for further indications on which principles drive the sentencing process day-to-day. This discussion will also draw together information on sentencing practice that previous chapters included when discussing specific criminal offences and the response to them.

Study exercise 10.9

Why do you think the government made the decision, in the Criminal Justice Act 2003, to allow courts to take a range of sentencing objectives into account when sentencing, instead of just requiring sentences to be proportionate, as the Criminal Justice Act 1991 had done?

Sentencing in practice: historical trends and the current 'bigger picture'

Joyce (2017: 346) describes a trend in criminal sentencing, in the later decades of the 20th century, whereby there was a move away from reductivist sentencing based on welfare provision, which was used alongside increases in usage of fines and suspended sentences (Bottoms 1983), and towards retributivist, just deserts-based sentencing. This trend reached its peak in the Criminal Justice Act 1991 in policy terms (discussed previously). However, the 1991 Act did not change the longer-term trend of increasing use of immediate custody, which rose slowly but steadily between 1975 and 2015 (Newburn 2017: 713). More recently, the proportion of people sent to immediate custody has remained stable at around 7% between 2008 and 2018, but the average custodial length has increased from 13 months to 17.2 months over the same period (Ministry of Justice 2019a). Usage of suspended sentences has increased slightly between 2008 and 2018, while usage of fines has remained stable, and usage of community sentences has continued to decline (ibid.). These figures point to a clear trend of moving away from retributivism and just deserts in sentences and moving towards reductivist aims such as deterrence and incapacitation.

However, reductivist aims have not taken over sentencing completely. Sentencing legislation has held onto the requirement of proportionality between crime and sentence, and non-supervisory sentences (that is, fines and discharges) are still used more than custody or supervisory penalties. Nor should the continuing role of discretion in sentencing be overlooked. There has been a range of evidence to suggest that sentencers in the Crown and magistrates' courts have a great deal of discretion in practice. In particular, it has been shown that sentences can depend on the individuals or groups of people doing the sentencing as much as on the law itself (Parker et al. 1989), and that irrelevant factors such as offenders' race can play a part in sentencing (Hood 1992). However, the move towards reductivism is still a significant feature of current sentencing in England.

Study exercise 10.10

Design a poster illustrating the advantages and disadvantages of immediate custody as a sentencing response to crime.

Punishment processes, responsibility for crime, and criminal justice

Financial and admonitory penalties

The discussion here starts with the fine. As Bottoms (1983) noted, the fine is the ultimate liberal, individualised form of punishment. It does not need any supervision of the offender, and it can easily be adjusted to reflect the seriousness of the offence being punished. However, the 'pure punishment' view of fines hides some of the issues which have been faced when imposing them in practice. Crow et al. (1989), for example, have illustrated that courts have been reluctant to use fines for unemployed offenders, because magistrates and judges do not see the point in fining the unemployed a small amount to reflect the fact that they do not have much disposable income. In addition, Raine et al. (2004) found that non-payment of fines was more to do with courts not obtaining enough information about offenders' ability to pay and not doing enough to help offenders to pay before criminalising non-payment, than with offenders deliberately not paying fines. Therefore, the evidence on fine enforcement in practice suggests that it can be both unfair to certain groups of offenders, and inefficient in terms of the unnecessary costs of enforcement and fine default.

Supervisory penalties and probation

The operation of public and private sector organisations responsible for managing community punishment must be examined more closely to find out how supervisory penalties operate in practice. The discussion here focuses on recent developments. Several key trends can be identified in current probation practice. The first trend is a continuing and increasing level of control of local probation practice by the government in a bureaucratic sense (Newburn 2017), which has meant that local-level probation workers have less discretion about the types of work they do with offenders. This has meant a series of structural and organisational changes for probation involving increasing levels of rapid policy change, as well as increasing accountability and bureaucracy (see Robinson and McNeill 2017). These include:

- The introduction of HM Prisons and Probation Service in 2017, returning to the previous National Offender Management Service (NOMS) structure that was introduced in 2003, with the aim of bringing Prison and Probation Services together and providing 'seamless' supervision, help, and treatment for those convicted of crime throughout and after their sentences;
- The replacement of local probation boards with probation trusts which have to compete with other public sector, private sector, and voluntary agencies for contracts to offer probation services (the so-called 'contestability' principle). Probation trusts are also responsible for employing probation officers in each area and ensuring that probation services are delivered;
- The reallocation of responsibility for community supervision work with the National Probation Service from spring 2021 onwards, reversing the 2014 policy of splitting supervision work between the National Probation Service and private sector Community Rehabilitation Companies (CRCs) (Grierson 2019). This follows highly critical assessment of CRC practice, such as the HM Inspectorate of Probation report of 2018. This report found severe overstretching of CRC staff in terms of workload, a tendency to replace face-to-face engagement with service users with phone conversations, a failure to appropriately enforce recall of service users to prison, and a drift into CRCs handling cases of medium seriousness rather than the low seriousness offences to which their staff were meant to respond (HM Inspectorate of Probation 2018).

Because of these developments, probation policy has moved closer to punitive and managerialist concerns and away from the traditional probation approach of help and treatment for those convicted of crime (Canton and Dominey 2018). The moves towards risk-based practice can be seen in two different ways. On the administrative level, the use of standardised electronic databases such as the Offender Assessment System (OASyS) to measure levels of risk has become a key part of probation practice. However, the ways in which these risk assessment tools are used in practice are still shaped by probation values at a local level and can be resisted by practitioners whose values conflict with a pure risk management approach (Robinson et al. 2014) despite the central role now played by risk management-based technology in shaping probation practice (Phillips 2017). There is evidence to show that managerialist approaches can actually damage probation officers' ability to bring about substantive compliance with probation from service users (Phillips 2016).

Thirdly, despite the trend towards risk management discussed previously, rehabilitation – the traditional focus of probation work – has continued to have an influence on probation practice, especially in the form of desistance theory (McNeill 2006). Desistance theory focuses on factors that prevent further offending in an individual. McNeill (2012) identified four kinds of desistance: judicial (removing labels associated with conviction), psychological (the development of self-confidence and resilience in terms of avoiding crime), social (building community relationships that make criminal behaviour less likely to occur), and moral (making amends for criminal responsibility through dialogue with the community). Under such an approach, risk assessment is negotiated between user and practitioner, and tasks are focussed on developing social capital rather than being imposed (Ward and Maruna 2007).

There is therefore more to probation practice than risk management, bureaucracy, and crime control. Robinson and Raynor (2006), for example, argue that rehabilitation and reform do and should play a continuing role in probation work, particularly in the form of social integration approaches which fuse individual responsibility for crime with the development of responses to social problems – such as poor education and drug abuse – which can create the context for offending. On this view, there is still evidence of discretion in probation practice being used to address social harm issues through rehabilitation and restorative justice.

Study exercise 10.11

What would you say should be the main aim of probation practice? Should it be managing the risks of criminal behaviour or promoting the reduction of future crime?

Custodial penalties

The discussion now moves on to look at prisons and how they punish those held responsible for crime. As with the earlier discussion on community penalties, the focus here is on current issues. Historical perspectives on the development of prison as a form of punishment for crime are discussed in Chapter 2. Prison Rules state that prisons should encourage and assist inmates to lead a good and useful life on release, that prisons should use no more restriction than necessary to require safe custody and order, and that prisons should promote 'self-respect' and 'personal responsibility' among inmates (Cavadino et al. 2013: ch.6). The Rules form the basis of the Prison Service's statement of purpose, which reflects the aims of security, basic standards, and rehabilitation, but has been added to with a framework of complex managerial aims, targets, and key performance objectives.

Cavadino et al. (2013) argue that the prison system in England and Wales is currently in crisis. Their arguments can be used to examine in more detail how prisons punish people, and how much focus is placed on individual responsibility for crime when doing so. Cavadino et al. identify seven separate areas of legitimacy crisis, which are linked to each other in terms of their causes:

- **The crisis of management**. This has been caused by the disconnection of authority and responsibility for prison management, the uncertainty caused by partial prison privatisation and the private sector issues of high staff turnover and inexperience (Ludlow 2017), and a focus on managerialist efficiency targets rather than issues like trust and loyalty.
- **The crisis of security**. Cavadino et al. argue that the 'dispersal system' approach, whereby category A prisoners were 'dispersed' across a number of prisons rather than all being contained in the same place, resulted in a noticeable increase in security and control measures for all prisoners in the dispersal prisons, not just the category A prisoners. One important result of this process has been the continuing problem of the rate of suicides in prison. In the year to June 2019, there were 86 suicides in English and Welsh prisons, up from 81 in the previous year, with record levels of self-harm in prisons (57,968) and assault in prisons (34,425) in the year to March 2019 (Ministry of Justice 2019b). Liebling and Arnold's (2004) research points to a link between low levels of decency and humanity in prisoner treatment and high rates of suicide and self-harm. They found different levels of humanity and decency in different prisons, driven by the attitudes of prison staff, showing that security, humanity, and decency can be balanced in the prison system.
- **The crisis of overcrowding**. On 6th September 2019, there were 83,327 people in prison – very close to the prison capacity of 85,069 (HM Prisons and Probation Service 2019). This means that the prison population has more than doubled in the space of 25 years. Overcrowding has a series of knock-on effects for people in prison, including poorer living conditions, fewer opportunities for work and training, and more transfers from one prison to another.
- **The crisis of conditions**, as described in the previous point. The constant movement of prisoners also has significant social and psychological effects on their families (Scott and Codd 2010) – for example, where the prisoner is moved to a place too far away for the family to be able to visit.
- **The crisis of control and authority**. This is characterised by discipline problems among prisoners and staff, restricted privileges for prisoners, and the resentment of prison officers towards increased professionalization from outside agencies.

- **The crisis of accountability**, or how effectively complaints and problems relating to the prison system are handled. Neither of the two channels of complaint for prisoners – Independent Monitoring Boards which hear and investigate complaints from individual prisoners at each prison, and the Prison Ombudsman who deals with complaints from all prisons – have any power to force prison authorities to change a decision or a particular prisoner's treatment (Coyle 2005: 127–8). Similarly, the Prisons Inspectorate monitors conditions in all prisons, but there is no requirement that the government has to take notice of its findings in policy terms. Individual legal challenges from prisoners have faced the problems of limited access to legal aid, and obstruction from those who manage prisons.

- **The crisis of legitimacy**. As explained earlier, this is the idea that prisoners feel that they are being treated fairly and with respect. Cavadino et al. (2013) argue that all of the crises discussed previously play a part in limiting the legitimacy of prison regimes in the view of prisoners. These limits on legitimacy strengthen the argument of critical writers such as Mathiesen (1990) that the aim of prisons is to exercise power and control, often in a psychologically and physically violent and damaging way, against powerless and socially excluded prisoners, rather than trying to treat them fairly or rehabilitate them. The evidence on the over-representation of BAME groups in prisons could also be said to support this view, as could the evidence presented by Cavadino et al. (2013: 173–4) on the over-representation of disadvantaged social groups such as the unemployed, care-leavers, those excluded from school, and those with recognised mental disorders. Christie (2000) argues that the powerful have turned prisons into a profit-making industry for controlling and socially excluding the powerless in society through introducing the privatisation of prisons. However, detailed empirical research (e.g. Sparks et al. 1996; Liebling and Arnold 2004; Crewe and Liebling 2017) has shown that prisons can have other punishment objectives, such as rehabilitation and due process justice for prisoners. The success of these objectives depends on prison staff acknowledging the power that prisoners have in maintaining order and discipline, by treating prisoners with respect and fairness so that prisoners see prisons as being morally legitimate. A good example of how this has been achieved in practice are the therapeutic regimes at HMP Grendon Underwood and HMP Dovegate, where even violent and sexual offenders have shown reduced reconviction rates compared with those in other prisons, and the reconviction rate was lower the longer a prisoner stayed (Cullen and Mackenzie 2011). Some writers have argued (e.g. Scott and Gosling 2016) that therapeutic communities are so successful in moving beyond punishment based on individual responsibility for crime to provide opportunities for rehabilitation that they should be used as an alternative to prison, rather than as a type of imprisonment, in certain circumstances.

Study exercise 10.12

Critically discuss the view that privatising more prisons will help to solve the prison crises that Cavadino et al. (2013) identify in their work.

Youth justice

Detailed consideration of youth justice, which responds to crime committed by young people between the ages of 10 and 17 inclusive, is outside the scope of this book. However, it is important to remember that youth justice operates separately to the criminal justice process for adults in England and Wales. Youth justice is also managed in a different way from adult justice. After the Crime and Disorder Act 1998 (s.38), each local authority area in England and Wales has its own Youth Offending Team (YOT), a multi-agency panel which must involve representation from the police, social services, education workers, and health workers, among others. The requirements on YOTs to submit an annual report on crime to the National Youth Justice Board (an organisation set up to monitor local practice and promote 'best practice' at the local level), and comply with a range of National Standards shows the influence of managerialism on youth justice under the New Labour government of 1997–2010 that remains in today's youth justice process (Smith 2014).

However, the trend of decreasing use of custody for young people since 2010, identified by Bateman (2012), has continued in the years since. Similarly, the number of first-time entrants to the youth justice process decreased by 85% between 2008 and 2018 (Ministry of Justice 2018). This indicates limits to punitivism in youth justice terms – although there are still a range of concerns over non-compliance of youth justice with international human rights frameworks, in terms of custody use and the setting of the minimum age of criminal responsibility at 10 (McAra 2017: 959–61). The introduction of youth justice sentences such as referral orders, as well as reparation requirements found in cautioning for young people since 2013, have encouraged youth justice practitioners to develop more restorative approaches to youth offending, such as mediation between offenders and victims and practical work done by offenders to help to repair the harm caused by their crime. There are (as shown earlier) still question marks about the values and purposes of restorative justice in practice (Muncie 2015: 323), and limitations on work which is restorative and related to the original offence in practice due to conflict with the 'top-down' pressure to be punitive (Crawford and Newburn 2003). However, the scope for reparative, rehabilitative, and diversionary work which recognises that young people should be seen as children first and offenders second (Haines and Case 2015) remains in youth justice practice. There is evidence to suggest that some discretion still exists in youth justice practice and that this discretion can be and is used for these restorative and inclusive aims in contrast to policy messages (Case 2018: ch.6). As such, a range of values and ideas are visible in youth justice practice in England and Wales.

Conclusions: linking discussion to the roadmap theories

This chapter has examined the issue of how criminal law and criminal justice use and limit ideas about who is responsible for crime from two different angles. The first perspective discussed how criminal defences limit responsibility for crime in certain circumstances. General defences in criminal law provide an exception to the liberal roadmap idea that people are held criminally responsible for their actions where it can be proved that they had the right actus reus and mens rea for the offence. Excusatory defences are also based around liberal principles – that people should not be held responsible for their actions if something about them makes it morally unacceptable to blame them for their criminal actions. However, the law has tried to restrict such limitations in recent times. We can see this in the morally based restrictions about particular types of duress scenario – most notably in *Howe* and *Gotts*, where the House of Lords decided that no threat could morally justify intentionally taking a life, or attempting to take one. On self-defence, the law again focuses on liberal roadmap ideas about proportionality between threat and action, and individual responsibility. However, in *Martin*, a case which attracted widespread publicity and debate, the Court of Appeal made an artificial distinction between perception of the facts of the scenario and perception of the danger involved to ensure that Tony Martin's conviction was not overturned. This could be seen as a decision aimed at holding onto the law's power in the face of what was seen as the threat of social unrest resulting from public sympathy for Tony Martin shooting intruders who were threatening his property. Finally, the courts have been extremely reluctant to allow anyone to use a defence of necessity. Norrie (2014: ch.8) argues that this is because the law does not want to acknowledge the inequality in society – in terms of poverty and unemployment especially – which narrows the choice people have not to commit crime. As a result, we can see the limits of the liberal roadmap, replaced by risk management approaches to those seen as dangerous to society, and radical roadmap ideas about law serving the interests of the powerful at the expense of the powerless in society.

In the criminal justice section of the chapter, the discussion of individual responsibility for crime focussed on the perspective of sentencing, which is based around the justification for allowing people to be punished by the State. The question here was whether, just as criminal law moves away from the idea of liberal roadmap-style individual responsibility in some situations to take into account more risk and power-based values, criminal justice also moves away from individual responsibility when it punishes the legally guilty. Although the liberal-retributive principle of proportionate sentencing that was the basis of the Criminal Justice Act 1991 is still part of criminal justice, policies based on crime control, deterrence, and incapacitation have also been introduced, most noticeably in the Criminal Justice Act 2003 (Cavadino et al. 2013). The results – more custodial sentences, the blurring of custodial and community punishment through suspended sentence orders, and reductions in the use of community sentences generally – are reflections of a move towards risk management-influenced reductivism in sentencing. However, this move ignores evidence on the limited effectiveness of deterrence (von Hirsch et al. 1999). Punishment processes have been heavily influenced by punitivism and risk-based managerialism (not least through privatisation), and the socially excluding nature of prisons reflects the values of the power-based radical roadmap. Even so, there is room for optimism in the form of restorative work in the community, in the form of the continuation of rehabilitative, desistance-based probation work (influenced by the deterministic roadmap), and in the form of the small number of prison-based therapeutic communities.

It is also significant that deterrence and incapacitation responses, like retributivism, generally focus on individual responsibility for crime. It has been more difficult for restorative roadmap values, in the form of reparative sentencing, which despite its limitations at least brings the opportunity for a more social and community-based approach to responding to crime, to become established in sentencing practice. This is true even where legislative measures have been introduced to encourage reparative justice, such as referral orders for young people in the Youth Justice and Criminal Evidence Act 1999. Even so, there is evidence that the restorative roadmap also plays a part in sentencing and punishment, especially in the youth justice context. This makes it difficult to explain criminal law and criminal justice in these areas other than through the radical hybrid realist roadmap. This is the only roadmap model that directly acknowledges the fact that there can be and is conflict and competition between different sets of values in both institutions, and also acknowledges that while the powerful have some influence over criminal law and criminal justice, their domination is not complete.

Key points

- Criminal law defences cover a wide range of scenarios and behaviours, and often move beyond straightforward liberal considerations of responsibility for crime to include risk or power-based concerns, by narrowing the scope of some defences, for example

- Criminal justice sentencing and punishment appear to focus on making those convicted of crime face individual responsibility for crime in a liberal way, but there are a range of other values playing a part in these processes, from the managerialism evident in privatisation and the power-based social exclusion in prisons, to the restorative work done with young people in the community, and the rehabilitative work done in prison-based therapeutic communities
- The radical hybrid realist roadmap is best at explaining the range of values evident in criminal law defences and criminal justice sentencing and punishment, while acknowledging the influence of power-based values in both

Further reading

Canton, R., and Dominey, J. (2018), *Probation* (2nd ed.). Abingdon: Routledge.

Easton, S., and Piper, C. (2016), *Sentencing and Punishment: The Quest for Justice* (4th ed.). Oxford: OUP.

Jewkes, Y., Bennett, J., and Crewe, B. (2016), *Handbook on Prisons* (2nd ed.). Abingdon: Routledge.

Norrie, A. (2014), *Crime, Reason and History* (3rd ed.): chs.8, 10 and 12. Cambridge: CUP.

Simester, A.P., Spencer, J.R., Stark, F., Sullivan, G.R., and Virgo, G.J. (2019), *Simester and Sullivan's Criminal Law: Theory and Doctrine* (7th ed.). Oxford: Hart.

References

Bateman, T. (2012), 'Who Pulled the Plug? Towards an Explanation of the Fall in Child Imprisonment in England and Wales', *Youth Justice*, **12**(1): 36–53.

Bottoms, A.E. (1983), 'Neglected Features of Contemporary Penal Systems', in Garland, D., and Young, P. (eds.), *The Power to Punish: Contemporary Penality and Social Analysis*. Aldershot: Gower.

Braithwaite, J. (1989), *Crime, Shame and Reintegration*. Cambridge: CUP.

Canton, R., and Dominey, J. (2018), *Probation* (2nd ed.). Abingdon: Routledge.

Case, S.P. (2018), *Youth Justice: A Critical Introduction*. Abingdon: Routledge.

Case, S.P., Johnson, P., Manlow, D., Smith, R., and Williams, K. (2017), *Criminology*. Oxford: OUP.

Cavadino, M., Dignan, J., and Mair, G. (2013), *The Penal System: An Introduction* (5th ed.). London: Sage.

Child, J.J., and Sullivan, G.R. (2014), 'When Does the Insanity Defence Apply? Some Recent Cases', *Criminal Law Review*: 788–801.

Christie, N. (2000), *Crime Control as Industry*. London: Routledge.

Coyle, A. (2005), *Understanding Prisons*. Maidenhead: Open University Press.

Crawford, A., and Newburn, T. (2003), *Youth Offending and Restorative Justice*. Cullompton: Willan.

Crewe, B., and Liebling, A. (2017), 'Reconfiguring Penal Power', in Liebling, A., Maruna, S., and McAra, L. (eds.), *The Oxford Handbook of Criminology* (6th ed.). Oxford: OUP.

Crow, I., Richardson, P., Riddington, C., and Simon, F. (1989), *Unemployment, Crime and Offenders*. London: Routledge.

Cullen, E., and Mackenzie, J. (2011), *Dovegate: A Therapeutic Community in a Private Prison and Developments in Therapeutic Work with Personality Disordered Offenders*. Hook, Hampshire: Waterside Press.

Easton, S., and Piper, C. (2016), *Sentencing and Punishment: The Quest for Justice* (4th ed.). Oxford: OUP.

Faulkner, D.E.R. (2006), *Crime, State and Citizen: A Field Full of Folk* (2nd ed.). Winchester: Waterside Press.

Finney, A. (2004), *Alcohol and Sexual Violence: Key Findings from the Research*. Home Office Research, Development and Statistics Directorate. London: Home Office.

Fletcher, G.F. (1978), *Rethinking Criminal Law*. Boston: Little, Brown and Co.

Grierson, J. (2019), 'Probation Will Be Renationalised After Disastrous Grayling Reforms', *The Guardian*, 26 May. Available online at: www.theguardian.com/society/2019/may/16/part-privatisation-probation-sevices-to-be-reversed-offender-management-nationalised-chris-grayling. Accessed 11 June 2019.

Hadfield, P. (2006), *Bar Wars: Contesting the Night in Contemporary British Cities*. Oxford: OUP.

Haines, K., and Case, S.P. (2015), *Positive Youth Justice: Children First, Offenders Second*. Bristol: Policy Press.

HM Inspectorate of Probation (2018), *Enforcement and Recall: A Thematic Inspection*. Available online at: www.justiceinspectorates.gov.uk/hmiprobation/wp-content/uploads/sites/5/2018/02/Enforcement-and-Recall-report.pdf. Accessed 17 August 2019.

HM Prisons and Probation Service (2019), *Prison Population Bulletin: Weekly*, 6 September. Available online at: www.gov.uk/government/statistics/prison-population-figures-2019. Accessed 10 September 2019.

Hood, R. (1992), *Race and Sentencing*. Oxford: Clarendon Press.

Jewkes, Y., Bennett, J., and Crewe, B. (eds.) (2016), *Handbook on Prisons* (2nd ed.). Abingdon: Routledge.

Johnstone, G. (2011), *Restorative Justice: Ideas, Values, Debates* (2nd ed.). Abingdon: Routledge.

Joyce, P. (2017), *Criminal Justice* (3rd ed.). Abingdon: Routledge.

Liebling, A., and Arnold, H. (2004), *Prisons and Their Moral Performance: A Study of Values, Quality and Prison Life*. Oxford: Clarendon Press.

Ludlow, A. (2017), 'Marketizing Criminal Justice', in Liebling, A., Maruna, S., and McAra, L. (eds.), *The Oxford Handbook of Criminology* (6th ed.). Oxford: OUP.

Mackay, R.D. (2012), 'Ten More Years of the Insanity Defence', *Criminal Law Review*: 946–55.

Mair, G. (2017), 'Community Sentences', in Harding, J., Davies, P., and Mair, G. (eds.), *An Introduction to Criminal Justice*. London: Sage.

Mathiesen, T. (1990), *Prison on Trial*. London: Sage.

McAra, L. (2017), 'Youth Justice', in Liebling, A., Maruna, S., and McAra, L. (eds.), *The Oxford Handbook of Criminology* (6th ed.). Oxford: OUP.

McNeill, F. (2006), 'A Desistance Paradigm for Offender Management', *Criminology and Criminal Justice*, **6**(1): 39–62.

McNeill, F. (2012), 'Four Forms of "Offender" Rehabilitation: Towards an Interdisciplinary Perspective', *Legal and Criminological Psychology*, **17**(1): 18–36.

Ministry of Justice (2018), *Youth Justice Annual Statistics: 2016–17*. London: Ministry of Justice.

Ministry of Justice (2019a), *Criminal Justice System Statistics Quarterly, September 2018 – Overview Tables*. Available online at: https://assets.publishing.service.gov.uk/government/uploads/system/uploads/attachment_data/file/780613/overview-tables-sept-2018.ods. Accessed 21 March 2019.

Ministry of Justice (2019b), *Safety in Custody Statistics, England and Wales: Deaths in Prison Custody to June 2019 Assaults and Self-harm to March 2019*. Available online at: https://assets.publishing.service.gov.uk/government/uploads/system/uploads/attachment_data/file/820627/safety-in-custody-q1-2019.pdf. Accessed 10 September 2019.

Muncie, J. (2015), *Youth and Crime* (4th ed.). London: Sage.

Newburn, T. (2017), *Criminology* (3rd ed.). Abingdon: Routledge.

Norrie, A. (2014), *Crime, Reason and History* (3rd ed.). Cambridge: CUP.

Parker, H., Sumner, M., and Jarvis, G. (1989), *Unmasking the Magistrates*. Milton Keynes: Open University Press.

Phillips, J. (2016), 'Myopia and Misrecognition: The Impact of Managerialism on the Management of Compliance', *Criminology and Criminal Justice*, **16**(1): 40–59.

Phillips, J. (2017), 'Probation Practice in the Information Age', *Probation Journal*, **64**(3): 209–25.

Raine, J., Dunstan, E., and Mackie, A. (2004), 'Financial Penalties: Who Pays, Who Doesn't, and Why Not?' *Howard Journal of Criminal Justice*, **43**(5): 518–38.

Robinson, G., and McNeill, F. (2017), 'Punishment in the Community: Evolution, Expansion and Moderation', in Liebling, A., Maruna, S., and McAra, L. (eds.), *The Oxford Handbook of Criminology* (6th ed.). Oxford: OUP.

Robinson, G., Priede, C., Farrall, S., Shapland, J., and McNeill, F. (2014), 'Understanding "Quality" in Probation Practice: Frontline Perspectives in England and Wales', *Criminology and Criminal Justice*, **14**(2): 123–42.

Robinson, G., and Raynor, P. (2006), 'The Future of Rehabilitation: What Role for the Probation Service?' *Probation Journal*, **53**(4): 334–46.

Scott, D.G., and Codd, H. (2010), *Controversial Issues in Prisons*. Maidenhead: Open University Press.

Scott, D.G., and Gosling, H.J. (2016), 'Before Prison, Instead of Prison, Better Than Prison: Therapeutic Communities as an Abolitionist Real Utopia', *International Journal for Crime, Justice and Social Democracy*, **5**(1): 52–66.

Simester, A.P., Spencer, J.R., Stark, F., Sullivan, G.R., and Virgo, G.J. (2019), *Simester and Sullivan's Criminal Law: Theory and Doctrine* (7th ed.). Oxford: Hart.

Smith, R. (2014), *Youth Justice: Ideas, Policy, Practice*. Abingdon: Routledge.

Sparks, R., Bottoms, A.E., and Hay, W. (1996), *Prisons and the Problem of Order*. Oxford: Clarendon Press.

von Hirsch, A., Bottoms, A.E., Burney, E., and Wikstrom, P.O. (1999), *Criminal Deterrence and Sentencing Severity*. Oxford: Hart.

Ward, T., and Maruna, S. (2007), *Rehabilitation: Beyond the Risk Paradigm*. Abingdon: Routledge.

Weaver, M. (2017), 'Justice Secretary Told To "Get a Grip" on Prisoners with No Release Date', *The Guardian*, Monday 14 August. Available online at: www.theguardian.com/society/2017/aug/14/liz-truss-get-grip-backlog-prisoners-held-beyond-interdeminate-sentence-ipp. Accessed 23 July 2019.

Wilson, W. (2017), *Criminal Law* (6th ed.). Harlow: Pearson.

Chapter 11

Conclusions

Chapter aims

After reading Chapter 11, you should be able to understand:

- Which of the theoretical models in Chapter 1 play a part in criminal law in practice and what part they play
- Which of the theoretical models in Chapter 1 play a part in criminal justice in practice and what part they play
- Current trends in the development of criminal law and criminal justice
- Key ideas on how criminal law and criminal justice could be reformed in the future

Introduction

This final chapter of the book returns to the key questions posed in Chapter 1. It summarises the evidence on what criminal law's functions are in society, what criminal justice's functions are in society, and how big the gap between them is, referring back to the roadmap theories put forward in Chapter 1. It will then move on to make some suggestions about how both criminal law and criminal justice could work more effectively in the future. Firstly, current trends in criminal law and criminal justice are summarised.

Where are criminal law and criminal justice going now?

Where is criminal law going?

As shown in the discussion of general principles of criminal law in Chapters 3, 4, and 10, criminal law gives the appearance of being based on principles of liberalism and individual responsibility that are characterised by the liberal roadmap theory introduced in Chapter 1. As Norrie (2014) has pointed out, many key principles within criminal law are based around these ideas. For example, in Chapter 3, actus reus, the behaviour required to be criminally liable for a particular offence, was seen to be defined by the law as about voluntary acts which the offender has played a part in causing through their behaviour. The different types of mens rea – especially intent and recklessness (after the decision in *G*) – discussed in Chapter 3, support principles of subjective planning, foresight and risk-taking concerning criminal consequences. The discussion of alternative forms of liability in Chapter 4 pointed to the focus on individual responsibility for assisting crime after *Jogee*, and the focus on intention to commit attempted crime after *Pace*. The discussion of criminal defences in Chapter 10 again pointed to liberal principles by showing the different circumstances in which the law removes criminal liability from people, even though they have the required actus reus and mens rea for an offence, because they were not fully responsible for their actions – because they were insane or acting in self-defence, for example.

However, a recent trend has appeared across a range of issues in criminal law that has displaced the liberal roadmap theory – the risk management roadmap theory. This approach involves attempts to reduce the risk of criminal behaviour occurring, especially by those viewed as being dangerous in society, using managerialist techniques of assessment. It also involves a punitive, harsh approach to criminalising what is seen as socially unacceptable or risky behaviour, as the analysis in the previous chapters showed. This trend has been a long-standing feature of criminal law, as the historical analysis in

Chapter 2 showed. However, the trend has accelerated in recent years – to give just three examples:

- The decision on the meaning of appropriation in theft in *Gomez* which makes any touching of property with the right mens rea an offence;
- The imposition of strict liability on Sexual Offences Act 2003 rape offences involving children of a similar age where the defendant has a reasonable belief that the victim is over 13 years old in *G;*
- The extension of fraud in the Fraud Act 2006 to cover situations where the defendant does not actually obtain any property from the victim but only has the intention to do so.

Criminal law has therefore moved increasingly towards a risk management-based roadmap in terms of intervening at an earlier stage to try to reduce the risk of that harm occurring by punitive means. However, as the analysis in previous chapters has shown, it would be wrong to say that criminal law is entirely dominated by this roadmap, or indeed by the liberal roadmap. As Norrie (2005, 2014) has shown, there is still more discretion in criminal law than either the risk-based or the liberal roadmaps suggest. No one set of values can explain everything. For example, the concept of intent goes further than just planning or aiming to do something, to cover situations where someone only has foresight of the illegal outcome being virtually certain to occur – but it is the jury's decision whether or not evidence of this level of foresight counts as intent. The scope of the defences of consent to offences of violence against the person, the defence of insanity, and the scope of criminal intent have all been defined by court decisions. The concept of dishonesty, which is fundamental to proving theft and other property offences, also has to be decided by the magistrates or jury in each case.

It is therefore clear that judges, magistrates, and juries have a great deal of scope to inject their own values into criminal law. As a result, criminal law can be about a range of other principles that show different sides to the liberal and risk management roadmaps, including:

- The imposition of morality in terms of blaming 'bad' people (*Brown* on consent) and excusing 'good' people (*Steane* on motive);
- The patriarchal protection of people who are viewed as being vulnerable in society (*Hinks* on theft);
- The deterrence of economically inefficient acts (*Corcoran v Anderton* on the wide scope of robbery);
- Or the maintenance of social order (the denial of a defence to criminal damage in political cases like *Jones and Milling*) at different times.

All of these are common law decisions, but different values can clearly be seen in statute law as well – such as:

- The Sexual Offences Act 2003 where there is a conclusive presumption or a rebuttable presumption that consent was not given in offences of rape, for example, where deceit as to identity is seen to be morally 'worse' than spiking someone's drink, and both are 'worse' than having non-consensual sex while voluntarily intoxicated;
- The limited effectiveness of the corporate manslaughter offence created by the Corporate Manslaughter and Corporate Homicide Act 2007 to regulate deaths caused by corporate wrongdoing.

Study exercise 11.1

Find three examples of new statutory criminal offences which have been introduced since 1997 and which could be described as risk-related criminal offences. For each one, explain why you think the offence tries to reduce the risk of future offending behaviour.

Where is criminal justice going?

The story of criminal justice's development is similar to the story of criminal law's development. Again, the basis of criminal justice principles lies in liberal roadmap ideas about due process, whereby punishment can only be imposed in cases where the defendant's liability has been proved beyond reasonable doubt. The police can only stop, search, and arrest based on 'reasonable suspicion'. The CPS can only prosecute where doing so is in the public interest and where there is a reasonable chance of obtaining a conviction. In court, there is a presumption in favour of releasing defendants on bail; defendants have the right to choose to have their case heard in either the magistrates' or the Crown Court if the offence is triable either way; convictions can only be made if there is proof of guilt beyond reasonable doubt; and custodial sentences can only be given if the court gives justification for the offence(s) being 'so serious' that only custody can be justified. Community punishment should involve rehabilitation and reparation as well as punishment based on responsibility, and the stated aim of prison is to help inmates to lead a good and useful life after release. In theory, the criminal justice process gives a series of rights to defendants and only punishes them when individual responsibility is proved, and in proportion with their responsibility.

As with criminal law, though, recent developments have signalled a move towards a risk-assessment roadmap model of criminal justice, based on managerialist risk assessment and an increasingly harsh and punitive criminal justice response to crime. These developments have included the following:

- The acceptance of forward-looking reductivist sentencing aims such as deterrence and protection of the public, under the Criminal Justice Act 2003, as well as the doubling of the prison population since 1992 due to more and longer prison sentences, as the discussion in Chapter 10 showed;
- The decreasing use of community sentences over the past decade, and the simultaneous increase in the use of suspended sentences, again as discussed in Chapter 10;
- The expansion of police powers to extend the 'normal' period of detention before charge to 36 hours, and remove the need for 'reasonable suspicion' when searching for items relating to terrorism under the Terrorism Act 2000, as discussed in Chapter 3;
- Evidence that the CPS may be screening out sexual assault cases where they think a jury is unlikely to convict, rather than building up an evidential case, as discussed in Chapter 8.

Successive chapters have also pointed to the presence of the radical roadmap model, in terms of the interests of the powerful in society being represented and enhanced through criminal justice. The radical model is particularly evident in cases of corporate wrongdoing, such as the Grenfell Tower fire of 14th June 2017 in which 72 people died. The Grenfell Tower block was cladded in material that was highly flammable and which was widely seen as being a cause of the rapid spread of the fire (Kentish 2019). Despite the apparent blameworthiness attached to the incident, police have confirmed that no charges are likely to be brought against anyone in connection with the Grenfell fire until at least 2021, and the associated inquiry report is not likely to be published until late 2020, over three years after the incident occurred (Crew 2019).

In addition, although there is not as much evidence of their influence as there is for the other roadmap models discussed previously, there is still some evidence of the deterministic and restorative models' presence in criminal law and criminal justice. The deterministic model is visible in criminal law's paternalistic prohibition of consensual violence in sexual circumstances (*Brown*), for example (see chapter 6), and in the kind of rehabilitative work done in the probation context (see Chapter 10). The restorative model plays an increasingly important role in a variety of criminal justice settings, such as state crime (see Chapter 4), sexual offences (see Chapter 8), and desistance-related probation and youth justice work (see Chapter 10).

However, as with criminal law, discretion still exists at every stage of the criminal justice process, as previous chapters have shown. The exercising of police powers is an inherently low profile, and the 'discretion gap' is sometimes filled using crime control values, or even using the aim of maintaining social order (McConville et al. 1991). The CPS Code for Crown Prosecutors has little influence on CPS discretion in terms of whether or not to prosecute.

Brown's (1991) work indicated that local 'court cultures', or decision-making patterns influenced by particular combinations of magistrates deciding cases, were more important in understanding variations in usage of bail and sentencing (Tarling 2006). Discretion in Crown Court sentencing can, in some cases, allow courts to increase social divisions by sentencing on the grounds of racism (Hood 1992). In terms of punishment, discretion over how punishment is carried out remains important, as shown by the continuing commitment to rehabilitation in probation practice despite the difficult recent transfer of some probation work into the private sector (Burke et al. 2017). Similarly, Crewe and Liebling's (2017) work shows the variation in staff-prisoner interaction across and within prisons of the same type and therefore demonstrates extensive low-level discretion.

As a result of the evidence on the range of values present in both criminal law and criminal justice, as well as the evidence of extensive discretion in both institutions, it is clear that while some roadmap models are more influential than others, there is no one model that can explain everything, or even most aspects, of either. Of the roadmap models explained in Chapter 1, only the radical hybrid realist model takes a variety of values into account, and accepts the presence of individual and group discretion, while also acknowledging the role played by power relations and inequalities in criminal law and criminal justice. One important message that the radical hybrid realist roadmap model gives is that the interests of the powerful do not always dominate criminal law and criminal justice. The recording of the deaths of the 96 victims of Hillsborough as unlawful killings after over 25 years of campaigning by families of the victims and survivors (mentioned in Chapter 7) is proof that this is true (Scraton 2016).

Study exercise 11.2

Should there be more or less discretion in criminal law and criminal justice than there currently is? Explain your answer.

The next section of the chapter looks at how criminal law and criminal justice can move in a more progressive direction in the future.

Where should criminal law and criminal justice go from here?

Reform from the inside: reorganisation on principled and substantive grounds

Ashworth (2000) argued that the scope of criminal law must be limited by clear principles relating to what it should do in order to comply substantively with human rights. Ashworth went on to argue that criminal law should be limited to censuring people who have committed substantial wrongdoing. As Reiner (2007, 2016) points out, there is no consensus on what counts as 'substantial wrongdoing', not least because most people commit some form of crime at some point in their lives. But the advantage of Ashworth's approach is that it would force those who have a say in developing criminal law to think not only about what they do now but also what they should do – a normative view, in other words. The approach is also flexible enough to apply to the very wide range of behaviour that criminal law regulates. The ECHR human rights – which are already part of criminal law in England and Wales under the Human Rights Act 1998 – could provide one way of implementing Ashworth's principle of limiting criminal law, if it was used to regulate the fairness of the substantive criminal law itself rather than to just correct procedural errors. A more radical approach might be organising criminal law around different levels of social harm caused by crimes (von Hirsch and Jareborg 1991; Pemberton 2015).

Cavadino et al. (2013: ch.10) argue for a similar reorientation process in criminal justice, again based on the principles of human rights and maximum possible liberty and autonomy for all of those in the criminal justice process, including prisoners. This leads them to make a series of recommendations for reforming criminal justice, such as a move back towards just deserts and away from incapacitation in sentencing, restrictions on the use of custodial remands, and enforceable ceilings on individual prison numbers. They also recommend greater use of restorative justice, in ways that could make people face up to the responsibility and motivations for their criminal behaviour, while giving victims a say in how to respond to offending and giving the opportunity to reintegrate offenders back into society following their 'shaming' (Braithwaite 1989). These reforms would again have the advantage of injecting humanity and decency back into criminal justice throughout the process (Rutherford 1993). As with criminal law, the reforms could be achieved by a 'strong' implementation of human rights that are already part of criminal justice in theory. However, these changes could not only be implemented by legislative and policy changes. There also would need to be a change in wider society – which forms the subject of the next recommendation.

Reform from the outside: moving beyond criminal law and criminal justice

It is important to recognise that important though criminal law and criminal justice are in society, there is only so much that either of them can do about crime, even if they are organised in a fairer way. Cavadino et al. (2013) argue that it is foolish as well as inhumane to look to punitive and risk-based criminal justice approaches to solve the problems of crime, given that such a small percentage of crime results in a criminal conviction and that the real amount of crime in today's society is unknown. The gap between criminal law and criminal justice remains wide. Exactly how wide it is remains unknown due to the limits of what is known about the extent of crime through police and Crime Survey for England and Wales data. That said, recent data (discussed in Chapter 8) suggest that the gap is wider than it has ever been in relation to rape. On the other hand, without criminal justice to enforce it, criminal law would have little impact on daily life.

Study exercise 11.3

List three ways in which you think the gap between criminal law and criminal justice could be narrowed.

Norrie (2014) has illustrated the conflicting values that compete with each other for influence over how criminal law develops, and the inconsistency in development and content which occurs as a result. This book has reached similar conclusions about criminal law and criminal justice. However, the major trends in both criminal law and criminal justice are based around individual responsibility and punishment on that basis. As Zedner (2004) has argued, the liberal and risk-based approaches are both individualistic, so that the move from liberalism to risk management is not really a radical move to a very different view of what criminal law and criminal justice should do. As a result, Hillyard and Tombs (2007) claim that criminal law and criminal justice pay too much attention to behaviour which does not cause significant social harm in most cases, such as minor antisocial behaviour. On the other hand, criminal law and criminal justice do not pay enough attention to behaviour which causes far more social harm, such as crime which is committed by states and corporations, like war crimes, torture, genocide, tax, or deaths in the workplace – all of which have been discussed in earlier chapters (Cohen 2001; Green and Ward 2017; Tombs 2017).

Worse still, other preventable social conditions which have the ability to damage or destroy people's lives, such as poverty, political exclusion, and a wide gap between rich and poor in society (Pemberton 2015) are completely ignored by criminal law and criminal justice because they are not seen as being criminal at all. This leads Hillyard and Tombs to argue that in order to understand how to make criminal law and criminal justice fairer, it is necessary to look beyond what is officially defined as 'crime'. Instead, on this view, we should examine the whole range of what Hulsman (1986) calls 'problematic situations' in society, where individuals or groups of people are suffering preventable physical, psychological, social, political, and/or economic harm.

This is not to argue that changes should be made to criminal law and criminal justice alone. Reiner (2007: ch.4) and Hall (2012) offer a range of evidence which shows a strong link between rising rates of crime (especially violent crime), harsher punishment, and socio-economic conditions. These authors argue that a complex combination of so-called 'neoliberal' economic policies which emphasise minimum regulation of financial markets and freedom for big business to make as much profit as possible, and social and cultural changes which emphasise selfishness, greed, and success through owning material goods, explains the expansion and harshness of criminal law and criminal justice since the 1970s. This socio-cultural mix promotes material gain as the primary measure of success in society but does not allow everyone the opportunity to achieve this material success, thereby encouraging selfishness and crime. It encourages corporate crime at the top of society because State regulation of financial business is weakened in order to allow people to achieve financial wealth. But it also encourages crime at the lower levels of society, through making people more selfish and more desperate to achieve material success that society and culture encourage them to want but will not let them have (Hall 2012).

A range of statistical evidence from writers like Dorling (2018), and Wilkinson and Pickett (2018) supports this argument. Such evidence also points to the links between social and cultural inequality, increased mental and physical health problems, and increasingly harsh punishment, especially in the current era of austerity in spending on criminal law and criminal justice. There is no shortage of evidence of the damaging effects of austerity in England in recent years: the increasing reliance on food banks, increasing poverty and homelessness, successive waves of cuts to public services responding to social issues like mental illness (Goodman 2018), and the fear and alienation leading to knife crime and other forms of violence. The riots of 2011 (Winlow et al. 2015) and the public vote in favour of Brexit (Dorling and Tomlinson 2019) can be seen as the results of public ignorance of this type of inequality, and of lower-class resentment of their perceived social and political exclusion, causing selfish individualism and xenophobia fuelled by a neoliberalist socio-economic approach and the right-wing media. All of these factors play a part in explaining the crime that law tries, and claims, to fight back against but cannot due to the inevitability of crime and harm in a neoliberal society. The result is a criminal law that fails to address the social harm generated by crime in terms of the great harm caused by it among the poorest in society, and in terms of the equally great harm caused by the actions of the most powerful in society. Another result is a criminal justice process that is unequal and discriminatory in terms of its gender and racial bias, for example (Reiner 2016). Lessons could be learned from other countries, such as the Scandinavian countries, with a stronger welfare system, a much smaller gap between rich and poor, and an apparently lower rate of crime and entrants to criminal justice (Cavadino and Dignan 2006; Lacey 2008).

As a result, if we want to make both criminal law and criminal justice fairer and more effective, it is not enough just to change their policies and practices. The historical analysis in Chapter 2 shows that the development of either is not inevitable or linear but is rather shaped by a wide range of social, political, moral, and economic values. As a result, we also need to change economic and social policies in ways that reduce social inequality and exclusion, and increase community cohesion and trust between individuals and groups in society – something which risk-based approaches fail to do. Further, these reforms need to occur in a transformative way, bringing 'deep' social and cultural changes. Such changes can be made for the better – but only this type of transformation can really make a positive difference to criminal law and criminal justice.

Study exercise 11.4

If you could make five changes to criminal law as it currently is in England and Wales, and five changes to criminal justice, what would those changes be and why?

Key points

- Both criminal law and criminal justice are shaped by a range of values, as well as by the interests of the powerful in society – as a result, the radical hybrid realist theory is the roadmap theory which comes closest to explaining both
- Both criminal law and criminal justice still contain considerable areas of discretion for those who operate them
- The most effective way of reforming both criminal law and criminal justice is to balance reforms of internal practice with wider socio-economic reforms which improve equality and fairness in wider society

---

Further reading

Cook, D. (2006), *Criminal and Social Justice*. London: Sage.

Garland, D. (2001), *The Culture of Control: Crime and Social Order in Contemporary Society*. Oxford: OUP.

Hall, S. (2012), *Theorizing Crime and Deviance*. London: Sage.

Hillyard, P., Pantazis, C., Tombs, S., and Gordon, D. (eds.) (2004), *Beyond Criminology: Taking Harm Seriously*. London: Pluto Press.

Reiner, R. (2016), *Crime: The Mystery of the Common-Sense Concept*. Cambridge: Polity Press.

References

Ashworth, A. (2000), 'Is the Criminal Law a Lost Cause?' *Law Quarterly Review*, **116**(2): 225–56.

Braithwaite, J. (1989), *Crime, Shame and Reintegration*. Cambridge: CUP.

Brown, S. (1991), *Magistrates at Work*. Buckingham: Open University Press.

Burke, L., Millings, M., and Robinson, G. (2017), 'Probation Migration(s): Examining Occupational Culture in a Turbulent Field', *Criminology and Criminal Justice*, **17**(2): 192–208.

Cavadino, M., and Dignan, J. (2006), *Penal Systems: A Comparative Approach*. London: Sage.

Cavadino, M., Dignan, J., and Mair, G. (2013), *The Penal System: An Introduction* (5th ed.). London: Sage.

Cohen, S. (2001), *States of Denial: Knowing About Atrocities and Suffering*. Cambridge: Blackwell.

Cook, D. (2006), *Criminal and Social Justice*. London: Sage.

Crew, J. (2019), 'Grenfell Tower: Police Carry Out 13 Interviews Under Caution as Part of Criminal Investigation', *The Independent*, 7 June. Available online at: www.independent.co.uk/news/uk/crime/grenfell-tower-police-investigation-fire-london-suspects-a8948861.html. Accessed 12 September 2019.

Crewe, B., and Liebling, A. (2017), 'Reconfiguring Penal Power', in Liebling, A., Maruna, S., and McAra, L. (eds.), *The Oxford Handbook of Criminology* (6th ed.). Oxford: OUP.

Dorling, D. (2018), *Peak Inequality: Britain's Ticking Time Bomb*. Bristol: Policy Press.

Dorling, D., and Tomlinson, S. (2019), *Rule Britannia: Brexit and the End of Empire*. Hull: Biteback Publishing.

Garland, D. (2001), *The Culture of Control: Crime and Social Order in Contemporary Society*. Oxford: OUP.

Goodman, P. (2018), 'The Big Squeeze: In Slow-Bleed Britain, Austerity Is Changing Everything', *The Independent*, 2 June. Available online at: www.independent.co.uk/news/long_reads/britain-austerity-changing-everything-prescot-food-banks-universal-credit-a8373851.html. Accessed 13 September 2019.

Green, P., and Ward, T. (2017), 'Understanding State Crime', in Liebling, A., Maruna, S., and McAra, L. (eds.), *The Oxford Handbook of Criminology* (6th ed.). Oxford: OUP.

Hall, S. (2012), *Theorizing Crime and Deviance*. London: Sage.

Hillyard, P., Pantazis, C., Tombs, S., and Gordon, D. (eds.) (2004), *Beyond Criminology: Taking Harm Seriously*. London: Pluto Press.

Hillyard, P., and Tombs, S. (2007), 'From "Crime" to "Social Harm"?' *Crime, Law and Social Change*, **48**(1): 9–25.

Hood, R. (1992), *Race and Sentencing*. Oxford: Clarendon Press.

Hulsman, L. (1986), 'Critical Criminology and the Concept of Crime', *Contemporary Crises*, **10**(1): 63–80.

Kentish, B. (2019), 'Government Warned of Another Grenfell-Type Disaster as 60,000 People Still Living in Buildings Covered in Same Flammable Material', *The Independent*, 5 June. Available online at: www.independent.co.uk/news/uk/politics/grenfell-tower-fire-material-high-rise-buildings-flat-block-a8946276.html. Accessed 12 September 2019.

Lacey, N. (2008), *The Prisoner's Dilemma: Political Economy and Punishment in Contemporary Democracies*. Cambridge: CUP.

McConville, M., Sanders, A., and Leng, R. (1991), *The Case for the Prosecution: Police Suspects and the Construction of Criminality*. London: Routledge.

Norrie, A. (2005), *Law and the Beautiful Soul*. London: GlassHouse.

Norrie, A. (2014), *Crime, Reason and History* (3rd ed.). Cambridge: CUP.

Pemberton, S. (2015), *Harmful Societies: Understanding Social Harm*. Bristol: Policy Press.

Reiner, R. (2007), *Law and Order: An Honest Citizen's Guide to Crime and Control*. Cambridge: Polity Press.

Reiner, R. (2016), *Crime: The Mystery of the Common-Sense Concept*. Cambridge: Polity Press.

Rutherford, A. (1993), *Criminal Justice and the Pursuit of Decency*. Oxford: OUP.

Scraton, P. (2016), *Hillsborough: The Truth*. Edinburgh: Mainstream Publishing.

Tarling, R. (2006), 'Sentencing Practice in the Magistrates' Courts Revisited', *Howard Journal of Criminal Justice*, **45**(1): 29–41.

Tombs, S. (2017), *Social Protection After the Crisis: Regulation Without Enforcement*. Bristol: Policy Press.

von Hirsch, A., and Jareborg, N. (1991), 'Gauging Criminal Harm: A Living-Standard Analysis', *Oxford Journal of Legal Studies*, **11**(1): 1–38.

Wilkinson, R., and Pickett, K. (2018), *The Inner Level: How More Equal Societies Reduce Stress, Restore Sanity and Improve Everyone's Wellbeing*. London: Allen Lane.

Winlow, S., Hall, S., Treadwell, J., and Briggs, D. (2015), *Riots and Political Protest: Notes from the Post-Political Present*. Abingdon: Routledge.

Zedner, L. (2004), *Criminal Justice*. Oxford: Clarendon Press.

Understanding basic legal skills

This appendix gives guidance on key study skills required for studying criminal law. In order to develop your knowledge of criminal law further, you will need to know how to find, understand, and interpret key sources of legal information. You will also need to know how to present essays about the law. The appendix focuses on specific legal skills, but you should always bear in mind more general study skills when tackling law assessments as well. These include managing your time effectively, taking notes in a way that works for you, writing clearly and accurately, and avoiding the plagiarism of others' work by referencing non-original ideas and material correctly.

Research skills

To find information about the law effectively, you need to start by becoming familiar with the law library at your place of study. Your law library is likely to have online resources for finding information about the law, as well as paper-based sources. Find out how to use your library's online resources and what is available.

Once you have done that, you need to identify and distinguish different sources of law. One useful way of doing this is to separate primary and secondary sources of law. Primary sources are what the law actually is, in the form of either statutory legislation (created and developed by Parliament as Acts) or law reports (records of legal decisions made by judges in different courts). Secondary sources are books, journal articles, and online legal databases like Westlaw and Lexis Library. Secondary sources are valuable in explaining what primary sources of law mean, but you need to study both types of sources to gain a full understanding of the law and how it works. When writing law-based essays and problem questions (see also the following discussion), always aim to use a mixture of primary and secondary sources as the base material for your answer. You need to understand what the law itself says (you can get this from the primary sources), but you also need to understand how the law works, why it works in the ways that it does, and how it could work better in the future. Secondary sources like books and journal articles will give you this type of information through their commentaries and analyses of the law. Make sure your sources are reliable, though – do not use unreliable and non-academic websites like Wikipedia and Law Teacher as sources. Instead, ask for guidance from your lecturers about the best books to read after this one, and choose trusted law journals such as *Criminal Law Review, Law Quarterly Review, Journal of Criminal Law,* or the *Modern Law Review.* Try different reading and note-taking styles to determine which one(s) work best for you.

When working with the different sources of law, a skill that you quickly need to develop is recognising different kinds of legal citation. Each case report has its own unique citation, in the form of the case name, date, and a series of letters and numbers. The citation can also tell you in which court the case being reported on was heard. For example, the citation *Gotts* [1992] 2 AC 412 tells you that this case was dealt with in the House of Lords, as it then was, because the abbreviation 'AC' stands for Appeal Cases, a series of reports which only covered cases heard in the House of Lords or the Supreme Court. The rest of the citation tells you in which volume of that year's report series the case was reported and on which page number the case report begins. Other types of citation cover more than one type of court, such as WLR (Weekly Law Reports), as in *Hughes* [2013] 1 WLR 2461, for example. More recent case citations (since 2001) do not relate to a particular report series but still have their own unique citation to enable you to find their case report on an online legal database such as Westlaw or Lexis Library (discussed earlier). An example of this type of neutral case citation would be *Golding* [2014] EWCA Crim 889, which simply tells you that the case was heard in the Court of Criminal Appeal. Another is *Jogee* [2016] UKSC 8. This citation tells you that the case was heard in the Supreme Court. These examples have all been primary legal sources, in the form of case reports, but some secondary sources have their own abbreviations, such as 'LQR' for the *Law Quarterly Review* (discussed earlier). For a full list of abbreviations, use an online database such as the Cardiff Index to Legal Abbreviations, available at www.legalabbrevs. cardiff.ac.uk.

When referencing legal sources in a law-based essay, you will probably be asked to use the Oxford Standard for the Citation of Legal Authorities (OSCOLA) as a referencing system. OSCOLA works differently from the Harvard referencing used in this book. Whereas Harvard referencing appears in the main text of what you write, OSCOLA referencing appears as a footnote at the bottom of each page of your work. A full guide to using OSCOLA referencing is available at www.law.ox.ac.uk/research-subject-groups/publications/ oscola.

Legal interpretation skills

Once you have found the right sources for the law-based research you are conducting, you then need to learn how to interpret those sources effectively.

With Acts of Parliament (statute law), bear in mind how the Act might have changed through Green Papers (consultation documents), White Papers (policy statements) and Parliamentary debate before becoming part of the law. Understanding this process of development can often help you to understand the true meaning of the statute. Courts also have to interpret statutes when the statute's meaning is not clear, for the purposes of deciding whether a criminal offence is strict liability, for example (see Chapter 3). Firstly, the courts consider the literal meaning of the words of the statute. Then, if the literal meaning produces a nonsensical result, the courts will look at the overall context of the statute (the 'golden rule' principle). If that does not work, then the courts will consider the problem or issue that the statute was designed to address (the 'mischief rule' principle).

When reading reports of cases, start by using reliable secondary sources, such as books and journal articles, as background reading for gaining an idea of what the case is about in general. Then, look at the headnote, which is the set of paragraphs at the start of each case report. In particular, note the name of the case, which type of legal issue the case is about, and which judges decided the case. This is all material that you might want to reference when writing about the case in an essay.

Then, note what the headnote tells you about precedent (or stare decisis), the system whereby decisions at the same level of the court 'ladder' have to be followed by later court decisions in cases on the same legal issue or point (see Figure 1.1 in Chapter 1 for more details on precedent). Also, note what the headnote tells you about the point(s) of law on which the decision in the case is based – in other words, the principles that explain or change the law in some way. This material is the ratio (short for ratio decidendi). The other parts of the decision that are not part of the ratio are known as obiter (obiter dicta). Do not only read the headnote, though. To reach a deep understanding not only of a decision itself but also of why the decision was made, and the potential problems with the decision, you need to read the actual judgments in each case. You do not need to read each case from beginning to end, though. Start with the parts of the judgment that form the ratio, then read as much of the material that surrounds the ratio as you need to in order to fully understand what the case is about and why it was decided as it was. Remember that cases can vary greatly in length and that it will not always be easy to find or understand the ratio. However, finding the ratio becomes easier the more cases you read.

Assessment skills

Remember that the marks you get on any law-based module or programme will depend on how well you perform in different types of assessment. Sometimes you will need to complete an essay on a legal topic. If you are asked to do this, remember that you need to make sure you are answering the specific question in every paragraph that you write. You also need to show that you have read a range of material that is reliable and relevant to the question that you are answering. You can demonstrate that you have done this not only by using key ideas in your discussion and argument but also by referencing others' material accurately (see earlier discussion for more on referencing). In addition, you need to make sure that the structure of your essay is clear and logical. Does it have a clear introduction mapping out the rest of the essay, a series of logically ordered points grouped into paragraphs in the main part, and a conclusion that summarises your arguments without providing any additional material? You also need to make sure that you write clearly and accurately, paying attention to spelling and grammar throughout your work.

You might also be asked to complete a problem question in relation to a legal topic. Here, your task is to identify the relevant law in a particular area and apply that law to a set of facts that have been given to you. If you are asked to complete a problem question, you are being asked to advise an imaginary client who is facing a particular legal issue. Start, in the introduction, by stating what your client wants to achieve through the legal process. Then discuss the law that is specifically relevant to the facts that you have been given, discussing one legal point per paragraph. Conclude by saying what you think the likely outcome would be in terms of how the case is likely to be decided. Remember that, depending on the type of legal issue under discussion and the facts that have been given to you, there might be more than one possible right answer. As long as you can back up your advice with primary legal source material in the form of relevant statute or case law, you will answer the problem question effectively.

In terms of preparing for other forms of assessment, like exams or oral presentations, the basic rules of preparation are the same – always focus on the question you are answering, bring in as much relevant source material as you can, and structure your answer clearly and logically while presenting it well.

Index